Fifth Edition

Avanzando

Grammar and Reading

Sara Lequerica de la Vega
Carmen Salazar

Los Angeles Valley College

WILEY

John Wiley & Sons, Inc.

ACQUISITIONS EDITOR	Helene Greenwood
MARKETING MANAGER	Gitti Lindner
SENIOR PRODUCTION EDITOR	Sujin Hong
SENIOR DESIGNER	Madelyn Lesure
PRODUCTION MANAGEMENT SERVICES	Lee Shenkman/Victory Productions, Inc.
COVER IMAGE	Photo Disc/Getty Images

This book was set in 10/12 Berkeley by Victory Productions, Inc., and printed
and bound by R.R. Donnelley. The cover was printed by Phoenix Color.

This book is printed on acid free paper.

ISBN 0-471-45638-1

Printed in the United States of America

10 9 8 7 6 5 4 3 2 1

Preface

Highlights of Avanzando: Grammar and Reading, Fifth Edition

- Now available in two versions, to address the needs of both native and non-native speakers of Spanish, Avanzando 5e features precise grammar explanations, engaging readings and a flexible organization. These are just a few reasons why **Avanzando: Grammar and Reading** is so effective in intermediate and advanced Spanish courses.
- Featuring an approach that has been tested and refined through four highly successful editions, **Avanzando** encourages students to build on their current Spanish literacy skills, focus on the finer details of the language, and expand their cultural knowledge.
- Grammar explanations, set in English, are simple, numbered, and grouped within one section of the chapter. The material, where applicable, is summarized in boxes for review and ease of identification.
- The text offers a selection of short stories by well-known Spanish and Latin American authors. Exercises at the end of each story encourage students to do a close reading of the text, stimulate critical thinking and class discussion, and introduce students to literary analysis techniques.
- The self-contained grammar review in each chapter allows instructors to follow a flexible sequence (for example, everything related to pronouns appears in chapter 7.)
- The *Cuaderno de ejercicios,* written entirely in Spanish, includes activities that help both native and non-native speakers of Spanish strengthen particular areas based on their needs.
- *Avanzando* can be used successfully in a variety of different courses, including one-semester courses at the intermediate, high-intermediate or advanced level, two-semester courses when the classes meet fewer than 4–5 hours per week, and advanced high school courses.

- The Fifth Edition includes the following **Appendices:**
  ~Spelling-changing verbs
  ~Irregular verbs
  ~List of irregular verbs
  ~Synopsis of a verb conjugation
  ~Practical vocabulary—false cognates

Organization

The content in each chapter is divided into three manageable sections: **Lectura, gramática,** and **composición.**

Lectura. Each chapter begins with one or two short reading selections of a cultural or literary nature, preceded by a vocabulary list of words and expressions that can sometimes be difficult for students. The readings are also enhanced with side glosses and are followed by three types of activities to help students with vocabulary expansion, reading comprehension, and oral practice.

Gramática. The grammatical explanations are presented in English in a brief and simplified manner with multiple examples and English translations. More contextualized and communicative-based exercises have been added to this edition, many of which focus on culture to enhance the topics presented in the **Lectura** section.

Composición. This reorganized component reviews and expands upon the rules of punctuation, capitalization, accentuation, and spelling introduced in the introductory chapter. The exercises corresponding to this section are included in the *Cuaderno de ejercicios.* Students are presented with a topic for an oral or written composition and an outline to help them develop their composition.

Supplements

- *Cuaderno de ejercicios* reinforces the grammatical structures presented in the text and helps students with problem areas. Numerous exercises of varying degrees of difficulty take into account each student's language background. The section **Para saber un poco más** is designed to help students recognize false cognates. As in the textbook, the exercises in the workbook have been contextualized whenever possible. An answer key at the end of the workbook allows students to check their own work.

- **Companion Web Site (www.wiley.com/college/delavega)**

For the Student

- Self tests (*Autopruebas*)
- Resources
- Países y gentilicios
- Abreviaturas

For the Instructor

- Testing program
- Textbook answer key

We wish to thank the reviewers who took the time and care to fill out the publisher's questionnaires with valuable comments and suggestions, and the editorial staff at John Wiley & Sons, Inc. for their help and interest in producing this text. We especially thank our project editor María F. García, Lee Shenkman of Victory Productions, Inc., Helene Greenwood and Christine Cordek, who diligently guided this text in its final stages.

Gloria Arjona, *University of Southern California*; Nancy Barclay, *Lake Tahoe Community College*; Teresa Boucher, *Boise State University*; Renatta Buscaglia, *East Los Angeles College*; Ellen M. Brennan, *Purdue University at Indianapolis*; John W. Griggs, *Glendale Community College*; Michael D. Finneman, *Augustana College*; Bill Hart, *Compton Community College*; Dorothy A. Gaylor, *California State University, San Bernardino*; Sonia López Blakely, *Colorado State University*; Irina Kappler-Crookston, *University of Idaho*; Iliana Mankin, *Stetson University*; Tina Pereda, *Nazareth College of Rochester*; Troy P. Prinkey, *University of Virginia*; Julie Stephens de Jonge, *Central Missouri State University*; Claire Ziamandanis, *The College of Saint Rose*

SARA LEQUERICA DE LA VEGA
CARMEN SALAZAR

Contenido

Parte I

Capítulo Preliminar — 3

Diphthongs and triphthongs	4
Division of syllables	4
Accentuation	6
Capital letters	11
Punctuation	12
Spelling rules	14
The sentence and its principal parts	16

Capítulo I — 20

Vocabulario	21
Lectura: "Una puerta hacia la historia"	22
Gramática	27
The verb: person, number, mood, and tense	27
Present indicative: regular verbs and irregular verbs	30
Reflexive verbs	38
The definite article	39
The indefinite article	42
Composición	45
Review of punctuation rules	45
Review of spelling rules: **c, s, z**	46

Capítulo 2 — 48

Vocabulario	49
Lectura 1: "Diversidad versus unidad"	50
Vocabulario	53
Lectura 2: "Apocalipsis" de Marco Denevi	54

Gramática 55
The past: preterite and imperfect indicative 55
Preterite: regular verbs and irregular verbs 56
Imperfect indicative: forms 61
Uses of the preterit and the imperfect indicative 62
Interrogatives 68
Composición 71
Review of punctuation rules 71
Review of spelling rules: **sc** 72

Capítulo 3 74

Vocabulario 75
Lectura 1: "Lección sobre ruedas" de Domitila Barrios de Chungara 76
Lectura 2: "Hombre pequeñito" de Alfonsina Storni 79
Gramática 80
Future and conditional 80
Past participles 85
Perfect tenses in the indicative mood 87
Uses of **ser** and **estar** 91
Uses of the verb **haber** 96
Gustar and other similar verbs 97
Composición 100
Review of punctuation rules 100
Review of spelling rules: **que, qui, cue, cui** 101

Capítulo 4 103

Vocabulario 104
Lectura 1: "Sor Juana Inés de la Cruz" 105
Vocabulario 108
Lectura 2: "Una palmera" de Rosario Castellanos 109
Gramática 110
Affirmatives and negatives 110
Indicative mood and subjunctive mood 114
Present subjunctive 114
The imperative mood 119
Imperfect subjunctive 124
Uses of the subjunctive: verbs that express doubt, will, or emotion 128
Composición 132
Review of capitalization rules 132
Review of spelling rules: **h** 132

Capítulo 5   134

Vocabulario   135
Lectura 1: "La América Central"   136
Vocabulario   140
Lectura 2: "Los mayas"   140
Vocabulario   141
Lectura 3: "El eclipse" de Augusto Monterroso   142
Gramática   144
Phrases and expressions that require the subjunctive   144
Present perfect subjunctive   147
Pluperfect subjunctive   149
Sequence of tenses   150
Other expressions that require the subjunctive   153
Si clauses   158
Expressions with **tener**   160
Composición   162
Review of capitalization rules   162
Review of spelling rules: **g, j**   162

Capítulo 6   164

Vocabulario   165
Lectura: "México y el arte muralista"   166
Gramática   170
The gerund or present participle   170
Possessive adjectives and pronouns   174
Demonstrative adjectives and pronouns   176
Adverbs   180
Impersonal verbs   182
Review of verbs that may be confusing   184
Prefixes **des-, in-, re-**   186
Composición   187
Review of capitalization rules   187
Review of spelling rules: **ll, y, -ío, -illo, -illa**   188

Capítulo 7   189

Vocabulario   190
Lectura 1: "Dos poetas chilenos: Mistral y Neruda"   191
Lectura 2: "Yo no tengo soledad" de Gabriela Mistral   194
Vocabulario   194
Lectura 3: "Poema 20" de Pablo Neruda   195

Gramática   196
Subject pronouns   196
Direct and indirect object pronouns   198
Double object pronouns   203
Reflexive pronouns   206
Prepositional pronouns   210
Expressions with **se**   212
Composición   215
Review of capitalization rules   215
Review of spelling rules: **gue, gui, güe, güi**   215

Capítulo 8   *217*

Vocabulario   218
Lectura 1: "Argentina"   219
Vocabulario   223
Lectura 2: "Sala de espera" de Enrique Anderson Imbert   223
Gramática   224
Nouns   224
Uses of the infinitive   233
Adjectives   236
Comparatives   240
Superlatives   244
Composición   246
Review of capitalization rules   246
Review of spelling rules: **b, v**   247

Capítulo 9   *249*

Vocabulario   250
Lectura 1: "Inmigraciones hispanas en los Estados Unidos" 251
Vocabulario   257
Lectura 2: "Recuerdo íntimo" de Lucha Corpi   257
Vocabulario   258
Lectura 3: "La mejor tinta" de Armando Valladares   259
Gramática   260
Prepositions   260
Uses of **por** and **para**   265
Uses of **pero** and **sino**   271
Verbs that are used with the preposition **a** followed by an infinitive,
    and the ones that are used without it   272
Verbs that are followed by prepositions   274
Composición   277
Review of accentuation   277
Review of spelling rules: **r, rr**   278

Capítulo 10   *280*

    Vocabulario   281
    Lectura 1: "Países en la costa del Pacífico: Ecuador, Perú y Chile"   282
    Vocabulario   287
    Lectura 2: "El nacimiento de la col" de Rubén Darío   288
    Gramática   289
    Relatives   289
    Passive constructions   296
    Verbs that express the idea of change or *to become*   300
    Phrases that denote obligation   302
    Expressions with **hacer. Hace** + time + **que**   303
    Review of prepositional phrases   307
    Idiomatic expressions   308
    Composición   309
    Review of accentuation   309
    Review of spelling rules: differences between Spanish and English 310

Parte 2

Lectura 1 "El ramo azul" de Octavio Paz   313

Lectura 2 "Pedro Salvadores" de Jorge Luis Borges   323

Lectura 3 "Abril es el mes más cruel" de Guillermo Cabrera Infante   331

Lectura 4 "El árbol de oro" de Ana María Matute   341

Lectura 5 "Noche de fuga" de María Manuela Dolón   352

Vocabulario   *361*

Apéndice   *383*

    Verbs with spelling changes   384
    Irregular verbs   386
    List of irregular verbs   398
    Synopsis of a verb conjugation   399
    Practical vocabulary—false cognates   400

Índice   *402*

Parte I

Gramática

Una villa maya cerca del mar. Mural en las ruinas de Chichén Itzá, Península de Yucatán, México.

- Diphthongs and triphthongs
- Division of syllables
- Accentuation
- Capital letters
- Punctuation
- Spelling rules
- The sentence and its principal parts

A Diphthongs and triphthongs

Strong vowels = **a, e, o.**   Weak vowels = **i, u.**

Diphthongs				*Triphthongs*	
A combination of a strong and a weak, a weak and a strong, or two weak vowels.				A combination of a strong vowel between two weak vowels.	
ai ia	**au ua**	**ei ie**		**iai iei**	**uai uei**
eu ue	**oi io**	**ou uo**	**iu ui**		
aire	gloria	autor	agua	apreciáis	pronunciéis
(air)	*(glory)*	*(author)*	*(water)*	*(you appreciate)*	*(you pronounce)*
reino	nadie	socio	cuota	Uruguay	buey
(kingdom)	*(nobody)*	*(member)*	*(share)*		*(ox)*

NOTE: The **i** changes to **y** whenever a diphthong or a triphthong ending in **i** comes at the end of a word.

hoy *(today)*   hay *(there is/are)*   ley *(law)*   Paraguay

The diphthongs **ue** and **ie** are written with **h (hue, hie)** when these occur at the beginning of a word.

hueso	huésped	huevo	hierro	hiena	hiel
(bone)	*(guest)*	*(egg)*	*(iron)*	*(hyena)*	*(gal)*
hueco	huerta	huella	hielo	hierba	hiedra
(hollow)	*(orchard)*	*(trace)*	*(ice)*	*(grass)*	*(ivy)*

Note the conjugation of the verb **oler** *(to smell)*: **huelo, hueles, huele, olemos, huelen.**

B Division of syllables

1. In dividing words into syllables, the prefix of a word is generally separated from the rest of the word although this separation may not coincide with division into syllables. Both ways are accepted.

   des i gual/de si gual   des in te re sa do/de sin te re sa do
   (uneven)   *(disinterested)*

   sub ra yar/su bra yar   in ú til/i nú til
   (underline)   *(useless)*

2. In words without prefixes, a single consonant between two vowels forms a syllable with the following vowel.

   A li cia *(Alice)*   e ne mi go *(enemy)*   o pe rar *(to operate)*
   a ma ne cer *(to dawn)*   u sar *(to use)*

3. Two consonants together are usually separated.

car ta (*letter*)   cuan do (*when*)   guan tes (*gloves*)   más ca ra (*mask*)
puer ta (*door*)   at le ta (*athlete*)

NOTE: In words derived from the Nahuatl language, the combination **tl** is not separated:
Ma za tlán.

4. The following are inseparable combinations:

ch, ll, rr	mu **cha** cha (*girl*) ca ba **llo** (*horse*) co **rrer** (*to run*)	**gl, gr**	con **glo** me ra do (*conglomerate*) a le **gre** (*happy*)
bl, br	ha **blar** (*to speak*) a **bri** go (*coat*)	**pl, pr**	re **plan** tar (*to replant*) a **pre** tar (*to tighten*)
cl, cr	a **cla** mar (*to acclaim*) re **cre** o (*recess*)	**dr, tr**	cua **dro** (*painting*) de **trás** (*behind*)
fl, fr	in **fluen** cia (*influence*) re **fres** co (*refreshment*)		

5. If there are three consonants between vowels, and the second consonant is an **s**, the division occurs after the **s**.

cons tar   ins ta lar   obs tá cu lo   abs ti nen cia
(*to consist of*)   (*to install*)   (*obstacle*)   (*abstinence*)

But when there is a combination of **consonant + l** or **r**, this combination joins the following vowel.

em ple ado   no viem bre   dis tri to
(*employee*)   (*November*)   (*district*)

6. If there are four consonants between two vowels, two consonants join the first vowel and two join the second.

cons truir   cons truc tor   ins cri bir   abs trac to
(*to construct*)   (*constructor*)   (*to inscribe*)   (*abstract*)

7. The only letters that are doubled are **c** and **n**; they are separated as in English.

ac ción   ac ce der   in ne ce sa rio

8. Diphthongs and triphthongs form a single syllable and are not separated.

bai lar   a gen cia   aun que   U ru guay

When the weak vowel is stressed, a written accent is placed over the vowel. In that case the diphthong becomes two syllables.

co mí a   o í do   le í do   i rí a   rí o   ve í a

NOTE: Syllables should not be separated in such a way that a single vowel stands alone at the beginning or the end of a line or a sentence.

Incorrect	Correct
a-demás	ade-más
simultáne-o	simultá-neo

Ejercicio

Divida las palabras en sílabas.

1. abril
2. diciembre
3. iría
4. cuarto
5. organizar

6. perro
7. vallecito
8. baile
9. tarde
10. usado

11. miércoles
12. automóvil
13. inspección
14. profesor
15. interesante

C   Accentuation*

All words of two or more syllables have one syllable that is pronounced with more stress than the others. This stressed syllable is called **sílaba tónica** in Spanish.

1. Most words that end in a **vowel, n** or **s,** are stressed on the next to the last syllable.

    gran de   **ha** blo   **co** mo   ca **mi** nan   **bai** las

2. Most words that end in a **consonant,** except **n** or **s,** are stressed on the last syllable.

    es pa **ñol**   a **rroz**   a **mor**   ca pa ci **dad**

3. If the pronunciation of the word does not follow the normal rules of stress as described above, a written accent is required on the syllable that is stressed.

    ca **fé**   a **llá**   **lá** piz   a **diós**   **Pé** rez

Depending on which syllable is stressed, words are divided into **agudas, breves** or **llanas, esdrújulas,** and **sobresdrújulas.**

---

*See Capítulos 9 y 10, Review of accentuation.

Agudas

The last syllable is the stressed syllable.

pa **sar**   a **mor**   ge ne **ral**   li ber **tad**   a **zul**   ca **paz**

A written accent is required when the word ends in a **vowel**, **n** or **s**.

ma **má**   can **té**   sa **lí**   pa **só**   hin **dú**   Ra **món**   na **ción**   es **tás**

Breves or llanas

The next to the last syllable is the stressed syllable.

ro sa   **co** me   ca **mi** no   lle **va** mos   es **cri** ban   **ca** sas

A written accent is required when the word ends in a **consonant**, except **n** or **s**.

dó lar   **ár** bol   Fer **nán** dez   ca **dá** ver   di **fí** cil   **Fé** lix

Esdrújulas

The stressed syllable is the third syllable counting back from the end of the word.

re **pú** bli ca   A **mé** ri ca   **pá** ja ro   re **gí** me nes   ven **dér** se la

These words always have a written accent.

Sobresdrújulas

The stressed syllable is the fourth syllable counting back from the end of the word.

llé ve se lo   es **crí** ba me lo   **lé** a me lo

These words always have a written accent. Note that these are verb forms with double object pronouns.

1. The accent mark is used to distinguish a difference in meaning and grammatical function in certain words that have identical forms.

aún *yet; still* (adverb)	**Aún** no ha pagado el carro. *He hasn't paid for the car yet.*
aun *even* (adverb)	**Aun** ella sabe ir al centro. *Even she knows how to go downtown*
dé *give* (verb)	Es posible que Pedro **dé** una fiesta mañana. *It's possible that Pedro may give a party tomorrow.*
de *of* (preposition)	La casa **de** María es grande. *Maria's house is large.*
él *he* (personal pronoun)	**Él** llegó ayer, ¿verdad? *He arrived yesterday, didn't he?*
el *the* (article)	**El** niño está llorando. *The child is crying.*
más *more* (adverb)	El niño quiere **más** helado. *The child wants more ice cream.*
mas *but* (conjunction and adverb)	No la vi, **mas** le escribí. *I didn't see her, but I wrote to her.*
mí *me* (prepositional pronoun)	Los boletos son para **mí**. *The tickets are for me.*
mi *my* (possessive pronoun)	**Mi** primo está en Sevilla. *My cousin is in Sevilla.*
sé *I know; be* (verb; command)	No **sé** la lección. *I don't know the lesson.* Hijo, **sé** un poco más cortés. *Son, be a little more courteous.*

se *himself, herself, him, her*   Ella **se** mira en el espejo.
(reflexive pronoun; indirect object)   *She looks at herself in the mirror.*
    Yo **se** lo dije a Luis. *I told it to Luis.*

sí *yes* (adverb)   ¿Quieres ir al baile? **Sí**, me gustaría mucho.
    Do you want to go to the dance? Yes, I'd like to very much.

si *if* (conjunction)   **Si** ella vino ayer, no la vi.
    If she came yesterday, I didn't see her.

sólo *only* (adverb)   Tenemos **sólo** un carro para toda la familia.
    We have only one car for the whole family.

solo *alone* (adjective)   Eliseo estaba **solo** en la fiesta.
    Eliseo was alone at the party.

té *tea* (noun)   Ya serví el **té**. *I already served the tea.*
te *you* (direct object pronoun;   Sonia **te** llamó ayer. *Sonia called you yesterday.*
indirect object pronoun;   **Te** daré los datos que quieres.
reflexive pronoun)   *I'll give you the data you need.*
    ¿A qué hora **te** levantas todos los días?
    At what time do you get up every day?

tú *you* (personal pronoun)   ¿Cuándo se van **tú** y Jorge?
    When do you and Jorge leave?

tu *your* (possessive pronoun)   Aquí está **tu** cuaderno. *Here is your notebook.*

2. Changes in the use of the accent mark when forming the plural of nouns.
    Words stressed on the last syllable (**agudas**) ending in **n** or **s** drop the accent mark
    because they are now stressed on the next to the last syllable (**llanas**).

    corazón → **corazones** (*hearts*)   nación → **naciones** (*nations*)
    francés → **franceses** (*French*)   alemán → **alemanes** (*Germans*)

    Words stressed on the next to the last syllable (**llanas**) that end in a consonant, except **s,**
    require an accent mark because the stress changes to the third from the last syllable
    (**esdrújulas**).

    examen → **exámenes**   árbol → **árboles**   lápiz → **lápices**

3. An accent mark is needed when the weak vowel is stressed, thus breaking a
    diphthong and creating two syllables. Compare the following words.

    dí a   co me **dia**   o **í**   **oi** go   pa **ís**   **pai** sa je

4. Interrogative and exclamatory words, both direct and indirect, require a written accent.

Direct	*Indirect*
¿**Qué** quieres?	No sé **qué** quieres.
(*What do you want?*)	(*I don't know what you want.*)
¿**Cómo** estás?	Ella preguntó **cómo estás**.
(*How are you?*)	(*She asked how you were.*)
¡**Qué** bello día!	Elsa dijo que **qué** día tan bello hacía.
(*What a beautiful day!*)	(*Elsa said what a beautiful day it was.*)

NOTE: The difference: **por qué** (*why*), **porque** (*because*).

5. Accentuation rules for the conjugation of verbs.

   a. The verb forms for **yo, Ud., él** and **ella** in the preterite tense of regular verbs always have a written accent.

(yo) compré	vendí	recibí
(Ud.) compró	vendió	recibió

   The irregular preterite forms, including **yo, Ud., él** and **ella**, do not have a written accent.

dije	puse	hice	tuve
dijo	puso	hizo	tuvo

   b. All **-er** and **-ir** verbs in the imperfect indicative tense have a written accent on the **i** (except **ser** and **ir**).

VENDER	RECIBIR	TENER
vendía	recibía	tenía
vendías	recibías	tenías
vendía	recibía	tenía
vendíamos	recibíamos	teníamos
vendíais	recibíais	teníais
vendían	recibían	tenían

   c. All forms of the conditional tense have a written accent on the **i**.

COMPRAR	SABER	IR
compraría	sabría	iría
comprarías	sabrías	irías
compraría	sabría	iría
compraríamos	sabríamos	iríamos
compraríais	sabríais	iríais
comprarían	sabrían	irían

   d. All forms of the future tense, except **nosotros**, have a written accent.

TRABAJAR	HACER	SALIR
trabajaré	haré	saldré
trabajarás	harás	saldrás
trabajará	hará	saldrá
trabajaremos	haremos	saldremos
trabajaréis	haréis	saldréis
trabajarán	harán	saldrán

   e. The past participles ending in **-ido** have an accent on the **i** if it is preceded by a strong vowel (**a, e, o**).

caer	**caído**	leer	**leído**	oír	**oído**

Ejercicios

I. Escuche la pronunciación de las siguientes palabras que leerá el profesor o la profesora. Subraye la sílaba que lleva el acento hablado y escriba los acentos necesarios.

1. dije	4. tendre	7. arboles	10. examenes
2. azucar	5. bailaria	8. comio	11. facil
3. leido	6. aire	9. ecribeselo	12. paciencia

II. Ponga el acento en las palabras que lo necesiten.

Agudas

nacion	saldras	almorce	frances	estas
amor	azul	dolor	ciudad	leyo

Breves o llanas

martes	verde	util	Perez	dificil
arbol	tuvo	dolar	escriben	famoso

III. Ponga el acento, cuando sea necesario, en las palabras subrayadas.

1. A el no le gusta el tener que viajar en avión.
2. ¿Cantas tu en el concierto mañana? Tu voz me gusta mucho.
3. ¿Quieres que te de una taza de te?
4. No se si se lo dije.
5. Carlos tiene solo un amigo. Por eso siempre está tan solo.

IV. Se han omitido los acentos en las siguientes oraciones. Cópielas y escriba los acentos donde sea necesario.

1. ¿Cuantas poesias leyo Rosalia?
2. Mi tio lo trajo para mi.
3. ¡Que problema! Tu hijo quiere que le de las llaves del carro nuevo.
4. Me gustaria visitar los paises de Sudamerica.
5. ¿De quien es el termometro?
6. El tren aun no ha llegado.
7. Salimos rapidamente despues del examen.
8. Ella pregunto como esta el Sr. Fernandez.
9. Ramon vendia seguros de vida (*life insurance*) cuando vivia en Mexico.
10. Cuando Maria llamo me dijo que recibio carta de su hermano.

V. Escuche el siguiente párrafo que va a leer el profesor o la profesora, prestando atención a la pronunciación. Después escriba las palabras que llevan acento escrito.

peoples / emigrating   El español ha sido uno de los pueblos° mas emigrantes° del mundo. Solo el ingles y el portugues pueden compararsele. La continua emigracion hispana hizo que la lengua española se extendiera por muchas partes del mundo.

D Capital letters*

1. A capital letter is used for the following:

a. Proper names of persons, animals, countries, cities, towns, rivers, lakes, mountains, etc.

Pedro López	España	el río Guadalquivir	los Andes
el gato Micifuz	Jalisco	el lago Titicaca	la Sierra Madre

b. The first word of the title of a book, article, poem, or play.

Lo que el viento se llevó
Bodas de sangre
La arena de los políticos

However, in the titles of newspapers or magazines the nouns and adjectives that form part of the title are capitalized as well as the first word.

El País
El Hogar y la Moda

c. The abbreviations for:

usted **Ud.** or **Vd.**	señor **Sr.**	señorita **Srta.**	doña **Da.**
doctor **Dr.**	señora **Sra.**	don **D.**	

d. Names of dignitaries and titles referring to employment when these refer to a specific person.

el Presidente	el Gobernador	el Papa	el Director
el General	Ministro	el Coronel	el Obispo

e. Names of institutions.

el Museo Arqueológico   la Real Academia Española

2. Unlike English, a capital letter is not used for the following:

a. Days of the week and months of the year: **martes, julio.**

b. Adjectives that denote nationality: **francés, alemana.**

c. Names of languages: **inglés, español.**

---

*See Capítulos 4, 5, 6, 7, y 8, Review of capital letters.

Ejercicio

En las siguientes oraciones se han omitido las letras mayúsculas. Escríbalas donde sea necesario.

1. el aconcagua es el pico más alto de américa y tiene 6.959 metros de altura. está en las montañas de los andes en la provincia de mendoza, en la argentina.
2. el venezolano simón bolívar, conocido como el libertador, dedicó su vida a la lucha por la independencia de su patria. murió en la pobreza el 17 de diciembre de 1830.
3. el café colombiano es muy apreciado en el mundo entero.
4. el español es la lengua oficial de casi todos los países de sudamérica, excepto el brasil, donde se habla portugués.
5. el ministro de educación, el sr. sánchez, está en su oficina sólo dos días a la semana: los lunes y los jueves.

E Punctuation*

punto, punto final	**period**	(.)
dos puntos	**colon**	(:)
punto y coma	**semicolon**	(;)
puntos suspensivos	**ellipsis**	(...)
coma	**comma**	(,)
signos de interrogación	**question marks**	(¿ ?)
signos de exclamación o admiración	**exclamation marks**	(¡ !)
comillas	**quotation marks**	(" ")
raya; guión	**dash; hyphen**	(-)
paréntesis	**parentheses**	( )

Punctuation in Spanish is similar to punctuation in English, except that in the case of the question mark and the exclamation point, an inverted mark is used at the beginning as well as the mark at the end of the sentence: (¿ ?) (¡ !).

1. The period (*punto*) is used with numbers to separate groups of three figures and the comma (*coma*) to separate decimals. The opposite occurs in English.

Spanish	*English*
1.234	*1,234*
5,6	*5.6*

---

*See Capítulos 1, 2, y 3, Review of punctuation rules.

2. The colon (*dos puntos*) is used:

   a. After the salutation in a letter.

   > Querido Ernesto: *Dear Ernesto:*   Muy estimada Sra. Rosas: *Dear Mrs. Rosas:*

   b. To introduce quotations from a text:

   > El Presidente dijo: "Estábamos al borde del abismo y hoy hemos dado un paso adelante".
   > *The President said: "We are on the edge of doom and today we have moved one step forward."*

   c. To list in a series the contents of something previously introduced, often after the word **siguiente** (*following*).

   > Juanito le pidió a los Reyes Magos lo siguiente: una bicicleta, un bate y un guante de pelota.
   > *Juanito asked the Three Wise Men for the following: a bicycle, a bat, and a baseball glove.*

3. The semicolon (*punto y coma*) is used to separate independent clauses in a sentence or longer complex clauses within a paragraph.

   > No quiero hablar con ese vendedor tan insistente; si llama le dices que no estoy.
   > *I don't want to talk to that insistent salesman; if he calls tell him I am not in.*

4. With regard to quotation marks (*comillas*), if the text within the quotations is a complete sentence, the period is placed inside the quotation marks; if the quoted text is part of a longer sentence, the period is placed after the closing quotations.

   > Entré en la sala y sentí un olor especial. "Caramba, se quemó la comida."
   > Fui corriendo a la cocina para ver qué pasaba.
   > *I entered the living room and sensed a peculiar odor. "Heavens, the food burned." I went running into the kitchen to see what was happening.*

   > En aquella reunión todo el mundo opinaba y discutía sobre su futuro que parecía indicar que "tenía todas las cualidades para ser una gran actriz".
   > *During the meeting everyone gave opinions and discussed her future which seemed to indicate that "she had all the qualities to be a great actress".*

5. The dash (*raya*) is used:

   a. In a dialogue, to indicate the person that speaks or a change of speaker. Note the quotation marks in English.

   > —¿Cómo te sientes? —le preguntó.   *"How do you feel?", she asked him.*
   > —Muy bien, ¿y tú?   *"Very well, and you?"*
   > —Muy bien también.   *"Very well also."*

   b. To separate incidental phrases, or a sudden change in thought, within a sentence. Commas or parentheses may be used in place of the dash.

   > El Sr. Suárez—el que llamó ayer para una reservación—dice que llegará el jueves en vez del martes.
   > *Mr. Suarez—the one who called yesterday for a reservation—says he will arrive on Thursday instead of Tuesday.*

6. If a question or exclamation occurs in the middle of a sentence, a capital letter is not used after the inverted mark that opens the question or exclamation.

> Sentimos que tocaban en la puerta y mi hermano me preguntó, ¿esperas a alguien?
> *We heard that someone was knocking at the door and my brother asked me, "Are you waiting for someone?"*

F   Spelling rules

Use:

b In the imperfect indicative endings of **-ar** verbs, and in the imperfect of the verb **ir**.

MIRAR		IR	
miraba	mirábamos	iba	íbamos
mirabas	mirabais	ibais	ibais
miraba	miraban	iba	iban

v In all forms of the preterite of the verbs **tener, estar, andar** and verbs derived from them (**retener, mantener,** etc.).

TENER	
tuve	tuvimos
tuviste	tuvisteis
tuvo	tuvieron

andar *(to walk, to go)* **anduve**   mantener *(to maintain, support)* **mantuve**
estar *(to be)* **estuve**   retener *(to retain)* **retuve**

c In **-zar** verbs, when **z** changes to **c** before **e**.

ALMORZAR

Preterite	*Present subjunctive*	
almorcé	almuerce	almorcemos
	almuerces	almorcéis
	almuerce	almuercen

In the plural of verbs that end in **z**, when **z** changes to **c**.

> luz → **luces**   lápiz → **lápices**   feliz → **felices**

In the diminutive endings **-cito** (**-os, -a, -as**) and **-cillo** (**-os, -a, -as**).

> vallecito   cochecitos   saloncito   pececillo

In the ending **-ción** (*-tion* in English).

> nación   relaciones

s In the ending **-sión** (*-ssion* and *-sion* in English).

> pasión   televisión

In the ending **-ísimo (-os, -a, -as)** of the abolute superlative.

carísimo   lindísimas

In the ending **-oso (-os, -a, -as)** to form adjectives.

famoso   valiosas

y   When the stem of **-er** and **-ir** verbs ends in a vowel, the **i** changes to **y** in the preterite endings (-ió > **-yó**, -ieron > **-yeron**), in the present participle and the past subjunctive.

	Preterite	*Present participle*		*Past subjunctive*	
CAER *(to fall)*	cayó, cayeron	cayendo	**LEER** *(to read)*	leyera	leyéramos
LEER *(to read)*	leyó, leyeron	leyendo		leyeras	leyerais
HUIR *(to flee)*	huyó, huyeron	huyendo		leyera	leyeran

j   In the preterite and past subjunctive of the verbs ending in **-decir** and **-ducir**.

MALDECIR *(to curse)*		**PRODUCIR** *(to produce)*	
Preterite		*Past subjunctive*	
maldije	maldijimos	produjera	produjéramos
maldijiste	maldijisteis	produjeras	produjerais
maldijo	maldijeron	produjera	produjeran

g   In the endings **-gio (-a)** and **-gía**.

colegio   magia   biología

r   At the beginning of a word and after **l**, **n** or **s** to represent the trilled sound **rr**.

rosa   alrededor   honra   israelita

rr   In all other cases to represent the trilled sound **rr**.

carro   perro   tierra

h   In all forms of the verbs **haber** and **hacer**.

HABER		**HACER**	
he de ir	**habremos** dicho	**hago**	**harían**
habían llegado	**habrían** hablado	**hicimos**	**haga**
hubo leído	**hubiera** visto	**hacían**	**hiciéramos**
		harán	**hecho**

The following words are written with **h** *(silent)*:

alhaja *(jewel)*   almohada *(pillow)*   azahar *(orange blossom)*

Ejercicios

I. Escriba las siguientes palabras escogiendo la letra correcta para completarlas. Si no está seguro, consulte el diccionario.

1. espa____io (c, z, s)
2. produ____ca (z, s)
3. hi____imos (c, s)
4. lu____es (z, c, s)
5. via____ero (j, g)
6. re____io (j, g)
7. tu____ieron (v, b)
8. canta____an (v, b)
9. ____orro (z, s)
10. valle____ito (c, s)
11. pa____iencia (c, s)
12. reci____imos (v, b)
13. andu____e (v, b)
14. tradu____e (g, j)
15. altí____imo (s, c)
16. comi____ión (s, c)
17. almor____é (s, c)
18. geolo____ía (j, g)
19. má____ico (j, g)
20. di____eron (j, g)

II. Escriba las siguientes oraciones escogiendo la letra correcta para completar las palabras. Si no hace falta ninguna letra, escoja el signo Ø. Si no está seguro, consulte el diccionario.

1. Cuando ha____e (c, s) calor me gusta ir a la pla____a (ll, y).
2. En el in____ierno (b, v) el río está ____elado (h, Ø).
3. ____abía (Ø, H) más de dos____ientas (c, s) personas en la fiesta.
4. Ayer re____ibí (c, s) la nota del examen de geolo____ía (j, g).
5. Tu____imos (b, v) que comprar almo____adas (h, Ø) para la cama.
6. Ese tra____e (g, j) cuesta mucho dinero.
7. Pedro lan____ó (s, z) la pelota con mucha fuer____a (s, z).

G The sentence and its principal parts

There are eight types of words that are used to form sentences: noun (*nombre or sustantivo*), article (*artículo*), adjective (*adjetivo*), verb (*verbo*), adverb (*adverbio*), pronoun (*pronombre*), preposition (*preposición*) and conjunction (*conjunción*).

- Noun: The name of a person, place, thing, or concept. **Juan, mesa, libertad**
- Article: Corresponds to *the, a, an, some.* Modifies a noun or its equivalent. **el** río, **unas** casas
- Adjective: Modifies a noun or its equivalent. Tells which one, what kind, or how many. rosa **blanca, cinco** programas
- Verb: Expresses the action or state of being and is the principal part of the sentence. Ella **juega.**
- Adverb: Modifies the verb, the adjective, or another adverb. Tells when, where, or how. Llega **tarde.**
- Pronoun: Substitutes the noun. **Ellos** salen.

- Preposition: Links words indicating the relationship between them. clase **de** español
- Conjunction: Joins clauses and other elements in a sentence generally in a parallel construction. Ellos tocan la guitarra **y** ellas cantan **y** beben refrescos **o** vino.

1. A sentence (*oración, frase*) is a word or group of words that expresses a complete thought. All sentences have two parts: a subject (*sujeto*) and a predicate (*predicado*). The subject is the person or thing that we talk about. The predicate is everything that is said about the subject.

<u>**El volcán Paricutín**</u> <u>**está en México**</u>.   <u>*The Paricutin volcano*</u> <u>*is in Mexico*</u>.
     sujeto   predicado   subject   predicate

<u>**El Río Grande**</u> <u>**nace en las montañas Rocallosas**</u>.
     sujeto   predicado

<u>*The Rio Grande*</u> <u>*originates in the Rocky Mountains*</u>.
    subject   predicate

2. Predicates may be nominative or verbal.

   a. A *predicate nominative* (*predicado nominal*) is the verb **ser** or **estar** + predicate complement (noun, pronoun, or adjective).

        predicado nominal   predicate nominative
   Mi madre <u>**es**</u> <u>**enfermera**</u>.   My mother <u>**is**</u> <u>**a nurse**</u>.
           verbo   sustantivo   verb   noun

         predicado nominal   predicate nominative
   Los jóvenes <u>**están**</u> <u>**tristes**</u>.   The young people <u>**are**</u> <u>**sad**</u>.
           verbo   adjetivo   verb adjective

NOTE: The verbs **ser** and **estar** are called *copulative* or *linking* verbs because they serve as a link between the subject and the predicate complement. The predicate complement qualifies or classifies the subject.

   b. A *verbal predicate* (*predicado verbal*) includes the verb + complements (direct, indirect, or circumstantial).

         predicado verbal   verbal predicate
   <u>**Le**</u> <u>**escribo**</u> <u>**una carta**</u> <u>**a mi novio**</u>. *I <u>write</u> <u>a letter</u> <u>to my boyfriend</u>*.
   complemento verbo complemento complemento   verb   direct   indirect object
     indirecto   directo   indirecto   object

         predicado verbal   verbal predicate
   El perro <u>**duerme**</u> <u>**en el patio**</u>. *The dog <u>sleeps</u> <u>on the patio</u>*.
          verbo complemento circunstancial   verb circumstantial complement

The verb in the predicate may be transitive or intransitive.

A transitve verb (*verbo transitivo*) requires a direct object to complete its meaning and generally receives action from the verb.

El viento **mueve las hojas.**   La madre **abraza a su hijo.**
*The wind **moves the leaves.***   *The mother **hugs her son.***

An intransitive verb (*verbo intransitivo*) does not require a direct object to complete its meaning, that is, it does not transmit action to a complement.

La niña **llora.** El avión **vuela.** La tierra **tiembla.**
*The child **cries.*** *The airplane **flies.*** *The earth **shakes.***

c. Objects (*Complementos*) complete the meaning of the verb. They may be direct, indirect, or circumstantial.

A direct object (complemento directo) is a word or words that receive the action of the transitive verb. In general, we can find the direct object by asking the question "what?" or "whom?" ("*¿qué?*" or "*¿a quién?*").

> Hacemos **el trabajo**. ¿Qué hacemos? El trabajo.
> *We do **the job**. What do we do? The job.*

> Llamé a **Elena**. ¿A quién llamé? A Elena.
> *I called **Elena**. Whom did I call? Elena.*

NOTE: The direct object is preceded by the preposition **a** when it refers to a person or a personified thing ("personal **a**").

Veo **a** Luis.	Veo las montañas.
I see Luis.	*I see the mountains.*
Conozco **a** tu primo.	Conozco el pueblo.
I know your cousin.	*I know the town.*

An indirect object (complemento indirecto) is the word or words that indicate to or for whom the direct object is intended. In general we can find the indirect object by asking "to whom?" or "for whom?" ("*¿a quién?*" o "*¿para quién?*").

Le llevamos las flores a **mi madre**.	¿A quién le llevamos flores? A mi madre.
We took the flowers to my mother.	*To whom did we take the flowers?* *To my mother.*
Traigo el abrigo para **Carolina**.	¿Para quién traigo el abrigo? Para Carolina.
I bring the coat for Caroline.	*For whom do I bring the coat?* *For Caroline.*

NOTE: When the indirect object is a noun, it is preceded by the preposition **a** or **para**. Direct and indirect objects may also be represented by a pronoun.

Los	conozco.	**Me**	escribió.
Nos	llamó.	**Le**	dijo.
complemento directo		complemento indirecto	
I know	**them.**	*He wrote*	**me.**
He called	**us.**	*She told*	**him (her).**
	direct object		indirect object

A circumstantial complement (complemento circunstancial) is the word or words that modify the meaning of the verb indicating a circumstance of place, time, manner, material, content, etc.

Salimos	**de la Ciudad de México**	**a las tres de la tarde.**
	complemento circunstancial de lugar	complemento circunstancial de tiempo
We left	**México City**	**at three in the afternoon.**
	circumstantial complement of place	circumstantial complement of time

Ejercicios

I. Indique en las siguientes oraciones el sujeto (S), el verbo (V) y los complementos (C): predicativo (pr), directo (dir), indirecto (ind), circunstancial (cir).

MODELO:

Ignacio Cervantes escribió muchas danzas.
　　　S　　　　　V　　　　　C-dir

1. Manuel de Falla fue un gran compositor español.
2. Falla escribió muchas obras importantes.
3. *El amor brujo* es un ballet muy conocido.
4. Falla le dejó una bella herencia musical al pueblo español.
5. Falla nació en 1876 y murió en 1946.

II. Complete las oraciones con los elementos gramaticales que se especifican. Use las palabras que Ud. desee.

1. Ayer _____ compré _____ .
　　　　　sujeto　　　　　　　　complemento directo

2. _____ es _____ .
　　sujeto　　　　　complemento predicativo

3. La muchacha _____ a su prima.
　　　　　　　　　　verbo

4. Pablo trajo las flores para _____ .
　　　　　　　　　　　　　complemento indirecto

5. Llevo _____ a la biblioteca.
　　　complemento directo

Capítulo

Acueducto de Segovia construido por los romanos en España.

LECTURAS
- Lectura: "Una puerta hacia la historia"

GRAMÁTICA
- The verb: person, number, mood, and tense
- Presente indicative: regular verbs and irregular verbs
- Reflexive verbs
- The definite article
- The indefinite article

COMPOSICIÓN
- Review of punctuation rules
- Review of spelling rules: c, s, z

Vocabulario

Antes de leer, repase el siguiente vocabulario que le ayudará a comprender la lectura.

Sustantivos

la belleza   beauty
el castillo   castle
el clima   climate
la convivencia   living together
el enriquecimiento   enrichment
el gobierno   government
la huella   trace
el idioma   language

la mezcla   mixture
la obra   work
el paisaje   landscape
el puente   bridge
el siglo   century
el/la testigo   witness
el valor   value

Verbos

actuar   to act
aterrizar (c)   to land
conocer (zc)   to know
demostrar (ue)   to show; to demonstrate
dejar   to leave behind; to permit
dirigir (j)   to direct
durar   to last
elegir (j)   to elect; to choose
encontrar (ue)   to find

hallar   to find
influir (y)   to influence
llegar   to arrive
llevar   to carry
merecer (zc)   to deserve
recordar (ue)   to remember; to remind
traer *irr.* **(traigo)**   to bring
venir (g) (ie)   to come

Adjetivos

hermoso   beautiful
majestuoso   majestic
mundial   worldwide

Frases

al aterrizar   upon landing
al aire libre   open air
al mismo tiempo   at the same time

cuerpo legislativo   legislative body
hoy día   nowadays
no sólo... sino que   not only . . . but

Cognates (Cognados). In the following reading selection you will recognize many words because of their similarity to English. Give the English equivalent for the following cognates and compare the spelling. Can you find other cognates in the reading?

catedral	acueducto	arquitectura	influencia
diversos	invadir	marca	religioso
fabuloso	funerario	monasterio	palacio

Reminder: an infinitive is used after a preposition. It is equivalent to the English *preposition + ing*.

Al aterrizar en Madrid…	*Upon landing in Madrid . . .*
Al traer el latín a la península…	*Upon bringing Latin to the peninsula . . .*
Al llegar a la ciudad…	*Upon arriving in the city . . .*
Después de haber tenido diversas formas de gobierno…	*After having had different forms of government . . .*

Uses of **se + verb** in impersonal expressions.

Se llega a una tierra de castillos…	*One arrives at a land of castles . . .*
Las huellas **se ven** en todos sus pueblos…	*One sees traces (Traces are seen) in all its towns . . .*
En El Escorial **se encuentran** las tumbas…	*One finds the tombs (The tombs are found) in El Escorial . . .*
En el museo **se hallan** magníficas colecciones…	*One finds magnificent collections (Magnificent collections are found in the museum) . . .*

ℒectura

Una puerta hacia la historia

Al aterrizar en el aeropuerto internacional de Barajas en Madrid, España, se llega a una tierra de castillos, catedrales góticas,° acueductos, puentes y pueblos medievales, donde el presente nos recuerda siglos de historia y lazos° culturales. La arquitectura es posiblemente el testigo más
5 importante de la historia de España al dejar° ver la influencia de los diversos pueblos que la invadieron—fenicios,° griegos, romanos, germanos, árabes—los que dejaron su marca, no sólo en la mezcla racial, sino en la superimposición de nuevos elementos culturales que influyeron en lo que hoy es el pueblo español. Al mismo tiempo, la convivencia de
10 tres grupos religiosos—los cristianos, los árabes y los judíos°—produjo° un enriquecimiento cultural de gran valor.

   Las huellas de las distintas° civilizaciones que vivieron en España se ven en todos sus pueblos y ciudades. Los romanos, cuya dominación duró casi seis siglos, no sólo dejaron monumentos fabulosos, como el acueducto de
15 Segovia, sino que al traer el latín a la Península Ibérica, contribuyeron a la formación del idioma español. Los árabes que estuvieron en España siete siglos, también dejaron hermosos ejemplos de arquitectura árabe, como lo son el palacio de la Alhambra, en Granada, y la Mezquita° de Córdoba. Asimismo, los judíos constituyeron uno de los grupos más influyentes en la
20 península y hoy día pueden apreciarse en Toledo bellos ejemplos de sinagogas, como la Sinagoga de Santa María la Blanca y el Tránsito.

Gothic

ties

allowing

Phoenicians

Jews / produced

different

Mosque

Entre° las grandes edificaciones° de España se encuentran la Catedral   *Among / buildings*
de Sevilla, de estilo gótico, y El Escorial, una mezcla de templo
funerario, iglesia,° monasterio y palacio, situado a unas treinta millas de   *church*
25 Madrid. Esta obra de un clasicismo majestuoso y severo fue construida
por Felipe II en el siglo XVI y en ella se encuentran las tumbas° de   *tombs*
varios reyes españoles. Contrastando con estos pueblos viejos, en la
ciudad de Bilbao, en el norte de España, se encuentra el Museo
Guggenheim, magnífico ejemplo de arquitectura moderna, construido a
30 finales del siglo XX y visitado anualmente por millones de turistas.

Al llegar a Madrid es casi imposible resistirse a la idea de visitar el
Museo del Prado, donde se hallan magníficas colecciones pictóricas° que   *pictorial*
incluyen obras de Francisco Goya, Diego Velázquez, Bartolomé Murillo,
Pablo Picasso, Salvador Dalí y otros muchos pintores de fama mundial.
35 Otro museo que merece ser visitado es el Museo Nacional Centro de
Arte Reina Sofía donde existen siempre importantes exhibiciones de arte
moderno.

En literatura, España ha producido figuras de alcance universal,
como Miguel de Cervantes (1547–1616) en la novela, y Lope de Vega
40 (1562–1635) en el teatro. Estas dos figuras, lo mismo que William
Shakespeare en Inglaterra, han servido de modelo y guía a todas las

Patio de los Leones en el palacio de la Alhambra, Granada, España.

generaciones posteriores a través de los siglos. Es dato interesante que Cervantes y Shakespeare murieron el mismo año, uno en Madrid y el otro en Inglaterra. Muchos nombres han brillado° en el   *have stood out*
45 campo de la poesía, y entre los más conocidos y admirados en el siglo XX está Federico García Lorca, poeta y dramaturgo que murió trágicamente en el año 1936, durante la Guerra Civil española.

La importancia que tiene la literatura para el español es evidente en los muchos monumentos que existen en las distintas ciudades de
50 España, empezando por el dedicado a Cervantes, en la Plaza de España en Madrid. Asimismo, muchas calles tienen nombres de escritores y poetas famosos, lo cual demuestra la importancia cultural que éstos tienen en la historia de este país.

España es rica en bellezas naturales, con montañas, costas y
55 playas muy apreciadas por los visitantes que vienen de todo el mundo. Existe gran diversidad de paisajes y climas y en las distintas regiones de España no sólo encontramos diferencias climáticas y topográficas, sino también diferencias en los bailes, la música, las comidas, la indumentaria° y las tradiciones folklóricas. La variedad   *clothing*
60 de bailes regionales es rica en contrastes y belleza y la sardana, la muñeira, la jota y la seguidilla son ejemplos de esta variedad. En la guitarra, nadie como el andaluz con su *cante jondo*, donde el guitarrista y el cantaor° expresan con vehemencia° las emociones   *el cantante / vehemently*
que llevan dentro.
65 Después de haber tenido diversas formas de gobierno, especialmente la monarquía absoluta que dejó sentir su peso° en el   *weight*
Nuevo Mundo durante la Conquista y la Colonización, el país hoy día está regido° por una monarquía parlamentaria-democrática   *ruled*
dirigida por el rey Juan Carlos I, quien actúa como Jefe de Estado.°   *Head of State*

Cubierta de la primera edición de Don Quijote de la Mancha, *publicada en Madrid en 1605.*

70 Existe también un presidente de gobierno, elegido dentro de las
reglas de la democracia española, y un cuerpo legislativo formado
por la Cámara de Diputados y el Senado.

    España es un mosaico de ricos colores, tanto en su historia como
en su paisaje. Al viajar por las distintas ciudades se recibe la
75 impresión de estar visitando museos al aire libre donde se pueden
ver todos los elementos que han contribuido a su historia y a lo que
hoy es el pueblo español.

Llene los espacios en blanco para completar las siguientes oraciones. Use los verbos que
necesite en infinitivo o en presente.

1. Al _____ en el aeropuerto internacional de Madrid, sentimos que
   hemos llegado a una tierra llena de historia.

2. Se puede _____ la historia de España por las _____
   dejadas por las distinas civilizaciones que la invadieron.

3. Los romanos, que estuvieron en España casi seis _____, no sólo
   dejaron catedrales, castillos y puentes, sino que al _____ el latín a la
   península contribuyeron a la formación del español.

4. La _____ de los judíos, los árabes y los cristianos produjo un
   _____ cultural de gran valor.

5. En El Escorial se _____ las tumbas de varios reyes españoles.

6. El _____ de España es variado y rico en _____ naturales con montañas y playas muy apreciadas por los visitantes.

7. Después de haber tenido diversas formas de gobierno, España _____ _____ _____ está regida por una monarquía parlamentaria democrática.

8. El autor dice que viajar por España es como visitar museos _____ _____ _____.

Preguntas sobre la lectura

1. ¿Cree Ud. que es importante conocer la historia de un país antes de visitarlo? Explique su respuesta.
2. ¿Por qué se dice que la arquitectura es el testigo más importante de la historia de España?
3. Después de leer "Una puerta hacia la historia", ¿qué información que Ud. no sabía le interesó? Explique las razones de su respuesta.
4. ¿Qué ejemplos de arquitectura árabe menciona el autor?
5. ¿Dónde se encuentran las tumbas de varios reyes españoles? ¿Quién construyó este monasterio?
6. ¿Qué importancia tiene la literatura en la cultura de España? Explique su respuesta.
7. ¿Cuáles son los tres museos que menciona el autor? Diga algo sobre ellos.
8. ¿Qué bailes regionales menciona el autor?
9. ¿De qué región de España es el *cante jondo*?
10. ¿Qué tipo de gobierno existe hoy en España?

Temas de conversación

1. El autor dice que España es un mosaico de ricos colores. ¿Cómo interpreta Ud. esta frase?
2. Fíjese en el mapa de España, página 23, y observe la posición que tiene con respecto al resto de Europa. ¿Cree Ud. que debido a su posición en el extremo occidental de Europa España debe sentirse aislada? Explique las razones de su respuesta. Localice en el mapa las siguientes ciudades: Madrid, Segovia, Toledo, Bilbao, Sevilla y Córdoba. ¿Qué puede decir de ellas?
3. Busque en el texto dónde se describe el tipo de gobierno que existe en España. ¿Le gustaría a Ud. vivir bajo una monarquía? Explique su respuesta. ¿Cuál cree Ud. que es la principal diferencia entre una monarquía y un gobierno democrático dirigido por un presidente?
4. ¿Ha visto Ud. un espectáculo (*show*) con bailes regionales de España? ¿Con bailes folklóricos de México? ¿Qué puede decir de estas dos manifestaciones folklóricas?
5. España atrae mucho turismo de todas las partes del mundo. ¿Por qué cree Ud. que ocurre esto?

Gramática

A The verb: person, number, mood, and tense

1. The verb expresses action, being, or state of being.

> Rafael **canta**.   *Rafael sings.*
> **Estoy** enferma.   *I am ill.*

a. The infinitive **(to + verb)** is the primary form of the verb and the one found in dictionaries and most vocabulary lists.

> comprar *(to buy)*   vender *(to sell)*   recibir *(to receive)*

b. The form of the verb changes to indicate person, number, tense, and mood. These changes are very significant because they indicate who does the action, when it occurs, and the attitude of the person who speaks with respect to the action.

> **compro:** first person singular present indicative *(I buy)*
> **compraran:** third person plural past subjunctive *(they may buy)*

c. In Spanish, verbs belong to one of three conjugations, depending on the ending of the infinitive:

> First conjugation: The infinitive ends in **-ar.**
> Second conjugation: The infinitive ends in **-er.**
> Third conjugation: The infinitive ends in **-ir.**

d. Regular verbs change according to a regular pattern for each conjugation. Most verbs change according to this regular model.

First conjugation	*Second conjugation*	*Third conjugation*
AMAR *(to love)*	**COMER** *(to eat)*	**ESCRIBIR** *(to write)*
amo amamos	como comemos	escribo escribimos
amas amáis	comes coméis	escribes escribís
ama aman	come comen	escribe escriben
Other verbs	*Other verbs*	*Other verbs*
cantar *(to sing)*	beber *(to drink)*	vivir *(to live)*
bailar *(to dance)*	leer *(to read)*	recibir *(to receive)*
comprar *(to buy)*	romper *(to tear)*	dividir *(to divide)*

e. Irregular verbs do not follow the pattern of regular verbs. Some verbs change in spelling while others have vowel changes in the root (stem) of the verb. In this textbook these changes are indicated in parentheses next to the infinitive.

perder (ie) (*to lose*) **pierdo**   volver (ue) (*to return*) **vuelvo**
pedir (i) (*to ask for*) **pido**   dirigir (j) (*to direct; to conduct*) **dirijo**
conocer (zc) (*to know*) **conozco**   vencer (z) (*to win; to defeat*) **venzo**

f. A few verbs in Spanish are highly irregular and do not easily lend themselves to classification. As we shall see later in this textbook, two of these irregular verbs are **ser** and **ir**.

2. When we conjugate a verb in class, we give the different forms or changes that indicate the person and number in the different tenses and moods.

a. The root or stem is the part that precedes the verb ending.

compr ar   **vend** er   **recib** ir

b. The ending is the part added to the root or stem. The ending indicates the person, number, tense, and mood.

compr **as** (*you buy*)   compr **aron** (*they bought*)

NOTE: Since the verb ending indicates the person and number, it is not necessary to give the corresponding subject noun or pronoun unless there is ambiguity in the subject.

(yo) converso   **yo** trabajaba
(nosotros) conversamos   **ella, él, Ud.** trabajaba

3. There are three persons: first, second, and third.

Grammatical person	Corresponding subject pronoun Singular	Plural	Person indicated by the grammatical form
1st	yo	nosotros (-as)	person who speaks
2nd	tú	vosotros (-as)	person(s) spoken to
	Ud.	Uds.	
3rd	él, ella	ellos (-as)	person(s) spoken about
	ello		object spoken about

NOTES: **Ud.** and **Uds.** are third person forms grammatically; they are used with the third person verb forms. Nevertheless, because of their meaning, **Ud.** and **Uds.** are second person forms since they indicate the person(s) **to whom one speaks**.

The subject pronoun determines the number and person of the verb form. In the conjugations that appear in this textbook, **Ud.** and **Uds.** are used to indicate the third person verb forms. Remember that these same verb forms are the ones used for other third person subject forms (**él, ella, ello, ellos, ellas**), for the names of persons (Srta. Suárez, Miriam y Encarnación, los Maldonado), and for nouns used as subjects (el árbol, los perros, el avión, los estudiantes).

4. Mood is a change in the verb that expresses the attitude or aspect of mood of the person who speaks toward an action or state of being. There are three moods: indicative mood, subjunctive mood, and imperative mood.

Indicative mood is used when the person who speaks states a fact or asks a question about an action or condition without expressing an attitude.

Leonor **habla** con Andrea por teléfono.	*Leonor is talking with Andrea on the telephone.*
Andrea **vive** en Sevilla.	*Andrea lives in Sevilla.*
Leonor y Andrea **son** primas.	*Leonor and Andrea are cousins.*

The different forms of the *subjunctive mood* are generally used in subordinate clauses to mention an action or a condition that may or may not be factual. The subjunctive mood is dependent upon the emotive state or attitude of the person who speaks in the main clause.

Main clause		*Subordinate clause*
Espero	que	Uds. **puedan** visitar el Museo del Prado en Madrid.
I hope	*that*	*you will be able to visit the Prado Museum in Madrid.*
Los turistas deseaban	que	los **llevaran** al museo.
The tourists wanted	*that*	*them to take them to the museum.*
Me alegro de	que	**hayan podido** ver los cuadros de Velázquez.
I am glad	*that*	*they've been able to see the paintings of Velazquez.*

The *imperative mood* is used to give instructions or commands to a person or a group of persons.

Jaime, **cierra** las ventanas, por favor.   *Jaime, please close the windows.*
Niños, no **hablen** en clase.   *Children, don't talk in class.*

5. *Tense* refers to the verb form that indicates when an action takes place. There are simple tenses and perfect tenses. The *simple tenses* do not need an auxiliary verb. The *perfect tenses* need the auxiliary verb **haber** *(to have)*.

a. The *indicative mood* has ten tenses.

Simple tenses		*Perfect tenses*	
Present:	**compro** *I buy*	Present perfect:	**he comprado** *I have bought*
Preterite:	**compré** *I bought*	Preterite perfect:	**hube comprado** *I had bought*
Imperfect:	**compraba** *I used to buy*	Pluperfect:	**había comprado** *I had bought*
Future:	**compraré** *I will buy*	Future perfect:	**habré comprado** *I will have bought*
Conditional:	**compraría** *I would buy*	Conditional perfect:	**habría comprado** *I would have bought*

b. The *subjunctive mood* has six tenses. The future and future perfect are hardly ever used these days and are rarely found in literature. For that reason they are not included in this textbook and we present only four tenses.

Simple tenses		*Perfect tenses*	
Present:	**compre** *may buy*	Present perfect:	**haya comprado** *may have bought*
Imperfect:	**comprara (comprase)** *might buy*	Pluperfect:	**hubiera comprado (hubiese comprado)** *might have bought*

c. The *imperative mood* has only two forms.

compra (tú) *Buy*   **comprad** (vosotros)

The imperative for **Ud., Uds.** and **nosotros** uses the forms corresponding to the present subjunctive.*

compre (Ud.) *Buy*.   **compren** (Uds.)   **compremos** *Let's buy*.

B Present indicative: regular verbs and irregular verbs

1. The present indicative is used:

- To express actions that occur at the moment one speaks.
  Hablo con mis amigos. *I talk (am talking) with my friends.*

- To express actions that will take place at a future moment.
  Mañana **salgo** para Barcelona. *I leave (am leaving, shall leave) for Barcelona tomorrow.*

- To express general truths.
  El cielo **es** azul. *The sky is blue.*

- To express actions that occur habitually.
  Van a la corrida de toros todos los domingos. *They go to the bullfight every Sunday.*

- To express the historic past.
  Cervantes **muere** en 1616. *Cervantes dies in 1616.*

- With the phrase **por poco** to express a past action that did not occur.
  Por poco **vengo** a verte ayer. *I almost came to see you yesterday.*

- To express a command.
  ¿Me **traes** un vaso de agua, por favor? *(Will you) bring me a glass of water, please?*

- To express the concept of *shall*.
  ¿Nos **vamos**? *Shall we go?*

2. Regular verbs

	Verbs ending in	
-ar	*-er*	*-ir*
COMPRAR	**VENDER**	**RECIBIR**
compr **o**	vend **o**	recib **o**
compr **as**	vend **es**	recib **es**
compr **a**	vend **e**	recib **e**
compr **amos**	vend **emos**	recib **imos**
compr **áis**	vend **éis**	recib **ís**
compr **an**	vend **en**	recib **en**

*See Capítulo 4, Present subjunctive, pages 114–119.

3. Irregular verbs

a. Spell-changing verbs. Certain verbs change spelling so that the pronunciation of the stem does not change when we add certain endings.

Verb ending	Change	Infinitive	Present indicative
-cer, -cir (with a consonant before the ending)	c → z before a, o	vencer (to defeat) ejercer (to practice)	(yo) venzo ejerzo
-ger, -gir	g → j before a, o	proteger (to protect) dirigir (to direct) escoger (to choose)	protejo dirijo escojo
-guir	gu → g before a, o	seguir (to continue) distinguir (to distinguish)	sigo distingo

b. Stem-changing verbs. Certain verbs change the vowel in the stem in the forms corresponding to **yo, tú, Ud.,** and **Uds., él, ella, ellos, ellas, ello** when the vowel is stressed. These changes occur in the present tense. As we shall see later, the change **e > i** also occurs in the preterite in **Ud.** and **Uds.*** These verbs are grouped according to the vowel change.

Change	Present indicative		Other verbs
	CERRAR (to close)		
e → ie	**cierro**	cerramos	apretar (to tighten), defender (to defend), divertirse (to have fun), mentir (to lie), gobernar (to govern), sentir (to feel), empezar (to begin), preferir (to prefer), pensar (to think), querer (to want), sugerir (to suggest)
	cierras	cerráis	
	cierra	**cierran**	
	ENCONTRAR (to find)		
o → ue	**encuentro**	encontramos	contar (to count), costar (to cost), dormir (to sleep), morir (to die), poder (to be able), volver (to return), rodar (to roll), recordar (to recall), rogar (to beg), mostrar (to show)
	encuentras	encontráis	
	encuentra	**encuentran**	
	PEDIR (to ask for)		
e → i	**pido**	pedimos	conseguir (to get), reír (to laugh), impedir (to impede), medir (to measure), reñir (to quarrel), repetir (to repeat), seguir (to follow), servir (to serve), vestirse (to get dressed)
	pides	pedís	
	pide	**piden**	

NOTE: Adquirir (to acquire), **inquirir** (to inquire) and **jugar** (to play) belong to this category. They change **i > ie** or **u > ue** in **yo, tú, Ud.** and **Uds., él/ella,** and **ellos/as/o.**

*These changes also occur in present subjunctive and in the **tú** form of the imperative.

ADQUIRIR		JUGAR	
adquiero	adquirimos	**juego**	jugamos
adquieres	adquirís	**juegas**	jugáis
adquiere	**adquieren**	**juega**	**juegan**

c. Other irregular verbs.

Irregularity	*Person*	*Infinitive*	*Present*
Verbs ending in **-cer, -cir** preceded by a vowel change **c → zc** before **a, o**	yo	aparecer (*to appear*) conocer (*to know*) merecer (*to deserve*) obedecer (*to obey*) padecer (*to suffer from*) traducir (*to translate*) producir (*to produce*)	(yo) **aparezco** **conozco** **merezco** **obedezco** **padezco** **traduzco** **produzco**
Verbs that take **g**	yo	hacer (*to do*) poner (*to put*) salir (*to leave*) traer (*to bring*) valer (*to be worth*) caer(se) (*to fall down*) decir (*to say*)	(yo) **hago** **pongo** **salgo** **traigo** **valgo** (me) **caigo** **digo**
Verbs ending in **-uir** change **i → y**	yo, tú, Ud.,Uds., él/ella, ellos/as/o	huir (*to flee*) incluir (*to include*)	**huyo** huimos **huyes** huís **huye** **huyen** **incluyo** incluimos **incluyes** incluís **incluye** **incluyen**

Other verbs that belong to this group are: **construir** (*to construct*), **destruir** (*to destroy*), **distribuir** (*to distribute*), **atribuir** (*to attribute*).

NOTE: The verbs **tener** and **venir**, in addition, change **e → ie**, and the verb **decir** changes **e → i** in the stem of the second and third person.

TENER		VENIR		DECIR	
tengo	tenemos	**vengo**	venimos	**digo**	decimos
tienes	tenéis	**vienes**	venís	**dices**	decís
tiene	**tienen**	**viene**	**vienen**	**dice**	**dicen**

d. The following verbs have their own irregularities.

IR (*to go*)		DAR (*to give*)		SER (*to be*)	
voy	**vamos**	**doy**	damos	**soy**	**somos**
vas	**vais**	das	dais	**eres**	**sois**
va	**van**	da	dan	**es**	**son**

ESTAR (*to be*)		SABER (*to know*)		HABER (*to have*)	
estoy	estamos	**sé**	sabemos	**he**	**hemos**
estás	estáis	sabes	sabéis	**has**	habéis
está	**están**	sabe	saben	**ha**	**han**

CABER (*to fit*)		CAER (*to fall*)		TRAER (*to bring*)	
quepo	cabemos	**caigo**	caemos	**traigo**	traemos
cabes	cabéis	caes	caéis	traes	traéis
cabe	caben	cae	caen	trae	traen

OÍR (*to hear*)	
oigo	oímos
oyes	oís
oye	**oyen**

e. Verbs derived from other verbs have the same irregularities as these in all tenses.

Such as **tener**:

MANTENER (*to maintain; support*)	
mantengo	mantenemos
mantienes	mantenéis
mantiene	**mantienen**

Such as **hacer**:

DESHACER (*to undo*)	
deshago	deshacemos
deshaces	deshacéis
deshace	deshacen

NOTE: The verb **satisfacer** is conjugated like **hacer**, substituting the **h** for **f**.

SATISFACER (*to satisfy*)	
satisfago	satisfacemos
satisfaces	satisfacéis
satisface	satisfacen

f. Changes in accentuation.

Some verbs ending in **-iar** and **-uar** (except **-guar**) require a written accent on the weak vowel when it is stressed.

ENVIAR (*to send*)		ACTUAR (*to act*)	
envío	enviamos	**actúo**	actuamos
envías	enviáis	**actúas**	actuáis
envía	**envían**	**actúa**	**actúan**

Other verbs:

ampliar (*to enlarge*)	continuar (*to continue*)
enfriar (*to chill*)	efectuar (*to carry out*)
guiar (*to guide*)	situar (*to locate*)
	acentuar (*to accentuate*)
	graduar(se) (*to graduate*)

NOTE: The same rule of accentuation applies to the present subjunctive and the **tú**, **Ud.**, and **Uds.** forms of the imperative.

ENVIAR		ACTUAR	
envíe	**envía tú**	**actúe**	**actúa tú**
envíes		**actúes**	
envíe	**envíe Ud.**	**actúe**	**actúe Ud.**
enviemos		actuemos	
enviéis		actuéis	
envíen	**envíen Uds.**	**actúen**	**actúen Uds.**

Ejercicios

I. Piense que Ud. es una estudiante norteamericana que está estudiando arquitectura en la Universidad de Barcelona. Un compañero de clase le hace una entrevista para publicarla en el periódico de la universidad. Conteste sus preguntas.

1. ¿Desde cuándo estás en Barcelona?
2. ¿Es la primera vez que estás en esta ciudad?
3. Hablas español muy bien. ¿Es el idioma que hablan en tu casa?
4. ¿De dónde son tus padres?
5. ¿Dónde vive tu familia en los Estados Unidos?
6. ¿Crees que la Universidad de Barcelona es un lugar bueno para estudiar arquitectura? ¿Por qué?
7. ¿Qué deseas hacer al terminar los estudios de arquitectura?
8. ¿Piensas viajar por España antes de regresar a los Estados Unidos?

II. En la oficina de correos. Trabaje con una compañero(a) de clase. Conteste las preguntas que le hace; después hágale las mismas preguntas que él (ella) debe contestar.

1. ¿Envías las cartas para tu padre por correo ordinario o por avión?
2. ¿Diriges las cartas a su oficina o a la casa?
3. ¿Tienes un apartado postal (*P.O. Box*)? ¿Dónde recoges la correspondencia: en la oficina de correos o la envían a tu casa?
4. ¿Dónde consigues los giros postales (*money orders*)?
5. ¿Certificas los paquetes que mandas o los aseguras (*insure*)?

III. De excursión por España. Complete el siguiente diálogo usando el presente de indicativo del verbo entre paréntesis.

Amigo: ¿Adónde (pensar) _____ ir Uds. este fin de semana?

Ud.: (Pensar) _____ hacer un breve recorrido por la costa del Mediterráneo.

Amigo: ¿(Ir) _____ a ir en tren o en auto?

Ud.: (Querer) _____ ir en auto porque así (poder) _____ parar donde nos guste.

Amigo: Si Uds. (almorzar) _____ en el camino yo les (sugerir) _____ comer una paella de mariscos (*seafood*) que siempre (ser) _____ muy buena en la costa.

Ud.: (Esperar) _____ salir bien temprano porque yo (preferir) _____ estar de regreso antes del anochecer y nosotros (desear) _____ ver muchas cosas.

IV. El Sr. García conversa con Basilio, el empleado de la estación de gasolina. Combine los elementos dados, de acuerdo con el modelo, para reproducir la conversación entre Basilio y el Sr. García.

MODELO: Basilio / trabajar / estación de gasolina / estar / la esquina.
Basilio trabaja en la estación de gasolina que está en la esquina.

Sr. García: (Yo) Querer / llenar / el tanque / estar vacío.
Basilio: ¿Querer / gasolina sin plomo?
Sr. García: Claro que sí. Yo / proteger / el medio ambiente.
Basilio: ¿Preferir / pagar / tarjeta de crédito, o en efectivo (*cash*)?
Ser / $28.
Sr. García: Aquí estar / tarjeta de crédito. ¡Qué cara / estar / la gasolina!
Costar / mucho más que el mes pasado.

V. Complete las frases con el presente de indicativo de los verbos que aparecen entre paréntesis. Observe el uso del presente histórico en el siguiente párrafo.

La dominación romana en España _____ (durar), aproximadamente, seis siglos (del II antes de Cristo hasta principio del V después de Cristo). Los romanos _____ (llevar) a la Península su civilización, cultura, costumbres y lengua. Más tarde, en el año 711, los árabes _____ (llegar) a España y _____ (establecer) su capital en Córdoba. En arquitectura los árabes _____ (introducir) y _____ (desarrollar) un nuevo estilo a base de arcos de herradura (*horseshoe arches*) y columnas delgadas. _____ (Construir) la Mezquita en Córdoba, la

Alhambra en Granada y la Giralda en Sevilla, todos monumentos ejemplares de la arquitectura árabe. La influencia árabe _____ (extenderse) mayormente en el sur y _____ (afectar) el espíritu, las costumbres y el idioma.

VI. Complete las frases con el presente de indicativo de los verbos que aparecen entre paréntesis.

Don Quijote de la Mancha _____ (ser) una obra universal en la que Miguel de Cervantes _____ (unir) lo trágico con lo cómico, y lo real con lo irreal en una forma maravillosa. Esta novela de caballerías (*book of chivalry*) _____ (divertir) y _____ (dar) gusto a todo el que la lee. En ella _____ (existir) gran profundidad psicológica y filosófica. Don Quijote, acompañado de su escudero (*shield bearer*) Sancho Panza, _____ (ir) de aventura en aventura por los caminos de España luchando contra los males y las injusticias que _____ (existir) en el mundo. Un gran sentido de justicia lo _____ (acompañar) siempre para defender sus ideales. La frase "luchar contra molinos de viento", que _____ (querer) decir luchar contra cosas imaginarias, _____ (proceder) de un episodio de esta novela. En este episodio Don Quijote _____ (pensar) que los molinos _____ (ser) gigantes y por más que Sancho le

Molinos de viento en La Mancha, España.

_____ (decir) que él no _____ (ver) gigantes sino

molinos, Don Quijote _____ (lanzarse) (*to throw oneself*) al ataque y

pronto _____ (rodar) (*roll*) por el suelo junto con su caballo Rocinante.

Cervantes _____ (morir) en 1616, pero la figura del caballero andante

(*knight errant*) _____ (ser) inmortal.

VII. Actividad oral o escrita. ¿Conoce Ud. a una persona que, como Don Quijote, lucha contra las injusticias y los males de la sociedad? Escriba unos dos o tres párrafos (o hable en clase) sobre esta persona y sus ideales.

VIII. En el siguiente párrafo se habla del famoso pintor español Pablo Picasso (1881–1974). Complételo usando el presente de los verbos que están entre paréntesis para expresar el presente histórico.

Aunque Pablo Picasso _____ (vivir) en Francia por muchos años, siempre

_____ (seguir) conectado con España, su patria de origen. Su fuerza

creadora _____ (influir) en los artistas de su época. La destrucción de

Guernica en 1937 por un bombardeo aéreo (*air raid*) le _____

(inspirar) su famoso cuadro que, ese mismo año, se _____ (exhibir) en

el pabellón español de la exposición de París. Picasso _____ (nacer) en 1881 en

la ciudad de Málaga y _____ (morir) en Francia en 1974.

IX. En este página aparece el cuadro *Guernica* de Pablo Picasso. Mírelo y conteste las siguientes preguntas.

Guernica (1937) de Pablo Picasso. Este cuadro está actualmente en el Centro de Arte Reina Sofía, en Madrid.

1. ¿Qué figuras puede Ud. encontrar en este cuadro?
2. ¿Qué animales aparecen?
3. ¿Qué sentimientos cree Ud. que expresan las bocas abiertas?

C Reflexive verbs*

Reflexive verbs are used with the following reflexive pronouns:

me te se nos os se

and in general indicate that the same subject that performs the action of the verb also receives it. The reflexive pronouns are placed:

before a conjugated verb:	**Me** afeito por la mañana. (afeitarse) *I shave in the morning.*
before a negative command:	No **se** siente ahí. (sentarse) *Don't sit there.*
attached to an infinitive:	¿Quieres levantar**te** temprano? (levantarse) *Do you want to get up early?*
attached to a gerund:	Estamos vistiéndo**nos** para ir a la fiesta. (vestirse) *We are getting dressed to go to the party.*
attached to an affirmative command:	¡Cállen**se**! (callarse) *Be quiet!*

Ejercicios

I. Actividad oral. Su amigo quiere que Ud. se inscriba con él en un programa de gimnasia. Dígale lo que Ud. hace diariamente, usando los verbos en presente, para explicarle que no le queda tiempo. Use como guía el siguiente vocabulario.

levantarse	pasear	periódicos	cine
bañarse	estudiar	biblioteca	novio(-a)
vestirse	hablar por teléfono	deportes	familia
irse al trabajo	escuchar las noticias	comida	siesta
jugar	preparar	tiendas	televisión

II. Usted se siente un poco enfermo y conversa con su amigo. Complete las frases con ideas originales usando el verbo que está entre paréntesis en el presente de indicativo.

MODELO: (tener) Voy a ver al médico porque…
Voy a ver al médico porque tengo un resfriado fuerte.

1. (estar) Tengo que tomar aspirina porque…
2. (toser) La doctora me hace una radiografía porque…
3. (cansarse) Creo que tengo anemia porque…
4. (sentirse) No voy al trabajo porque…
5. (padecer) Tengo que dejar de fumar porque…

*See Capítulo 7, pages 206–207 for other uses of the reflexive verbs and pronouns.

D The definite article

In Spanish there are four forms for the definite article *the*, plus the neuter article **lo**.

	Masculine	*Feminine*
Singular	**el**	**la**
Plural	**los**	**las**

1. The definite article agrees with the noun in gender and number.

> **el** amor   **la** mujer
> **los** perros   **las** flores

   a. The definite article **el** is used, instead of **la**, with feminine nouns that begin with a stressed **a** or **ha**.

> **el** agua fresca   **las** aguas frescas
> **el** hambre   **mucha** hambre

   b. In Spanish there are only two contractions, **al** and **del**, combining a preposition and an article.

> a + el = **al**   Vamos **al** teatro. *Let's go (We're going) to the theatre.*
> de + el = **del**   Ésta es la casa **del** Sr. Vidales. *This is Mr. Vidales' home.*

2. The definite article is used:

   a. When the noun is something definitive or specific.

> **El** poncho de Carmelina es de lana. *Carmelina's poncho is made of wool.*

   b. When the noun refers to something in its totality, in a general, abstract, or collective sense. (This construction is not used in English.)

> **El** pan es un buen alimento.   *Bread is good nourishment.*
> **El** amor es ciego.   *Love is blind.*
> **Los** gatos son animales felinos.   *Cats are feline animals.*
> **El** tiempo es oro.   *Time is money (gold).*
> **La** envidia es un defecto humano.   *Envy is a human defect.*
> No me gusta **el** invierno.   *I don't like winter.*

   c. With parts of the body and articles of clothing, especially with reflexive verbs. Note that English uses possessive adjectives.

> Ella movió **la** cabeza.   *She moved her head.*
> Me puse **el** abrigo.   *I put on my coat.*
> Me lavé **las** manos.   *I washed my hands.*
> Se quitó **los** zapatos.   *He took off his shoes.*

   d. With the days of the week, except after the verb **ser**. Note that the definite article corresponds to *on* in English.

> Hoy es sábado; siempre vamos a la discoteca **los** sábados, pero esta semana iremos **el** domingo.
> *Today is Saturday; we always go to the disco on Saturdays,*
> *but this week we will go on Sunday.*

e. With **Sr., Sra., Srta., Dr., Dra.** and other titles, followed by the name of the person about whom we speak.

El Sr. Jiménez enseña en la Escuela Superior.	*Mr. Jiménez teaches in high school.*
La Sra. Felicidad Ramírez se está desayunando.	*Mrs. Felicidad Ramírez is having breakfast.*
¿De dónde es **la Srta.** Salazar?	*Where is Miss Salazar from?*
Voy al consultorio de **la Dra.** Milanés.	*I am going to Dr. Milanés's office.*

NOTE: The definite article is not used when addressing a person.

Sr. Rodríguez, pase Ud. por favor.	*Mr. Rodríguez, please come in.*
¿Quiere Ud. un café, Sra. Lazo?	*Would you like some coffee, Mrs. Lazo?*

f. When referring to the meals of the day; and when telling time.

Tomo café en **el** desayuno.	*I drink coffee for breakfast.*
El almuerzo es a las doce.	*Lunch is at twelve.*
¿Quién preparó **la** cena?	*Who prepared supper?*
Son **las** tres de la tarde.	*It's three o'clock in the afternoon.*

3. The definite article is not used:

a. With nouns that express an indefinite amount or quantity of a thing.

No tengo dinero.	*I don't have money.*
Compramos pan, vino y queso.	*We buy bread, wine, and cheese.*
Necesitamos cortinas.	*We need curtains.*

b. With the names of languages if they immediately follow the verb **hablar** or the prepositions **de** and **en**. The use of the definite article is optional if the names of languages follow **aprender, estudiar,** or **escribir.**

Hablan portugués en el Brasil.	*They speak Portuguese in Brazil.*
Tomo un curso de español.	*I'm taking a Spanish course.*
La conferencia fue en japonés.	*The lecture was in Japanese.*
Me gustaría aprender (**el**) noruego.	*I would like to learn Norwegian.*

NOTE: Use the definite article if an adverb follows the verb.

Angelina habla **fluidamente el** italiano.	*Angelina speaks Italian fluently.*

c. With the titles **don, doña, Santo, San, Santa, sor,** and **fray.**

Ayer llamó **don** Pedro y habló con **doña** Berta.
(*Yesterday don Pedro called and talked with doña Berta.*)
San Antonio es el santo preferido de las chicas solteras.
(*San Antonio is the single girls' preferred saint.*)

d. With roman numerals that denote the numeric order of sovereigns and pontiffs.

Carlos V (Carlos Quinto) (*Charles the Fifth*)
Enrique VIII (Enrique Octavo) (*Henry the Eighth*)

4. The definite article is used with some countries, though often omitted these days. The names of most countries, however, do not require the definite article.

México	**la** Argentina
Colombia	**el** Perú
Chile	**el** Brasil
España	**el** Ecuador
Inglaterra	**el** Canadá
Suiza	**los** Estados Unidos
Suecia	**la** China
Alemania	**la** India
Rusia	**el** Japón

NOTE: The article is required if the geographic name is modified by an adjective.

El México precolombino es fascinante.   *Pre-Columbian México is fascinating.*

5. The definite article is generally used with the names of mountains, rivers, seas, and oceans.

Los Andes están cubiertos de nieve.   *The Andes are covered with snow.*
El Amazonas está en el Brasil.   *The Amazon is in Brazil.*
El Caribe es un mar de aguas cálidas.   *The Caribbean is a sea of warm waters.*
El Pacífico baña las costas de Chile.   *The Pacific washes the coast of Chile.*

6. The neuter article **lo** is used before an adjective or a participle to express a quality or an abstract idea.

Lo grotesco me disgusta.   *The grotesque disgusts me.*
Lo ocurrido no tiene importancia.   *What occurred is not important.*
Creo **lo** mismo que Ud.   *I believe the same as you.*
Lo malo es que no puedo ir.   *The bad thing is that I can't go.*

NOTE: Lo + adjetive or adverb + **que** is equivalent to the English expression *how.*

Me sorprende **lo bueno que** es Pepe.   *I'm surprised how good Pepe is.*
No puedo creer **lo tarde que** es.   *I can't believe how late it is.*
Ella me dijo **lo divertida que** es esta clase.   *She told me how much fun this class is.*
Me sorprendió **lo bien que** habla español.   *It suprised me how well she speaks Spanish.*

Ejercicios

I. Decida en cuál de las siguientes oraciones se necesita el artículo definido. Después, escriba la forma del artículo definido que sea necesaria para completarlas.

1. La familia habla _____ español en la casa.

2. Salió para la escuela a _____ ocho de la mañana.

3. Ellos beben _____ agua pura de las montañas.

4. Luisa y René van a bailar todos _____ viernes.

5. Prefiero _____ otoño a _____ primavera.

6. Hoy es _____ sábado.

7. Necesitamos _____ vino y queso para _____ cena.

8. Enrique _____ VIII tuvo muchas esposas.

9. A Juan le duele _____ cabeza.

10. _____ vegetales son necesarios para el cuerpo humano.

II. Conteste las preguntas usando las palabras entre paréntesis y el artículo definido, si es necesario.

> **MODELO:** ¿Qué países visitó Ud.? (Argentina y Bolivia)
> **Visité la Argentina y Bolivia.**

1. ¿Qué hablan en Nicaragua? (español)
2. ¿Qué idioma habla bien Fermín? (portugués)
3. ¿Quién llamó por teléfono? (Srta. Suárez)
4. ¿Qué libro quieres? (libro de historia)
5. ¿Qué venden en esa tienda? (perfumes y jabones)
6. ¿De quién es esa casa? (Sres. Rangel)
7. ¿Qué sentimiento predomina en *Romeo y Julieta*? (amor)
8. ¿Qué le duele a Fermín? (espalda)

III. Complete el párrafo con las contracciones **al** o **del**.

Los jóvenes hablaron _____ juego de tenis y se fueron

_____ club a tomar un refresco. Allí se encontraron con los hijos

_____ Sr. Alfonso que estaban jugando _____ dominó.

E The indefinite article

The indefinite article has four forms.

	Masculine	*Feminine*
Singular	**un** (*a*)	**una** (*a*)
Plural	**unos** (*some*)	**unas** (*some*)

1. The indefinite article agrees with the noun in gender and number.

un árbol	**una** idea
unos caballos	**unas** amigas

The indefinite article **un**, instead of **una**, is used with the feminine nouns that begin with a stressed **a** or **ha**.

un alma (soul) buena	**unas** almas buenas
un hacha (ax) nueva	**unas** hachas nuevas

2. Uses of the indefinite article.

   a. In general, the indefinite article is used to refer to a nonspecific person, place, or thing.

   Dame **un** lápiz.   *Give me a pencil.*

   b. **Unos** and **unas** express an indefinite amount or quantity. The English equivalent is *some* or *about*. If used with numbers, they express the idea of *approximately*.

Compré **unos** discos viejos.	*I bought some old records.*
Había **unas** cien personas en la recepción.	*There were about one hundred people at the reception.*

   c. The indefinite article may be used to refer to a quality that characterizes an individual.

   Mi hermano es **un** perezoso. (His main quality or characteristic is laziness)
   My brother is a lazy one.

3. The indefinite article is not used:

   a. With nouns referring to a profession, occupation, nationality, religion, or political affiliation when these nouns are not modified.

Fernando es abogado y su hermano es electricista.	*Fernando is a lawyer and his brother is an electrician.*
Ellos son peruanos.	*They are Peruvian.*
Eugenio es budista.	*Eugenio is a Budhist.*
Patricia es republicana.	*Patricia is a Republican.*

NOTE: The indefinite article is used when the noun is modified.

Mi hermano es **un** piloto experto.	*My brother is an expert pilot.*
Benito Juárez fue **un** mexicano que luchó contra la intervención francesa en México.	*Benito Juarea was a Mexican who fought against the French intervention in Mexico.*
Ellos son **unos** católicos fervientes.	*They are fervent Catholics.*
Samuel es **un** verdadero demócrata.	*Samuel is a true Democrat.*

   b. With the words **cien, mil, otro, tal** (*such*) and **¡qué...!** (The article is used in English in this type of construction)

Tenemos cien libros.	*We have a hundred books.*
Necesito mil dólares.	*I need a thousand dollars.*
Mis padres compraron otra casa.	*My parents bought another house.*
No dije tal cosa.	*I did not say such a thing.*
¡Qué hombre!	*What a man!*

Ejercicios

I. Conteste las preguntas usando las palabras entre paréntesis y el artículo indefinido, si es necesario.

> **MODELO:** ¿Qué es Alberto? (piloto comercial)
> **Alberto es un piloto comercial.**

1. ¿Qué es tu hermano? (comunista furioso)
2. ¿Qué tienes que hacer? (mil cosas)
3. ¿De dónde son los hermanos Gómez? (paraguayos)
4. ¿Había muchas personas en el estadio? (aproximadamente diez mil)
5. ¿Qué quiere Ramona? (otro vaso de vino)
6. ¿Qué tienes? (dolor de cabeza muy fuerte)

II. En el siguiente párrafo se habla del pintor español Salvador Dalí (1904–1989). Complete este párrafo con los artículos definidos o indefinidos que sean necesarios.

Salvador Dalí es _____ pintor famoso cuyo arte surrealista presenta

_____ mundo lleno de imágenes alucinatorias. Dalí estudió en

_____ Escuela de Bellas Artes de Madrid. En 1928 se fue a París y allí se

puso en contacto con _____ movimiento surrealista. Colaboró con

_____ director de cine español Luis Buñuel en _____

cuantas películas. Dalí usaba _____ bigote enroscado (*twisted*) a los lados

que le daba _____ apariencia _____ poco extravagante.

III. Temas de conversación.

1. Su prima quiere ir de vacaciones y no sabe adónde ir. Como Ud. viaja tanto, ella le pide informes sobre algún lugar interesante para ir. Déle la información necesaria de los lugares que Ud. conoce para que ella pase unas buenas vacaciones.
2. Imagine que Ud. tiene un amigo en Costa Rica que piensa venir a vivir a los Estados Unidos. Él desea saber cómo es la vida en un pueblo pequeño o en una ciudad grande de este país. Ud. le va a dar la información que él pide.
3. Su profesor desea saber por qué Ud. estudia español. Explique sus razones. También explique si Ud. necesita el español en su trabajo o profesión, y si alguien en su familia habla este idioma.

 **omposición**

Antes de escribir, repase las siguientes reglas sobre la puntuación y la ortografía.

 ## A Review of punctuation rules

1. The *period* (*punto*) is used:

   - At the end of a declarative sentence or a paragraph.
     Rosa llegó a las tres de la tarde. *Rosa arrived at three.*

   - With numbers, to separate groups of three figures (English uses a comma). It should be noted, however, that this use is not standard across the Spanish-speaking world.
     2.000; 5.345 (2,000; 5,345)

   - With abbreviations*
     Srta. (señorita); **Atte.** (atentamente)

2. The *comma* (*coma*) is used:

   - To separate the name of the person addressed from the rest of the sentence.
     Josefina, llámame el lunes. Llámame el lunes, **Josefina,** no el martes.
     Josefina, call me on Monday. Call me on Monday, Josefina, not on Tuesday.

   - To separate words or phrases in a series.
     Entró, se sentó, habló por teléfono y luego salió.
     He entered, sat down, talked on the telephone, and then left.

   - To separate expressions such as **al parecer** (*apparently*), **por consiguiente** (*consequently*), **ahora bien** (*now then*), **al menos** (*at least*).
     No la vi el martes; **por consiguiente**, no le di las noticias.
     I didn't see her on Tuesday, consequently, I did not give her the news.

   - To avoid the repetition of a verb.
     Ramona cenó en casa; Rubén, en la cafetería.
     Ramona had supper at home, Ruben, in the cafeteria.

   - To separate decimals (English uses a decimal point). This use is not standard in the Spanish-speaking world.
     2,6 (2.6 in English)

3. The *semicolon* (*punto y coma*) is used to separate long phrases or clauses within a sentence.

     Todos estuvieron allí a la hora acordada; saben que para el director la puntualidad es importante.
     Everyone got there at the agreed time; they know that punctuality is very important for the director.

---

*See the website for a list of abbreviations in Spanish.

B Review of spelling rules: *c, s, z*

1. The letter **c** is used in the following cases:

   - verbs ending in **-cer** y **-cir**:
     aparecer, conocer, producir except: **ser, toser** (*to cough*), **coser** (*to sew*)
   - words ending in **-ancia** or **-ancio**:
     ignorancia, distancia, cansancio except: **ansia** (*anxiety*)
   - words ending in **-encia**:
     emergencia, inteligencia except: **Hortensia**
   - words ending in **-icia, -icio, -icie**:
     avaricia, servicio, superficie (*surface*)
   - the diminutive forms ending in **-cita, -cito, -cico, -cillo, -cilla**:
     rinconcito (*little corner*), **Carmencita, panecillo**
   - nouns ending in **-ción** corresponding to the English **-tion**:
     conversación, mención
   - words ending in **-acia, -acio**:
     democracia, espacio

2. The letter **s** is used in the following:

   - nouns ending in **-ulsión**:
     propulsión, expulsión
   - adjectives ending in **-oso, -osa, -esco, -esca, -sivo, -siva**:
     famoso, preciosa, burlesco, comprensiva except: **nocivo** (*harmful*), **lascivo** (*lustful*)
   - nouns referring to nationalities ending in **-ense**:
     nicaragüense, estadounidense, canadiense except: **vascuence** (*Basque language*)
   - the ending **-ísimo** or **-ísima**:
     bellísima, muchísimo
   - nouns ending in **-sión** corresponding to the English **-sion**:
     ocasión, explosión

3. The letter **z** is used in the following:

   - words ending in **-anza**:
     confianza (*confidence*), **esperanza** (*hope*) except: **mansa** (*meek*), **gansa** (*gander*)
   - abstract nouns ending in **-ez** and **-eza**:
     niñez (*childhood*), **grandeza** (*greatness*)

- surnames ending in **-ez, -iz, -oz:**
    Chávez, Muñiz, Muñoz
- the endings **-uzco, -uzca, -azo:**
    negruzco (*darkish*), **portazo** (*door slam*)
- the feminine ending **-iz:**
    actriz, emperatriz

4. Nouns ending in **z** change the **z > c** to form the plural:
    lápiz, lápices; vez, veces

 ## Note the use of *c, s, z* in the following words

coser (*to sew*) **cocer (ue)** (*to cook*)	**casa** (*house, marries*) **caza** (*hunts*)
ciento (*hundred*) **siento** (*I feel*)	**has** (*you have*) **haz** (*do*)
ves (*you see*) **vez** (*time*)	**cierra** (*closes*) **sierra** (*mountain range*)
abrazar (*to embrace*) **abrasar** (*to burn*)	**asta** (*mast*) **hasta** (*until*)
cenado (*dined*) **senado** (*senate*)	**asar** (*to roast*) **azar** (*chance*)

NOTE: The exercises corresponding to this section are included in the *Cuaderno de ejercicios*, Capítulo 1.

Ejercicio de composición (opcional)

Haga una composición, oral o escrita, sobre el tema que se da a continuación. Use el esquema siguiente.

TEMA: La importancia del estudio del español en los Estados Unidos.

INTRODUCCIÓN: La población hispana en los Estados Unidos. Las relaciones comerciales con los países de Hispanoamérica. México, el país vecino más cercano al sur de los Estados Unidos.

DESARROLLO: La importancia del español en las siguientes profesiones y trabajos: médicos, enfermeros, trabajadores sociales, secretarios, policías. Explique por qué. Aspectos de la vida diaria en los Estados Unidos donde se nota la influencia hispana. Los estados y las ciudades donde viven más hispanos.

CONCLUSIÓN: Ventajas que tiene el hablar español para obtener trabajo. ¿Qué otros aspectos positivos tiene para Ud. el poder hablar español?

Monumento de Cristobal Colón frente a la catedral de Santo Domingo, República Dominicana.

LECTURAS
- Lectura 1: "Diversidad vs. Unidad"
- Lectura 2: "Apocalipsis" de Marco Denevi

GRAMÁTICA
- The past: preterite and imperfect indicative
- Preterite: regular verbs and irregular verbs
- Imperfect indicative: forms
- Uses of the preterite and the imperfect indicative
- Interrogatives

COMPOSICIÓN
- Review of punctuation rules
- Review of spelling rules: **sc**

Vocabulario

Antes de leer, repase el siguiente vocabulario que le ayudará a comprender la lectura.

Sustantivos

el ayuntamiento   city hall
la costumbre   custom; practice, habit
el desarrollo   development
el ejército   army
la fuente   source
el habitante   inhabitant

la herencia   heritage; inheritance
la patria   homeland
la pobreza   poverty
el poder   power
la siesta   nap
la sobremesa   sitting at the table after dinner

Verbos

alcanzar (c)   to reach
aparecer (zc)   to appear
aumentar   to augment, increase
compartir   to share
dejar   to leave behind
desarrollar   to develop
enriquecer (zc)   to enrich

heredar   to inherit
negar (ie)   to deny
rezar (c)   to pray
seguir (i)   to continue
sentir (ie, i)   to feel
unirse   to get together

Adjetivos

cualquier   any

Frases

así como   as well as
asimismo   likewise
a pesar de   in spite of
de repente   suddenly

nivel de vida   standard of living
ni siquiera   not even
y por lo tanto   and therefore

Related words (Palabras relacionadas). The meaning of some words may be determined by thinking of related words familiar to you. Can you give in English the meaning of the underlined words derived from the words in parentheses?

1. (mejor)…importantes reformas para mejorar el nivel de vida
2. (pobre)…muchos viven en la pobreza
3. (rico)…posee un gran potencial de riqueza económica
4. (habitar)…los habitantes hablan, piensan, sienten y rezan en español
5. (gobernar)…el poder del ejército para establecer gobiernos militares

Cognates (Cognados). The ending **-dad** is equivalent to the English **-ty**. Look in the reading for the cognates that end in **-dad** and give their English equivalent.

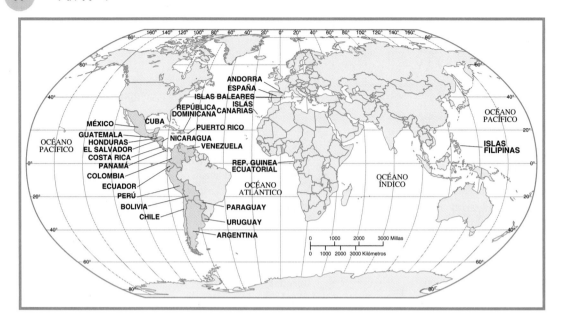

Lectura 1

Diversidad versus unidad

A pesar de la gran diversidad que presenta Hispanoamérica, los países
que la forman tienen un patrimonio° histórico común y, por lo tanto, la   *heritage*
misma tradición hispana. La unidad de su historia hace de
Hispanoamérica una gran patria para todos sus habitantes, los cuales
5 hablan, piensan, sienten y rezan en español.
     La organización de los pueblos y ciudades de Hispanoamérica es
típicamente española, teniendo siempre una plaza central con la iglesia a
un lado y el ayuntamiento, o palacio municipal, al otro. En cualquier
ciudad de Hispanoamérica se puede apreciar la huella que España dejó en
10 sus calles, en sus casas con patios interiores, en sus ventanas enrejadas,° en   *latticed windows*
sus catedrales y en sus claustros.° Asimismo, son parte de la herencia   *cloisters*
española ciertas costumbres y tradiciones, como la siesta del mediodía,
las cenas tardes y las sobremesas largas. También forman parte de esta
herencia ciertas celebraciones, como el Día de los Difuntos (Día de los
15 Muertos), el 2 de noviembre. Esta es una fecha de recordación de las
personas desaparecidas y los cementerios se llenan de gente que lleva
flores a las tumbas de sus familiares.

Celebración del Día de los Muertos en la Ciudad de México.

    Esta marcada influencia española tomó distintas formas al unirse con
otras culturas en el Nuevo Mundo. El substrato° azteca y maya en   *substratum, origin*
20 México y en Guatemala, y el inca en el Perú, así como la cultura
africana en el Caribe, fueron las principales fuentes de enriquecimiento
que contribuyeron a formar un mundo con formas, colores y música
genuinamente propio de Hispanoamérica. ¿Quién puede negar la
influencia indígena que aparece en las artes populares de muchos países
25 de Hispanoamérica? ¿Y no es en la música y los bailes donde aparece
más completa la fusión de lo español con la cultura indígena y la cultura
africana? Ciertos países crearon y desarrollaron ritmos nuevos
enriqueciendo aún más el rico folklore heredado de España. Por
ejemplo, en México surgió el corrido, en la region del Caribe el danzón,
30 el son y la rumba, en Venezuela el joropo, en Colombia la cumbia, en
Chile la tonada y en la Argentina el tango que a principios del siglo XX
invadió los salones de Europa con sus melodías.
    Los pueblos de Hispanoamérica son pueblos individualistas, de gran
vitalidad y, por lo tanto, difíciles de gobernar. Esto explica los golpes de
35 estado° que se han producido en algunos países, así como el poder del   *coups d'etat*
ejército para establecer gobiernos militares, interrumpiendo un
desarrollo democrático estable. Los países de Hispanoamérica son
repúblicas cuyo jefe de gobierno es un presidente elegido por el voto de
los ciudadanos. Cuba es la excepción donde el régimen de gobierno es
40 una dictadura comunista que lleva 43 años en el poder.

El contraste entre las clases sociales en Hispanoamérica sigue siendo muy marcado. La clase con mayores medios° económicos representa una minoría y la clase media todavía no predomina en la mayor parte de los países. Una gran mayoría, tanto en el campo como en la ciudad, vive en la pobreza. En
45 algunos países se han introducido importantes reformas para mejorar el nivel de vida de sus habitantes.

means

Actualmente,° se están haciendo grandes esfuerzos por desarrollar y aumentar la economía de ese conglomerado de naciones que comparte la misma tradición histórica, que tiene inmensas reservas espirituales, y que
50 posee un gran potencial de riqueza económica, lo cual promete un futuro lleno de esperanzas.

At present

Llene los espacios en blanco con la palabra que sea correcta.

1. No se puede negar la _____ hispana que existe en Hispanoamérica. Las huellas que dejaron los españoles se ven en todas las ciudades.
2. El alcalde (*mayor*) de la ciudad tiene la oficina en el _____.
3. Cuando la familia acaba de comer se queda conversando en la mesa. Hacen siempre unas _____ largas.
4. Todos los días la abuela dormía la _____ al mediodía.
5. Los salarios han aumentado y la situación económica ha mejorado en el país. Por lo tanto, ha subido el _____ de los habitantes.
6. El ejército dio un _____ y estableció un gobierno militar que interrumpió el proceso democrático del país.
7. El _____ económico del país fue grande al abrirse nuevas industrias y aumentar la exportación de sus productos.

Preguntas sobre la lectura

1. ¿Por qué se dice que Hispanoamérica es como una gran patria común para sus habitantes?
2. ¿En qué manifestaciones en Hispanoamérica se nota la herencia española?
3. ¿En qué aspectos de la cultura hispanoamericana se nota la influencia de las culturas indígenas y africanas?
4. Dé ejemplos de los ritmos que surgieron en México, el Caribe, Chile, Venezuela, Colombia y Argentina.
5. ¿Existe una clase media grande en muchos países de Hispanoamérica? Explique su respuesta.

Temas de conversación

1. ¿Cómo cree Ud. que se podría mejorar la riqueza económica de algunos países de Hispanoamérica?
2. ¿Cree Ud. que sería posible unir todos los países de Sudamérica bajo un gobierno federal central como existe en los Estados Unidos? Explique su respuesta.
3. ¿Cómo es el centro de la ciudad donde Ud. vive? ¿Dónde está el ayuntamiento?
4. ¿Existe influencia africana en la música de los Estados Unidos? Dé ejemplos.
5. ¿Qué música popular de Hispanoamérica conoce Ud.? ¿Cuál le gusta más? Explique por qué.
6. ¿Qué países de Hispanoamérica desea Ud. visitar? ¿Qué le interesaría ver si viaja por Hispanoamérica?

Vocabulario

Antes de leer, repase el siguiente vocabulario que le ayudará a comprender la lectura.

Sustantivos
la máquina   machine
la mitad   half
el sillón   chair, rocking chair

Verbos
alcanzar (c)   to reach
apretar (ie)   to push
bastar   to be enough
prevalecer (zc)   to prevail
quedar   to remain, end up; to be left behind
tropezar (ie)   to bump into

Adjetivos
disponible   available

Frases
la tienda de antigüedades   antique shop
ni siquiera   not even
ellos mismos   they themselves
ya no   no longer

Lectura 2

Marco Denevi

Marco Denevi nació en Buenos Aires, Argentina, en 1922. Su primer libro *Rosaura a las diez* mereció el primer premio en un concurso celebrado por la Editorial Kraft, en 1955. Este libro fue el comienzo de su brillante carrera literaria que abarca (*covers*) el campo de la novela, el cuento corto y el teatro. En muchas de sus obras prevalece cierta sátira social, así como su preocupación por el progreso tecnológico del mundo actual. La pequeña fantasía que sigue pertenece a la colección *Ceremonia secreta y otros cuentos*, de 1965.

El palacio presidencial, la Casa Rosada, al frente de la Plaza de Mayo con el obelisco en el centro, Buenos Aires.

Apocalipsis

La extinción de la raza de los hombres se sitúa aproximadamente a fines del siglo XXXII. La cosa ocurrió así: las máquinas habían alcanzado tal perfección que los hombres ya no necesitaban comer, ni dormir, ni leer, ni hablar, ni escribir, ni hacer el amor, ni siquiera pensar. Les bastaba
5 apretar botones y las máquinas lo hacían todo por ellos. Gradualmente fueron desapareciendo las Biblias, los Leonardo da Vinci,[1] las mesas y los sillones, las rosas, los discos con las nueve sinfonías de Beethoven,[2] las tiendas de antigüedades, el vino de Burdeos,[3] las oropéndolas,° los   *golden orioles* tapices flamencos,° todo Verdi,[4] las azaleas, el palacio de Versalles. Sólo   *Flemish tapestries*
10 había máquinas. Después los hombres empezaron a notar que ellos mismos iban desapareciendo gradualmente, y que, en cambio, las máquinas se multiplicaban. Bastó poco tiempo para que el número de los hombres quedase° reducido a la mitad y el de las máquinas   *end up* aumentase al doble.° Las máquinas terminaron por ocupar todo el   *increase doubly*
15 espacio disponible. Nadie podía moverse sin tropezar con una de ellas. Finalmente, los hombres desaparecieron. Como el último se olvidó de desconectar las máquinas, desde entonces seguimos funcionando.

[1]*Leonardo da Vinci (1452–1519), artista italiano que se distinguió en la pintura y en otros campos del saber humano.*
[2]*Ludwig van Beethoven (1770–1827), famoso compositor alemán.*
[3]*Burdeos, región de Francia famosa por sus vinos.*
[4]*Giuseppe Verdi (1813–1901), célebre compositor italiano, autor de muchas óperas.*

Preguntas sobre la lectura

1. En esta pequeña fantasía, ¿cuándo cree el autor que se extinguirá la raza humana?
2. ¿Qué aspecto del mundo actual critica el autor?
3. ¿Qué usa el autor para representar la religión, la pintura, la música y la arquitectura?
4. ¿Por qué cree Ud. que el autor dice al final "seguimos funcionando"?

Gramática

A The past: preterite and imperfect indicative

In Spanish there are two simple tenses to express events in the past: the preterite and the imperfect. Their use depends on the idea that the speaker wishes to communicate.

In general, the *preterite* expresses an action, state of being, or condition that is completed in the past at a specific moment in time. It focuses on the beginning or end of the action or event.

The *imperfect* describes a scene and expresses an action, state of being, or condition that was continuous or in progress. It focuses on the middle of the event, without specifying a moment in time.

Past	
Preterite	Imperfect
La semana pasada **fui** a la playa. (*Last week I went to the beach.*)	**Hacía** una mañana hermosa. (*It was a beautiful morning.*)
Salí de casa a las diez. (*I left home at ten.*)	**Me sentía** feliz. (*I felt happy.*)
Cuando **llegué me senté** en la arena. (*When I arrived I sat on the sand.*)	Las olas **eran** suaves. (*The waves were gentle.*)
Después **nadé** un rato. (*Later, I swam for a while.*)	El mar **estaba** claro y tibio. (*The sea was clear and warm.*)
Volví a casa a las cuatro. (*I came home at four.*)	Cuando **regresaba** a casa en el coche **pensaba** que **debía** ir a la playa con más frecuencia. (*When I was coming back home in the car I was thinking that I should go to the beach more often.*)

B Preterite: regular verbs and irregular verbs

1. Regular verbs.

Verbs ending in

-ar	-er	-ir
COMPRAR	VENDER	RECIBIR
compr **é** *(I bought)*	vend **í** *(I sold)*	recib **í** *(I received)*
compr **aste**	vend **iste**	recib **iste**
compr **ó**	vend **ió**	recib **ió**
compr **amos**	vend **imos**	recib **imos**
compr **asteis**	vend **isteis**	recib **isteis**
compr **aron**	vend **ieron**	recib **ieron**

2. Irregular verbs.

  a. Verbs of the second and third conjugation (**-er** and **-ir** verbs) whose stem ends in a vowel change the endings **-ió, -ieron** to **-yó, -yeron**.

Infinitive		*Preterite*
caer	(Ud.) **cayó**	(Uds.) **cayeron**
creer	(Ud.) **creyó**	(Uds.) **creyeron**
leer	(Ud.) **leyó**	(Uds.) **leyeron**
oír	(Ud.) **oyó**	(Uds.) **oyeron**
huir	(Ud.) **huyó**	(Uds.) **huyeron**
incluir	(Ud.) **incluyó**	(Uds.) **incluyeron**
construir	(Ud.) **construyó**	(Uds.) **construyeron**
atribuir	(Ud.) **atribuyó**	(Uds.) **atribuyeron**

  b. There is one group of verbs that has the following endings in the preterite:

-e	-imos
-iste	-isteis
-o	-ieron

Note that the endings for **yo** and **Ud., él, ella** are **-e, -o** (instead of **-í, -ió**) and omit the accent mark.

Infinitive			*Preterite*		
poder	(yo)	**pude**	(él/ella/Ud.)		**pudo**
poner		**puse**			**puso**
saber		**supe**			**supo**
caber		**cupe**			**cupo**
haber		**hube**			**hubo**
tener		**tuve**			**tuvo**
estar		**estuve**			**estuvo**
andar		**anduve**			**anduvo**
querer		**quise**			**quiso**
hacer		**hice**			**hizo**
venir		**vine**			**vino**

c. Verbs ending in **-decir** and **-ducir**, have a **j** in the ending.

The verb **traer** is included in this category. Note that the endings for these verbs, whose stem ends in **j**, changes from **-ieron** to **-eron**. Note also that the endings for these irregular verbs are not accented.

DECIR		**PRODUCIR**		**TRAER**	
dije	**dijimos**	**produje**	**produjimos**	**traje**	**trajimos**
dijiste	**dijisteis**	**produjiste**	**produjisteis**	**trajiste**	**trajisteis**
dijo	**dijeron**	**produjo**	**produjeron**	**trajo**	**trajeron**

d. The verbs **ser**, **ir**, and **dar** are irregular in the preteterite. Note that **ser** and **ir** have identical forms.

SER		**IR**		**DAR**	
fui (*I was*)	**fuimos**	**fui** (*I went*)	**fuimos**	**di** (*I gave*)	**dimos**
fuiste	**fuisteis**	**fuiste**	**fuisteis**	**diste**	**disteis**
fue	**fueron**	**fue**	**fueron**	**dio**	**dieron**

e. Stem-changing **-ir** verbs have the following changes in the **Ud.** and **Uds.** forms. The endings are regular.

Change	*Infinitive*		*Preterite*		
e → i	pedir (*to ask for*)	(Ud.)	**pidió**	(Uds.)	**pidieron**
	preferir (*to prefer*)		**prefirió**		**prefirieron**
o → u	morir (*to die*)		**murió**		**murieron**
	dormir (*to sleep*)		**durmió**		**durmieron**

Other **-ir** verbs that have this stem-change are:

mentir (*to lie*)	**servir** (*to serve*)	**seguir** (*to follow*)
sentir (*to feel*)	**teñir** (*to tint*)	**impedir** (*to impede*)
conseguir (*to get*)	**repetir** (*to repeat*)	**reñir** (*to fight, to argue*)
divertir(se)	**despedir(se)**	**desvestir(se)**
(*to enjoy oneself*)	(*to say farewell*)	(*to undress*)

f. Verbs of the third conjugation (**-ir** verbs) whose stem ends in **ñ**—such as **reñir** and **teñir**—drop the **i** of the endings in the following forms:

preterite (Ud., Uds.): **riñó, riñeron**
imperfect subjunctive (all forms): **riñera, riñeras…**
present participle: **riñendo**

> Los niños **riñeron** en la calle. *The children quarreled on the street.*
> Lupe se está **tiñendo** el pelo. *Lupe is tinting her hair.*

g. Verbs ending in **-car**, **-gar**, and **-zar** have a spelling change in the **yo** form so that the pronunciation of the consonant in the stem does not change. The endings are regular.

Spelling change	Infinitive	Preterite
c → qu	sacar (*to take out*)	(yo) **saqué**
	atacar (*to attack*)	**ataqué**
g → gu	llegar (*to arrive*)	**llegué**
	pagar (*to pay*)	**pagué**
z → c	empezar (*to begin*)	**empecé**
	almorzar (*to have lunch*)	**almorcé**

h. The **yo** form of the verb **averiguar** requires a diaeresis (two dots) over the **u** to indicate that the **u** is pronounced.

> (yo) **averigüé** (*I found out*)

Ejercicios

I. Haga nuevas oraciones usando en pretérito los verbos entre paréntesis.

MODELO: García Lorca vivió en Granada. (nacer) (estudiar) (morir)
García Lorca nació en Granada.
García Lorca estudió en Granada.
García Lorca murió en Granada.

1. El ladrón entró por la ventana. (salir) (huir) (saltar)
2. Ellos bailaron mucho. (divertirse) (lastimarse) (reñir)
3. Ella leyó la noticia ayer por la mañana. (oír) (traducir) (saber)
4. Compré las entradas para el concierto. (pagar) (obtener) (traer)
5. Abelardo salió en el avión de las cinco. (venir) (ir) (llegar)

II. Imagine que·Ud. ha ido a almorzar con un amigo que hace tiempo que no ve y conversan durante el almuerzo. Complete el diálogo usando el pretérito de los verbos que están entre paréntesis.

Amigo: ¿Qué me cuentas de tu prima Luisita?

Ud.:   Tengo muchas noticias que darte. Figúrate, que hace un año ella

_____ (sacarse) la lotería y _____ (andar) de viaje

por toda Sudamérica durante seis meses. Cuando _____ (ir) a

Bariloche, en la Argentina, en el mes de agosto que, como sabes, es invierno

allí, _____ (tener) un accidente serio.

Amigo: No me digas, ¿qué le _____? (pasar)

Ud.:   A ella le encanta esquiar y _____ (quebrarse) una pierna y

_____ (lastimarse) una vértebra.

Amigo: ¡Pobre Luisita! ¿_____ (quedarse) en Bariloche hasta estar bien

o _____ (regresar) a los Estados Unidos?

Ud.:   Al principio, _____ (estar) en un hospital en Bariloche dos

semanas y cuando _____ (poder) hacer el viaje

_____ (decidir) irse a Buenos Aires a casa de unos amigos que la

quieren mucho.

Amigo: Menos mal, porque un viaje de Buenos Aires a los Estados Unidos con una

pierna quebrada y una vértebra lastimada es horrible. Son muchas horas de

avión.

Ud.:   Dímelo a mí, que _____ (volar) a Buenos Aires para traerla a

casa y _____ (salir) de aquí un lunes y _____

(volver) el miércoles con ella.

Amigo: ¿Y ya está completamente bien?

Ud.:   Sí, y dice ahora que va a ir a Suiza para esquiar en los Alpes. Ya le

_____ (decir) que si le pasa algo yo no voy a buscarla.

III. Rafael y Adelaida tienen que escribir un informe sobre los españoles que han recibido el Premio Nobel. Complete el párrafo con el pretérito de los verbos entre paréntesis para enterarse (to know) de la conversación de ellos.

Rafael: ¿Sabes que Santiago Ramón y Cajal _____ (recibir) el Premio

Nobel en Medicina en 1906?

Adelaida: Sí, él _____ (ser) un médico e investigador notable y además

un escritor que _____ (publicar) varios libros que

_____ (tener) gran aceptación en su época. Recuerdo también que Severo Ochoa _____ (compartir) el Premio Nobel en Medicina en 1959 por los estudios que _____ (hacer) sobre las enzimas (*enzymes*).

Rafael: Dos poetas que _____ (obtener) también este Premio _____ (ser) Juan Ramón Jiménez, en 1956, y Vicente Aleixandre, en 1977.

Adelaida: Yo creo que la obra de Juan Ramón Jiménez *Platero y yo* es una verdadera joya literaria. Yo la _____ (leer) muchas veces y siempre la _____ (gozar) mucho.

Rafael: En el teatro hay otros dos españoles que recibieron este Premio: José Echegaray, matemático y dramaturgo, en l904, quien _____ (publicar) primero obras científicas y más tarde _____ (alcanzar) gran celebridad con sus obras teatrales; y Jacinto Benavente, con su abundante producción teatral, que _____ (contribuir) a ganar este valioso Premio.

Adelaida: El último español que _____ (conseguir) recibir el Premio Nobel _____ (ser) el novelista Camilo José Cela, en 1989.

Rafael: ¿Qué sabes de los Premios Nobel de Hispanoamérica? _____ (haber) muchas personas a quienes se les _____ (otorgar) ese Premio. Recuerdo que en 1992 le _____ (dar) a Rigoberta Menchú el Premio Nobel de la Paz por su lucha cívica en favor de los pueblos (*people*) indígenas y mestizos de Guatemala.

Adelaida: Como sabes, los dos poetas chilenos Gabriela Mistral y Pablo Neruda _____ (ganar) el Premio Nobel, la primera en 1945 y el segundo en 1971.

Rafael: Y el Premio Nobel de Literatura en 1982 _____ (caer) en el colombiano Gabriel García Márquez quien _____ (producir) una de las mejores muestras de realismo mágico con su obra *Cien años de soledad*.

Adelaida: Fue una alegría el saber que el escritor mexicano Octavio Paz _____ (ser) el elegido (*selected*) para el Premio Nobel de Literatura en 1990. La crítica ocupa un lugar importante en su obra, como puede verse en *El laberinto de la soledad*. Este gran escritor también _____ (recibir) el importante Premio Cervantes en 1981.

IV. Composición dirigida (oral o escrita). Imagine que Ud. hizo un viaje el verano pasado y ahora sus amigos quieren que Ud. les diga cómo fue porque ellos piensan hacer lo mismo. Use para su narración los verbos en pasado y la guía que se da a continuación.

1. El viaje en avión. Sobre el mar o sobre tierra.
2. El vuelo directo o con escala.
3. El precio del pasaje. Pasaje de ida y vuelta, o pasaje de ida nada más.
4. El tiempo que estuvo de viaje.
5. Los lugares que visitó.
6. Las cosas que compró.
7. Los restaurantes y hoteles donde estuvo.
8. Las personas que conoció.

Comience así: **El verano pasado fui a...**

V. Temas de conversación. Coméntele a un(a) compañero(a) lo que ocurrió en las siguientes situaciones. Continúe la idea y dé por lo menos tres ejemplos para cada tema.

1. Ayer ocurrió algo muy interesante. El Secretario de Educación estuvo en la universidad y...
2. Ayer me quedé en casa todo el día, pero hice muchas cosas...
3. Pasé unas Navidades (o unos días festivos) muy buenas el año pasado porque...

C Imperfect indicative: forms

1. Regular verbs.

Verbs ending in

-ar	-er	-ir
COMPRAR	**VENDER**	**RECIBIR**
compr **aba** (*I used to buy*)	vend **ía** (*I used to sell*)	recib **ía** (*I used to receive*)
compr **abas**	vend **ías**	recib **ías**
compr **aba**	vend **ía**	recib **ía**
compr **ábamos**	vend **íamos**	recib **íamos**
compr **abais**	vend **íais**	recib **íais**
compr **aban**	vend **ían**	recib **ían**

2. There are only three irregular verbs in the imperfect indicative.

SER		IR		VER	
era (*I was*)	éramos	iba (*I used to go*)	íbamos	veía (*I used to see*)	veíamos
eras	erais	ibas	ibais	veías	veíais
era	eran	iba	iban	veía	veían

D Uses of the preterite and imperfect indicative

1. Uses of the *preterite*. The preterite tense is used to express an action, state of being, or condition completed at a specific time in the past.

> El terremoto de San Francisco **fue** en 1906.
> *The San Francisco earthquake was in 1906.*
> Cristina García **escribió** su primera novela en inglés.
> *Cristina García wrote her first novel in English.*
> Los problemas que tiene hoy el país **comenzaron** en 1992.
> *The problems that the country has today began in 1992.*
> El año pasado **fuimos** tres veces a México.
> *Last year we went to México three times.*
> Cuando le **hice** la pregunta a mi padre, me dijo que sí.
> *When I asked my father the question, he said yes.*
> Mis amigos **estuvieron** en Bogotá el año pasado.
> *My friends were in Bogota last year.*

2. Uses of the *imperfect indicative*. The imperfect indicative is used:

   a. To describe the scene of an action, state of being, or condition in progress in the past.

   > El viento **soplaba** muy fuerte cuando cerré todas las ventanas.
   > *The wind was blowing very hard when I closed all the windows.*
   > Los niños **jugaban** en el parque con sus amiguitos.
   > *The children were playing in the park with their little friends.*

   b. To express what used to happen or what happened repeatedly in the past.

   > Siempre **íbamos** de vacaciones a Puerto Vallarta.
   > *We always used to go on vacation to Puerto Vallarta.*
   > Mi padre **escribía** todos los domingos; él venía aquí frecuentemente.
   > *My father used to write every Sunday; he used to come here often.*

   c. To describe the physical condition or characteristics of persons or things in the past.

   > Su mujer **era** joven y linda. *His wife was young and beautiful.*
   > El cielo **estaba** cubierto de nubes negras. *The sky was covered with dark clouds.*

   d. To describe a state of mind, feeling, desire, or opinion.

   > Julia no **se sentía** contenta en el trabajo. *Julia did not feel happy at work.*
   > Ellos **querían** visitar varias fábricas en Monterrey.
   > *They wanted to visit several factories in Monterrey.*
   > Yo **creía** que Salvador **vivía** en Taxco.
   > *I thought that Salvador was living in Taxco.*

   e. To express time and age in the past.

   > **Eran** las doce del día cuando salí de la biblioteca.
   > *It was eleven in the morning when I left the library.*
   > **Tenía** veinte años cuando me casé.
   > *I was twenty years old when I got married.*

3. Differences between the preterite and the imperfect indicative.
    Choosing the preterite or imperfect, or the use of both tenses in a single sentence, depends on what the speaker wishes to communicate.

    a. Compare the following examples.

Preterite	*Imperfect indicative*
Él **estuvo** enfermo la semana pasada. (He is no longer ill.)	Él **estaba** enfermo cuando lo visité la semana pasada. (Describes the condition of the person at the time of my visit last week.)
He was ill last week.	*He was ill when I visited him last week.*
Cuando **tuvo** dinero **gastó** mucho. (It suggests that the fact of having money and of spending a lot is finished.)	Cuando **tenía** dinero gastaba mucho. (During the indefinite period of time when he had money he used to spend a lot)
When he had money he spent a lot.	*When he would have money he would spend a lot.*
Yo **tuve** que ir al médico porque **estaba** enferma. (The visit to the doctor took place [finished action] due to the condition of being ill.)	Yo **tenía** que ir a la escuela pero **me quedé** dormida. (I had the moral obligation to go to school, but I didn't go because I overslept.)
I had to go to the doctor because I was ill.	*I had to go to school but I overslept.*
El almuerzo **fue** a la una. (Lunch took place at one.)	El almuerzo **era** a la una. (Lunch was announced for one o'clock.)
Lunch was (took place) at one.	*Lunch was at one.*
Ella **enseñó** en la universidad. (It indicates that at a certain moment the action of teaching was interrupted.)	Ella **enseñaba** en la universidad. (Describes what she used to do during an indefinite period of time.)
She taught at the university.	*She used to teach at the university.*

    b. Some verbs communicate a different meaning when used in the preterite or in the imperfect. Among these verbs are **poder, saber, querer,** and **conocer.** Note the change in meaning in the following examples.

Preterite	*Imperfect indicative*
Él **pudo** trabajar. (He succeeded in working.)	Él **podía** trabajar. (He was able to work.)
He did manage to work.	*He was able to work.*
Supieron la noticia. (They discovered the news.)	**Sabían** la noticia. (They had knowledge of the knews.)
They found out the news.	*They knew the news.*
Yo no **quise** hacerlo. (I refused and didn't try to do it.)	Yo no **quería** hacerlo. (I didn't have the desire to do it.)
I refused to do it.	*I did not want to do it.*

Él **quiso** venir.
(He made every effort (tried) to come.)
He wanted to come. He tried to come.

Él **quería** venir.
(He had the desire, the mental attitude, to come.)
He wanted to come.

Conocí a tu hermana el año pasado.
(I was introduced to your sister last year.)
I met your sister last year.

Yo **conocía** a tu hermana.
(Suggests knowing your sister in an indefinite manner.)
I used to know your sister. I knew your sister.

Ejercicios

I. Ud. hace una solicitud (*application*) para una beca (*scholarship*) y su consejero (*counselor*) desea tener alguna información suya. Conteste las preguntas usando en sus respuestas los verbos en imperfecto.

1. ¿Qué deportes hacía cuando era niño o niña?
2. ¿Qué hacía durante los veranos cuando no había clases?
3. ¿Qué hacía para ganar algún dinero?
4. ¿Qué hacía en su casa para ayudar a sus padres?
5. ¿Qué hacía cuando los fines de semana no podía salir?

II. Complete las oraciones con ideas originales usando el verbo que está entre paréntesis en el imperfecto de indicativo para indicar lo que estas personas hacían en las siguientes situaciones.

MODELO: (fumar) Siempre tosía porque…
   Siempre tosía porque fumaba muchos cigarrillos.

1. (acostarse) Luis siempre se levantaba tarde porque…
2. (querer) Adelaida estaba a dieta porque…
3. (tener) No podíamos comprar la casa porque…
4. (ser) Marta tenía muchos amigos porque…
5. (estudiar) Siempre sabía las lecciones porque…

III. Combine los elementos dados y haga oraciones completas usando los verbos en el imperfecto de indicativo para hacer una descripción del calendario azteca.

MODELO: En el calendario azteca / año / consistir / dieciocho meses.
   En el calendario azteca el año consistía en dieciocho meses.

1. Cada mes / tener / veinte días / representarse / con símbolos.
2. En ese calendario / haber / cinco días / mala suerte.
3. Los aztecas / creer / estos días / ser / peligrosos.
4. Ellos / tratar de / actuar con mucho cuidado.
5. Siempre / evitar / irse lejos / casas.

IV. Complete las oraciones con el pretérito o el imperfecto de indicativo de los verbos entre paréntesis para narrar lo que su hermano hizo cuando necesitaba empleo.

1. (necesitar / leer / estar) Mi hermano _____ encontrar empleo y _____ en el periódico que _____ buscando personal en la nueva sucursal (*branch*) del Banco de América.

2. (llamar / pedir) _____ por teléfono y _____ una entrevista.

3. (sentir / recibir / pasar) El día de la entrevista se _____ muy nervioso, pero cuando el gerente (*manager*) lo _____ en forma amable se le _____ el nerviosismo.

4. (decir / necesitar) El gerente le _____ que _____ una persona para trabajar de cajero (*cashier*).

5. (ser / querer / tardar / hacer) El trabajar de cajero en un banco _____ lo que mi hermano _____, así que no _____ en aceptar la proposición que el gerente le _____.

Interior de la nueva Basílica de Guadalupe, en la Ciudad de México.

V. El 12 de diciembre se hace una gran celebración en México dedicada a la Virgen de Guadalupe, que es la patrona del país. En las siguientes oraciones se habla de la aparición de la Virgen en el cerro del Tepeyac. Complételas con el pretérito o el imperfecto de indicativo de los verbos entre paréntesis.

1. (vivir) Un indiecito humilde que se llamaba Juan Diego _____ con su tío.

2. (ayudar) Lo _____ a cuidar las ovejas y a sembrar maíz y frijol.

3. (caer / salir) Una vez el tío _____ enfermo y Juan Diego _____ solo al campo.

4. (oír / llamar) De repente _____ una voz que lo _____.

5. (subir / ver / tender) _____ al cerro y _____ en medio de una luz brillante a una dama preciosa que le _____ la mano.

6. (empezar) Juan Diego _____ a correr lleno de miedo.

7. (volver / aparecer) A la mañana siguiente _____ al cerro y la dama _____ de nuevo.

8. (hablar / decir / querer) Le _____ a Juan Diego y le _____ que ella _____ una iglesia en ese cerro para proteger y velar por (*to look after*) los indios.

9. (arrodillarse (*to kneel*) / decir) Juan Diego _____ y le _____: "Madrecita linda, soy tu siervo (*servant*) y voy a obedecerte."

10. (ser / construir) Así _____ como se _____ la primera Basílica de la Virgen de Guadalupe al pie del cerro del Tepeyac, en la Ciudad de México.

VI. En el siguiente párrafo se habla del escritor argentino Jorge Luis Borges (1899–1986). Complete las oraciones con el pretérito o el imperfecto de indicativo de los verbos entre paréntesis.

Jorge Luis Borges _____ (nacer) en Buenos Aires, Argentina, en 1899. Su abuela paterna _____ (ser) inglesa y con ella _____ (aprender) el inglés al mismo tiempo que el español. Desde muy niño le _____ (gustar) leer y siempre _____ (entretenerse) leyendo libros en español e inglés. Borges _____ (comenzar) sus estudios en Buenos Aires y los _____ (continuar) en Suiza. Después que _____ (terminar) la Primera Guerra Mundial _____ (ir) a Londres y a España. Entre los años 1930 y 1955 Borges _____ (producir) las colecciones de cuentos que lo _____ (hacer) famoso entre los autores de Hispanoamérica.

VII. La fiesta en casa de Gloria. Complete las oraciones en español con el pretérito o el imperfecto de indicativo de los verbos que aparecen en inglés.

1. (met) Anoche yo _____ a los primos de Gloria.
2. (did not know) Yo no _____ que ellos eran tan simpáticos.
3. (found out) Yo _____ la noticia de la fiesta cuando me llamó Roberto para invitarme.
4. (knew) También estaba en la fiesta Julio Iglesias. Él _____ a todos los que estaban allí.
5. (refused) Él _____ cantar porque dijo que tenía dolor de garganta (*sore throat*).

VIII. Composición dirigida oral. El chico que Ud. conoció en la fiesta de graduación se ha interesado mucho en Ud. y quiere saber más detalles de Ud. y de su familia. Le ha pedido a Ud. que hable de los siguientes tópicos. En su narración use los verbos en pretérito o en imperfecto de indicativo.

1. Sus abuelos. Mencione el aspecto físico, lugar de donde eran, cualidades o defectos que tenían, lo que hacían, etc.
2. Todo lo que Ud. hacía cuando era niño o niña.
3. Las actividades en que Ud. tomaba parte cuando estaba en la escuela secundaria.
4. Las cosas que hacía su familia cuando iba de vacaciones.
5. Algún hecho especial, dramático o divertido, de su vida.

E Interrogatives

Invariable	Variable
qué *what*	**cuál** (-es) *which*
cuándo *when*	**quién** (-es) *who*
cómo *how*	**cuánto** (-os, -a, -as) *how much; how many*
dónde *where*	

Interrogatives (question words) always have an accent mark, whether in a direct or an indirect question.

¿**Qué** compraste?	Dime **qué** compraste.
What did you buy?	*Tell me what you bought.*
(direct question)	(indirect question)

Interrogatives may be used alone or with a preposition.

¿**Cuándo** te casas?	*When do you get married?*
¿**Para dónde** vas?	*Where are you going?*
¿**Dónde** está Remigio?	*Where is Remigio?*
¿**Cómo** sigue su abuelo?	*How is his grandfather?*
¿**A cómo** están las naranjas?	*How much are the oranges?*

1. ¿**Qué**? Asks for a definition, identification, explanation, or other information.

> ¿**Qué** es un mango? Es una fruta tropical.
> *What is a mango? It is a tropical fruit.*
> ¿En **qué** ciudad nació Ud.? Nací en La Habana.
> *In what city were you born? I was born in Havana.*
> ¿**Qué** hiciste? Nada. *What did you do? Nothing.*

   a. ¿**Qué**? before a noun generally asks for information or an explanation.

> ¿**Qué** obra de Juan Rulfo le gusta más? Me gusta más *Pedro Páramo*.
> *Which work by Juan Rulfo do you like best? I like Pedro Páramo.*
> ¿**Qué** zapatos compraste? Los de charol.
> *Which shoes did you buy? The patent leather ones.*
> ¿**Qué** día es hoy? Hoy es lunes. *What day is today? Today is Monday.*
> ¿**Qué** fecha es hoy? Hoy es el veinte de septiembre.
> *What is today's date? Today is September 20ᵗʰ.*

   b. ¿**Qué**? + **tal** is equivalent to ¿**cómo**?

> ¿**Qué tal** estás? Estoy bien. *How are you? I am fine.*
> ¿**Qué tal** estuvo el concierto? Muy bueno. *How was the concert? Very good.*

2. ¿**Cuál**? is used before the verb **ser** when it asks for a choice or selection.

> ¿**Cuál** es el cuadro que le gusta más? El del muralista Diego Rivera.
> *Which is the painting that he likes best? The one by the muralist Diego Rivera.*
> ¿**Cuál** de ellos es Guillermo? El que tiene bigote.
> *Which one of them is Guillermo? The one who has a moustache.*

¿**Cuáles** son los meses de más calor? Junio, julio y agosto.
Which are the hottest months? June, July, and August.

NOTE: Use ¿**qué**? and not ¿**cuál**? before **ser** with nouns such as **día, hora, fecha, estación, mes.**

3. ¿**Quién (-es)**? refers only to persons and may be used alone or with a preposition.

¿**Quién** es ese señor? Alberto Gómez. *Who is that man? Alberto Gomez.*
¿**A quiénes** viste? A todos mis amigos. *Whom did you see? All my friends.*
¿**De quién** es este pantalón? De mi marido.
Whose pants are these? My husband's.
¿**Para quién** es la medicina? Para Claudia.
Who is the medicine for? For Claudia.

4. ¿**Cuánto (-a)**? means *how much?* ¿**Cuántos (-as)**? means *how many?*

¿**Cuánto** cuesta el mantel? *How much is the table cloth?*
¿**Cuántas** personas había en el juego de pelota?
How many persons were there at the ball game?

5. Some of these question words may also be used as exclamations. They also require an accent mark.

¡**Qué** barbaridad!   *Good heavens!*
¡**Cuánto** lo siento!   *I am so sorry! How sorry I am!*
¡**Cómo** no!   *Of course!*

6. ¡**Qué**! used with a noun is equivalent to *what!*

¡**Qué** jugador tan bueno!   *What a good player!*

¡**Qué**! used with an adjective or an adverb is equivalent to *how!*

¡**Qué** sabroso!   *How tasty!*
¡**Qué** bien baila!   *How well she dances!*

Ejercicios

I. Construya una pregunta que tenga por respuesta las palabras subrayadas.

MODELO: <u>Mónica</u> viene mañana.
          ¿Quién viene mañana?

1. Los muchachos van a las montañas <u>este fin de semana</u>.
2. Prefiero <u>las corbatas estrechas</u>.
3. Mi abrigo <u>es el de lana azul</u>.
4. Digo <u>que hace calor</u>.
5. Las vacaciones fueron <u>muy divertidas</u>.
6. Quiero <u>dos libras</u>.
7. El libro está <u>en el librero</u>.
8. El sarape cuesta <u>veinte pesos</u>.

II. Escriba las preguntas que Ud. hace para las siguientes respuestas que le da un compañero.

1. ¿_____? Vivo en la residencia de la universidad.

2. ¿_____? Mi consejero es el Sr. Álvarez.

3. ¿_____? Estoy tomando cinco cursos este semestre.

4. ¿_____? Me gusta más la clase de filosofía.

5. ¿_____? El decano (*dean*) de humanidades es muy inteligente.

6. ¿_____? El que está vestido de negro es el rector (*president*).

7. ¿_____? Todos los días tengo clases.

8. ¿_____? Este fin de semana voy a tomar el examen de latín.

9. ¿_____? La copiadora que tengo es de mi tío Pepe.

10. ¿_____? Esta carta es para mi prima Claudia.

III. Composición dirigida (oral o escrita). Haga tres o cuatro preguntas adecuadas según la situación.

MODELO: En la tienda. Ud. va a comprar un televisor.
¿Cuánto cuesta este televisor?
¿Cuántas pulgadas tiene la pantalla (*screen*)?
¿Cuál marca es mejor, ésta o aquélla?
¿Cuándo pueden entregármelo?

1. En el correo. Ud. necesita enviar varias cartas y paquetes al extranjero.

2. En la farmacia. Ud. necesita una medicina para el dolor de garganta.

3. En el aeropuerto. Ud. fue a recoger a un amigo que viene de Honduras.

4. En casa de unos amigos. Le han presentado a una chica de Costa Rica.

5. En la calle. Un policía lo ha parado porque Ud. iba a mucha velocidad.

IV. Temas de conversación.

1. Piense que Ud. está en el acto de graduación de una universidad (en un juego de pelota, en una playa, en un museo). Construya oraciones exclamativas comentando lo que Ud. ve.

2. Usted piensa comprar un ordenador (una computadora). Prepare unas preguntas para hacerle al vendedor usando **¿qué?** y **¿cuál?**, pidiendo definición y selección.

Composición

Antes de escribir, repase las siguientes reglas sobre la puntuación y la ortografía.

A Review of punctuation rules

1. The *colon* (*dos puntos*) is used:

   - In the salutation of letters, to introduce quotations and to begin a listing.

     Querida Rosita: *Dear Rosita:*

     Muy señor mío: *Dear Sir:*

     El refrán que se le aplica reza así: "No dejes para mañana lo que puedes hacer hoy."
     The refrain that applies to it says this: "Don't leave for tomorrow what you can do today."

     Las capitales de Bolivia son dos: Sucre y La Paz.
     There are two capitals of Bolivia: Sucre and La Paz.

   - In dialogues between characters after the words **explicó, dijo, contestó,** etc.

El chico le preguntó al amigo:	*The boy asked his friend:*
—¿Dónde compraste el violín?	*"Where did you buy the violin?"*
Y éste le contestó:	*And he answered:*
—No lo compré. Me lo regalaron mis padres.	*"I didn't buy it. My parents gave it to me."*

   - To summarize a listing.

     Se portó como todo lo que es: un caballero.
     He behaved like everything that he is: a gentleman.

2. *Ellipses points* (*puntos suspensivos*) are used:

   - To indicate that the listing continues.

     Allí se encontraban profesores, estudiantes, directores...
     There one could find professors, students, directors...

- When a sentence is left unfinished, in suspense, or when that which follows is understood.

  Yo le insistí, pero… bueno, no vale la pena repetirlo.
  I insisted, but...well, it's not worth repeating it.

- To indicate fear, doubt, or uncertainty

  Pues… no sé que más pueda decir…
  Well...I don't know what else to say…

- To indicate that certain passages from a text that is transcribed have been omitted. In this case the ellipses points are enclosed in brackets […] or in parentheses (…).

  El día de su encuentro con Marta […] tuvo la sensación de que todo había pasado ya.
  The day of his meeting with Martha […] he had the feeling that everything had happened before.

B Review of spelling rules: *sc*

Use **sc**:

- In verbs formed by the prefix **des-** and another word that begins with **ce-** or **ci-**: **descifrar** (*to decipher*), **descentrar** (*to put off center*)

- In verbs whose infintive ends in **-cender: ascender** (*to ascend*) except: **encender** (*to light*)

- In the words **doscientos** (*two hundred*), **trescientos** (*three hundred*), **seiscientos** (*six hundred*)

- In the following words that have **sc** in English:

adolescencia	*adolescence*
disciplina	*discipline*
discípula	*disciple*
escena	*scene*
obsceno	*obscene*
miscelánea	*miscellaneous*
reminiscencia	*reminiscence*
susceptible	*susceptible*
consciente	*conscious*

NOTE: The exercises corresponding to this section are included in the *Cuaderno de ejercicios*, Capítulo 2.

Ejercicio de composición (opcional)

Haga una composición, oral o escrita, sobre el tema que se da a continuación. Use el esquema siguiente.

TEMA: La influencia hispana en el suroeste de los Estados Unidos.

INTRODUCCIÓN: Enriquecimiento cultural ocurrido en el suroeste de los Estados Unidos. Principales inmigraciones de habla hispana que han venido. ¿En qué parte del país es más fuerte la influencia hispana?

DESARROLLO: Cambios que se han producido en las costumbres, en la ropa, en las comidas. Incorporación de nuevas palabras en el vocabulario. Los efectos de estas influencias en la sociedad, en la educación y en la familia.

CONCLUSIÓN: Dé su opinión personal de los resultados, positivos o negativos, producidos por La mezcla de las culturas.

3 *Capítulo*

Plaza Mayor en la ciudad de La Paz, Bolivia.

LECTURAS

- Lectura 1: "Lección sobre ruedas" de Domitila Barrios de Chungara
- Lectura 2: "Hombre pequeñito" de Alfonsina Storni

GRAMÁTICA

- Future and conditional
- Past participles
- Perfect tenses in the indicative mood
- Uses of **ser** and **estar**
- Uses of the verb **haber**
- **Gustar** and other similar verbs

COMPOSICIÓN

- Review of punctuation rules
- Review of spelling rules: **que, qui, cue, cui**

Vocabulario

Antes de leer, repase el siguiente vocabulario que le ayudará a comprender la lectura.

Sustantivos

la cita   appointment
el compañero   companion
el derecho   right
el esclavo   slave
la igualdad   equality
la lucha   fight
el quehacer   chore
la rueda   wheel

Verbos

burlarse   to make fun
charlar   to chat
contar (ue)   to tell
cuidar   to take care
luchar   to fight
morirse (ue)   to die
quedarse   to stay
tomar   to take

Adjetivos

cansado   tired
casado   married
soltero   single
bastante   much, enough

Frases

acabar de + inf.   to have just + past participle
de ninguna manera   by no means
en vez de   instead of
hacerse cargo   to be in charge
mientras tanto   meanwhile
ponerse colorado   to blush

Cognates (Cognados). As you read, look for the word or phrase that has the same meaning as the underlined words.

1. No me acuerdo de su nombre.

2. El chofer era un poco viejo.

3. El señor se rio de nosotras.

4. Dice que es imposible cuidar a los hijos.

5. A mi esposa la quiero, la respeto y no quisiera que se muera.

6. Hace de todo. Trabaja mucho.

Hace de todo vs. **Hace todo.** La esposa del chofer hace de todo. Both phrases may be translated as *she does everything*. The first phrase may be interpreted to mean that she is a very able person and knows how to do many things. *She does all sorts of things.* The second phrase focuses more on the amount, that is, all the work.

Eso sí que no lo creo vs. **Eso no lo creo.** The word **sí** is used to give emphasis to the idea and means *indeed*.

Lectura I

Domitila Barrios de Chungara

Domitila Barrios de Chungara nació en Bolivia en 1937. Es una mujer que cree en la igualdad del hombre y la mujer, y ha luchado frente a la sociedad de su patria por defender los derechos de la mujer. "Lección sobre ruedas" aparece en su libro, escrito con la cooperación de David Acebey, *¡Aquí también, Domitila!*

Lección sobre ruedas

Una vez en Quito tomamos un taxi para ir a una cita. Estábamos con Blanquita, Rosita y otra compañera que no recuerdo su nombre. El chofer era ya un poco maduro° y empezó a charlar. Nos preguntó de dónde veníamos y Rosita le contó que éramos de otros países y todo eso, ¿no?

5 Entonces el señor se burló de nosotras y nos preguntó si éramos casadas. Rosita le dijo que sí, que teníamos varios hijos y que habíamos venido a

somewhat old

esta conferencia sobre la "Participación de la mujer en la lucha por la democracia."

Entonces el señor nos preguntó: —¿Y quién está cuidando a sus hijos
10 mientras Uds. están en estas actividades? Y peor todavía si vienen de tan lejos —que tenía mucha compasión de nuestros maridos porque se habían quedado cuidando a nuestros hijos.

Entonces la Rosita[1] le dijo: —Si aquí hay una democracia, ¿qué clase de demócrata es Ud.? Ud. debe de ser uno de esos señores que no permiten
15 que su mujer participe.

—Las mujeres tienen que quedarse en su casa —dijo él.

—Entonces Ud. en vez de mujer tiene una esclava —dijo ella.

—¡No! De ninguna manera —dijo él. Yo a mi esposa la quiero, la estimo y no quisiera que se muera, porque ella cuida a mis hijos, trabaja
20 bastante. Ella hace de todo. Yo lo reconozco y le doy su lugar.

—¿Y el derecho a organizarse y a participar? —le pregunta ella.

—No —dice él—. Ella tiene quehacer en la casa.

—¿Pero por qué Ud. no podría quedarse un día en su casa mientras ella va a organizarse?

25 Entonces él dijo que viene muy cansado y que es imposible que se haga cargo de los hijos más.

—¡Ah, sí! —le dijo la Rosita—. ¡Eso sí que no le creo, señor! Porque Ud. acaba de decirme que tiene muchos hijos y que viene del trabajo muy cansado. ¿Y cómo hizo los hijos si Ud. estaba tan cansado?

30 El pobre señor se puso muy colorado y no sabía qué decir.

[1]Es común en español usar el artículo definido con los nombres de pila (first names).

Complete el párrafo llenando los espacios en blanco con la palabra correcta. Use los verbos en el tiempo que sea necesario.

Las muchachas tenían que ir a una _____ y tomaron un taxi. El chofer _____ mucho con ellas y les preguntó si eran solteras. Ellas le dijeron que no, que eran _____ y que eran de otros países. Tenían que ir a una conferencia sobre la _____ de la mujer en la lucha por la democracia. El chofer _____ un poco de ellas al saber que mientras ellas estaban de viaje los maridos _____ en casa _____ de los niños. Las chicas creían que la esposa del chofer era una _____ porque hacía todos los _____ de la casa, cuidaba a los niños y trabajaba mucho. El chofer _____ cuando las muchachas le hicieron la pregunta de cómo tuvo tantos hijos si trabajaba tanto y estaba tan cansado cuando llegaba a su casa.

Preguntas sobre la lectura

1. Explique el significado del título. ¿A qué lección se refiere la autora? ¿Por qué es una lección sobre ruedas?
2. ¿Cuál de las tres muchachas, Blanquita, Rosita o Domitila, mantiene un diálogo con el chofer?
3. ¿Cómo se imagina Ud. a Rosita?
4. ¿Qué palabras usa el chofer para decir que él respeta mucho a su esposa?
5. ¿Está Ud. de acuerdo con las ideas del chofer? ¿Por qué?
6. ¿Qué piensa Ud. del final de este relato?
7. Comente sobre los aspectos feministas del cuento.

Temas de conversación

1. ¿Hay algunas personas en su familia que no estén de acuerdo con las ideas feministas de hoy? ¿Qué opina Ud.?
2. Hay personas que piensan que las mujeres con familia no deben trabajar fuera de la casa. ¿Qué cree Ud. sobre esto?
3. ¿Qué problemas pueden presentarse cuando una mujer con hijos trabaja fuera de la casa?

Antes de leer, repase la siguiente orientación (*guidance*) que le ayudará a comprender la lectura.

¿Qué nos dice el poeta?

La lectura de una poesía es siempre más difícil que la lectura de un párrafo en prosa. Una poesía, generalmente, despierta en el lector sensaciones diversas que afectan los diferentes sentidos,° produciendo en la mente multitud de   *senses*
emociones, sentimientos e imágenes.

5   En la poesía, muchas veces el orden gramatical de las palabras aparece invertido y por eso para poder entender la oración tenemos que organizarla gramaticalmente. Note el siguiente ejemplo:

estrofa
{
Anoche cuando dormía ◄———— verso
Soñé ¡Bendita ilusión! ———► rima
que una colmena tenía ———► rima
dentro de mi corazón
}

10

Organizada gramaticalmente: Anoche cuando yo dormía soñé que yo tenía una colmena° dentro de mi corazón.   *beehive*

Note los términos literarios de *verso, estrofa* y *rima. Verso* es cada línea de un
15   poema; *estrofa* es el grupo de versos que se repite; *rima* es la igualdad o semejanza de los sonidos finales de dos o más versos. Puede haber poesías con versos libres o sueltos (también llamados versos blancos), es decir, que no tienen rima.

Lectura 2

Alfonsina Storni

Alfonsina Storni (1892–1938), poeta argentina y mujer de gran inteligencia e imaginación, denuncia en su poesía las injusticias y las dificultades de ser mujer frente a una sociedad dominada por el hombre. Cuando le diagnosticaron que tenía un cáncer incurable se suicidó en el balneario (*beach resort*) de Mar del Plata. Tenía 46 años.

Hombre pequeñito

Hombre pequeñito, hombre pequeñito,
Suelta° a tu canario que quiere volar...   *Set free*
Yo soy el canario, hombre pequeñito,
Déjame saltar.

Estuve en tu jaula,° hombre pequeñito,   *cage*
Hombre pequeñito que jaula me das,
Digo pequeñito porque no me entiendes,
Ni me entenderás.

Tampoco te entiendo, pero mientras tanto°   *meanwhile*
ábreme la jaula, que quiero escapar;
Hombre pequeñito, te amé media hora,
No me pidas más.

De *Irremediablemente* (1919)

Preguntas sobre la lectura

1. ¿A quién se dirige la poeta?
2. ¿Qué quiere la autora que haga el hombre pequeñito?
3. ¿Por qué llama al hombre "pequeñito"?
4. ¿Qué simbolizan la jaula y el canario?
5. ¿Cómo interpreta Ud. los dos versos finales del poema?
6. ¿Cuál es el tema principal de este poema?

Vista de la playa del Mar del Plata, Argentina.

ramática

A Future and conditional

1. Regular verbs.

Infinitive	Future		Conditional	
comprar	comprar **é** (*I will buy*)	comprar **emos**	comprar **ía** (*I would buy*)	comprar **íamos**
	comprar **ás**	comprar **éis**	comprar **ías**	comprar **íais**
	comprar **á**	comprar **án**	comprar **ía**	comprar **ían**
vender	vender **é**	vender **emos**	vender **ía**	vender **íamos**
	vender **ás**	vender **éis**	vender **ías**	vender **íais**
	vender **á**	vender **án**	vender **ía**	vender **ían**
recibir	recibir **é**	recibir **emos**	recibir **ía**	recibir **íamos**
	recibir **ás**	recibir **éis**	recibir **ías**	recibir **íais**
	recibir **á**	recibir **án**	recibir **ía**	recibir **ían**

Note that in the future tense the only form that does not have a written accent is the nosotros form. In the conditional all forms have a written accent.

2. Irregular verbs.

Some verbs have an irregular stem in the future and the conditional. The regular endings are added to these stems.

Infinitive	Stem	Future	Conditional
salir	**saldr-**	saldré	saldría
venir	**vendr-**	vendré	vendría
poner	**pondr-**	pondré	pondría
tener	**tendr-**	tendré	tendría
poder	**podr-**	podré	podría
valer	**valdr-**	valdré	valdría
haber	**habr-**	habré	habría
saber	**sabr-**	sabré	sabría
caber	**cabr-**	cabré	cabría
hacer	**har-**	haré	haría
decir	**dir-**	diré	diría
querer	**querr-**	querré	querría

3. Uses of the future.

a. The future tense is used to indicate that the action, state of being, or condition will occur after the present moment.

Saldré para el aeropuerto dentro de una hora.	*I will leave for the airport within an hour.*
Iremos antes del anochecer.	*We will go before nightfall.*

b. The future is also used to express conjecture, probability, or doubt of an action, state of being, or condition, either at the present time or in the future. It is equivalent to the English *I wonder, I suppose, probably.*

¿Qué hora **será**?	*I wonder what time it is. What time can it be?*
Serán las dos.	*It's probably two o'clock.*
¿**Llegará** Gustavo a tiempo?	*I wonder if Gustavo will arrive on time?*

c. The future may also be used to give an order or a command.

Niños, les repito que no **saldrán** esta tarde.	*Children, I repeat, you will not go out this afternoon.*
Escribirás la carta en seguida.	*You will write the letter at once.*

4. There are three ways to express a future action:

a. With **ir a** + an infinitive.

Voy a aprender a esquiar.	*I am going to learn to ski.*

b. With the verb in the present tense.

> Mañana **salgo** para Haití y Santo Domingo.
> *I leave for Haiti and Santo Domingo tomorrow.*

c. With the verb in the future tense.

> El Sr. Ventura me **llevará** al juego de pelota.
> *Mr. Ventura will take me to the ball game.*

5. Uses of the conditional.

a. The conditional tense is used to express an idea or an action that takes place in the future with respect to a past moment.

> Evelio me prometió que me **llevaría** a ver el Ballet Folklórico de México.
> *Evelio promised me that he would take me to see the Ballet Folklorico de México.*
> Él dijo que **compraría** las entradas. *He said he would buy the tickets.*

b. The conditional is also used to express what would occur if it were not for some other circumstance.

> **Iría** contigo, pero no tengo tiempo.   *I would go with you, but I don't have time.*
> **Pagaría** la cuenta, pero no tengo dinero.   *I would pay the bill, but I don't have money.*

c. In conditional statements with **si**, the conditional tense is used in conjunction with the past subjunctive*

Imperfect subjunctive	Conditional
Si Pepe **llamara,**	**hablaría** con él.
If Pepe were to call	*I would talk with him.*

d. The conditional is used to express conjecture, probability, or doubt of an action, state of being or condition in the past. It is equivalent to the English *I wonder, I suppose, probably.*

> **Serían** las dos cuando él llegó.   *It was probably two o'clock when he arrived.*
> ¿**Iría** Antonio al baile anoche?   *I wonder if Antonio went to the dance last night?*

e. Note the following combinations of time: the present with the future; the conditional with the preterite or imperfect indicative.

Present → Future	Preterite or Imperfect → Conditional
Él **dice** que **vendrá**.	Él **dijo** que **vendría**.
He says he will come.	*He said he would come.*
Sé que él **llamará**.	**Sabía** que él **llamaría**.
I know he will call.	*I knew he would call.*

f. The conditional is often used with verbs such as **desear, querer, poder,** and **deber** to express an idea in a more courteous or delicate manner.

> ¿**Podrías** prestarme $10?   *Could you lend me $10?*
> **Deberías** visitar a tus abuelos.   *You should visit your grandparents.*

---

*See Capítulo 5, page 158.

Ejercicios

I. Una huelga (*strike*). Complete el siguiente diálogo usando el futuro de indicativo del verbo que está entre paréntesis.

Cliente: Me han dicho que (haber) _____ una huelga de pilotos la semana que viene.

Agente: Así es, señor.

Cliente: ¿Entonces no (salir) _____ ningún vuelo?

Agente: Mire Ud. En este momento (yo) no (poder) _____ decirle con seguridad. Lo siento.

Cliente: Le dejo mi teléfono. Si fuera tan amable de llamarme…

Agente: Por supuesto. Le (decir) _____ a mi secretaria que anote su número y ella lo (llamar) _____ en cuanto sepamos algo definitivo.

II. Su amiga Amelia va a ir de pesca (*fishing*) con unos amigos. Pregúntele a un(a) compañero(a) qué va a hacer Amelia. Su compañero(a) debe contestar las preguntas indicando lo que harán.

MODELO: ¿Cuándo va a salir de pesca Amelia? (el sábado)
Saldrá de pesca el sábado.

1. ¿Dónde va a reunirse con sus amigos? (en Acapulco)
2. ¿A qué hora va a salir el barco que piensan tomar? (de madrugada)
3. ¿Cómo va a ser el barco? (grande y cómodo)
4. ¿En cuánto van a alquilar el equipo de pesca? (en unos $100)
5. ¿Crees que van a divertirse? (Sí)
6. Van a tener una experiencia diferente, ¿verdad? (Claro)

III. Cambie los verbos que están en presente y futuro al pasado y al condicional.

MODELO: Dice que no tomará la medicina.
Dijo que no tomaría la medicina.

1. Pienso que Ernesto me llamará.
2. Creo que ellos vendrán en tren.
3. Dice que no gastará tanto dinero.
4. Anuncian que habrá nieve en las montañas.
5. Creo que ellos me invitarán.

IV. Complete las frases usando el futuro o el condicional del verbo entre paréntesis.

1. (poner) Ellos me dicen que (ellos) _____ los libros en el librero.
2. (venir) La Srta. Badillo dijo que (ella) no _____.
3. (ser) ¿ _____ las cinco ahora?

4. (ser) _____ las dos cuando ella se fue.

5. (ir) Yo _____ contigo, pero tengo que estudiar.

6. (haber) Sé que _____ una reunión mañana.

7. (poder) ¿ _____ Ud. cambiarme este billete?

8. (invitar) Yo _____ a Luisita pero ella no está en la ciudad.

9. (salir) Si ellos pudieran, _____ de viaje.

10. (querer) ¿ _____ Ud. salir a dar un paseo?

V. Complete las oraciones usando el futuro o el condicional del verbo entre paréntesis para indicar conjetura o probabilidad.

1. (tener) Ella parece muy joven. ¿Qué edad _____?

2. (estar) No encuentro las llaves. ¿ _____ en el carro?

3. (ser) Anoche sonó el teléfono a las tres de la mañana. ¿Quién _____?

4. (ir) ¿Con quién _____ Luisa al teatro anoche?

5. (ser) No tenemos reloj. ¿Qué hora _____?

VI. Va a haber un partido de fútbol en la Universidad de Texas. Prepare con un(a) compañero(a) un diálogo en el que Ud. le pida la siguiente información. Usen en sus preguntas y en las respuestas de su compañero(a) el verbo en futuro.

1. El lugar del partido.
2. La hora del partido.
3. El precio de la entrada.
4. El lugar de estacionamiento.
5. El costo del estacionamiento.

VII. Una compañera le hace varias preguntas sobre los programas de televisión porque va a escribir un informe para la clase de periodismo (*journalism*). Conteste sus preguntas.

1. ¿Qué cambios piensa Ud. que deberían hacer los productores de televisión?
2. ¿Qué programas cree Ud. que beneficiarían más a la juventud?
3. ¿Qué tipo de programas eliminaría Ud. de la televisión?
4. ¿Cómo podría la televisión ser un medio muy eficaz (*effective*) de educación?
5. ¿Qué programas le gustaría ver con más frecuencia?

VIII. Composición dirigida (oral o escrita). ¿Qué haría Ud. en las siguientes situaciones?

1. ¿Qué haría Ud. al recibir una herencia de un millón de dólares?
2. ¿Qué haría Ud. para darle una sorpresa a su amiga(o)?

3. ¿Qué haría Ud. para convencer a su jefe que le pague más?
4. ¿Qué haría Ud. al ser despedido de su trabajo?
5. ¿Qué haría Ud. para celebrar su graduación de la universidad?

IX. Su amigo cree que Ud. puede predecir el futuro. Ud. le va a dar sus predicciones futuras para las siguientes cosas que él le ha preguntado.

1. El consumo de drogas entre la juventud en los próximos cinco años.
2. La casa del futuro.
3. Medios de transporte en el año 2100.
4. Posibilidades de descubrir una cura para el cáncer y el SIDA.

X. Unos amigos lo han invitado a pasar una semana en las montañas durante las vacaciones de Navidad. Descríbales a sus compañeros de clase las cosas que harán. (Use los verbos en el futuro y el siguiente vocabulario como guía.)

Comience así: **En el mes de diciembre iré...**

subir	divertirse	lago helado
esquiar	funicular	frío
patinar	esquí	ropa de lana
cenar	patines	crema protectora
usar	viento	restaurante

B Past participles

comprar compr **ado** (*bought*)   vender vend **ido** (*sold*)   recibir recib **ido** (*received*)

Past participles (*participios pasados*) that end in **-ido** have an accent mark on the **i** if it is preceded by a strong vowel (**a, e, o**).

caer **caído** (*fallen*)   leer **leído** (*read*)   oír **oído** (*heard*)

NOTE: The past participles of the verbs ending in **-uir** do not have an accent mark.

huir **huido** (*fled*)   destruir **destruido** (*destroyed*)

1. Some verbs have irregular past participles.

Infinitive	Past participle	Infinitive	Past participle
abrir	**abierto** (*opened*)	volver	**vuelto** (*returned*)
cubrir	**cubierto** (*covered*)	poner	**puesto** (*put*)
escribir	**escrito** (*written*)	morir	**muerto** (*died*)
romper	**roto** (*torn*)	decir	**dicho** (*said; told*)
ver	**visto** (*seen*)	hacer	**hecho** (*done; made*)
resolver	**resuelto** (*resolved*)		

The verbs **bendecir** (*to bless*) and **freír** (*to fry*) have two past participle forms, one regular and one irregular. (**Freído** is less common than **frito**.)

Regular	*Irregular*
bendecido	**bendito**
freído	**frito**

NOTE: The irregular forms of the past participles are used mainly as adjectives.

En la iglesia hay agua **bendita**.	*There is holy water in the church.*
Me gustan las papas **fritas**.	*I like French fries.*

2. Uses of the past participle.*

   a. With the different tenses of the verb **haber** to form the perfect tenses.**

he llegado (*I have arrived*)	**había salido** (*she had left*)
habremos visto (*we will have seen*)	**haya dicho** (*he may have said*)

   b. Used as an adjective. In this case the past participle agrees in gender and number with the noun or pronoun it modifies.

profesor **aburrido** (*boring profesor*)	ventanas **abiertas** (*open windows*)

Ejercicios

I. Ud. habla con su amigo, quien va a ir a Venezuela, sobre la importancia del petróleo en la economía de ese país. Complete el párrafo con el participio pasado de los verbos que están entre paréntesis.

La economía venezolana está _____ (basar) principalmente en el petróleo. Los pozos de petróleo del lago de Maracaibo estuvieron bajo una compañía extranjera hasta el primero de enero de 1976, fecha en que el gobierno adquirió el control de estos pozos y de todo el petróleo del país. Se han _____ (extraer) muchos billones de barriles de petróleo del suelo de Venezuela, y la mayor parte de él ha _____ (salir) del fondo (*bottom*) del lago de Maracaibo.

II. La fiesta en casa de Ismael fue buena. Descríbeles a sus amigos cómo fue. Para completar el párrafo, use como adjetivos los participios pasados de los verbos que están en paréntesis.

La fiesta en casa de Ismael fue muy (divertir) _____ . Las personas (invitar) _____ eran de distintos países y cada invitado parecía (interesar) _____ en la cultura del otro. Los músicos (seleccionar) _____ para esta reunión tocaron muy bien y la comida que sirvieron estaba muy bien (preparar) _____ . En fin, la fiesta no fue nada (aburrir) _____ . Al contrario, fue todo un éxito.

---

*See Capítulo 10 for other uses of the past participle.
**See pages 87–88 of this capítulo.

C Perfect tenses in the indicative mood

1. *Present perfect* (*presente perfecto*). The present perfect is formed using the present tense of **haber** (**he, has, ha, hemos, habéis, han**) + the past participle.

> **he comprado** (*I have bought*)
> **hemos vendido** (*we have sold*)
> **han recibido** (*they have received*)

The present perfect tense is used to express an action that has ended in the past but whose effect extends up to the present. In general it refers to an action that took place in the past but continues into the present.

> Mi hija **ha crecido** mucho este año.
> *My daughter has grown a lot this year.*
> Andrés y Felipe **han trabajado** mucho, pero no **han ahorrado** ningún dinero.
> *Andrés and Felipe have worked a lot, but they have not saved any money.*

NOTE: In Spanish the two verbs are not separated as they are in English.

> ¿**Ha llegado** María?   *Has María arrived?*
> Siempre **he hecho** lo mismo   *I have always done the same thing.*

2. *Pluperfect* (*pluscuamperfecto*). The pluperfect tense is formed using the imperfect tense of **haber** (**había, habías, había, habíamos, habíais, habían**) + the past participle.

> **habías comprado** (*you had bought*)
> **habíamos vendido** (*we had sold*)
> **habían recibido** (*they had received*)

The pluperfect is used to express a past action that was completed prior to another past action.

> Ellos ya **habían comido** cuando   *They had already eaten when*
>   yo llamé.   *I called.*
> Ella ya **había visto** esa película. *She had already seen that movie.*

3. *Preterite perfect* (*pretérito anterior*). The preterite perfect is formed by using the preterite of **haber** (**hube, hubiste, hubo, hubimos, hubisteis, hubieron**) + the past participle.

> **hube comprado** (*I had bought*)
> **hubimos vendido** (*we had sold*)
> **hubo recibido** (*he had received*)

This tense is seldom used and it appears generally in sentences that are currently expressed with the verb in the preterite tense.

> Tan pronto como **hubimos llegado** empezó el programa.
> *As soon as we had arrived the program began.*
> Tan pronto como **llegamos** empezó el programa.
> *As soon as we arrived the program began.*

4. *Future perfect* (*futuro perfecto*). The future perfect is formed by using the future tense of **haber** (**habré, habrás, habrá, habremos, habréis, habrán**) + the past participle.

> **habré comprado** (*I will have bought*)   **habrá vendido** (*he will have sold*)
> **habrán recibido** (*they will have received*)

a. The future perfect is used to express a future action that will occur prior to another future moment. It refers to an action or event that will have been completed in the future.

> **Habré terminado** el libro para esa fecha.   *I will have finished the book by that date.*
> **Habremos preparado** las maletas   *We will have packed the suitcases by*
>   para mañana.   *tomorrow.*

b. The future perfect is also used to express probability, conjecture, or doubt. In this case it is equivalent to the English form of present perfect + *probably* or *I wonder, I suppose.*

> Ya **habrán salido**.   *They have probably gone out already.*
> ¿Qué le **habrá pasado** a Susana?   *I wonder what has happened to Susana?*

5. *Conditional perfect* (*condicional perfecto*). The conditional perfect is formed by using the conditional of **haber** (**habría, habrías, habría, habríamos, habríais, habrían**) + the past participle.

> **habría comprado** (*he would have bought*)
> **habrías vendido** (*you would have sold*)
> **habríamos recibido** (*we would have received*)

a. The conditional perfect is used to express what would have happened if another action had not occured. It refers to an action or an event that would have been completed.

> Yo les **habría hablado**, pero no los vi.
> *I would have talked to them, but I did not see them.*

b. The conditional perfect is also used to express probability, conjecture, or doubt in the past.

> Pensé que **habrías ido** a la playa.
> *I thought that you had probably gone to the beach.*
> ¿**Habría ganado** Elisa el primer premio?
> *I wonder if Elisa would have won the first prize?*

c. In conditional sentences with **si**, the conditional perfect is used with the imperfect subjunctive to express a contrary-to-fact statement in the past.*

> Imperfect subjunctive   Conditional perfect
> Si **hubiera venido**,   →   lo **habría visto**
> *If he had come, I would have seen him.*
>
> Si no **hubiera llovido, habría ido** al juego de pelota.
> *If it had not rained, I would have gone to the baseball game.*

---

*See Capítulo 5.

Ejercicios

I. Ud. entrevistó a una profesora de español sobre la educación en los Estados Unidos. Complete las respuestas que le dio la profesora con el presente perfecto de indicativo de los verbos que están entre paréntesis.

Estudiante entrevistando a una profesora de SUNY en Oswego, Nueva York.

Ud.:   ¿Qué idioma extranjero cree Ud. que es más necesario en los Estados Unidos?

Profesora: El español se _____ (hacer) cada vez más necesario en este país.

Ud.:   ¿Cómo es la educación con respecto a ese idioma?

Profesora: Ésta _____ (cambiar) en muchos aspectos. Muchas instituciones _____ (establecer) programas bilingües y muchas universidades _____ (abrir) cursos sobre la cultura chicana y la cultura hispanoamericana en general.

Ud.:   ¿Qué puede decir de la literatura que _____ (producir) las diferentes inmigraciones hispanas en los Estados Unidos?

Profesora: Creo que todos los grupos, los chicanos, los puertorriqueños y los cubanos, _____ (crear) una literatura propia que cada vez es más leída y apreciada.

II. Haga las oraciones, según el modelo, cambiando el primer verbo de la frase al pluscuamperfecto de indicativo para indicar una acción terminada antes de otra acción pasada.

> MODELO: Salí cuando él llegó.
> **Ya había salido cuando él llegó.**

1. Nos acostamos cuando empezó a llover.
2. Te despertaste cuando ladró el perro.
3. Preparé la cena cuando llamó Esteban.
4. Ellos se durmieron cuando empezó el programa.
5. La televisión se rompió cuando empezó a hablar el Presidente.

III. Su amigo le hace varias preguntas que Ud. va a contestar empezando sus respuestas con: **No sé**. Después, usando las palabras entre paréntesis, va a decirle quién probablemente hizo la acción.

> MODELO: ¿Quién lavó el carro? (mi hermano)
> **No sé. Lo habrá lavado mi hermano.**

1. ¿Quién arregló el motor? (el mecánico)
2. ¿Quién cambió el aceite? (Tomás)
3. ¿Quién compró la batería? (mi padre)
4. ¿Quién ajustó los frenos? (Juanito)
5. ¿Quién puso en el carro las gomas nuevas? (Ramón)

IV. Complete las oraciones con el condicional perfecto de los verbos entre paréntesis para expresar una acción contraria a la realidad en el pasado.

1. (aprender) Si hubieran vivido en México, _____ español.
2. (traer, yo) _____ muchos objetos de plata de Taxco si hubiera podido.
3. (visitar, nosotros) _____ a tu hermano si hubiéramos tenido su dirección.
4. (ser) Si Cristina hubiera estudiado francés, _____ intérprete.
5. (distribuir) Si Leopoldo hubiera tenido mucho dinero, lo _____ entre los pobres.

V. Complete las oraciones con la traducción al español de las frases que están en inglés.

1. (*have learned*) Ellos ya _____ a manejar el camión.
2. (*would have gone*) Pensé que tú _____ con ellos.
3. (*had told*) Eusebio me _____ que volvería temprano.

4. (*I will have finished*) (Yo) _____ la construcción del edificio para fines de año.

5. (*probably have arrived*) Ellos ya _____.

6. (*I would have seen them*) (Yo) Los _____ si hubieran venido.

VI. Conteste las preguntas elaborando las respuestas en forma original.

> **MODELO:** ¿Dónde ha dejado Ud. las llaves?
> **Probablemente las he perdido porque siempre las he tenido dentro de la bolsa y ahora no están.**

1. ¿Qué experiencias personales ha tenido Ud. este año?
2. Ud. ha sentido un ruido grande en la cocina de su casa. ¿Qué cree Ud. que habrá pasado?
3. La policía ha encontrado a un hombre herido en la calle donde Ud. vive. ¿Qué cree Ud. que le habrá pasado?

VII. Temas de conversación.

1. ¿Qué cosas cree Ud. que ocurrirán en su vida en los próximos diez años?
2. ¿Qué cree Ud. que pasará en los Estados Unidos si continúan viniendo inmigrantes de otros países?
3. ¿Qué cree Ud. que pasará con los problemas de la contaminación del medio ambiente?
4. ¿Qué cambios cree Ud. que habrán ocurrido en el panorama económico, político y social de los Estados Unidos para el año 2010?

D   Uses of *ser* and *estar*

1. **Ser** is used:

   a. With the preposition **de** to express place of origin, ownership, or material from which something is made.

Rosita le contó que **éramos de** otros países.	*Rosita told him that we were from other countries.*
Estos vinos **son de** Chile.	*These wines are from Chile.*
El perro **es de** Antonio.	*The dog belongs to Antonio.*
¿**De quién** será esa casa?	*I wonder whose house that is.*
Su blusa **es de** seda.	*The blouse is made of silk.*
Las paredes **son de** adobe.	*The walls are made of adobe.*

   b. With adjectives to express basic or inherent characteristics or qualities of persons and things.

El chofer **era** muy conversador.	*The chauffeur was very talkative.*
El edificio **es** moderno.	*The building is modern.*
Los limones **son** ácidos.	*Lemons are acid.*

c. To express the idea that an event will take place.

> El banquete **será** en el Hotel Tamanaco de Caracas y el concierto que lo precede **será** a las seis, también en el Hotel Tamanaco.
> *The banquet will be (take place) at the Tamanaco Hotel in Caracas and the concert that precedes it will be at six, also at the Tamanaco Hotel.*

d. To express the passive voice.*

> La ciudad **fue destruida** por la erupción del volcán.
> *The city was destroyed by the eruption of the volcano.*
> Todo **fue descrito** en los periódicos de ayer.
> *Everything was described in yesterday's newspapers.*

e. When the predicate is a noun, pronoun, or adjective used as a noun.

> Ellos **son** amigos.
> *They are friends.*
> La inteligente **es** ella y el perezoso **es** él.
> *The intelligent one is she and the lazy one is he.*

f. To indicate time and other temporal expressions.

> ¿**Será** muy tarde ya? No lo creo. **Son** las dos.
> *I wonder if it's too late already. I don't think so. It is two o'clock.*
> Caramba, no recuerdo qué día **es** hoy.
> *Heavens, I don't remember what day today is.*
> Hoy **es** el quince de marzo.
> *Today is March 15th.*

g. With impersonal expressions.

> **Es necesario** llegar a tiempo al concierto.
> *It is necessary to arrive on time to the concert.*
> **Es lástima** si no escuchamos el principio.
> *It is a pity if we don't listen to the beginning.*

2. **Estar** is used:

a. To express location or position of persons or things.

> El calendario azteca **está** en el Museo Nacional de Antropología en la Ciudad de México. Ayer **estuvimos** allí y también en el Parque de Chapultepec que **está** al lado del museo.
> *The Aztec calendar is in the National Museum of Anthropology in México City. Yesterday we were there and also at Chapultepec Park which is located next to the museum.*

---

*See Capítulo 10, passive voice.

b. With adjectives to describe the current condition of a person or thing, and with past participles—used as adjectives—to express the result of an action and describe the state or condition of the subject.

Current or temporary condition	Result of an action
Ana **está** enferma. *Ana is ill.*	El hombre **está** muerto. Murió una hora después del accidente. *The man is dead. He died one hour after the accident.*
El café **está** frío. *The coffee is cold.*	La puerta **está** cerrada. Creo que la cerró Carlos. *The door is closed. I think Carlos closed it.*

c. With present participles (the **-ndo** form) to form the progressive tenses.*
(This construction is used less in Spanish than in English)

Bernabé **está recogiendo** los juguetes y los niños **están estudiando**.
Bernabé is picking up the toys and the children are studying.

d. In the following idiomatic expressions:**

estar a oscuras	*to be in the dark*	**estar de acuerdo**	*to be in agreement*
estar de buen (mal) humor	*to be in a good (bad) mood*	**estar de cabeza**	*to do a headstand*
		estar de espaldas	*to be facing away*
estar de frente	*to be facing forward*	**estar de incógnito**	*to be incognito*
estar de lado	*to be sideways*	**estar de moda**	*to be fashionable*
estar de pie	*to be standing*	**estar de prisa**	*to be in a hurry*
estar de regreso	*to be back*	**estar de rodillas**	*to be kneeling*
estar de vacaciones	*to be on vacation*	**estar de viaje**	*to be traveling, on a trip*
estar de vuelta	*to be back*	**estar en estado**	*to be pregnant*
estar listo	*to be ready*	**estar para**	*to be about to*
estar por	*to be in favor of*		

3. Note in the following sentences how the adjective differs in meaning when used with **ser** or **estar**:

SER	ESTAR
Beatriz **es** bonita. *Beatriz is a pretty girl.*	Beatriz **está** bonita. *Beatriz looks pretty.*
Soy listo. *I am smart.*	**Estoy** listo. *I am ready.*
Joaquín **es** aburrido. *Joaquín is a boring person.*	Joaquín **está** aburrido. *Joaquín is bored.*
Esta fruta **es** dulce. *This (kind of) fruit is sweet.*	Esta fruta **está** dulce. *This fruit tastes very sweet.*
Juanito **es** un chico nervioso. *Juanito is a nervous kid.*	Juanito **está** nervioso por el examen. *Juanito is nervous about the exam.*

---

*See Capítulo 6, the gerund or present participle, page 171.
In Spanish there are other verbs that have the preposition **de. See Capítulo 9.

Ejercicios

I. Complete las oraciones con el presente de indicativo de **ser** o **estar**, de acuerdo con el sentido de las frases.

1. Pedro _____ un hombre neurótico.

    Pedro _____ neurótico porque ha perdido una gran suma de dinero.

2. Asela _____ aburrida de tanto trabajar.

    Asela _____ aburrida; es imposible estar con ella.

3. Él _____ una persona saludable; nunca está enfermo.

    Él _____ saludable; no ha tenido que llamar al médico este mes.

4. Ese hombre _____ impaciente porque quiere irse.

    Ese hombre _____ una persona impaciente.

5. Silvia _____ lista todos los días cuando la vamos a buscar.

    Silvia _____ muy lista. Salió bien en todos los exámenes.

6. Ella _____ bonita con ese traje.

    Ella _____ la más bonita de las hijas.

7. Javier _____ de Puerto Rico; nació en San Juan.

    Javier _____ en Quito de visita.

8. Mi hermano _____ arquitecto.

    Mi hermano _____ con el arquitecto en su oficina.

9. Carmen _____ en estado.

    Carmen _____ del estado de Arizona.

10. El diccionario _____ en el librero.

    El diccionario _____ del profesor Ramírez.

II. Complete las siguientes oraciones usando una de las expresiones idiomáticas con **estar**, de acuerdo con el contexto. Use la forma verbal que sea necesaria.

1. Jorge _____ . Lleva gafas oscuras para que nadie lo reconozca.

2. Anselmo y yo raras veces discutimos. Casi siempre _____ .

3. Cuando entramos en la iglesia nadie estaba sentado. Unas personas _____ y otras _____ .

4. Hoy en día _____ llevar más de un arete (*earring*) en cada oreja.

5. No podemos quedarnos a charlar más. Ya son las diez y (nosotros) _____ .

6. Tiene las manos en la tierra y los pies en el aire. ¿Por qué crees tú que ese hombre _____ ?

7. Los Pérez se fueron a Madrid en mayo y no _____ hasta el mes próximo.

8. La esposa del Sr. Jiménez _____. Dice que va a tener gemelos.

9. ¿Por quién vas a votar? ¿(Tú) _____ el partido republicano o el partido demócrata?

10. Nuestra amiga Petra es muy simpática. Siempre está contando chistes y parece _____.

III. Complete las oraciones con el tiempo apropiado de **ser** o **estar**, según el sentido de la frase.

1. Cuando llegamos la casa _____ abandonada. Todas las ventanas _____ rotas.

2. Cuando yo _____ ayer en el portal, vi que mi vecina _____ hablando con un policía.

3. El año pasado los naranjos (*orange trees*) _____ llenos de azahares (*orange blossoms*). Me gusta el perfume de estas flores porque _____ suave y delicado.

4. A Juan no le gusta hablar; él _____ muy callado (*quiet*).

5. Elsa siempre conversa mucho, pero anoche durante la comida _____ muy callada.

6. Las manzanas que _____ en el árbol no se pueden comer todavía _____ muy verdes.

7. Los estudiantes _____ hoy de mal humor porque tienen un examen.

8. El edificio _____ muy antiguo y _____ deteriorado porque no lo cuidan.

9. Ocho por cinco _____ cuarenta.

10. El hombre tuvo un ataque al corazón y _____ muerto cuando llegó la ambulancia.

11. Estas maletas me gustan más porque _____ de piel.

12. ¿Quién _____ la muchacha que _____ ayer con Esteban?

IV. Un ladrón entró en su casa y robó varias cosas. Explíquele Ud. al policía cómo encontró la casa. Use **estar** + participio pasado en sus respuestas.

MODELO: (Policía) ¿Cómo estaban las ventanas? (cerrar)
(Ud.) **Las ventanas estaban cerradas.**

1. ¿Cómo estaba el garaje? (abrir)
2. ¿Cómo estaban las luces? (apagar)
3. ¿Cómo estaba la puerta del patio? (romper)
4. ¿Cómo estaba la alarma de la casa? (descomponer)

V. Composición dirigida (oral o escrita). Complete las frases en forma original.

MODELO: Marcos está muy triste…
> **Marcos está muy triste porque han cerrado el negocio donde trabaja. Ahora está sin trabajo y sin dinero. La gran ironía es que Marcos siempre ha sido optimista, pero ahora está muy pesimista.**

1. Rodolfo y Rolando están muy contentos…
2. Estoy construyendo una casa nueva…
3. Maricusa es muy popular en la universidad…
4. La familia Benítez es de origen español…
5. La fiesta del cuatro de julio…

VI. Temas de conversación.

1. Descríbale a su amiga la boda de su prima. Describa a los novios, la ceremonia, la iglesia, etc.
2. Piense que Ud. está en el hipódromo (*racetrack*) mirando las carreras de caballos. Describa el lugar, los caballos, el público, etc.
3. Imagine que Ud. acaba de llegar de un viaje y le describe a sus compañeros la ciudad que visitó.
4. Su amiga, que vive en Panamá, quiere saber cómo es su novio o novia y Ud. se lo va a describir.

E Uses of the verb *haber*

1. The third person singular of the verb **haber** (*to be*), is used in all tenses that may be necessary to express the concept of *there is/are*. The plural forms are not used. Note the following equivalencies.

hay	(*there is/there are*)	**hay** un estudiante **hay** diez estudiantes
había	(*there was/there were* [existed])	**había** una persona **había** mil personas
hubo	(*there was/there were* [occurred])	**hubo** una fiesta **hubo** muchas fiestas
habrá	(*there will be*)	**habrá** un baile **habrá** varios bailes
habría	(*there would be*)	**habría** un carro **habría** cientos de carros
ha habido	(*there has been/there have been*)	**ha habido** una revolución **ha habido** muchas revoluciones
había habido	(*there had been*)	**había habido** un presidente **había habido** otros presidentes

2. The rule above applies to sentences that require the subjunctive: only the third person singular is used.

> Tal vez **haya** una exhibición de carros este mes y espero que **haya** muchos modelos baratos porque necesito comprar un carro nuevo.
> *There may be a car exhibit this month and I hope there are many inexpensive models because I need to buy a new car.*
> Sentí que no **hubiera** más personas en el desfile.
> *I was sorry there weren't more people at the parade.*

Ejercicio

Ud. conversa con una compañera sobre las celebraciones que tendrán en su escuela y sobre la visita que Ud. hizo al museo. Complete las narraciones traduciendo las frases que están en inglés.

1. _____ (*there will be*) muchas celebraciones el Día de la Independencia. Esta semana _____ (*there were*) dos reuniones en la escuela para planear las festividades. _____ (*there is*) mucho entusiasmo y _____ (*there are*) muchas personas que están trabajando en el programa que van a presentar.

2. Fui al museo y _____ (*there were*) miles de personas viendo la exposición de los cuadros de Frida Kahlo. Anteriormente _____ (*there had been*) otra exhibición con dibujos de distintos pintores mexicanos. Espero que _____ (*there are*) otras exposiciones con artistas de Hispanoamérica.

F *Gustar* and other similar verbs

1. The verb **gustar,** like other verbs that belong to the same category, requires a special construction.

   a. In general, only the third person singular or plural is used with an indirect object pronoun.

   > **Me gusta** la música de Carlos Chávez. *I like the music by Carlos Chavez.*
   > ¿**Te gustan** las fresas? *Do you like strawberries?*
   > **Le gustan** las ciudades grandes. *He likes big cities.*
   > **Nos gustan** las películas de misterio. *We like mystery films.*
   > **Les gusta** viajar en avión. *They like to travel by plane.*
   > **Me gustan** el español, el portugués y el italiano.
   > *I like Spanish, Portuguese, and Italian.*
   > **Me gustan** mucho tres cosas: comer, beber y bailar.
   > *I like three things very much: to eat, to drink, and to dance.*

NOTE: When we say in Spanish **Me gusta la casa**, the literal translation is *The house is pleasing to me.*

b. A prepositional phrase (**a** + prepositional pronoun) is often used for clarification or emphasis of the indirect object pronoun.

> **A mí** me pareció fantástico. *It seemed fantastic to me.*
> **A Ud.** le gusta hablar en público. *You like to speak in public.*
> **A José** le gustan todas las chicas. *Jose likes all the girls.*
> **A ella** le gusta el té helado. *She likes iced tea.*
> **A ellos** les gusta montar en bicicleta. *They like to ride a bicycle.*

c. If **gustar** is followed by a reflexive verb, the corresponding reflexive pronoun follows and is attached to the infinitive.

> **Me gusta cepillarme** el pelo. *I like to brush my hair.*
> ¿**Te gusta sentarte** en el balcón? *Do you like to sit in the balcony?*
> A Gilberto **le gusta ponerse** sombrero. *Gilberto likes to wear a hat.*
> **Nos gusta acostarnos** tarde. *We like to go to bed late.*
> **Les gusta levantarse** al amanecer. *They like to get up at dawn.*

NOTE: The following construction: ¿**Te gusto**? Sí, claro, **me gustas**, querido. *Do I please you? Yes, of course, you please me, dear.* [*Do you like me? Yes, of course I like you, dear.*]

d. Other verbs that are used like **gustar** are:

asustar (*to frighten*)	**interesar** (*to interest*)
divertir (*to amuse*)	**parecer** (*to seem*)
doler (*to hurt, ache*)	**preocupar** (*to worry*)
enojar (*to anger*)	**quedar** (*to fit; to have left over*)
encantar (*to "love"*)	**sobrar** (*to have extra*)
faltar (*to lack*)	**sorprender** (*to surprise*)
importar (*to matter*)	**tocar** (*to be one's turn*)

> A los niños **les encantó** ver al payaso. *The children loved seeing the clown.*
>
> **Nos parece** imposible que tengas seis hijos.
> *It seems impossible to us that you have six children.*
>
> **Me queda** una semana de vacaciones. *I have one week of vacation left.*
>
> **Nos ha sorprendido** tu respuesta. *Your answer has surprised us.*
>
> Ya tú jugaste, ahora **me toca** a mí. *You already played, now it's my turn.*

e. The following expressions are used like **gustar**.

dar igual	¿Qué prefieres comer, carne o pescado? **Me da igual**. *What do you prefer to eat, meat or fish? It's all the same to me.*
hacer daño	¿**Le hizo daño** al niño lo que comió anoche? *What did the child eat last night to harm him?*

hacer falta	**Nos hace falta** un carro nuevo.
	We need (lack) a new car.
caer bien (mal)	referring to people: *to like (dislike)*
	Me caen bien los nuevos vecinos.
	I like the new neighbors.
	referring to food: *to agree (disagree)*
	¿**Te cayó mal** la cena ayer?
	Did supper disagree with you yesterday?

Ejercicios

I. Complete los minidiálogos.

A. Use el pronombre que sea necesario.

1. —¿ _____ gustaría (a ti) ir de compras mañana?
   —Sí, _____ gustaría, pero _____ duelen mucho los pies.

2. —¿ _____ gustaría a su hermana sentarse en la arena o en la terraza?
   — _____ encantaría sentarse en la terraza, no _____ gusta coger mucho sol.

3. —¿ _____ gustó a Uds. el concierto?
   —No, _____ disgustó. No _____ gusta la música de rock.

4. —¿ _____ gustaría a los chicos ir al lago o a la playa?
   — _____ divertiría más ir a la playa.

B. Use el presente del verbo que está entre paréntesis.

1. —¿Le (gustar) _____ a Ud. los camarones?
   —Sí, me (encantar) _____ y también me (gustar) _____ el pescado.

2. —¿Qué cosa les (faltar) _____ a ellos en la mesa?
   —Les (faltar) _____ los tenedores.

3. —¿Qué le enoja a Josefina?
   —Le (enojar) _____ comer tarde.

4. —¿Te (interesar) _____ las comidas exóticas?
   —No, me (disgustar) _____ esas comidas.

II. Conteste las preguntas usando en la respuesta la información que está entre paréntesis.

MODELO: ¿Qué le pasa a Simón? (doler los pies)
Le duelen los pies.

1. ¿Qué piensan Uds. de esa pareja? (parecer muy aburrida)
2. ¿Por qué gritas? (enojar lo que haces)
3. ¿Qué vestido prefieres? (gustar el blanco de algodón)
4. ¿Por qué enciende ella todas las luces? (asustar la oscuridad)
5. ¿Por qué se ríen ellos? (divertir los chistes)
6. ¿Le gusta a tu amigo hablar de política? (No, al contrario, disgustar)
7. ¿Les gustaría a Uds. ir al cine? (encantar ver una buena película)
8. ¿Le gustaría a Ud. correr una milla? (hacer daño tanto ejercicio)

III. Para conocer mejor a su compañero(a) de clase, hágale las siguientes preguntas. Después conteste las preguntas que él (ella) le hará.

1. ¿Qué te interesa más, el cine o el teatro?
2. ¿Qué tipo de película te gusta más?
3. ¿Qué te parecen las películas del oeste (*westerns*)?
4. ¿Qué te encanta hacer en tu tiempo libre?
5. ¿Te hace falta dinero para hacer lo que deseas?
6. ¿Te preocupan los problemas de tus amigos?

IV. Traduzca al español las siguientes frases.

1. *I like my neighbor.* (Hay dos posibilidades.)
2. *We love to try on new clothes.*
3. *I don't like big cities.*
4. *She likes iced coffee.*
5. *Does your arm hurt?*
6. *We had a lot of wine left.*

omposición

Antes de escribir, repase las siguientes reglas sobre la puntuación y la ortografía.

A Review of punctuation rules

1. *Parentheses* (*paréntesis*) are used:

   • To enclose words or expressions that clarify a text.

   Leímos los párrafos asignados **(páginas 30–35)** antes de contestar las preguntas.
   We read the assigned paragraphs (pages 30–35) before answering the questions.
   Visitó varias ciudades **(Guanajuato, Morelia y Zacatecas)** cuando estuvo en México.
   He visited several cities (Guanajuato, Morelia, and Zacatecas) when he was in Mexico.

• In dramatic scripts, to indicate stage directions.

> Doña Marta: (**En voz baja**) No es que quiera criticar, pero…
> Doña Ana: Bueno, bueno. Vámonos ya. (**Salen por el lado izquierdo.**)
> *Doña Marta: (**In a low voice**) It's not that I want to criticize, but…*
> *Doña Ana: Alright, alright. Let's go now. (**They exit on the left.**)*

NOTA: Note that the period is placed inside the parentheses.

2. *Quotation marks (comillas) are used:*

• To quote literally from a text.

> El famoso libro de Cervantes empieza así: "**En un lugar de la Mancha,
> de cuyo nombre no quiero acordarme…**"
> *The famous book by Cervantes begins like this:* "**En un lugar de la Mancha,
> de cuyo nombre no quiero acordarme…**"

• For titles of short stories, films, works of art, articles from a newspaper, poems.

> "**El árbol**" es un cuento de Elena Garro. La película "**Recuerdos del
> porvenir**" está basada en su novela del mismo nombre.
> "**El árbol**" *is a short story by Elena Garro. The film* "**Recuerdos del porvenir**" *is
> based on her novel by the same name.*

• To introduce foreign words, or expressions with an ironic or sarcastic tone.

> Su hermano Juan, el "**ojitos**" del barrio, era un "**yuppie**" que trabajaba
> sin cesar.
> *Her brother Juan, the "little eyes" of the neighborhood, was a "yuppie" who
> worked incessantly.*

• In literary works, to express a character's thoughts.

> Raúl salió lentamente, pensando: "**¿Cómo he de explicar esto a Ana María?**"
> *Raul went out slowly, thinking: "How am I to explain this to Ana Maria?"*

B Review of spelling rules: *que, qui, cue, cui*

1. The hard sound of **c** with the vowels **e, i** is written **que, qui**. The **u** is silent.

   banquete, orquesta, queso, pequeñito, quitar, esquiar, quinto

2. The **u** is pronounced in the combinations **cue, cui**.

   cuenta, frecuente, acuerdo, cuidado, circuito, descuido *(carelessness)*

3. The letter **k** is used in words of foreign extraction.

   kilo, kimono, kiosko

   These words may also be written with **que** or **qui**:

   quilo, quimono, quiosco

Ejercicio de composición (opcional)

Haga una composición, oral o escrita, sobre el tema que se da a continuación. Use el esquema siguiente.

TEMA: Nuevo concepto de la unión entre el hombre y la mujer.

INTRODUCCIÓN: Actualmente los jóvenes prefieren vivir juntos sin casarse.
                      Ventajas y desventajas que tiene este modo de vida.
                      Concepto de la sociedad sobre esta unión voluntaria de las parejas.

DESARROLLO: ¿Existe más responsabilidad si los jóvenes se casan?
                      Facilidad para terminar la relación cuando no quieren seguir juntos.
                      El divorcio y los requisitos legales.
                      Responsabilidades que se presentan cuando se forma una familia con hijos.
                      La independencia económica del hombre y la mujer cuando no están casados.

CONCLUSIÓN: ¿Cree Ud. que eventualmente no existirá más el matrimonio?
                      ¿Cree Ud. que el hombre y la mujer vivirán más felices sin casarse?
                      Dé su opinión sobre lo que pasará con los hijos.

Universidad Nacional Autónoma de México, en la capital mexicana.

LECTURAS

- Lectura 1: "Sor Juana Inés de la Cruz"
- Lectura 2: "Una palmera" de Rosario Castellanos

GRAMÁTICA

- Affirmatives and negatives
- Indicative mood and subjunctive mood
- Present subjunctive
- The imperative mood
- Imperfect subjunctive
- Uses of the subjunctive: verbs that express doubt, will, or emotion

COMPOSICIÓN

- Review of capitalization rules
- Review of spelling rules: **h**

Vocabulario

Antes de leer, repase el siguiente vocabulario que le ayudará a comprender la lectura.

Sustantivos

la afición   liking
el alma   soul
el ambiente   environment
la belleza   beauty
el cura   priest
la época   epoch, era
el grado   degree
el magisterio   teaching profession

la monja   nun
el obispo   bishop
el pecado   sin
el quehacer   chore
la razón   reason
el saber   knowledge
la soledad   solitude
la vanidad   vanity

Verbos

acoger (j)   to welcome, to receive
acusar   to accuse
adquirir (ie)   to acquire
asistir   to attend
atraer (atraigo)   to attract
buscar (qu)   to look for
crecer (zc)   to grow
culpar   to blame
ejercer (z)   to practice a profession

fundar   to found
hallar   to find
mostrar (ue)   to demonstrate, to show
perseguir (i)   to persecute
regañar   to scold
rogar (ue)   to beg
sobresalir (sobresalgo)   to stand out
vestirse (i)   to get dressed

Adjetivos

bello   beautiful

impuesto   imposed

Frases

al mismo tiempo   at the same time
en contra de   against

en cuanto a   in regard to

Related words (Palabras relacionadas). The meaning of some words may be determined by thinking of related words familiar to you. Can you give in English the meaning of the underlined words derived from the words in parentheses?

1. (pasión) (dominar) Su temperamento apasionado estaba controlado por el dominio de la razón.

2. (acusar) (vanidad) En esta carta Sor Juana Inés rebatió la acusación de vanidosa que le hacía el obispo.

3. (justo) … un documento en contra de las injusticias de la época.

4. (contestar) Sor Juana Inés escribió una contestación al obispo…

False cognates (Cognados falsos). Note the meaning of the following words that are false cognates:

asistir *to attend*   grado *degree*

atender *to assist*   nota *grade*

ℒectura 1

Sor Juana Inés de la Cruz: voz feminista de Hispanoamérica

En el año 1651 nació, a poca distancia de la Ciudad de México, Inés de Asbaje y Ramírez, más conocida por su nombre conventual° de Sor Juana Inés de la Cruz. Esta mujer notable sobresalió como poeta brillante y defendió con convicción la dignidad y los derechos de la
5 mujer en una época en que ésta estaba relegada° a los quehaceres domésticos. Aunque las costumbres de la época en el virreinato° de México y las restricciones impuestas por un dogma religioso no eran favorables para el desarrollo intelectual de una mujer interesada en la poesía, la música y las ciencias, Sor Juana mostró siempre unos deseos
10 intensos de saber y pasó toda su vida tratando de adquirir cultura para comprender las ciencias y las letras.

En el siglo XVII existía en México un ambiente intelectual estimulante y la universidad, fundada en 1553, atraía a miles de estudiantes que deseaban recibir los grados de bachiller,° o de licenciado
15 o de doctor. En este ambiente de curiosidad intelectual creció Sor Juana. Ella nos dice en una página de su "Respuesta a Sor Filotea" que ella tenía unos seis o siete años cuando oyó hablar de la Universidad de México y de las Escuelas donde se aprendían las ciencias. Como° ya sabía leer y escribir, le rogaba a su madre, con gran insistencia, que la
20 vistiera de muchacho para así poder asistir a la universidad. Aun° a esa edad, ella sabía que como mujer nunca podría entrar allí.

Desde muy niña, Sor Juana tuvo acceso a los libros de su abuelo, y así adquirió y desarrolló su enorme afición e interés por la lectura. Cuando siendo una adolescente fue a vivir a casa de su tía en la Ciudad
25 de México, llamó la atención de todos los que la conocieron por su curiosidad intelectual y gran aptitud para defender sus ideas y responder a las preguntas que le hacían en la corte del virreinato de México.

La vanidad de la corte de México en aquella época no le atraía a la joven, y siempre buscaba la soledad para dedicarse tranquilamente a la
30 lectura y a la investigación. En 1669 Inés de Asbaje y Ramírez decidió entrar en un convento de monjas para vivir el resto de su vida en la pobreza, sin poseer ningún bien material, y dedicarse a meditar, a estudiar y a escribir. La poeta que había en ella empezó a desarrollarse

monastic

relegated
viceroyalty

bachelor

Since

Even

y escribió versos que empezaron a circular y a publicarse, siendo muy
35 bien acogidos en México y en España.

Hay dos características constantes que marcan todo el proceso de la
obra de Sor Juana Inés de la Cruz: la pasión y la razón. Su
temperamento apasionado estaba controlado por el dominio de la
razón y ella misma lo explica, con gran sinceridad, en los siguientes
40 versos:

> *En dos partes dividida*
> *tengo el alma en confusión:*
> *una, esclava a la pasión,*
> *y otra, a la razón medida.°*

°controlled by reason

Sor Juana Inés de la Cruz.

45   Sus poemas más conocidos son sus famosas "Redondillas" donde hace una defensa de la mujer, culpando a los hombres de los pecados de las mujeres, ya que son ellos los que las llevan al mal.

    Pero la vida de la monja-poeta se vio ensombrecida° cuando el   *darkened*
obispo de Puebla, contestando una carta que Sor Juana Inés de la Cruz
50 escribió discutiendo un sermón pronunciado por un cura jesuita, la
regañó públicamente y la criticó por su vanidad. Sor Juana Inés
escribió una contestación al obispo que ha pasado a la historia como
un documento en contra de las injusticias de la época. En esta carta
Sor Juana Inés rebatió° la acusación de vanidosa que le hacía el obispo   *refuted*
55 y, al mismo tiempo, defendió los derechos de la mujer para aprender y
ejercer el magisterio. Asimismo, defendió la libertad de opinión,
oponiéndose a la intolerancia de la época. En cuanto a la poesía que
escribió, Sor Juana Inés de la Cruz expresó: "he buscado muy de
propósito que los versos pueden hacer daño y no lo he hallado."
60   Sor Juana Inés murió en 1695 cuando una epidemia azotó° el   *hit*
convento en que ella vivía. Esta notable mujer fue víctima del
antagonismo y de la hostilidad que existían contra los intelectuales y,
especialmente, contra la mujer. En el primer cuarteto de uno de sus
famosos sonetos Sor Juana Inés expresó:

65   *En perseguirme,° Mundo, ¿qué interesas?*   *persecuting me*
   ¿En qué te ofendo cuando sólo intento
   poner belleza en mi entendimiento°   *mind, reasoning*
   y no mi entendimiento en las bellezas?

Llene los espacios en blanco con la palabra que sea correcta. Use los verbos en el tiempo que sea necesario.

1. A Sor Juana le gustaba mucho leer. Tenía gran _____ por la lectura.

2. Las _____ viven en el convento.

3. El _____ dijo la misa en la iglesia del pueblo.

4. El libro fue muy bien _____ por el público.

5. Los estudiantes deben _____ a clase todos los días.

6. Los _____ domésticos son muy aburridos.

7. En el siglo XVII las mujeres no enseñaban en las escuelas. Sor Juana Inés defendió los derechos de la mujer para ejercer el _____ .

8. En una de sus "Redondillas", Sor Juana Inés _____ a los hombres de los pecados de las mujeres.

9. La sociedad la _____ por las ideas de liberación feminista que tenía.

10. Ella era tan inteligente que _____ siempre en todo lo que estudió.

Preguntas sobre la lectura

1. ¿Por qué considera el autor que Sor Juana Inés fue una feminista notable?
2. ¿Fue Sor Juana Inés una joven diferente a las demás de su época? ¿En qué se diferenciaba?
3. Cuando Sor Juana Inés era una niña, ¿qué le pidió a su madre con gran insistencia?
4. ¿Qué dice Sor Juana Inés en las "Redondillas" con respecto a los hombres?
5. ¿Por qué decidió Sor Juana Inés entrar en el convento?
6. ¿Qué ideas expresó Sor Juana Inés en la carta que le escribió al obispo de Puebla?
7. Si Sor Juana Inés hubiera vivido en el siglo XX, ¿habría sufrido el ataque de la sociedad al expresar sus ideas? Explique por qué.
8. ¿Cómo era el ambiente intelectual en México en el siglo XVII? Si Ud. conoce actualmente a alguna mujer similar a Sor Juana Inés, hable sobre ella.

Temas de conversación

1. ¿Cómo cree Ud. que es la vida de una monja? ¿Aburrida, triste, interesante, divertida, libre de preocupaciones? Explique su respuesta.
2. ¿Qué profesión o trabajo le interesa más a Ud.? Explique por qué. ¿Le gustaría tener un negocio? ¿Qué negocio?
3. ¿Qué piensa Ud. de las personas que critican a sus amigos? ¿Conoce Ud. a alguien con esa característica? ¿Pertenece Ud. a ese grupo de personas? ¿Piensa Ud. que la crítica puede ser positiva en muchas situaciones? Explique su respuesta.
4. ¿Conoce Ud. a alguna mujer similar a Sor Juana Inés? Describa a esa persona.

Vocabulario

Antes de leer, repase el siguiente vocabulario que le ayudará a comprender la lectura.

Sustantivos

el cielo	sky	**la llanura**	flat land
la cintura	waist	**la oración**	prayer
la copa	tree-top; goblet	**el viento**	wind
la garza	heron	**el vuelo**	flight

Adjetivos

desnudo	naked	**único**	unique

Verbos

mecer (mezo)	to rock	**verter (ie)**	to pour; to flow

Lectura 2

Rosario Castellanos

Rosario Castellanos (1925–1974), poeta, novelista, dramaturga y profesora mexicana. A través de su obra se ven el interés y la preocupación por la mujer en la sociedad mexicana. Al igual que la poeta argentina, Alfonsina Storni, Rosario Castellanos muere bastante joven, a los 49 años.

Una palmera

Señora de los vientos,
garza de la llanura
cuando te meces canta
tu cintura.

5　Gesto de la oración
o preludio del vuelo,
en tu copa se vierten uno a uno
los cielos.

Desde el país oscuro de los hombres
10　he venido a mirarte de rodillas,
alta, desnuda, única,
poesía.

De *El rescate del mundo* (1952)

Preguntas sobre la lectura

1. ¿Cómo describe Rosario Castellanos la palmera?
2. ¿Qué palabras usa para trasmitirnos su percepción de la palmera?
3. ¿Ve la autora características femeninas o masculinas en la palmera? Explique su respuesta.
4. En el segundo grupo de versos, ¿qué palabras hacen referencia a un sentimiento religioso?

ramática

A   Affirmatives and negatives

Reference	Affirmative	Negative
things	**algo** (*something*)	**nada** (*nothing; anything*)
persons	**alguien** (*someone; somebody*)	**nadie** (*no one; nobody; anyone, anybody*)
persons and things	**alguno** (**-os, -a, -as**), **algún** (*some*)	**ninguno** (**-a**), **ningún** (*none; any*)
time	**siempre** (*always*)	**jamás, nunca** (*never*)
conjunctions	**o** (*either; or*)	**ni** (*neither; nor*)
adverbs	**también** (*also*)	**tampoco** (*neither*)

Mi hermano sabe **algo** de física, pero yo no sé **nada**.
My brother knows something about physics, but I don't know anything.
Alguien tocó en la puerta y cuando abrí no vi a **nadie**.
Someone knocked at the door, and when I opened it I didn't see anyone.
Algunas de las fotografías quedaron muy bien.
Some of the photographs came out very well.
No llamé a **ninguno** de los amigos. *I didn't call any of my friends.*
Siempre dices que sí pero después **nunca** cumples tu palabra.
You always say yes but afterwards you never keep your word.
No le pongo **ni** azúcar **ni** crema al café.
I put neither sugar nor cream in my coffee.
Este verano **también** estuvimos en Guayaquil.
This summer we were also in Guayaquil.
Hoy no pude salir de compras; **tampoco** podré ir mañana.
Today I couldn't go shopping; nor can I go tomorrow.

1. In Spanish, the double negative is very common.

   a. Negatives may be placed before or after the verb. In general, the negative precedes the verb. However, negatives follow the verb if the word **no** precedes the verb.

      Nadie me vino a ver así que **nada** sabemos de lo ocurrido.
      No me vino a ver **nadie** así que **no** sabemos **nada** de lo ocurrido.
      No one came to see me, thus we know nothing of what happened.

      Josefina **nunca** escribe y **tampoco** llama por teléfono.
      Josefina **no** escribe **nunca** y **no** llama **tampoco** por teléfono.
      Josefina never writes, and she never calls on the telephone either.

   b. In contrast to English, several negative words may be used in the same sentence.

      José **nunca** le da **nada** a **nadie**.   *José never gives anything to anyone.*

2. The personal **a** is used with **alguien** or **nadie** when these are direct object pronouns.

> Espero **a alguien** esta tarde. *I'm waiting for someone this afternoon.*
> No veo **a nadie** en la calle. *I don't see anyone on the street.*

3. **Alguno** and **ninguno**, when used as adjectives, drop the final **-o** when placed before a masculine singular noun.

> **Algún día** me sacaré la lotería. *Some day I will win the lottery.*
> No me gusta **ningún** cuadro. ¿Y a ti? *I don't like any painting. And you?*

NOTE: Ninguno may not be used in the plural.

4. When **alguno (-a)** follows a noun, the meaning is equivalent to **ninguno**.

> No he recibido noticia **alguna** de ellos.
> (No he recibido **ninguna** noticia de ellos.)
> *I have received no news from them.*

NOTE: Alguna vez is equivalent to the English *ever*.

> ¿Has estado **alguna vez** en San Miguel de Allende?
> *Have you ever been in San Miguel de Allende?*

5. **Ni** connects two negative elements: clauses or parts of speech (nouns, verbs, adjectives, etc.).

> No quiero salir **ni** ver a nadie. *I don't want to go out or to see anyone.*
> Felipe **ni** escribió **ni** llamó. *Felipe neither wrote nor called.*

NOTE: Ni siquiera, and sometimes **ni**, are equivalent to the English *not even*.

> Julián **ni siquiera** me miró.   *Julian did not even look at me.*
> Ella no quiere **ni** hablar con él.   *She doesn't even want to talk to him.*

6. **También** (*also, too, in addition*) is used in affirmative sentences. **Tampoco** (*neither, either*) is used in negative sentences.

> Nosotros **también** iremos a la reunión de padres y maestros.
> *We will also go to the parent-teacher meeting.*
> Ofelia no quiere asistir a la reunion; yo **tampoco** iré.
> *Ofelia doesn't want to attend the meeting; I won't go either.*

7. Note the translation of the following expressions.

más que nunca	*more than ever*
más que nada	*more than anything*
alguna vez	*ever*
mejor que nadie	*better than anyone*
sin + infinitivo + nada	*without + present participle + anything*

> He trabajado este año **más que nunca**. *This year I have worked more than ever.*
> Le gusta bailar **más que nada**. *He likes to dance more than anything.*
> ¿Ha tomado **alguna vez** sangría? *Have you ever had sangria?*
> Conozco a Arturo **mejor que nadie**. *I know Arturo better than anyone.*
> Se pasa el día **sin hacer nada**. *He spends the day without doing anything.*

8. **Nunca jamás** is a strong *expresión* of negation and is equivalent to the English *never ever* or *never again*. **Nunca más** is also equivalent to *never again*.

> **Nunca jamás** me volveré a casar.   *I'll never ever marry again.*
> **Nunca más** saldré contigo.   *Never again will I go out with you.*

When **jamás** is used in superlative expressions, it is equivalent to the English *ever*.

> Es la catedral más linda que **jamás** he visto.
> *It is the most beautiful cathedral I have ever seen.*

Ejercicios

I. Enrique y Felipe son gemelos, pero siempre hacen cosas opuestas. Dé una oración negativa para indicar el contraste entre los dos.

> **MODELO:** Felipe siempre camina por el parque.
> **Enrique nunca camina por el parque.**
> **Enrique no camina por el parque nunca.**

1. Felipe siempre hace ejercicios por la mañana.
2. También le gusta correr por la tarde.
3. Felipe algunas veces nada o en el mar o en la piscina.
4. Generalmente algún amigo va a nadar con él.
5. Felipe prepara todo la noche anterior.

II. Ahora trabaje con un(a) compañero(a) y conteste las siguientes preguntas que le hace usando dos negativos. Después él/ella va a contestar las preguntas que Ud. le hace.

> **MODELO:** ¿Le han dicho algo?
> **No, no me han dicho nada.**

1. ¿Tú siempre haces ejercicios en el gimnasio?
2. ¿Has hecho algo para adelgazar?
3. ¿Sales a correr o haces algún deporte?
4. ¿Vas a caminar algunos días?
5. ¿Crees que alguien haga ejercicio por gusto solamente?

III. Complete las oraciones con el equivalente en español de las palabras que están en inglés. Use las palabras negativas necesarias.

1. (*no one*) _____ es perfecto.
2. (*more than ever*) Ahora, _____ , me preocupo por los problemas sociales.
3. (*either*) Los niños no quieren comer _____ .
4. (*not even*) Jorge _____ me llamó una vez.
5. (*ever*) ¿Ha estado _____ en Barcelona?
6. (*any*) No me gusta _____ vestido en esta tienda.

Paseo de la Reforma en la Ciudad de México.

7. (*none*) _____ de los muchachos aceptó la invitación.

8. (*more than anything*) Lo que deseo, _____ , es terminar mis estudios.

9. (*never again*) _____ volveré a ir a ese lugar.

10. (*anyone*) No llamé a _____ cuando estuve en San Francisco.

IV. Irma le pidió a su hermano que fuera al mercado para comprar algunas cosas que ella necesitaba. Complete el diálogo entre ellos dos con los negativos necesarios.

Irma: No trajiste _____ de las cosas que te pedí.

Hermano: No me explico, pues llevé la lista que me diste. ¿Qué cosas faltan?

Irma: No compraste _____ la mantequilla _____ la margarina y _____ trajiste el queso crema. Eres la persona más distraída que _____ he visto.

Hermano: Por esa razón _____ _____ debes mandarme al mercado.

B Indicative mood and subjunctive mood

The *indicative mood* is used when the speaker gives information about an action or condition, in the present, past, or future, without commenting or expressing an attitude. It expresses a verbal action as a factual or objective reality. The indicative may be used in main clauses and subordinate clauses.

The *subjunctive mood* is used to refer to an action or condition as a concept, commented upon in the main clause. It presents a verbal action in a doubtful or hypothetical form and is the subjective expression of the speaker's attitude or thought. The subjunctive is generally used in subordinate clauses introduced by **que**.

Main clause		*Subordinate clause*	
Sé	que	ella **viene** hoy.	It is certain that she will come today.
Espero	que	ella **venga** hoy.	There is a hope that she will come today, but there is no assurance.

NOTE: In the examples above the subject of the main clause is different from the subject of the subordinate clause.

As we shall see later, the subjunctive is used when verbs of doubt, will, emotion, or certain impersonal phrases appear in the main clause, commenting on the concept expressed in the subordinate clause. Note the following examples.

> **Dudo** que **compremos** la casa.
> *I doubt we will buy the house.*
> Alfredo **prefiere** que **alquilemos** un apartamento.
> *Alfredo prefers that we rent an apartment.*
> **Tal vez** mi hijo **consiga** un condominio.
> *Perhaps my son will get a condominium.*
> **Será necesario** que **vendamos** la cabaña del lago.
> *It will be necessary for us to sell the lake house.*

The subjunctive mood has two simple tenses: present and past; and two perfect tenses: present perfect and past perfect. The use of the subjunctive is more common in Spanish than in English.

C Present subjunctive

1. Forms

   a. To form the present subjunctive, drop the final **-o** of the first person singular (**yo**) of the present indicative and add the present subjunctive endings.

Verbs ending in			
	-ar	*-er*	*-ir*
	COMPRAR	VENDER	RECIBIR
Indicative	compr **o**	vend **o**	recib **o**
Subjunctive	compr **e**	vend **a**	recib **a**
	compr **es**	vend **as**	recib **as**
	compr **e**	vend **a**	recib **a**
	compr **emos**	vend **amos**	recib **amos**
	compr **éis**	vend **áis**	recib **áis**
	compr **en**	vend **an**	recib **an**

b. Verbs with irregularities in the stem of the first person singular (**yo**) of the present indicative usually have the same irregularity in all the forms of the subjunctive.

Infinitive	*Present indicative*		*Present subjunctive*	
hacer	(yo)	**hago**	(yo, Ud.,	**haga**
salir		**salgo**	él, ella)	**salga**
oír		**oigo**		**oiga**
traer		**traigo**		**traiga**
venir		**vengo**		**venga**
valer		**valgo**		**valga**
conocer		**conozco**		**conozca**
producir		**produzco**		**produzca**
traducir		**traduzco**		**traduzca**
huir		**huyo**		**huya**
construir		**construyo**		**construya**
coger		**cojo**		**coja**
dirigir		**dirijo**		**dirija**
caber		**quepo**		**quepa**
cerrar		**cierro**		**cierre**
comenzar		**comienzo**		**comience**
contar		**cuento**		**cuente**
encontrar		**encuentro**		**encuentre**
pedir		**pido**		**pida**
servir		**sirvo**		**sirva**
seguir		**sigo**		**siga**
vencer		**venzo**		**venza**

Examples:

HACER		ESCOGER		PEDIR	
haga	hagamos	escoja	escojamos	pida	pidamos
hagas	hagáis	escojas	escojáis	pidas	pidáis
haga	hagan	escoja	escojan	pida	pidan

c. Verbs that change spelling in the first person of the preterite tense to retain the pronunciation of the infinitive have the same spelling change in all persons of the present subjunctive.

Spelling change	Infinitive		Present subjunctive
c → qu	buscar	(yo, Ud.,	busque
	tocar	él, ella)	toque
g → gu	llegar		llegue
	pagar		pague
z → c	cruzar		cruce
	comenzar		comience

d. Stem-changing verbs ending in **-ar** and **-er** that change the **e** to **ie** and the **o** to **ue** in the present indicative have the same changes in the present subjunctive in **yo**, **tú**, **Ud.**, and **Uds.** but not in **nosotros, vosotros**.

CERRAR		CONTAR	
cierre	cerremos	**cuente**	contemos
cierres	cerréis	**cuentes**	contéis
cierre	**cierren**	**cuente**	**cuenten**

e. Stem-changing verbs ending in **-ir** have another change that does not occur in the present indicative. In the present subjunctive the **e** changes to **i** and the **o** to **u** in **nosotros** and **vosotros**.

SENTIR		DORMIR	
sienta	**sintamos**	duerma	**durmamos**
sientas	**sintáis**	duermas	**durmáis**
sienta	sientan	duerma	duerman

Other verbs that belong to this group are:

mentir   preferir   divertirse   morir

f. The following verbs have their own irregularities:

DAR		ESTAR		SER	
dé	demos	**esté**	estemos	sea	seamos
des	deis	**estés**	estéis	seas	seáis
dé	den	**esté**	**estén**	sea	sean

SABER		HABER		IR	
sepa	sepamos	haya	hayamos	vaya	vayamos
sepas	sepáis	hayas	hayáis	vayas	vayáis
sepa	sepan	haya	hayan	vaya	vayan

2. The tense of the verb used in the main clause serves as a guide to determine the tense used in the subordinate clause. In general, the present subjunctive is used in the subordinate clause if the verb in the main clause is in present tense or future tense. Note the following examples:

> **Quiero** que **lleves** la carta al correo.
> *I want you to take the letter to the post office.*
> **Dudo** que el cartero **recoja** la correspondencia hoy.
> *I doubt that the mail carrier will pick up the mail today.*

Jóvenes estudiando en la biblioteca de la Universidad Nacional Autónoma de México.

Ejercicios

I. Escriba las oraciones cambiando los verbos en la cláusula subordinada de acuerdo con los nuevos sujetos entre paréntesis.

> **MODELO:** Leopoldo desea que cierres la puerta. (nosotros) (Uds.)
> **Leopoldo desea que cerremos la puerta.**
> **Leopoldo desea que Uds. cierren la puerta.**

1. Es importante que Uds. se despierten temprano. (tú) (nosotros)
2. Miguel teme que pierdas las llaves. (nosotros) (mis hijos)
3. Espero que ella encuentre trabajo pronto. (Uds.) (nosotros)
4. Ojalá que se diviertan mucho. (tú) (Ud.)
5. ¿Quiere que sirva el café? (nosotros) (las chicas)

II. Complete las oraciones, según el modelo, usando el presente de subjuntivo de los verbos entre paréntesis.

> **MODELOS:** Deseamos que Ud. _____ .
> (venir con nosotros)
> **Deseamos que Ud. venga con nosotros.**
>
> (ser presidente)
> **Deseamos que Ud. sea presidente.**

Espero que Ud. _____ .

1. (venir a la fiesta)
2. (traer los discos)
3. (llegar a las siete)

Dudo que ellos _____ .

4. (saber lo que pasó)
5. (hacer la acusación)
6. (buscar un abogado)

Es necesario que nosotros _____ .

7. (ir al restaurante)
8. (almorzar con el director)
9. (pagar la cuenta del almuerzo)

Deseo que tú _____ .

10. (conocer a Luis)
11. (sentarse a su lado)
12. (seguir conversando con él)

III. Sus amigos piensan ir a un partido de fútbol. Conteste las preguntas usando en las respuestas el verbo en el presente de subjuntivo.

1. ¿Qué desea Ud. que hagan sus amigos durante el partido?
2. ¿Duda Ud. que vayan también los padres de sus amigos?
3. ¿Qué espera Ud. que pase en el partido de fútbol de su universidad? ¿Cree Ud. que gane su equipo (team)?
4. ¿Lamenta Ud. no poder ir con ellos?
5. ¿Qué les sugiere Ud. que hagan después del partido?

IV. Es posible que Uds. hagan un viaje a Guadalajara. Ud. tiene ciertas dudas. Exprese posibilidad o duda cambiando las siguientes frases. Comience las oraciones con la expresión **tal vez**.

1. Vamos a Guadalajara.
2. Convenzo a mi amigo para hacer el viaje.
3. Anita viene también.
4. Todos caben en nuestro carro.
5. Podemos escuchar a los mariachis.
6. Compramos blusas bordadas y ollas de barro (*clay pots*).

V. Un profesor amigo suyo le habla de la posibilidad de una huelga (*strike*) de maestros. Usando los verbos que siguen en el presente de subjuntivo, complete las oraciones.

ocurrir   tener   aumentar   ser   servir   obtener

Es posible que _____ una huelga este mes. Me preocupa que los

profesores _____ que pasar por esa situación. Ellos piden que les

_____ el salario y que las clases _____ más pequeñas.

¡Ojalá que la huelga _____ su propósito y que los maestros

_____ lo que quieren!

VI. Imagine que Ud. conversa con un grupo de estudiantes sobre la ecología y los problemas del medio ambiente. Usando las frases que siguen, continúe las oraciones para expresar sus opiniones. Use los verbos en el presente de subjuntivo.

MODELO: Espero que todo el mundo…
Espero que todo el mundo evite usar los productos que contaminan el medio ambiente.

1. Recomiendo que el gobierno…
2. Sugiero que las compañías de autos…
3. Lamento que las personas…
4. Aconsejo que…
5. Propongo que…

D   The imperative mood

The imperative mood is used for affirmative and negative commands. There are imperative forms for the familiar **tú** or **vosotros(as)** and other forms for the formal **Ud.** or **Uds.** There are also forms for **nosotros(as)**. The present subjunctive forms are used for **Ud., él, ella, Uds., ellos(as)** and **nosotros(as)** in affirmative and negative commands. The only command that does not use a subjunctive form is the affirmative **tú** command.

1. Affirmative commands for the familiar **tú** and **vosotros**. Note that the **tú** form is the same as the third person singular of the present indicative.

compr **a** (tú)	vend **e** (tú)	recib **e** (tú)
compr **ad** (vosotros)	vend **ed** (vosotros)	recib **id** (vosotros)

2. Negative commands for **tú** and **vosotros**. The forms are the same as in the present subjunctive.

		Imperative	
Infinitive	_Present subjunctive_	_Affirmative_	_Negative_
comprar	tú compres	**compra** (tú)	**no compres**
	Ud. compre	**compre** (Ud.)	**no compre**
	nosotros compremos	**compremos** (nosotros)	**no compremos**
	vosotros compréis	**comprad** (vosotros)	**no compréis**
	Uds. compren	**compren** (Uds.)	**no compren**
vender	tú vendas	**vende** (tú)	**no vendas**
	Ud. venda	**venda** (Ud.)	**no venda**
	nosotros vendamos	**vendamos** (nosotros)	**no vendamos**
	vosotros vendáis	**vended** (vosotros)	**no vendáis**
	Uds. vendan	**vendan** (Uds.)	**no vendan**
recibir	tú recibas	**recibe** (tú)	**no recibas**
	Ud. reciba	**reciba** (Ud.)	**no reciba**
	nosotros recibamos	**recibamos** (nosotros)	**no recibamos**
	vosotros recibáis	**recibid** (vosotros)	**no recibáis**
	Uds. reciban	**reciban** (Uds.)	**no reciban**

Lee las frases.	**No leas** las frases.	_Read (don't read) the sentences._
Abra las ventanas.	**No abra** las ventanas.	_Open (don't open) the windows._
Esperemos a Elisa.	**No esperemos** a Elisa.	_Let's wait (not wait) for Elisa._
Firmen los documentos.	**No firmen** los documentos.	_Sign (don't sign) the documents._

NOTE: The following are examples of affirmative commands with the verb **estar**. Note also that the affirmative commands for reflexive verbs use **te** in the familiar.

> **Esté** Ud. seguro de que se hará el negocio. **Estése** tranquilo, Sr. Pérez, que todo saldrá bien.
> _Be assured that the business will get done. Be calm/Don't worry, Mr. Perez, everything will turn out fine._
> Pepito, **estáte** quieto y **estáte** callado por cinco minutos.
> _Pepito, be calm/don't move and be quiet for five minutes._

3. Irregular verbs. The imperative has the same irregularities as the present subjunctive.

> **Cierra** esa puerta y **durmamos** la siesta. _Close that door and let's take a nap._
> **Conduzcan** con cuidado, **vayan** al aeropuerto y **traigan** al tío Francisco que llega esta noche.
> _Drive carefully, go to the airport, and pick up uncle Francisco who arrives tonight._
> **Sepa** Ud. que me voy mañana. _Know that I am leaving tomorrow._

Note the following examples with the verbs **saber** and **saberse** in affirmative commands with **tú**.

> **Sábelo** bien, no vas a salir esta noche.
> *Know this well, you are not going out tonight.*
> **Sábetelo** de memoria para mañana.
> *Know it (all) by heart (memory) by tomorrow.*

4. The following verbs have irregular forms in the affirmative **tú** commands.

Infinitive	Imperative	Infinitive	Imperative
salir	**sal** tú	decir	**di** tú
venir	**ven** tú	hacer	**haz** tú
poner	**pon** tú	ser	**sé** tú
tener	**ten** tú	ir	**ve** tú

> **Sal** en seguida, **ve** a la tienda y **haz** todas las compras.
> *Leave at once, go to the store, and do all the shopping.*

The negative forms of these verbs are the same as the present subjunctive forms.

> No te **preocupes** tanto y no **seas** tan pesimista.
> *Don't worry so much and don't be so pessimistic.*

5. The English expression *let's* is expressed in Spanish with the **nosotros** form of the present subjunctive.

> **Cantemos** esa canción.   *Let's sing that song.*
> No **pidamos** tantas cosas.   *Let's not ask for so many things.*

NOTE: *Let's* may also be expressed in the affirmative by using **vamos a** + infinitive.

> **Vamos a** cantar esa canción.   *Let's sing that song.*

The verb **ir** has an irregular form in the affirmative commands. In the negative, it follows the rule for the subjunctive.

> **Vamos**, ya va a empezar   *Let's go, the program is going to*
>   el programa.   *begin already.*
> No **vayamos** con Luciano.   *Let's not go with Luciano.*

6. Direct and indirect object pronouns as well as reflexive pronouns follow and are attached to affirmative commands. They precede negative commands.

> Dá**melo**.   No **me lo** des.   *Give (don't give) it to me.*
> Díga**selo**.   No **se lo** digan.   *Tell (don't tell) it to him/her/them.*
> Acués**tate**.   No **te** acuestes.   *Go (don't go) to bed.*
> Hagámos**lo**.   No **lo** hagamos.   *Let's (not) do it.*

NOTE: Note the use of the written accent when adding pronouns to the affirmative commands.

hágalo	díselo	ábranlas
hágamelo	dígaselo	póntelos
vámonos	dánoslo	despiértate

The accent mark is not needed in one-syllable commands that add only one pronoun.

ponte   dime   danos   hazlo

a. Reflexive verbs drop the final **-s** of the **nosotros** form in the affirmative commands. In the negative they follow the form of the present subjunctive.

lavemos + nos = **lavémonos**   **no nos lavemos**   *Let's (not) get washed.*
sentemos + nos = **sentémonos**   **no nos sentemos**   *Let's (not) sit down.*

b. Reflexive verbs drop the final **-d** of the **vosotros** form in affirmative commands. In the negative they follow the form of the present subjunctive.

lavad + os = **lavaos**   **no os lavéis**

c. Instead of the imperative, Spanish frequently uses a more courteous form using the verb in the present indicative in an interrogative sentence. Note the following examples.

Tráeme un vaso de agua.
Bring me a glass of water.
¿**Me traes** un vaso de agua, por favor?
Will you bring me a glass of water, please?
Cállate.
Be quiet.
¿**Te callas**, por favor?
Will you be quiet, please?

Ejercicios

I. Imagine que Ud. es instructor en una clase de manejar. Cambie las siguientes instrucciones a órdenes formales que Ud. le da a su estudiante.

MODELO: Es importante mantener su carro en buenas condiciones.
Mantenga su carro en buenas condiciones.

1. Es necesario disminuir la velocidad al doblar una esquina.
2. Tiene que parar para dejar cruzar a los peatones (*pedestrians*).
3. Debe encender las luces al atardecer.
4. Es importante no correr a más de la velocidad indicada.
5. No debe manejar si toma bebidas alcohólicas.
6. Tiene que ponerse siempre el cinturón de seguridad.
7. No es bueno quitar las manos del volante (*steering wheel*).

II. Su hermana le hace varias preguntas relacionadas con la fiesta que piensan dar. Conteste las preguntas con órdenes afirmativas y negativas, usando pronombres y el verbo en la forma familiar.

> **MODELO:** ¿Mando las invitaciones?
> **Sí, mándalas.**
> **No, no las mandes.**

1. ¿Hago el ponche?
2. ¿Pongo las mesas en el patio?
3. ¿Traigo las enchiladas?
4. ¿Invito al profesor de español?
5. ¿Sirvo café con leche?

III. Sustituya la construcción **ir a + un infinitivo** por una orden.

> **MODELO:** Vamos a escuchar las noticias.
> **Escuchemos las noticias.**

1. Vamos a hablar español.
2. Vamos a tocar la guitarra.
3. Vamos a dormir la siesta.
4. No vayamos a dar un paseo.
5. No vayamos a construir una casa.

IV. Conteste las preguntas con órdenes afirmativas y negativas usando pronombres.

> **MODELO:** ¿Abrimos las ventanas?
> **Sí, ábranlas.**
> **No, no las abran.**

1. ¿Apagamos las luces?
2. ¿Pedimos un taxi?
3. ¿Leemos el artículo?
4. ¿Hacemos los ejercicios?
5. ¿Llamamos a Ernesto?

V. Complete las oraciones con el imperativo afirmativo o negativo de los verbos entre paréntesis.

1. (decir) Jorge, _____ (tú) lo que pasó.

2. (Empezar / esperar) _____ (Uds.) a comer, no me

   _____ .

3. (llamar) No _____ (tú) al médico, ya me siento mejor.

4. (Probarse) _____ (Ud.) el traje.

5. (Hacer) _____ (tú) lo que yo digo, pero no lo que yo hago.

VI. Ud. va a cuidar a los niños de su hermana este sábado. Ella le deja una lista de cosas que quiere que ellos hagan. Transforme en órdenes lo que la hermana quiere que hagan los niños.

Hermana: Dile a Ramoncito que se levante temprano; que se bañe, que se pruebe la chaqueta nueva, y que se la pruebe con el suéter, y que ordene su cuarto.
Ud.:   Ramoncito…
Hermana: Diles a Gabriel y a Anita que se pongan los zapatos de tenis; que se los pongan con calcetines; que se desayunen antes de salir; y que se den prisa porque deben visitar a la abuela.
Ud: Gabriel y Anita…

VII. Ramoncito, Gabriel y Anita, los hijos de su hermana, están jugando en el patio. ¿Qué les dice ella si quiere que hagan o no hagan ciertas cosas? Cambie el infinitivo que está entre paréntesis y continúe la oración con una idea original.

> **MODELO:** Niños, (no gritar) tanto porque…
> **Niños, no griten tanto porque van a despertar al bebé.**

1. Niños, (ponerse) el traje de baño…
2. Niños, (no jugar) en la calle…
3. Ramoncito, (no cruzar) por el jardín…
4. Anita, (no dejar) salir al perro porque…
5. Gabriel, (tener cuidado)…

E Imperfect subjunctive

1. Forms

   a. The imperfect subjunctive has two forms: one with **-ra** and the other with **-se**. In general, the **-ra** form is more common. This tense is formed by deleting the **-ron** of the third person plural of the preterite and adding one of the past subjunctive endings.

ALL VERBS

COMPRAR compraron		**VENDER** vendieron	
compra **ra**	compra **se**	vendie **ra**	vendie **se**
compra **ras**	compra **ses**	vendie **ras**	vendie **ses**
compra **ra**	compra **se**	vendie **ra**	vendie **se**
comprá **ramos**	comprá **semos**	vendié **ramos**	vendié **semos**
compra **rais**	compra **seis**	vendie **rais**	vendie **seis**
compra **ran**	compra **sen**	vendie **ran**	vendie **sen**

RECIBIR   recibie**ron**

recibie **ra**	recibie **se**
recibie **ras**	recibie **ses**
recibie **ra**	recibie **se**
recibié **ramos**	recibié **semos**
recibie **rais**	recibie **seis**
recibie **ran**	recibie **sen**

b. The **-ra** and **-se** forms of the imperfect subjunctive are interchangeable. The **-ra** form is more commonly used.

c. Verbs that are irregular in the **Uds.** form of the preterite are also irregular in the past subjunctive.

Infinitive		Preterite	Stem	Past subjunctive
decir	(Uds.)	**dijeron**	**dije-**	**dijera**
producir		**produjeron**	**produje-**	**produjera**
traer		**trajeron**	**traje-**	**trajera**
poner		**pusieron**	**pusie-**	**pusiera**
saber		**supieron**	**supie-**	**supiera**
tener		**tuvieron**	**tuvie-**	**tuviera**
estar		**estuvieron**	**estuvie-**	**estuviera**
andar		**anduvieron**	**anduvie-**	**anduviera**
ir, ser		**fueron**	**fue-**	**fuera**
hacer		**hicieron**	**hicie-**	**hiciera**
haber		**hubieron**	**hubie-**	**hubiera**
querer		**quisieron**	**quisie-**	**quisiera**
leer		**leyeron**	**leye-**	**leyera**
sentir		**sintieron**	**sintie-**	**sintiera**
pedir		**pidieron**	**pidie-**	**pidiera**
preferir		**prefirieron**	**prefirie-**	**prefiriera**
dormir		**durmieron**	**durmie-**	**durmiera**
morir		**murieron**	**murie-**	**muriera**
caber		**cupieron**	**cupie-**	**cupiera**
huir		**huyeron**	**huye-**	**huyera**
construir		**construyeron**	**construye-**	**construyera**

2. The past subjunctive is used in the subordinate clause when the verb in the main clause is in the past (preterite, imperfect, or conditional indicative). Note the following examples.

No **quise** que ella **vendiera** su auto.
I didn't want her to sell the car.
Yo **dudaba** que le **pagaran** el precio que pedía.
I doubted that they would pay the price she was asking.

Ejercicios

I. Complete las oraciones, según el modelo, usando el imperfecto de subjuntivo de los verbos entre paréntesis.

MODELOS: Ellos querían que yo _____ .
(ir a la playa)
Ellos querían que yo fuera a la playa.
(jugar en la arena)
Ellos querían que yo jugara en la arena.

Dudaba que Magdalena _____ .

1. (saber cocinar)
2. (hacer el pastel)
3. (traer los ingredientes)
4. (tener una buena receta)

Era imposible que nosotros _____ .

5. (leer la novela en un día)
6. (traducir los apuntes de clase)
7. (poder escribir el informe)
8. (estar listos para tomar el examen)

II. Complete las oraciones con el presente y el imperfecto de subjuntivo, respectivamente, según sea necesario.

MODELO: (hacer) Desean que yo **haga** el trabajo.
Deseaban que yo **hiciera** el trabajo.

1. (entrar) Dígales a los chicos que _____ .
   Les dijo a los chicos que _____ .
2. (venir) Se alegran de que Ud. _____ a la boda.
   Se alegraron de que Ud. _____ a la boda.
3. (influir) Desean que Ud. _____ en la decisión.
   Deseaban que Ud. _____ en la decisión.
4. (construir) Es imposible que ellos _____ ese edificio.
   Era imposible que ellos _____ ese edificio.
5. (traer) Espero que ellos _____ los refrescos.
   Esperaba que ellos _____ los refrescos.

III. Cuando Claudio decidió ir a México Ud. le hizo varias recomendaciones. Complete el párrafo llenando los espacios en blanco con el imperfecto de subjuntivo de los verbos entre paréntesis.

Le recomendé a Claudio que _____ (visitar) algunos lugares en México. Yo deseaba que él

_____ (conocer) la Plaza del Zócalo. Quería que él

_____ (apreciar) la amplitud del lugar. Le dije que

La catedral de México en la Plaza del Zócalo.

_____ (entrar) en la catedral que está en la plaza. Era importante que él _____ (ver) el bello altar barroco. Le pedí que _____ (sacar) fotografías de la catedral y del Palacio Nacional.

IV. En las siguientes frases se habla del drama de la literatura española *Don Juan Tenorio*, escrito por José Zorrilla (1817–1893). El personaje de don Juan, que originalmente apareció en una antigua leyenda española, se convirtió en una figura de carácter universal.

Usando el presente de subjuntivo haga nuevas oraciones empezando con las frases que están entre paréntesis.

1. Vamos al teatro el próximo sábado. (Es posible)
2. Ponen un famoso drama de la literatura española. (Me alegro de)
3. La obra *Don Juan Tenorio* se pone en España todos los años en el mes de noviembre. (Es sorprendente)

Ahora use el imperfecto de subjuntivo.

4. Todos los estudiantes de español leyeron este drama. (Recomendé)
5. Doña Inés murió de dolor por don Juan. (Sentí)
6. Don Juan tuvo un final trágico. (Fue justo)

V. Composición dirigida (oral o escrita). Basándose en los temas, complete las oraciones en forma original usando los verbos en el imperfecto de subjuntivo.

MODELO: Tema: Las cosas que le permitían hacer sus padres cuando Ud. era niño o niña.

Cuando yo era niño…

Cuando yo era niño mis padres permitían que yo hiciera deportes, que fuera a un campamento todos los veranos, que comiera lo que quisiera y que fuera a pescar todos los fines de semana.

1. Tema: Las cosas que sería conveniente que Ud. hiciera este fin de semana.
   Sería conveniente que yo…
2. Tema: Las cosas que desearía que su amigo hiciera cuando sale con Ud.
   Desearía que mi amigo…
3. Tema: Las cosas que le aconsejaba su profesor o profesora de inglés en la escuela secundaria.
   Mi profesor de inglés en la escuela secundaria me aconsejaba que (yo)…

F Uses of the subjunctive: verbs that express doubt, will, or emotion

When the verb in the main clause expresses doubt, will, or emotion with relation to the concept expressed in the subordinate clause, the verb in the subordinate clause is generally in the subjunctive. Note that the subject of the main clause must be different from the subject of the subordinate clause.

Main clause: Verb in indicative		*Subordinate clause:* Verb in subjunctive
Ella **duda**	que	**salgas** bien en el examen.
She doubts	*that*	*you will pass the exam.*
(Yo) **Espero**	que	Ud. **llegue** bien.
I hope	*that*	*you arrive well.*

If there is no change of subject, the infinitive is used and not the subjunctive.

Yo deseo que Luisa **obtenga** el empleo.	*I want Luisa to get the job.*
Yo deseo **obtener** el empleo.	*I want to get the job.*

1. Verbs that express doubt, will, or emotion.

dudar *to doubt*	rogar *to beg*	impedir *to impede*
desear *to wish*	suplicar *to plead*	lamentar *to lament; be sorry*
querer *to want*	necesitar *to need*	temer *to fear*
preferir *to prefer*	permitir *to permit*	anhelar *to desire*
esperar *to hope*	prohibir *to forbid*	alegrarse de *to be happy*
proponer *to propose*	aprobar *to approve*	sentir *to feel; to regret*
recomendar *to recommend*	ordenar *to order*	exigir *to demand*
pedir *to request*	aconsejar *to advise*	
insistir *to insist*	sugerir *to suggest*	

+ que + subjuntive

El Sr. Espinosa **quiere** que **pasemos** a su oficina.
Mr. Espinosa wants us to go into his office.
La secretaria nos **rogó** que **saliéramos** del cuarto.
The secretary begged us to leave the room.
Lamento que no **podamos** firmar el contrato.
I'm sorry that we cannot sign the contract.

2. When the verbs **decir** or **escribir** appear in the main clause expressing a command, the subjunctive is used in the subordinate clause.

Ana te dice que **vengas**.   *Ana tells you to come.*
Me escribió que le **enviara** el dinero.   *She wrote to me to send her the money.*

When these verbs appear in the main clause stating a fact or merely informing, the indicative is used in the subordinate clause.

Ana dice que ellos **vienen**.   *Ana says they are coming.*
Me escribió que le **envió** el dinero.   *She wrote me that she sent him the money.*

Ejercicios

I. Complete las siguientes oraciones usando el verbo en el presente de subjuntivo.

MODELO: Mi primo viene mañana.
Espero que mi primo…
Espero que mi primo venga mañana.

1. Tenemos que limpiar la casa.
Temo que nosotros…
2. La casa es grande y cómoda.
Espero que la casa…
3. Ellos no pueden mudarse hasta el mes que viene.
Siento que ellos no…
4. Ellos compran las entradas para la ópera.
Deseo que ellos…
5. El vestido cuesta mucho dinero.
Dudo que el vestido…
6. Pedro quiere salir a las ocho.
Quiero que Pedro…

II. Ud. le cuenta a un amigo acerca de la celebración del aniversario de bodas de sus padres. Complete las oraciones usando los verbos entre paréntesis en indicativo o en subjuntivo, según convenga.

1. (desear) (cocinar) Mi madre _____ que yo _____ una paella para celebrar su aniversario de boda.
2. (dudar) (tener) Ella _____ que (yo) _____ suficiente dinero para comprar todos los mariscos (*seafood*).
3. (esperar) (ayudar) Yo _____ que mi hermano me _____ con los gastos (*expenses*).

4. (salir) (venir) Espero que la paella _____ bien porque toda la familia _____ a cenar ese día.

5. (preferir) (servir) Mi padre _____ que nosotros _____ sangría con la paella.

III. Su amiga tiene que ir a una entrevista para un puesto de secretaria. Todo el mundo le da distintos consejos. Escriba estos consejos, según el modelo, usando el presente o el imperfecto de subjuntivo.

MODELO: hermano / recomienda / pedir un buen sueldo
Su hermano le recomienda que pida un buen sueldo.

1. madre / dice / no ponerse nerviosa
2. padre / aconsejó / contestar las preguntas con claridad
3. hermana / sugiere / vestirse y peinarse bien
4. profesor de español / recomendó / hablar despacio
5. mejor amigo / dijo / mostrar mucho interés en obtener el puesto

IV. Traduzca al español usando el presente de subjuntivo.

1. *We prefer that you (Ud.) do the work.*
2. *I suggest that you (Ud.) leave early.*
3. *I want you (tú) to tell the truth.*
4. *They want me to go to the bank.*
5. *She hopes that John will pass the exam.*

V. Traduzca al español usando el imperfecto de subjuntivo.

1. *He ordered me to write the report.*
2. *Mr. Cortina asked me to sign the check.*
3. *I advised him to visit Sevilla.*
4. *They wanted us to go to the wedding.*
5. *Manuel allowed his son to go to Las Vegas.*

VI. Ud. es un buen amigo y un buen consejero. Cuando sus amigos le cuentan sus problemas Ud. les hace algunas recomendaciones.

Amigo N°. 1:   No estudié para el examen.

     Ud.:   Dudo que _____ . Te recomiendo que

        _____ .

Amigo N°. 2:   Me duelen las piernas por el mucho ejercicio.

     Ud.:   Siento que _____ . Te aconsejo que _____ .

Amigo N°. 3:   Fui al médico y me dijo que estoy demasiado gordo.

    Ud.:   Es una pena que _____ . Te sugiero que

_____ .

Amigo N°. 4:   Hablé con mi amiga y no puede acompañarme al baile de graduación.

    Ud.:   Es una lástima que _____ . Te recomiendo que

_____ .

VII. Exprese su reacción emocional ante los siguientes hechos. Use verbos como **sentir, desear, esperar, dudar, alegrarse,** etc.

MODELOS: María y Juan van a casarse.
> **Me alegro de que María y Juan se casen.**
> Pedro perdió el dinero en el negocio.
> **Sentí que Pedro perdiera el dinero en el negocio.**

1. Elisa no viene mañana a vernos.
2. La semana pasada mi primo se sacó la lotería.
3. Los recién casados van a comprar una casa.
4. Hace mal tiempo y los jóvenes no pueden ir a esquiar.
5. Mis abuelos fueron de viaje el año pasado.

VIII. Combine las dos oraciones en una según el modelo. Use el presente o el imperfecto de subjuntivo.

MODELO: Isabel quiere. Ricardo trae a los primos.
> **Isabel quiere que Ricardo traiga a los primos.**

1. Él desea. Ella los llama.
2. Será mejor. Ellos toman un taxi en el hotel.
3. Ella recomendó. Ellos alquilaron un carro.
4. Él temió. Ellos no encontraron la dirección.
5. Isabel y Ricardo sienten. Los primos se van mañana.

IX. En el siguiente párrafo se habla del escritor y poeta mexicano Octavio Paz (1914–1998). Llene los espacios en blanco con el tiempo correcto del verbo que está entre paréntesis.

Sentí mucho que ayer Uds. no _____ (oír) la conferencia sobre el escritor y

poeta mexicano Octavio Paz. Es importante que los estudiantes de español

_____ (conocer) su obra para que _____ (poder) apreciar su valor. Sería

bueno que Uds. _____ (leer) algunas de sus muchas obras. Entre sus obras en

prosa les recomiendo que _____ (buscar) *El laberinto de la soledad* y *Tiempo

nublado*. Su obra poética es muy importante también. Me alegró que por fin, en

1990, le _____ (dar) el Premio Nobel de Literatura.

Composición

Antes de escribir, repase las siguientes reglas sobre las mayúsculas y la ortografía.

A Review of capitalization rules

Remember that a capital letter is used:

- At the beginning of a sentence and after a period:

    Recibió un 98. Una buena nota.

- With proper names, nicknames, geographic names, institutions:

Sara H. López	**Paquito**	**río Amazonas**
Sierra Nevada	**la Casa Blanca**	**el Seguro Social**

- With nouns and pronouns referring to deity

Nuestro Señor Jesucristo	**la Virgen Santísima**
el Espíritu Santo	**el Divino Redentor**

B Review of spelling rules: *h*

Because the **h** is silent in Spanish, the spelling of some words is confusing. Note the spelling of the following words:

a	*(to; at)*	**¡Ah!** *Ah*		**asta** *flagpole*	**hasta** *until*
		ha *has*			
ojear	*to stare*	**hojear** *to leaf through*		**echo** *I throw*	**hecho** *made*
ora	*prays*	**hora** *hour*		**ola** *wave*	**hola** *hello*

Study the following rules. Write with an **h**:

1. words that begin with **hipo-, hidr-, hiper-:**

    hipótesis (*hypothesis*), **hidráulico** (*hydraulic*), **hipertensión** (*hypertension*)

2. words that begin with **hie-, hia-:**

    hielo (*ice*), **hiato** (*hiatus*)

3. words that begin with the sound **hue-**, **hui-**:

    huevos (*eggs*), **huido** (*fled*)

4. words that begin with **hexa-**, **hepta-**, **hect-**:

    hexágono (*hexagon*), **heptasílabo** (*heptasyllable*), **hectárea** (*hectare*)

5. words derived from the verbs **haber** (*to have*) and **hacer**:

    habían, han, haciendo

6. the exclamations ¡ah!, ¡eh!, ¡oh!

NOTE: The exercises corresponding to this section are included in the *Cuaderno de ejercicios*, Capítulo 4.

Ejercicio de composición (opcional)

Haga una composición sobre el tema que se da a continuación. Use el esquema siguiente.

TEMA:	Evolución y cambios producidos por el movimiento feminista.
INTRODUCCIÓN:	Cambios en la forma de vida de la mujer.
	Dilemas que tiene: la crianza (*raising*) de los hijos y las exigencias de su trabajo.
	El papel del padre en el hogar, antes y ahora.
	Libertades que tienen hoy las mujeres que no tenían sus abuelas.
DESARROLLO:	Los trabajos que hace hoy la mujer que antes sólo hacían los hombres.
	¿Cómo aceptan los hombres que las mujeres estén en el mismo campo laboral que ellos?
	Cambios en la relación entre el hombre y la mujer.
	Idea que existía de que la mujer pertenecía al sexo débil y el hombre al sexo fuerte.
CONCLUSIÓN:	Dé su opinión sobre los cambios producidos por el movimiento feminista y los efectos de éstos en la sociedad. ¿Cómo cree Ud. que será la vida de la mujer dentro de cincuenta años?

5 *Capítulo*

Plaza Libertad, San Salvador, El Salvador.

LECTURAS

- Lectura 1: "La América Central"
- Lectura 2: "Los mayas"
- Lectura 3: "El eclipse" de Augusto Monterroso

GRAMÁTICA

- Phrases and expressions that require the subjunctive
- Present perfect subjunctive
- Pluperfect subjunctive
- Sequence of tenses
- Other expressions that require the subjunctive
- **Si** clauses
- Expressions with **tener**

COMPOSICIÓN

- Review of capitalization rules
- Review of spelling rules: **g, j**

Vocabulario

Antes de leer, repase el siguiente vocabulario que le ayudará a comprender la lectura.

Sustantivos

el bosque forest	**la papa** potato
el crecimiento growth	**el plátano** banana
el desarrollo development	**la población** population
el eslabón link	**el porcentaje** percentage
el éxito success	**el sentido** sense
el fango mud	**el tamaño** size
la franja strip	**el trigo** wheat

Verbos

abrazar (c) to embrace	**crecer (zc)** to grow
aparecer (zc) to appear	**morir (ue)** to die
azotar to beat	**prevalecer (zc)** to prevail
condenar to condemn	**probar (ue)** to prove

Adjetivos

acogedor hospitable	**hermoso** beautiful
ancho wide	**hondo** deep
estrecho narrow	**libre** free

Frases

al mismo tiempo at the same time	**así como** as well as
alzar la voz to raise the voice	**llevar a cabo** to carry out

Related words (Palabras relacionadas). The meaning of some words may be determined by thinking of related words familiar to you. Can you give the meaning of the underlined words derived from the words in parentheses?

1. (rico) La principal fuente de <u>riqueza</u> de estos países centroamericanos es la agricultura…
2. (escribir) … Rigoberta Menchú, en sus <u>escritos</u>, ataca el racismo y la discriminación…
3. (saber) Asturias … recordaba un Dios ancestral lleno de <u>sabiduría</u>.
4. (cerca) Al final de la clase el profesor <u>se acercó</u> a Asturias…
5. (emoción) … el <u>emocionado</u> profesor lo abrazó con entusiasmo…

Preliminary view of some expressions (Vista preliminar de algunas expresiones).

1. Note the translation of the following sentence:

   Notó que éste no le quitaba los ojos de encima.
   He noticed that the latter did not take his eyes off of him.

2. Note that some cognates may have more than one definition and that the meaning may be determined according to the context in which it is used:

provocar *to provoke; to cause; to tempt*
… movimientos sísmicos que han provocado grandes desastres…
. . . seismic movements that have caused great disasters . . .

conservar *to conserve; to preserve; to keep; to remain*
… el elemento indígena se conserva en una proporción alta…
. . . the indigenous element remains proportionately high . . .

quedar *to remain; to be left behind; to fit; to be*
La construcción del Canal que quedó terminado en 1914…
The construction of the Canal, which was finished in 1914 . . .

False cognates (Cognados falsos). Note the meaning of the following words that are false cognates.

éxito	*success*	recordar	*to recall; to remind*
salida	*exit*	grabar	*to record*

*L*ectura I

La América Central

La América Central es el eslabón que une las dos Américas, la del Norte
y la del Sur, y en esa franja de tierra, ancha en su comienzo y estrecha
en el sur, viven más de treinta y cinco millones de habitantes. Ocupa
una zona volcánica que ha sido azotada por movimientos sísmicos que
5   han provocado grandes desastres y, al mismo tiempo, ofrece hermosos
paisajes de montañas, volcanes, lagos y playas acogedoras. Está formada
por los siguientes países: Guatemala, Honduras, El Salvador, Nicaragua,
Costa Rica y Panamá.

Un fuerte sentido nacionalista prevalece en estas pequeñas repúblicas,
10   que representan una unidad geográfica y económica donde el
crecimiento y el desarrollo son inestables, teniendo extremos de gran
riqueza y de gran pobreza. La política volátil, los conflictos entre
liberales y conservadores, la frecuente intervención del ejército, así como
los regímenes autocráticos, son características comunes en los países de
15   Centroamérica, con excepción de Costa Rica, que ha tenido éxito en
mantener una tradición democrática, con elecciones libres, y donde el
ejército tiene poca influencia.

El país de mayor población es Guatemala, sede° de la civilización maya,   *center*
donde el elemento indígena puro (indios mayas-quichés) se conserva en
20   una proporción alta. La población mestiza es abundante en todos los

países, excepto en Costa Rica, donde el 95% de la población es blanca, predominando el elemento de origen español, y donde el porcentaje de indios puros es insignificante.

25 La principal fuente de riqueza de estos países centroamericanos es la agricultura, siendo el café y los plátanos los productos más importantes de exportación. En los bosques de Honduras crecen hermosos cedros° y *cedars* caobas° y en las regiones elevadas de Guatemala se cultiva el trigo, la *mahogany trees* cebada° y la papa. *barley*

Panamá ocupa la franja más estrecha del istmo centroamericano y es el
30 punto de unión con la América del Sur. La fuerte presencia económica de los Estados Unidos se ha dejado sentir° en estos países, especialmente en *has been felt* Panamá con la construcción del Canal que quedó terminado en 1914. En la Zona del Canal la población, en su mayoría, es bilingüe (español e inglés), lo que no ocurre en ninguna de las otras repúblicas donde el
35 idioma que se habla, además de las lenguas indígenas, es el español.

Estos países son pequeños en tamaño, pero ricos en su arte, folklore y literatura. Fue Nicaragua el país que le dio al mundo un poeta cuya influencia se extendió a todas las literaturas de lengua castellana. Rubén Darío, al frente del movimiento Modernista, influyó hondamente° en *deeply*
40 España, y sus innovaciones métricas, el gusto refinado, y el ritmo y la

Fuente de agua en un pequeño pueblo de Guatemala.

armonía de sus versos aparecieron en todas las literaturas del idioma español.

Dos autores centroamericanos —los dos de Guatemala— han recibido el Premio Nobel: Miguel Ángel Asturias, el de Literatura, en
45   1967, y Rigoberta Menchú, en 1992, el de la Paz. Tanto Asturias como Menchú han condenado los males sociales y políticos que afectan a los países centroamericanos y han alzado la voz° en defensa de los   *raised their voices* indígenas. En sus obras literarias, Asturias ha combinado el misticismo de los mayas con el mundo de protesta moral y social, y Rigoberta
50   Menchú, en sus escritos, ataca el racismo y la discriminación contra los indígenas.

Asturias era un hombre de figura grande, de ojos estrechos, y recordaba a un Dios ancestral lleno de sabiduría. Cuando terminó sus estudios de Derecho en Guatemala se fue a París a estudiar en la
55   Sorbona.[1] El primer día en la clase del profesor Raynaud —quien hablaba varios idiomas indios y quien había traducido al francés el *Popol Vuh*[2]— notó que éste no le quitaba los ojos de encima. Al final de la clase el profesor se acercó a Asturias y le preguntó: "¿Es Ud. maya?". Al contestarle que era de Guatemala el emocionado profesor lo abrazó
60   con entusiasmo y se lo llevó a su casa para probarle a su esposa que los mayas existían.

[1]*University of Paris; the Sorbonne.*
[2]*Libro sagrado de los quichés de Guatemala.*

Llene los espacios en blanco con la palabra que sea correcta. Use los artículos cuando sea necesario.

1. Los productos más importantes de exportación de la América Central a Estados Unidos son el café y _____ .

2. El desarrollo es inestable, ya que hay extremos de gran pobreza y gran

   _____ .

3. En los _____ de Honduras hay maderas hermosas como cedro y caoba.

4. Dos escritores centroamericanos _____ la voz para condenar los males que afectan a la América Central.

5. Los países de la América Central son pequeños en _____ pero ricos en su arte, folklore y literatura.

6. En la Zona del Canal la mayor parte de la _____ es bilingüe.

7. La franja de tierra que une las dos Américas es ancha en su comienzo y

   _____ en el sur.

8. Costa Rica ha tenido _____ en mantener una tradición democrática.

Preguntas sobre la lectura

1. ¿Por qué dice el autor que la América Central es un eslabón?
2. ¿Qué características comunes existen en los países de Centroamérica?
3. Explique las diferencias entre Costa Rica y los otros países de Centroamérica.
4. ¿Por qué es importante Rubén Darío dentro del panorama de la literatura hispanoamericana?
5. Miguel Ángel Asturias y Rigoberta Menchú son dos figuras importantes de Guatemala. Explique por qué.
6. Narre la anécdota que se cuenta en la lectura sobre Miguel Ángel Asturias en París.

Temas de conversación

1. En su opinión, ¿cuáles son los principales problemas que tienen los inmigrantes que vienen a Estados Unidos de Centroamérica? ¿Pueden compararse estos problemas con los que tienen los inmigrantes de otros países de la América del Sur y del Caribe? Explique su respuesta.
2. ¿Qué país le interesaría más visitar: Guatemala o Panamá? Explique por qué.
3. El autor nos dice que Costa Rica es el único país de Centroamérica que ha podido mantener una tradición democrática con elecciones libres. ¿Por qué cree Ud. que existe esta excepción si todos los países representan una unidad geográfica con características comunes?
4. ¿Le gustaría a Ud. ver algunos de sus programas favoritos de televisión doblados al español? ¿Cree Ud. que serían populares entre los muchos hispanos que viven en Estados Unidos? ¿Qué le parece la idea de producir programas nuevos escritos originalmente en español? Explique sus respuestas.

Vocabulario

Antes de leer, repase el siguiente vocabulario que le ayudará a comprender la lectura.

Sustantivos

el conocimiento   knowledge   **el nivel**   level
el conquistador   conqueror   **el rasgo**   characteristic

Verbos

caer (caigo)   to fall   **establecer (zc)**   to establish   **predecir (j)**   to predict
desconocer (zc)   to not know   **levantar**   to raise   **sorprender**   to surprise

Adjetivos

avanzado   advanced   **sorprendente**   surprising

Lectura 2

Los mayas

El origen de los mayas se desconoce. Se cree que probablemente, durante
muchos años, llevaron° una vida nómada hasta que se establecieron en lo   *they had*
que hoy es Yucatán, Guatemala, parte de Honduras y El Salvador. El nivel
más alto de esta civilización ocurrió del siglo IV al siglo XI d.C.° Los mayas   *A.D.*
5   están considerados como los "griegos° de América" y fue la civilización   *Greeks*
más avanzada del Nuevo Mundo, contando con refinados artistas, hombres
de ciencia, astrónomos y excelentes arquitectos. El sistema astronómico
que tenían era de gran precisión, y los astrónomos mayas podían predecir
los eclipses solares y lunares valiéndose° del conocimiento que tenían de las   *to make use of*
10   órbitas de los planetas. El desarrollo de las matemáticas era sorprendente, y
tenían conocimiento del concepto matemático del cero mucho antes que los
europeos. La precisión del calendario maya era también superior al
europeo, porque coincidía con más exactitud con el año solar.

Numerosas ciudades-estados, con una lengua común y similares rasgos
15   culturales, integraban esta civilización. Durante la época de su crecimiento
se levantaron las grandes ciudades de Tikal, Uaxactum, Chichén Itzá,
Palenque y Copán.

La guerra civil hacia fines del siglo XII, y más tarde otra en el siglo XV,
entre mayas e itzás,* contribuyeron a la decadencia en que se encontraba
20   el pueblo maya cuando cayó bajo la dominación de los conquistadores
españoles en los siglos XVI y XVII.

Itzás, indios centroamericanos de la familia maya, supuestos fundadores de Chichén Itzá.

Vocabulario

Antes de leer, repase el siguiente vocabulario que le ayudará a comprender la lectura.

Sustantivos

el desdén disdain	**la esperanza** hope	**la selva** jungle; forest
el lecho bed	**el rostro** face	**el temor** fear

Verbos

conferir (ie) to give	**disponerse (g)** to get ready	**parecer (zc)** to seem
confiar to trust	**engañar** to deceive	**perder (ie)** to lose
descansar to rest	**intentar** to try	**prever** to foresee

Adjetivos

aislado isolated	**perdido** lost	**rodeado** surrounded
fijo fixed	**poderoso** powerful	

Cuadro de Salvador Dalí (1904–1989) que representa el descubrimiento de América por Cristóbal Colón. (Salvador Dalí, "The Discovery of America by Christopher Columbus", 1958–1959. Oil on canvas. (161¹/₂ x 122¹/₈ inches.) Collection of The Salvador Dali Museum, St. Petersburg, Florida. Copyright 2001 Salvador Dali Museum, Inc.)

Lectura 3

Augusto Monterroso

Augusto Monterroso (1921–2003), nacido en Guatemala, es autor de numerosos y variados cuentos cortos. "El eclipse" es del libro *Obras completas y otros cuentos*. En él, Monterroso presenta el encuentro del mundo indígena de América con el mundo cultural europeo.

El eclipse

Cuando fray° Bartolomé Arrazola se sintió perdido, aceptó que ya nada podría salvarlo. La selva poderosa de Guatemala lo había apresado,° implacable y definitiva. Ante su ignorancia topográfica se sentó con tranquilidad a esperar la muerte. Quiso morir allí sin ninguna
5 esperanza, aislado, con el pensamiento fijo en la España distante, particularmente en el convento de Los Abrojos, donde Carlos V condescendiera una vez a bajar de su eminencia para decirle que confiaba en el celo° religioso de su labor redentora.°

Al despertar se encontró rodeado por un grupo de indígenas de
10 rostro impasible que se disponían a sacrificarlo ante un altar, un altar que a Bartolomé le pareció como el lecho en que descansaría, al fin, de sus temores, de su destino, de sí mismo.

Tres años en el país le habían conferido un mediano dominio de las lenguas nativas. Intentó algo. Dijo algunas palabras que fueron
15 comprendidas.

Entonces floreció° en él una idea que tuvo por digna° de su talento y de su cultura universal y de su arduo° conocimiento de Aristóteles.* Recordó que para ese día se esperaba un eclipse total de sol. Y dispuso, en lo más íntimo, valerse de aquel conocimiento para engañar a sus
20 opresores y salvar la vida.

—Si me matáis —les dijo— puedo hacer que el sol se oscurezca en su altura.°

Los indígenas lo miraron fijamente° y Bartolomé sorprendió° la incredulidad en sus ojos. Vio que se produjo un pequeño consejo,° y
25 esperó confiado, no sin cierto desdén.

Dos horas después el corazón de fray Bartolomé Arrazola chorreaba° su sangre vehemente sobre la piedra de los sacrificios (brillante bajo la opaca luz de un sol eclipsado), mientras uno de los indígenas recitaba sin ninguna inflexión de voz, sin prisa, una por una, las infinitas fechas
30 en que se producirían eclipses solares y lunares, que los astrónomos de la comunidad maya habían previsto y anotado en sus códices° sin la valiosa ayuda de Aristóteles.

Aristóteles, célebre filósofo griego (384–322 a.C.).

friar

had captured

zeal / redemptive

appeared / worthy
difficult

darken the sky
fixedly / caught
council

was gushing

old manuscripts

Llene los espacios en blanco traduciendo al español las palabras que están en inglés.

1. Fray Bartolomé se sintió apresado en la _____ (*jungle*) de Guatemala, y

   como estaba completamente _____ (*isolated*) perdió toda la

   _____ (*hope*) de salvarse.

2. Cuando despertó se encontró _____ (*surrounded*) por los indígenas que

   _____ (*were getting ready*) a sacrificarlo.

3. Decidió _____ (*make use of*) sus conocimientos para

   _____ (*deceive*) a los opresores.

4. Los conocimientos astronómicos que tenían los mayas les permitían

   _____ (*foresee*) los eclipses solares y lunares.

5. El altar le _____ (*seemed*) a fray Bartolomé el _____ (*bed*)

   donde _____ (*he would rest*).

Preguntas sobre la lectura

1. ¿Qué le pasó a fray Bartolomé en la selva?

2. ¿En qué pensó el fraile cuando se sintió aislado y perdió la esperanza de salvarse?

3. ¿Qué le iban a hacer los indígenas a fray Bartolomé?

4. ¿Qué les dijo fray Bartolomé a sus opresores para que no lo mataran?

5. ¿Qué sabían los astrónomos mayas que iba a pasar?

Temas de conversación

1. ¿Conoce Ud. alguna leyenda de los indios de Norteamérica? Si la conoce, nárrela. ¿Puede contar alguna otra leyenda que Ud. conozca?

2. ¿Es Ud. una persona supersticiosa? ¿En qué supersticiones cree Ud.? ¿Conoce Ud. algunas supersticiones que traen mala suerte como la del número 13, o la de no abrir una sombrilla (*umbrella*) dentro de la casa, o la de no pasar por debajo de una escalera (*ladder*)? Menciónelas.

3. ¿Qué opina Ud. de las prácticas de brujería (*witchcraft*)? ¿Cree Ud. que una persona inteligente y educada puede creer en brujería? Explique su respuesta.

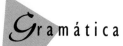

Gramática

A Phrases and expressions that require the subjunctive

When the expressions from the following list appear in a main clause commenting on the concept expressed in the subordinate clause, the subjunctive is used in the subordinate clause.

1. Impersonal expressions that express uncertainty, doubt, probability, necessity, emotion, or desire

es posible	es aconsejable (*advisable*)
es probable	es raro
es importante	es suerte
es dudoso	es sorprendente
es lástima	es de temerse
es natural	es conveniente
es necesario	es triste
es mejor	más vale
es bueno	quiera Dios
es malo	ojalá

+ **que** + subjunctive

Es conveniente que **digan** la verdad.
It is advisable that they tell the truth.
Fue necesario que **llamaran** al médico.
It was necessary that they call the doctor.
Quiera Dios que **tengas** éxito.
God willing you will be successful.
No **es probable** que **llueva** mañana.
It is not probable that it will rain tomorrow.
No **es necesario** que me **lleves** a la universidad.
It is not necessary that you take me to the university.
No **es bueno** que **salgas** sin abrigo. Hace mucho frío.
It is not good that you go out without a coat. It is very cold.

NOTE: These expressions, affirmative or negative, always require the subjunctive.

Sentences with the expression **ojalá** may express an idea referring to the present, the past, or the future. When **ojalá** is used in a sentence that has a verb in the present or the imperfect subjunctive, the idea expressed refers to the present or the future.

Ojalá que Raquel **llame.**   *I hope Raquel calls.*
Ojalá que Raquel **llamara.**   *I wish Raquel would call.*

When **ojalá** is used in a sentence that has a verb in the present perfect or the past perfect subjunctive, the idea expressed refers to the past.
(The present perfect and the past perfect appear later on in this chapter.)

Ojalá que ellos **hayan llegado** anoche.
I hope (that) they arrived last night.

Ojalá que ellos **hubieran estado** aquí.
I wished (that) they had been here.

NOTE: **Que** may be omitted, especially when the subject is not expressed.

Ojalá nieve mañana.	*I hope it snows tomorrow.*
Ojalá vengan.	*I hope they come.*

2. Negative expressions that express doubt or uncertainty

$$\left.\begin{array}{l} \text{no es cierto} \\ \text{no es seguro} \\ \text{no es claro} \\ \text{no es verdad} \\ \text{no es evidente} \\ \text{no creo} \end{array}\right\} + \textbf{que} + \text{subjunctive}$$

No es seguro que **vayamos** a la tienda.
It isn't certain that we will go to the store.

No es verdad que ella **saliera** anoche con Pedro.
It isn't true that she went out with Pedro last night.

No creo que Paco **gane** el premio.
I don't think that Paco will win the prize.

NOTE: These phrases in the affirmative require the indicative, because they do not express doubt.

Indicative	Subjunctive
Es cierto que Ud. **habla** mucho.	**No es cierto** que Ud. **hable** mucho.
It's true that you talk a lot.	*It isn't true that you talk a lot.*
Es seguro que él **viene** mañana.	**No es seguro** que él **venga** mañana.
It is certain that he will come tomorrow.	*It isn't true that he will come tomorrow.*
Es verdad que ella **gasta** mucho.	**No es verdad** que ella **gaste** mucho.
It is true that she spends a lot.	*It isn't true that she spends a lot.*

3. Subordinate clauses with **por** + adjective or adverb + **que** require a subjunctive verb when they express an idea that refers to the present or to the future.

Por mucho que hable la gente,
no creo lo que dicen de él.
No matter how much people talk, I don't believe what they say about him.

Por rápido que vayamos,
no **llegaremos** a tiempo.
No matter how fast we go, we will not arrive on time.

NOTE: When the idea refers to the past, the subjunctive is not used.

Por mucho que explicó, no **entendí** lo que dijo.
No matter how much he explained, I did not understand what he said.

Ejercicios

I. Haga nuevas oraciones empezando con las frases que están entre paréntesis.

MODELO: Mañana voy a visitar a mis amigos. (Es posible que…)
   Es posible que mañana yo vaya a visitar a mis amigos.

1. Mi amigo me invita a ir a El Salvador. (Es probable que…)
2. No pude ir porque tenía mucho trabajo. (Fue una lástima que…)
3. Mi amigo tiene una casa grande en San Salvador, la capital. (Es probable que…)
4. Mi amigo vivió por muchos años en Costa Rica. (Fue una suerte que…)
5. Él habla muy bien el español. (Ojalá que…)

II. Su amigo tiene ciertas opiniones acerca del nuevo candidato a la presidencia. Ud. tiene ideas opuestas y lo contradice.

MODELO: Amigo: Es verdad que Alfonso Hernández es el mejor candidato para la presidencia.

   Ud.:   **No es verdad que Alfonso Hernández sea el mejor candidato para la presidencia.**

1. Es evidente que tiene todas las cualidades necesarias para ser presidente.
2. Es probable que él inicie nuevos programas de educación.
3. No es cierto que él esté en contra de los movimientos ecológicos.
4. Es seguro que él quiere combatir la inflación.
5. No es verdad que él reciba dinero de las grandes compañías de petróleo.
6. Creo que él va a ganar las elecciones.
7. Es necesario que él tenga un buen vicepresidente.
8. No es seguro que él pueda mejorar la situación económica del país.

III. Repase las frases y expresiones que requieren el subjuntivo. Con su compañero(a) de clase, completen los siguientes minidiálogos usando la forma verbal que corresponda.

1. —¿Cuándo llega Horacio?
   —No sé, ojalá que _____ mañana.
   —¿Sabes si viene solo o con Patricia?
   —No me dijo, pero es posible que _____ con ella.

2. —¿Es seguro que vas en el verano a Puerto Rico?

—No, no es seguro que _____ porque tengo que tomar unos cursos que necesito para graduarme.

—¿Podrás ir en las Navidades?

—Sí, es probable que _____ hacer el viaje en diciembre.

3. —¿Fuiste a comprar las entradas para ir a ver *El fantasma de la ópera*?

—Fue imposible que yo _____ a comprarlas porque tuve una reunión esta tarde.

—Si vas mañana, ¿las conseguirás para el próximo sábado?

—¡Quiera Dios que las _____ !

IV. Conteste las preguntas comenzando con las frases que están entre paréntesis y continuando con una cláusula subordinada original. Note que todas las frases requieren el uso del subjuntivo en la cláusula subordinada.

1. ¿Lloverá esta tarde? (Quiera Dios que…)
2. ¿A qué hora van a salir? (Ojalá que…)
3. ¿Llegarán a tiempo al teatro? (Por rápido que…)
4. ¿Va Pepe al juego de pelota? (No es seguro que…)
5. ¿Qué dice Manuel? (Dice que es bueno que…)

V. María e Isabel conversan sobre el matrimonio y expresan las ideas que se dan a continuación. Usando las expresiones que están entre paréntesis escriba otras opiniones sobre lo que dicen las muchachas. Use el verbo en indicativo o en subjuntivo de acuerdo con la expresión usada en cada oración.

MODELO: El matrimonio ahora es diferente. (Es posible…) (Es cierto…)

Es posible que el matrimonio ahora sea diferente.

Es cierto que el matrimonio ahora es diferente.

1. Los jóvenes tienen ideas erróneas sobre el matrimonio. (Tal vez…) (Es verdad…)
2. Los jóvenes no piensan en las responsabilidades. (Es triste…) (Es evidente…)
3. Ellos no se conocen bien antes del matrimonio. (Es posible…) (Es cierto…)
4. Ellos se casan sin terminar los estudios. (Es lástima…) (No es verdad…)
5. Muchos matrimonios acaban en divorcio. (No es cierto…) (Es seguro…)

B Present perfect subjunctive

1. The present perfect subjunctive is formed with the present subjunctive of the verb **haber** + the past participle of the verb to be conjugated.

haya	
hayas	
haya	comprado
hayamos	vendido
hayáis	recibido
hayan	

2. The present perfect subjunctive is used in the subordinate clause when the verb in the main clause comments in the present on a concept expressed in the subordinate clause that refers to a previous moment. Note the following examples:

> Joaquín **ha leído** el libro.
> *Joaquín has read the book.*

> **Dudo** que Joaquín **haya leído** el libro.
> *I doubt that Joaquín has read the book.*

Ejercicios

I. Complete las oraciones, según el modelo, usando el verbo en el presente perfecto de subjuntivo en la cláusula subordinada.

MODELO: Benito ha vuelto.
Espero que Benito...
Espero que Benito haya vuelto.

1. Carolina ha salido temprano.
   Dudo que Carolina...
2. Hemos escrito la carta.
   Esperan que...
3. Has estado enferma.
   Siento que...
4. Uds. no han visto el desfile.
   Es lástima que Uds. no...
5. Ellos han salido tarde.
   Es posible que ellos...

II. Elisa desea trabajar en el Banco Mundial (*World Bank*). Para saber lo que ella ha hecho, complete las oraciones con la traducción al español de los verbos que están en inglés. Use el presente perfecto de indicativo o el presente perfecto de subjuntivo, según el contenido de la frase.

1. (*has written*) Elisa _____ una carta de solicitud para un puesto en el Banco Mundial.
2. (*has written*) Dudo que ella _____ la solicitud en español.
3. (*has read*) Es posible que el gerente _____ la recomendación.
4. (*has read*) Ella _____ mucho sobre ese banco.
5. (*has arrived*) Es importante que la solicitud _____ a tiempo (*on time*).
6. (*has arrived*) La respuesta _____ por correo electrónico.

III. Su primo le ha dado a Ud. las siguientes noticias. Exprese su reacción personal sobre las cosas que se mencionan más abajo usando expresiones tales como **es posible, es bueno, es una lástima, es importante, tal vez, dudo, me alegro (de), me sorprende, siento, espero**.

> **MODELO:** Isabel ha perdido el trabajo.
> **Siento que Isabel haya perdido el trabajo.**
> **Es una lástima que Isabel haya perdido el trabajo.**

1. Las condiciones sociales han cambiado.
2. Mis padres han decidido ir a Puerto Rico.
3. Ha llovido mucho el fin de semana.
4. Mi hermana ha pasado el examen de geometría.
5. Mi tío Alfonso ha venido a comer con nosotros.
6. El profesor ha cancelado la clase de español.

C Pluperfect subjunctive

1. The pluperfect subjunctive is formed with the imperfect sujunctive of the verb **haber** + the past participle of the verb that is conjugated.

hubiera	(hubiese)		
hubieras	(hubieses)		comprado
hubiera	(hubiese)	+	vendido
hubiéramos	(hubiésemos)		recibido
hubierais	(hubieseis)		
hubieran	(hubiesen)		

2. The pluperfect subjunctive is used in the subordinate clause when the verb in the main clause comments in the past on a concept in the subordinate clause that refers to a time much prior to the past time of the verb in the main clause. Note the following examples:

> Le **dije** que ellos **habían ido** al museo.
> *I told him they had gone to the museum.*

> Yo **esperaba** que ellos **hubieran ido** al museo.
> *I was hoping that they had gone to the museum.*

Ejercicios

I. De acuerdo con el contenido de las frases, llene los espacios en blanco con la forma apropiada de **haber (haya o hubiera)**.

1. Me alegro de que Gustavo _____ podido recibir hoy mi recado.
2. Gustavo temía que yo me _____ olvidado de llamarlo.
3. Es bueno que él _____ visitado a sus primos.
4. Me daba miedo de que él no _____ traído la dirección.

II. Ud. fue a ver al médico ayer. Su amigo quiere saber qué le dijo y le hace a Ud. algunas preguntas. Contéstelas usando los verbos en el pluscuamperfecto de subjuntivo.

MODELO: ¿De qué se alegró el médico? (ir a verlo)
De que yo hubiera ido a verlo.

1. ¿Qué esperaba el médico? (tomar las medicinas)
2. ¿Qué dudaba el médico? (seguir sus instrucciones)
3. ¿Qué le disgustó al médico? (aumentar de peso) (*to gain weight*)
4. ¿Qué le preocupaba al médico? (no continuar los ejercicios)
5. ¿Qué le sorprendió al médico? (no tener un ataque al corazón) (*heart attack*)

III. El siguiente párrafo está narrado con los verbos de las cláusulas principales en presente. Cambiando estos verbos al pasado (pretérito o imperfecto de indicativo) vuelva a narrar el párrafo.

Siento que no hayas escuchado la conferencia del arqueólogo en la universidad. Ojalá que todos los alumnos hayan oído la explicación sobre las ruinas mayas de Tikal. Es una lástima que no hayamos grabado la conferencia. Es una suerte que hayamos leído sobre la civilización maya. El profesor espera que los estudiantes hayan visto las fotos de las ruinas.

D   Sequence of tenses

As shown in the following diagram, the verb tense (present or past) in the main clause determines the tense of the subordinate clause.

Main clause: *Verb in indicative*	Subordinate clause: *Verb in subjunctive*
Present Future Present Perfect Imperative	Present or Present Perfect
Dudo **Dudaré** **He dudado** **Dude Ud.**	lo que Adolfo **diga.** or lo que Adolfo **haya dicho.**
Preterite Imperfect Conditional Pluperfect Conditional Perfect	Imperfect or Pluperfect
Dudé **Dudaba** **Dudaría** **Había dudado** **Habría dudado**	que Adolfo **saliera.** or que Adolfo **hubiera salido.**

Use the combination of tenses that is necessary in order to express the idea that the speaker wishes to communicate.

Espero que **lleguen** bien.	*I hope they arrive well.*
Espero que ya **hayan llegado**.	*I hope they have arrived.*
Esperaban que **fuéramos** con ellos.	*They hoped we would go with them.*
Dudaba que **hubieras salido** hoy.	*She doubted that you would have gone out today.*

NOTE: It is possible to combine the present indicative with the imperfect subjunctive to express an idea or action already completed:

Siento que **estuvieras** enferma la semana pasada.
I'm sorry you were sick last week.

Ejercicios

I. De acuerdo con el modelo, haga nuevas oraciones que contengan dos cláusulas. Use en la cláusula subordinada el sujeto que está entre paréntesis.

MODELO: Lamento vender la casa. (Luisa)
Lamento que Luisa venda la casa.

1. Prohíben caminar en la autopista. (las personas)
2. Raúl siente no ir a la fiesta. (ella)
3. Querían proteger el museo. (la policía)
4. ¿Deseas almorzar ahora? (nosotros)
5. Esperaba conocer a tus padres. (Elsa)

II. Complete las frases usando el tiempo correcto del subjuntivo de los verbos que están entre paréntesis.

1. (visitar) Ellos me han pedido que yo _____ a Federico.
2. (poder) Lamento que él no _____ venir con nosotros.
3. (enfermarse) Siento que Federico _____ la semana pasada.
4. (divorciarse) Él sintió mucho que sus padres _____ cuando él era niño.
5. (terminar) Él siempre había dudado que yo _____ la carrera.

III. Traduzca al español las siguientes oraciones.

1. *I hope the new house is big and comfortable.*
2. *I am sorry you (tú) have a headache.*
3. *The doctor advised me to take aspirin.*
4. *I hope you (Ud.) have not had any problem.*
5. *I will call Rosa when I receive the letter.*
6. *He wished they had come last night.*

IV. Trabaje con un(a) compañero(a) de clase. Hágale las siguientes preguntas que él/ella debe contestar en forma original. Después él/ella le hará las mismas preguntas para que Ud. las conteste.

1. Cuando almuerzas en la cafetería, ¿qué quiere el cajero que hagas?
   Cuando terminas de almorzar, ¿qué desea el empleado que hagas con los platos sucios?

2. Cuando vas a comprar un carro, ¿qué esperas que el vendedor haga?
   Cuando escoges el carro, ¿qué espera el vendedor que tú hagas?

3. Cuando Luis jugaba fútbol en la universidad, ¿qué deseaba el entrenador que él hiciera?
   Cuando terminaba la temporada de fútbol, ¿qué les aconsejaba el entrenador a todos los jugadores del equipo?

4. Cuando no tienes dinero, ¿qué deseas que tu hermano haga?
   Cuando una persona te da dinero, ¿qué espera ella que tú hagas?

5. Cuando de niño o niña ibas a la playa con tus padres, ¿qué querían ellos que hicieras?
   Cuando había muchas olas, ¿qué te aconsejaban ellos?

Barco pasando por la esclusa (lock) *de Miraflores en el Canal de Panamá.*

V. Los siguientes párrafos tratan del Canal de Panamá. Complete las frases con el tiempo correcto del subjuntivo del verbo entre paréntesis.

1. (comunicar) (ser) Es un dato curioso que la primera persona que propuso la construcción de un canal que _____ el océano Atlántico con el Pacífico _____ Hernán Cortés.

2. (hacer) El Emperador Carlos V se entusiasmó, pero su sucesor, Felipe II, recomendó que no se _____ tal cosa.

3. (estudiar) En 1898 el gobierno norteamericano aconsejó que se _____ el plan de construcción.

4. (llevar) (comprar) Como era preciso que se _____ a cabo el proyecto, el Congreso de los Estados Unidos le autorizó al presidente Teodoro Roosevelt que _____ los derechos (*rights*) de la Nueva Compañía del Canal de Panamá.

5. (reconocer) (anular) La construcción del Canal de Panamá se inició en 1904 y quedó terminada en 1914. En 1975 Panamá y los Estados Unidos acordaron firmar un tratado, ratificado en 1977. Era importante que se _____ la soberanía de Panamá en la zona del canal y que además se _____ el tratado de 1903.

6. (existir) (mantener) Es necesario que _____ relaciones amigables entre los Estados Unidos y Panamá, puesto que es vital para el mundo entero que se _____ el control de este canal libre de los conflictos y tensiones de la política internacional.

E Other expressions that require the subjunctive

The subjunctive is used in the following cases:

1. With conjunctions that denote time, purpose, or condition

antes de que (*before*)		
a fin de que (*so that*)		La llamaré **para que venga** a comer.
a menos que (*unless*)		*I will call her so that she will come to eat.*
para que (*so that*)		Salió **sin que** yo la **viera**.
con tal (de) que (*provided that*)	+ subjunctive	*She left without my seeing her.*
sin que (*without*)		Usaré tu carro **en caso de que tenga** que salir.
en caso de que (*in case that*)		*I'll use your car in case I have to go out.*
a condición de que (*on condition that*)		

2. Adverbial conjunctions of time. The subjunctive is used in the subordinate clause when the verb refers to an action that has not yet occurred.

cuando (*when*)	**mientras que** (*while*)	**después (de) que** (*after*)
en cuanto (*as soon as*)	**tan pronto como** (*as soon as*)	**así que** (*as soon as*)
luego que (*as soon as*)	**hasta que** (*until*)	**siempre que** (*provided that*)

Yo le hablaré a él **cuando venga**.
I will talk to him when he comes.
Les daré el recado **tan pronto como lleguen**.
I will give them the message as soon as they arrive.
Después de que llegues, llámame.
Call me after you arrive.

But the indicative is used if the sentence refers to an action that occurs generally or to one that has already occurred.

Le hablo **cuando** él **viene**. *I talk to him when he comes.*

Le hablé **cuando** él **vino**. *I talked to him when he came.*

Les di el recado **tan pronto como llegaron**.
I gave them the message as soon as they arrived.

Ellos llegaron **después de que** yo **había comido**.
They arrived after I had eaten.

NOTE: In conversational speech, the preposition **de** is often omitted in the expressions **antes (de) que, con tal (de) que**, and **después (de) que**.

3. Expressions of certainty or uncertainty. The expressions **quizás, tal vez,** and **aunque** may be used with the indicative or the subjunctive, depending on whether the speaker wishes to communicate doubt or certainty. Note that the subjunctive indicates an uncertain, doubtful action. The indicative expresses certainty.

Uncertainty or probability: *Subjunctive*	Certainty: *Indicative*
Quizá **salgamos** esta noche. *Perhaps we will go out tonight.* [But I doubt it]	Quizá **regresarán** mañana. *Perhaps they will return tomorrow.* [I'm relatively sure they will return tomorrow.]
Quizá Pedro no **esté** en la casa. *Perhaps Pedro is not at home.* [But I am not sure]	Quizá ella **salió** un momento. *Perhaps she went out for a moment.* [I'm almost certain she went out for a short time.]
Tal vez **hayan ido** al banco. *Maybe they've gone to the bank.* [But I can't be sure.]	Tal vez **has trabajado** mucho. *Maybe you've worked too much.* [I'm sure you've worked too much.]
Él vendrá aunque **haga** mal tiempo. *He will come although the weather may be bad.* [I don't know about the weather.]	Él vendrá aunque **hace** mal tiempo. *He will come even though the weather is bad.* [The weather is bad.]
Aunque **viniera** no le hablaría. *Although she might come I wouldn't speak to her.* [But I doubt she's coming.]	Aunque **vino** no le hablé. *Although she came, I didn't speak to her.* [She did come.]
Aunque **llueva** iré a la universidad. *Although it may rain I will go to the University.* [It may or may not rain.]	Aunque **llovió** fui a la universidad. *Even though it rained I went to the university.* [It did rain yesterday.]

4. Indefinite antecedent. The subjunctive is used in the subordinate clause if the antecedent, that is, the person or thing it modifies, is indefinite or nonexistent. The indicative is used if the antecedent is definite.

Indefinite or nonexistent antecedent: *Subjunctive*	Definite antecedent: *Indicative*
Necesito un amigo que me comprenda. *I need a friend who may undertand me.*	Tengo un amigo que me comprende. *I have a friend who understands me.*
Buscaba una casa que tuviera dos cuartos. *He was looking for a house that might have two bedrooms.*	Encontró la casa que quería. *He found the house that he wanted.*
Llamaré a un mecánico que sepa cómo arreglar mi carro. *I will call a mechanic who knows how to fix my car.*	Llamaré al mecánico que sabe cómo arreglar mi carro. *I will call the mechanic who knows how to fix my car.*
No hay nada que me guste más. *There is nothing that I like better.*	Hay algo que me gusta más. *There is something that I like better.*
No había nadie que hablara japonés. *There was no one who spoke Japanese.*	Conozco a alguien que habla japonés. *I know someone who speaks Japanese.*

5. Indefinite expressions. The following expressions require the subjunctive when used in a subordinate clause: **quienquiera, cuandoquiera, comoquiera, cualquier (-a).** **Dondequiera** requires the subjunctive when the idea expressed refers to a future time.

> **Dondequiera** que vayas verás flores en Xochimilco.
> *Wherever you may go you will see flowers in Xochimilco.*
> Lo haré **comoquiera** que sea. *I'll do it however it may be.*
> Dígale a **quienquiera** que sea, que no puedo recibirlo.
> *Tell whoever it may be that I cannot receive him.*

NOTE: The plural of **quienquiera** is **quienesquiera,** but it is not commonly used in modern Spanish.

In subordinate clauses with **dondequiera,** the indicative is used when referring to an idea in the present or the past.

Dondequiera que **vamos** vemos flores.	*Wherever we go we see flowers.*
Dondequiera que **fuimos** vimos flores.	*Wherever we went we saw flowers.*
Dondequiera que **íbamos** veíamos flores.	*Wherever we would go, we would see flowers.*

6. After **como si,** use only the imperfect or the pluperfect subjunctive.

Él habla **como si fuera** el dueño de la casa.	*He speaks as if he were the master of the house.*
El niño parece **como si hubiera tenido** una pelea.	*The child looks as if he had had a fight.*

7. The imperfect and the pluperfect subjunctive are used in expressions with the word **quién** to express a wish or desire by the speaker.

¡Quién pudiera bailar como tú!	*If only I could dance like you!*
¡Quién fuera Plácido Domingo!	*If only I were Plácido Domingo!*
¡Quién lo **hubiera sabido**!	*If only I had known it!*

Ejercicios

I. Las siguientes oraciones contienen cláusulas adverbiales de tiempo que pueden usarse con el verbo en subjuntivo o en indicativo según el significado de la oración. Complételas con el subjuntivo o el indicativo del verbo que está entre paréntesis, según lo requiera el contexto.

1. (salir) Te llamaré cuando (yo) _____ de la oficina.
2. (estar) Le di el pasaporte a Luisa cuando (yo) _____ en su casa.
3. (conseguir) Tan pronto como _____ los pasajes, saldré para México.
4. (hacer) En cuanto _____ las maletas, salí para el aeropuerto.
5. (poder) Viajaré mientras que _____ .
6. (tener) Fui piloto de aviación hasta que _____ sesenta años.

II. La siguiente narración tiene dos párrafos. En el primer párrafo se habla del hombre que Lolita busca para casarse. En el segundo párrafo se narra la suerte de Lolita cuando encontró a Roberto. Escriba el tiempo correcto, en subjuntivo o en indicativo, de los verbos que están entre paréntesis.

Lolita busca un marido que _____ (ser) inteligente y sincero. Además ella

quiere que _____ (tener) un buen empleo, que la _____

(comprender) y que cuando _____ (tener) hijos que él _____

(ser) un buen padre. Son muchas las cualidades que Lolita _____ (querer) y

ojalá que _____ (encontrar) al hombre de sus sueños.

Al fin, hace dos años, Lolita _____ (encontrar) al hombre de sus sueños.

Se llama Roberto y lo _____ (conocer) en un viaje que ella

_____ (hacer) al Uruguay. Ellos _____ (enamorarse) a primera

vista (*at first sight*) y _____ (casarse) a los dos meses de conocerse.

Roberto y Lolita _____ (ser) muy felices y _____ (tener) un

niño que _____ (llamarse) Robertico.

III. Un(a) compañero(a) de clase le presenta las siguientes situaciones. ¿Qué le sugiere Ud.?

MODELO: Tengo un examen mañana.
Te sugiero que estudies.

1. Tengo sueño.
2. Estoy muy aburrido(a).
3. Estoy enfermo(a).
4. Estoy muy cansado(a).
5. Tengo hambre y sed.
6. Tengo mucho frío.

IV. Hay muchos problemas en la oficina donde trabaja su amigo. ¿Qué le recomienda Ud. para solucionarlos?

1. El aire acondicionado no enfría bastante.
2. El secretario siempre llega tarde.
3. Las computadoras se descomponen muy frecuentemente.
4. La supervisora tiene muy mal genio y grita mucho.
5. Hay muchos papeles sin archivar (*to file*) porque no hay donde ponerlos.

V. Complete las frases con el tiempo correcto del indicativo o del subjuntivo de los verbos entre paréntesis.

1. (poder) Ojalá que ellos _____ ir de vacaciones.

2. (tocar) Es sorprendente que el niño _____ tan bien el violín.

3. (correr) Por mucho que _____ Elisa, no podrá llegar a tiempo.

4. (venir) Le daré la carta cuando él _____ mañana.

5. (llamar) Ella me dio el recado cuando yo la _____ ayer.

6. (ir) Dondequiera que _____ , nos recibieron muy bien.

7. (comprar) Dondequiera que _____ el vestido, te costará caro.

8. (dar) Aunque yo le _____ la cuenta, él no me pagó.

9. (invitar) Aunque Juan me _____ , no iré con él.

10. (ser) Quiero un marido que _____ inteligente, guapo y rico.

11. (ser) Tengo un marido que _____ muy bueno.

12. (llevar) Busco a alguien para que me _____ al centro.

13. (llevar) Tengo un amigo que siempre me _____ al centro.

VI. Complete las frases con el tiempo correcto del indicativo o del subjuntivo del verbo entre paréntesis.

1. (decir) Me alegré cuando él me _____ que me había ganado la beca.

2. (irse) Nos dará gran tristeza cuando él _____ .

3. (mandar) Le prometí que le escribiría cuando él _____ la dirección.

4. (bajar) Parece que el costo de la vida va a bajar. Aunque _____ el costo de la vida no podré cubrir los gastos.

5. (saber) Elisa toca la guitarra muy bien. Sin embargo, aunque Elisa _____ tocar la guitarra, no quiere tocar hoy.

6. (invitar) Aunque Alfonso me _____ anoche, no pude salir con él.

VII. Escoja el verbo correcto para completar la oración.

1. Tal vez Dora _____ mañana.
   (llegue / llegaba)

2. Quizá Carmelina _____ ayer.
   (llegue / llegó)

3. Llamaré al muchacho que _____ en la gasolinera.
   (trabaja / trabaje)

4. Busco un secretario que _____ español.
   (sabe / sepa)

5. Dígales que se _____ .
   (sientan / sienten)

6. Es verdad que él _____ muchas tonterías.
   (dice / diga)

7. Parece que va a llover, pero Ramón dice que vendrá aunque _____ .

(llueva / llueve)

8. Le escribiré tan pronto como _____ .

(puedo / pueda)

VIII. Composición dirigida (oral o escrita). Ud. es una persona que va a ir a Centroamérica a trabajar con el Cuerpo de Paz. Haga una narración breve exponiendo sus dudas, deseos, temores, posibilidades, etc. Use como guía las siguientes frases.

El Cuerpo de Paz necesita	Me aconsejan	Desean que yo
Mis amigos dudan	Es posible que	El gobierno no quiere
Temo que	Es una suerte	
No es seguro	Quiera Dios	

Si clauses

Clauses with **si** (*if*) are used in conditional statements in combination with a result clause. The **si** clause expresses a condition that may be either probable or contrary to fact, in either the present or the past. If the situation is likely or probable, the indicative is used. If the situation is contrary to fact, the subjunctive is used in the **si** clause.

Probable condition: *Indicative*	Result: *Indicative*
Si **quieres**, *If you want,*	te **presto** mi secadora de pelo. *I'll lend you my hair dryer.*
Si **tengo** dinero, *If I have money,*	**iré** a Madrid. *I will go to Madrid.*
Si Mirta **escribió**, *If Mirta did write,*	no **llegó** la carta. *the letter didn't arrive.*
Si él **caminaba** tanto, *If he used to walk so much,*	**era** porque **quería** hacer ejercicio. *it was because he wanted to exercise.*
Si mi marido **llama**, *If my husband calls,*	le **dices** que **salí**. *tell him I went out.*

Unlikely or contrary-to-fact situation in the present: *Imperfect subjunctive*	Result: *Conditional*
Si **tuviera** tiempo, *If I had time,*	**iría** hoy a la playa. *I would go to the beach today.*
Si **comiera** menos, *If I ate less,*	**estaría** más delgado. *I would be thinner.*

Unlikely or contrary to fact situation in the past: *Pluperfect subjunctive*	Result: *Conditional perfect or pluperfect subjunctive*
Si ellos se **hubieran conocido** antes, *If they had met before,*	se **habrían** (**hubieran**) **casado**. *they would have gotten married.*
Si **hubieras traído** el traje de baño, *If you had brought the swim suit,*	**habríamos** (**hubiéramos**) **ido** a nadar. *we would have gone swimming.*

Ejercicios

I. Complete las oraciones según los modelos empleando la forma correcta del verbo entre paréntesis.

Condiciones probables.

> **MODELO:** (necesitar) Si (tú) _____ mis botas, te las doy.
> **Si necesitas mis botas, te las doy.**

1. (llamar) Si mi mujer _____ dentro de una hora, le das el recado.
2. (salir) Si ellos _____ mañana temprano, llegarán antes de las seis.
3. (venir) Si Úrsula _____ ayer, no la vi.
4. (ir) Si Vicente _____ al cine anoche, no me invitó.

Condiciones poco probables y contrarias a la realidad presente o pasada.

> **MODELO:** (poder) Si yo _____ , viajaría el próximo verano.
> **Si yo pudiera, viajaría el próximo verano.**

1. (pedir) Si (tú) me _____ un favor, te lo haría.
2. (estar) Si ella _____ en casa, me recibiría.
3. (avisar) Si (nosotros) les _____ anoche, ellos habrían venido a jugar al póquer.
4. (tener) Si yo _____ el libro, se lo habría prestado.

II. Composición dirigida (oral o escrita). El siguiente ejercicio tiene dos partes.

Continúe las frases con ideas originales usando el verbo en el tiempo que necesite (subjuntivo o indicativo) para expresar su pensamiento.

1. Si yo tuviera mucho dinero...
2. Si mi amiga viene esta noche...
3. Si yo hubiera tenido tiempo...
4. Si yo pudiera...
5. Si Elisa hubiera ido a España...

Complete la primera parte de las frases con ideas originales usando el verbo en el tiempo que sea necesario (subjuntivo o indicativo) para expresar su pensamiento.

1. Si yo..., compraría un carro nuevo.
2. Si ellos..., iré con ellos a la fiesta de fin de año.
3. Si Fernando... en el equipo de la universidad, habrían ganado el campeonato.
4. Si yo..., sacaría muy buenas notas.
5. Si yo..., me habría divorciado en seguida.

III. Su amiga cree que se deben hacer cambios en los programas de televisión. Para conocer la opinión de ella, complete el párrafo con la forma correcta del subjuntivo de los verbos entre paréntesis.

Deseo que los productores de televisión _____ (aumentar) el número de programas educativos. Se beneficiaría más la juventud si _____ (mostrarse) programas científicos y culturales y _____ (disminuirse) los anuncios. Espero que las estaciones _____ (mostrar) más programas históricos y que _____ (presentar) biografías de gente notable en el campo de la ciencia, la música y el arte. Propongo que _____ (sustituirse) la violencia por música y arte.

IV. Temas de conversación.

1. Si Ud. fuera un productor de Hollywood, ¿qué tipo de películas haría Ud.?
2. Si a Ud. le ofrecieran el puesto de gerente de la General Motors, ¿qué salario y qué condiciones de trabajo pediría Ud.?
3. Piense en una compañía que comparte las ganancias anuales con sus empleados. ¿Con qué fin cree Ud. que hace esto?
4. Piense que Ud. es la presidenta de una corporación y tiene un secretario. ¿Qué órdenes le daría Ud. al secretario?
5. ¿Qué haría Ud. si fuera presidente de los Estados Unidos?
6. ¿Qué haría Ud. si fuera el profesor o la profesora de esta clase?

G Expressions with *tener*

tener en cuenta	to take into account	tener derecho	to have the right
tener que ver con	to have to do (with)	tener razón	to be right
tener… años	to be . . . years old	tener éxito	to be successful
tener lástima	to have pity	tener sed	to be thirsty
tener calor	to be hot	tener frío	to be cold
tener lugar	to take place	tener sueño	to be sleepy
tener catarro	to have a cold	tener ganas de	to feel like
tener miedo	to be afraid	tener suerte	to be lucky
tener celos	to be jealous	tener hambre	to be hungry
tener presente	to keep in mind	tener vergüenza	to be ashamed
tener cuidado	to be careful	tener la culpa	to bear the blame
tener prisa	to be in a hurry		

Ejercicios

I. Seleccione de la lista la expresión adecuada y complete las oraciones de acuerdo con el sentido de éstas. Use el tiempo verbal que sea necesario.

tener celos	tener catarro
tener éxito	tener cuidado
tener vergüenza	tener prisa
tener la culpa	tener sueño
tener lugar	tener derecho

1. ¡ _____ Alfonso, que estás al borde de un precipicio!

2. Él es muy celoso, _____ hasta de su sombra.

3. Ellos son los herederos (*heirs*) directos, por lo tanto, _____ a la herencia.

4. Los políticos han perdido el sentido de la decencia y la honradez; no _____ .

5. ¿Quién crees que es culpable de todo lo que pasó? No estoy seguro pero creo que es tu hermano quien _____ .

6. Agapito _____ porque quiere llegar al banco antes de que cierren.

7. Frida Kahlo fue una artista que _____ .

8. Elena no fue a la escuela porque está enferma; _____ .

9. El concierto se celebrará el diez de octubre: _____ en el Palacio de Bellas Artes.

10. Me voy a acostar temprano porque _____ .

II. Usando frases con **tener**, complete las oraciones según las indicaciones en inglés.

1. (*I don't feel like*) _____ ver esa película. Me dicen que es mala.

2. (*he is right*) Pedro siempre cree que _____ .

3. (*he is lucky*) Cada vez que Octavio va a Las Vegas gana dinero; _____ .

4. (*I'm very careful*) Cuando manejo en la autopista _____ .

5. (*take into account*) Hay que _____ todo lo que ella hizo por él.

6. (*he is afraid*) El niño no quiere que le apaguen la luz porque _____ .

7. (*will take place*) El concierto _____ en la universidad.

8. (*I am in a hurry*) _____ y no puedo seguir conversando contigo.

9. (*have the right*) Ellos _____ a la herencia del tío Antonio.

10. Juan Carlos (*has to do with*) _____ todos los negocios de su padre.

Composición

Antes de escribir, repase las siguientes reglas sobre las mayúsculas y la ortografía.

A Review of capitalization rules

1. Use a capital letter:

   • With titles and names of dignitaries when these refer to a specific person

el Presidente	**la reina Sofía**	**Isabel la Católica**
el Papa	**el Coronel**	**Su Santidad**

   • In the first word of the title of a book, article, poem, or dramatic work

   Bodas de sangre de Federico García Lorca

   El laberinto de la soledad de Octavio Paz

   • For the names of institutions

   el Museo del Prado   la Real Academia Española   la Cruz Roja

B Review of spelling rules: *g, j*

1. The following words are written with **g**:

   • Verbs ending in **-ger** and **-gir** and their derived forms, except when the ending changes to **-a, -o**:

   proteger, escoger, dirigir, proteja, escojo, dirijo except: **tejer** (*to weave*), **crujir** (*to creak*)

   • The endings **-gía, -gia, -gio, -gión**:

   antología, magia, religión except: **bujía** (*spark plug*), **mejía** (*mixed*), **lejía** (*bleach*)

   • The syllable **-gen**:

   origen, margen, gente except: **comején** (*termite*)

2. The following words are written with **j**:

   • The ending **-jero**:

   viajero, pasajero except: **ligero** (*not heavy*)

- The ending **-aje:**

  aprendizaje *(apprenticeship)*, **mestizaje** *(crossbreeding)*

- The sounds **ja, jo, ju:**

  jarro *(vase)*, **joya, jugo**

- The endings for the preterite indicative and the imperfect subjunctive of the verbs ending in **-decir** and **-ducir:**

  dijeron, tradujéramos

NOTE: The syllables **ge, gi, je, ji** have the same sound: **gelatina, gimnasio, jefe** *(boss)*, **cajita** *(little box)*

NOTE: The exercises corresponding to this section are included in the *Cuaderno de ejercicios*, Capítulo 5.

Ejercicio de composición (opcional)

Escriba una composición sobre el tema que se da a continuación. Use el esquema siguiente.

TEMA: Efectos producidos por el cine y la televisión en la sociedad actual.

INTRODUCCIÓN: La violencia que hay en las películas se refleja en la sociedad.
Efecto que causa en los niños y jóvenes el ver tantas cosas horribles en el cine y la televisión.
Protesta de muchas personas contra este tipo de película.
Necesidad de un cambio.

DESARROLLO: Cómo influir para que se produzca un cambio.
Necesidad de usar el cine y la televisión como un medio educativo.
Necesidad de destacar los valores morales y éticos en el cine y la televisión.

CONCLUSIÓN: ¿Cuál es su opinión sobre este tema?
¿Cree que el cine y la televisión pueden usarse como un medio de educación cultural?
¿Qué tipos de programas culturales podrían ser muy educativos?

6 Capítulo

Mural de Diego Rivera hecho en 1931, el cual se encuentra en el Museo de Arte de Filadelfia.

LECTURAS

- Lectura: "México y el arte muralista"

GRAMÁTICA

- The gerund or present participle
- Possessive adjectives and pronouns
- Demonstrative adjectives and pronouns
- Adverbs
- Impersonal verbs
- Review of verbs that may be confusing
- Prefixes **des-, in-, re-**

COMPOSICIÓN

- Review of capitalization rules
- Review of spelling rules: **ll, y, -ío, -illo, -illa**

164

Vocabulario

Antes de leer, repase el siguiente vocabulario que le ayudará a comprender la lectura.

Sustantivos

la ayuda help	**el levantamiento** uprising
el campesino peasant	**la patria** native land; country
el campo field	**la pintura** painting
el clavel carnation	**la preocupación** worry
el cuadro painting	**el renacer** rebirth
la dictadura dictatorship	**el vecino** neighbor
el fracaso failure	**la ventaja** advantage

Verbos

alcanzar (c) to attain	**iniciar(se)** to begin
animar to encourage	**lloviznar** to drizzle
complacer (zc) to please	**nombrar** to appoint, to name; to elect
destacar(se) (qu) to stand out	**pasear** to stroll, to take a walk
disfrutar to enjoy	**pelear** to fight, to quarrel
donar to donate	**pertenecer (zc)** to belong
escampar to stop raining	**pintar** to paint
esclavizar (c) to enslave	**proporcionar** to provide
fracasar to fail	**realizar (c)** to achieve, to accomplish

Adjetivos

ambicioso ambitious	**juguetón** playful
fiel faithful	

Frases

a mano by hand	**al extremo que** to the extent that
a partir de since	**punto de vista** point of view

Cognates (Cognados). In the reading that follows, you will recognize many words because of their similarity to English. Give the English equivalent for the following cognates and compare the spelling. Can you find other examples in the reading?

-tion	<u>educational</u>	**-ción**	<u>educacional</u>
-tion	_____	**-ción**	unificación
-sion	_____	**-sión**	explosión
-sc-	_____	**-esc-**	escuela
-st-	_____	**-est-**	estilo; estimular
-sp-	_____	**-esp-**	espacio
-mm	_____	**-nm**	inmortalizar
-ff	_____	**-f**	efecto

Be careful with the following words:

realizar	*to achieve, to accomplish*	**darse cuenta de**	*to realize*
pelear	*to fight, to quarrel*	**luchar**	*to fight for; to struggle*
crear	*to create*	**criar**	*to raise*

Lectura

México y el arte muralista

Geográficamente, México pertenece a la América del Norte, pero culturalmente, es una nación separada de sus vecinos. En ella, la unificación de dos culturas —la indígena y la española— es tan fuerte que ha llegado a formar una nueva cultura: la mexicana. La evolución histórica
5 de este país ha proporcionado muchos de los elementos que han contribuido a darle forma y carácter a esta cultura.

La Revolución Mexicana de 1910 marca el final de una época que comenzó en 1876 con la dictadura de Porfirio Díaz. Durante su gobierno, el país aparentemente disfrutaba de paz, pero la represión política y social
10 culminó° en la explosión revolucionaria. En esa época, que se conoce   *culminated*
como el porfiriato, se imitaba lo europeo en la forma de vida y también en la educación, donde muchas de las ideas educacionales resultaron un fracaso en las escuelas mexicanas, ya que gran parte de la población siguió en la ignorancia y en la pobreza.
15 En las artes y en las letras,° la influencia europea se hizo aún más   *literature*
visible. Todo el que pasee por el Paseo de la Reforma, en la Ciudad de México, verá las casas de estilo francés construidas en esa época. En la literatura, la influencia francesa era muy fuerte, al extremo que el conocido poeta modernista Amado Nervo (1870–1919) decía que "su
20 alma venía de Francia." En el campo de la música, prevalecía° la   *prevailed*
influencia alemana, y todo el que conozca el vals "Sobre las olas," de Juventino Rosas, notará la influencia del famoso compositor austriaco Johann Strauss (1825–1899).

Al llegar la Revolución de 1910 todo este deseo de imitar lo europeo
25 desapareció. Apareció una nueva generación de intelectuales, entre ellos, José Vasconcelos (1882–1959) y Alfonso Reyes (1889–1959), quienes contribuyeron a formar el mundo de ideas que animó y dio forma a la Revolución. Como consecuencia de esta revolución política, el mundo de ideas y las artes sufrió una renovación completa. Se inició un período de
30 libertad filosófica y artística que no se hizo sentir,° como una verdadera   *was not felt*
revolución intelectual, hasta después de 1920.

Donde más se sintió el efecto del cambio producido por la Revolución fue en el campo del arte, especialmente en la pintura mural, que había sido muy importante en el siglo XVI, cuando se pintaban frescos con
35   temas religiosos. A partir de 1920, el arte se identificó con lo social y los artistas desarrollaron un marcado interés por la pintura mural que el Gobierno, en su deseo de hacer popular la Revolución, protegía y estimulaba. El Ministerio de Educación llamó a los artistas para que pintaran los muros de la Escuela Nacional Preparatoria y, más tarde, los
40   del Palacio Nacional, los del Palacio de Cortés en Cuernavaca, los del Hospicio° de Guadalajara y los de Chapingo.   *orphanage*

Tres importantes artistas de ese momento se destacaron, llegando a alcanzar fama internacional: Diego Rivera (1886–1957), David Alfaro Siqueiros (1898–1974) y José Clemente Orozco (1883–1949). De los tres,
45   Diego Rivera es el que realizó en sus pinturas la síntesis de la Revolución Mexicana, y en su arte se ve su preocupación por lo "mexicano," desde la época anterior a la Conquista hasta el siglo XX. Diego Rivera es quien estimula un renacer° de la pintura muralista, no sólo en México sino en   *rebirth* otros países de Latinoamérica, y aun en los Estados Unidos.
50   Diego Rivera utilizó su arte para expresar la realidad mexicana en un estilo vigoroso, presentándole al pueblo en sus murales la historia de la

Zapatistas, óleo de José Clemente Orozco.

patria. Su obra más ambiciosa y gigantesca es la historia épica de México
hecha para el Palacio Nacional. En los muros del Palacio de Cortés, en
Cuernavaca, Rivera pintó el levantamiento de Emiliano Zapata,
55   inmortalizando la figura de Zapata, junto a su hermoso caballo blanco,
como defensor y protector de los campesinos mexicanos.

  David Alfaro Siqueiros, lo mismo que Diego Rivera, puso su arte al
servicio de la Revolución usando el concepto de espacio de los murales
para crear, en colores chocantes, grandes masas de gente y objetos. En su
60   pintura se mezcla el realismo con la fantasía, llegando a crear un mundo
imaginario. Uno de sus muchos murales, "Marcha de la humanidad," tiene
50.000 pies cuadrados y le llevó más de cuatro años pintarlo, necesitando
la ayuda de muchas manos extras.

  José Clemente Orozco nació dentro de una familia prominente de
65   Ciudad Guzmán y, siendo muy joven, perdió la mano izquierda en un

accidente en un laboratorio. Este hecho hizo que abandonara los estudios
de agronomía° y se dedicara a la pintura.   *agriculture*

Para apreciar la obra monumental de Orozco hay que visitar
Guadalajara. En los murales del Hospicio, Orozco une la historia de
70 México a la historia del hombre contemporáneo que lucha siempre por la
libertad. Es en estos murales, con los dioses indios y sus sacrificios
humanos, los conquistadores que esclavizan, los dictadores, los
trabajadores, los frailes° franciscanos y Cervantes (creador del *Quijote*), donde   *friars*
se puede apreciar la profundidad y riqueza imaginativa de este gran artista.
75 Orozco vivió en los Estados Unidos de 1927 a 1932 y durante ese
tiempo pintó importantes murales en diferentes lugares del país,
especialmente en Dartmouth College, en New Hampshire.

Junto a Rivera, Siqueiros y Orozco, Rufino Tamayo (1899–1991)
contribuyó a definir claramente el arte moderno mexicano. Sus pinturas,
80 con los colores y la luz de la tierra mexicana, tienen la influencia de su
origen zapoteca* y de los estudios que hizo del arte precolombino° y   *pre-Columbian*
folklórico. Sus muchos murales adornan las paredes del Palacio de Bellas
Artes y las de muchos otros edificios dentro y fuera de México.

Rufino Tamayo donó su magnífica colección de arte, junto con sus
85 pinturas, al museo que lleva su nombre en la Ciudad de México.

*Pueblo indígena de México que se estableció en el estado de Oaxaca y desarrolló una brillante
cultura.*

Llene los espacios en blanco con la palabra correcta para completar la oración.

1. La exhibición que el artista tuvo en París le _____ la oportunidad de
darse a conocer. Al final de su vida sus _____ estaban en muchos
museos importantes del mundo.

2. Rufino Tamayo tenía una magnífica colección de arte que _____ al
museo que tiene su nombre en la Ciudad de México.

3. Las personas que visitan el Hospicio en Guadalajara pueden disfrutar los murales
que Orozco _____ allí.

4. Emiliano Zapata, protector de los _____ mexicanos, es la figura que
aparece, junto a su caballo blanco, en un famoso _____ de Diego Rivera.

5. Siqueiros usó colores _____ para crear un mundo alucinante en sus
cuadros.

6. En el arte de Diego Rivera se ve su _____ por lo mexicano. Él fue
quien estimuló un renacer de la pintura muralista.

Preguntas sobre la lectura

1. ¿Qué elementos han contribuido a formar la cultura mexicana?
2. ¿Qué cosas son características del porfiriato en México?
3. ¿Cómo eran la arquitectura y la literatura de esa época?
4. ¿Por qué dice el autor que la Revolución Mexicana marca el final de una época?
5. ¿Qué cambios ocurrieron en México como consecuencia de la Revolución?
6. Mencione los cambios que ocurrieron en el arte a partir de 1920.
7. ¿Qué expresión artística utilizó el gobierno para hacer popular la Revolución?
8. ¿Quiénes son los tres primeros muralistas de la Revolución?
9. ¿Qué temas usa Diego Rivera en sus murales?
10. ¿En qué forma contribuye David Alfaro Siqueiros a la Revolución?
11. ¿Qué circunstancia de la vida de José Clemente Orozco contribuyó a que se dedicara a la pintura?
12. ¿Cuál es el tema que predomina en los murales del Hospicio de Guadalajara?
13. ¿Qué otro artista mexicano ha contribuido al enriquecimiento de la pintura muralista en México?

Temas de conversación

1. ¿Ha visto Ud. algunos murales de estos artistas en México o en los Estados Unidos? Comente la impresión que le causaron.
2. Actualmente se pueden ver muchos murales en sitios públicos en los Estados Unidos. ¿Sabe Ud. quién pintó estos murales? ¿Por qué cree Ud. que surgió un movimiento muralista en los Estados Unidos en la década de los setenta?
3. ¿Puede mencionar a alguna mujer que haya influido en la vida política y social de los Estados Unidos? Hable sobre ella. ¿Qué otras mujeres conoce Ud. que hayan pasado a la historia de sus países? ¿Cree que Eva Perón fue una de esas mujeres? Explique su respuesta.

Gramática

A   The gerund or present participle

The gerund or present participle (**-ing** form) is formed by adding the endings **-ando** or **-iendo** to the stem of the verb.

comprar **comprando**   vender **vendiendo**   recibir **recibiendo**

Verbs of the second and third conjugation (**-er** and **-ir**) whose stem ends in a vowel, change the **i** of **-iendo** to **y**.

leer	**leyendo**	creer	**creyendo**
caer	**cayendo**	oír	**oyendo**
huir	**huyendo**	traer	**trayendo**

NOTE: The present participle of **ir** is **yendo**.

Yendo por ese camino demorarás mucho.
By going on that road you will take long.

Third conjugation verbs that change **e** to **ie** or **e** to **i** in the present indicative, also change **e** to **i** in the present participle.*

Infinitive	Present	Gerund
sentir	siento	**sintiendo**
mentir	miento	**mintiendo**
preferir	prefiero	**prefiriendo**
servir	sirvo	**sirviendo**
pedir	pido	**pidiendo**
repetir	repito	**repitiendo**
seguir	sigo	**siguiendo**
conseguir	consigo	**consiguiendo**
reír	río	**riendo**
decir	digo	**diciendo**

The verbs **poder, dormir,** and **morir** change the **o** to **u.**

poder **pudiendo**   dormir **durmiendo**   morir **muriendo**

1. Uses of the present participle

   a. The main use of the present participle is with the verb **estar** to form the progressive tenses and to indicate that an action is in progress.

Estoy leyendo.	**Han estado trabajando.**
I'm reading.	*They have been working.*
Estuvo estudiando.	**Habíamos estado caminando.**
He was studying.	*We had been walking.*
Estaba bañándome.	Ojalá que mañana **esté nevando.**
I was taking a bath.	*I hope it will be snowing tomorrow.*

   The object or reflexive pronouns can go in front of **estar** or can be attached to the present participle, though in spoken Spanish pronouns generally precede the form of **estar.**

   Lo estaba sirviendo. Estaba sirviéndo**lo**. *She was serving it.*

   Unlike English, the verbs **ir, venir,** and **andar** are seldom used in the present progressive. It is more common to use the present indicative.

   Mira, ahí **viene** Ignacio.
   Look, Ignacio is coming.

   En este momento él **va** hacia tu casa.
   At this moment he is going towards your house.

NOTE: In Spanish the present progressive is used much less than in English because its meaning may be expressed with a simple present tense.

*See Capítulo 1, page 31.

b. The present participle can be used with the verbs **andar**, **seguir**, and **continuar** to give the idea of continuity.

Fermín **anda buscando** trabajo.	*Fermin is looking for work.*
Ellos **siguen viviendo** en San Antonio.	*They keep on living in San Antonio.*
José **continúa coleccionando** sellos.	*Jose continues collecting (to collect) stamps.*

c. The present participle is used as an adverb to describe the action of another verb.

El chico viene **corriendo**.	*The boy comes running.*
Ellos vuelven **cantando**.	*They come back singing.*
Los soldados pasaron **marchando**.	*The soldiers went marching by.*

d. The present participle used by itself serves as an explanatory expression subordinated to another verb.

Conociendo a mi marido, no lo esperé.	*Knowing my husband, I didn't wait for him.*
Estando en Santa Fe, decidimos ir a Albuquerque.	*While in Santa Fe, we decided to go to Albuquerque.*

Plaza de las Tres Culturas en la Ciudad de México.

Ejercicios

I. Complete las frases con el gerundio (participio presente) de los verbos que están entre paréntesis.

1. (vestirse) Alicia estaba _____ cuando su amigo vino a buscarla.

2. (levantarse) Por tres años ella estuvo _____ a las cinco de la mañana.

3. (dormir) Ellos están _____ en un hotel del centro.

4. (decir) ¿Qué está _____ el locutor de radio?

5. (pedir) ¿Cuánto está _____ el vendedor por la casa?

6. (reírse) Las chicas están _____ con los chistes de Fermín.

II. Ud. pasa la mañana en el parque y describe las actividades que ocurren a su alrededor. Llene los espacios en blanco con el presente del verbo **estar** y el gerundio del verbo que está entre paréntesis.

Mientras yo _____ _____ (leer) sentado en un banco del

parque, _____ _____ (ver) a mucha gente que, lo mismo

que yo, _____ _____ (disfrutar) del ambiente agradable de los árboles,

las flores y el aire fresco de la mañana. Hay muchos niños que _____

_____ (saltar), _____ (correr), _____ y

_____ (jugar) al mismo tiempo que otros más pequeñitos

_____ _____ (dormir) en sus cochecitos junto a los

padres. Un grupo de jóvenes, cerca de mí, _____ _____

(comer) y _____ (beber) vino. _____ _____

(reírse) y _____ _____ (divertirse) mucho.

III. Imagine que Ud. es un actor o una actriz de cine y se encuentra con un amigo que hace tiempo que no ve. Conteste las preguntas que él le hace usando el progresivo y la información que aparece entre paréntesis.

> **MODELO:** ¿En qué trabajas ahora? (en una película de guerra)
> **Estoy trabajando en una película de guerra.**

1. ¿Qué película filmas ahora? (una comedia romántica)
2. ¿Qué director dirige la película? (un director italiano)
3. ¿Dónde hacen la filmación? (en Nápoles y en Roma)
4. ¿Dónde vives mientras haces la película? (en una villa romana cerca de Roma)
5. ¿Qué piensas hacer cuando termines? (casarme con el actor o la actriz que hace la película conmigo)
6. Caramba, ¿qué dices? (que voy a casarme)

IV. Temas de conversación.

1. Piense que Ud. está mirando un juego de baloncesto (*basketball*). Diga todas las cosas que están haciendo los jugadores y las personas que están mirando también el juego.
2. Piense que Ud. está en la playa. Diga todas las cosas que están haciendo las personas que están allí.
3. Piense que Ud. está en un aeropuerto. Diga todas las cosas que están ocurriendo allí.

B Possessive adjectives and pronouns

POSSESSIVES

Owner	Adjective when preceding the noun	Adjective when following the noun	Pronoun
yo	mi, mis	mío (-os, -a, -as)	el (los, la, las) mío (-os, -a, -as)
tú	tu, tus	tuyo (-os, -a, -as)	el (los, la, las) tuyo (-os, -a, -as)
él, ella, Ud., cosa	su, sus	suyo (-os, -a, -as)	el (los, la, las) suyo (-os, -a, -as)
nosotros (-as)	nuestro (-os, -a, -as)	nuestro (-os, -a, -as)	el (los, la, las) nuestro (-os, -a, -as)
vosotros (-as)	vuestro (-os, -a, -as)	vuestro (-os, -a, -as)	el (los, la, las) vuestro (-os, -a, -as)
ellos (-as), Uds., cosas	su, sus	suyo (-os, -a, -as)	el (los, la, las) suyo (-os, -a, -as)

1. *Possessive adjectives.* The possessive adjective is used with a noun to express ownership. It agrees with the thing possessed and not with the owner, in contrast to English usage.

   a. As you can see in the diagram, there are two forms of possessive adjectives: one short and another long. The short form is used in front of nouns. **Mi, tu, su** agree in number with the noun; **nuestro** and **vuestro** agree in gender and number.

mi hermano (*my brother*)	**tus** casas (*your houses*)
nuestros amigos (*our friends*)	**sus** ideales (*his/her/your ideals*)

   The long form is used after the noun, after the verb **ser**, and alone. It agrees in gender and number with the noun.

¿Es éste el abrigo **suyo**?	*Is this coat yours?*
El televisor es **tuyo**.	*The television set is yours.*
¿De quién es esta camisa? **Mía**.	*Whose shirt is this? Mine.*

   b. **Su, sus,** and **suyo** (-os, -a, -as) may present some ambiguity. For clarity the preposition **de** + the personal pronoun can be used.

   su amigo
   {
   el amigo **de él**
   el amigo **de ella**
   el amigo **de Ud.**
   el amigo **de ellos**
   el amigo **de ellas**
   el amigo **de Uds.**
   }

   la casa suya
   {
   la casa **de él**
   la casa **de ella**
   la casa **de Ud.**
   la casa **de ellos**
   la casa **de ellas**
   la casa **de Uds.**
   }

NOTE: Remember that in Spanish the definite article is used with parts of the body and articles of clothing.*

Me lavo **las** manos.	*I wash my hands.*
¿Te pusiste **las** botas?	*Did you put on your boots?*

2. *Possessive pronouns.* Possessive pronouns are formed using the definite articles + the long forms **mío, tuyo, suyo, nuestro, vuestro,** and **suyo.** They agree in number and gender with the thing possessed.

Mi abrigo es azul; **el tuyo** es rojo.	*My coat is blue; yours is red.*
Su casa costó poco; **la nuestra**, mucho.	*Your house cost little; ours a lot.*
Mi hermana es bella; **la tuya** también.	*My sister is beautiful; yours, too.*
¿Cuál es tu taza? Ésta es **la mía**.	*Which is your cup? This one is mine.*

3. *Neuter forms.* The neuter forms **lo mío, lo tuyo, lo suyo, lo nuestro, lo vuestro,** and **lo suyo** are used to express abstract ideas or concepts.

Lo nuestro no tiene solución.	*Ours has no solution.*
Ellos explicaron **lo suyo**.	*They explained theirs (situation or thing).*

Ejercicios

I. Ud. le habla a una amiga suya acerca de su familia. Cambie las oraciones sustituyendo la forma corta de los posesivos por la forma larga.

MODELO: Mis amigos son puertorriqueños.
Los amigos míos son puertorriqueños.

1. Nuestra familia es muy complicada.
2. Mi hijo es pacifista.
3. Mi esposo es coronel del ejército y trabaja en el Ministerio de Guerra.
4. Mi hermano ha sido siempre anarquista. Mi hermana mayor es monja.
5. ¿Es tu familia tan colorida (*colorful*) como mi familia?

II. Cambie las oraciones sustituyendo la construcción con **de** + pronombre por el posesivo **su** o **suyo**.

MODELOS: El marido de ella quiere ir al cine.
Su marido quiere ir al cine.
La culpa es de ella.
La culpa es suya.

1. El amigo de Ud. está de mal genio porque los tíos de él no le han hecho nunca un regalo y siempre lo están llamando para que los ayude.
2. Pedro cree que el dinero es de él y no de los padres de él. Las propiedades de ellos valen mucho y Pedro espera que la casa de la familia sea de él y no de la hermana de él.
3. Pero la hermana dice que la casa es de ella porque ella nació allí y allí también nacieron los hijos de ella.

---

*See Capítulo 1, page 39.

III. Cambie las oraciones sustituyendo las palabras subrayadas por un pronombre posesivo.

MODELO: Mis padres son mexicanos; <u>tus padres</u> son cubanos.
Mis padres son mexicanos; los tuyos son cubanos.

1. Su tía y <u>mi tía</u> salieron juntas.
2. Éstos son mis guantes. ¿Dónde están <u>tus guantes</u>?
3. ¿Tiene Ud. mi cartera o <u>su cartera</u>?
4. Tus hijos salieron con <u>nuestros hijos</u>.
5. Mi bicicleta es americana y <u>su bicicleta</u> es japonesa.

IV. Traduzca al español los posesivos que están en inglés y complete las frases.

1. (*mine/yours* [Ud.]) No me interesa el trabajo _____ sino

   _____ .

2. (*my*) Ella no es _____ amiga.

3. (*Our/yours/mine*) _____ generación era muy diferente. ¿Cuál te

   gusta más, _____ o _____ ?

4. (*ours*) ¿De quiénes son estas gafas? Son _____ .

5. (*his*) No acepto _____ excusas.

6. (*his*) Este programa es _____ .

7. (*their*) Ellos discuten _____ planes.

8. (*my/theirs*) Ésas no son _____ ideas; son _____ .

9. (*My/yours* [tú]) _____ familia habla español; _____

   habla inglés.

10. (*mine*) El artículo fue escrito por una profesora _____ .

 C Demonstrative adjectives and pronouns

DEMONSTRATIVES

| Adjectives | | Pronouns | | |
Singular	Plural	Singular	Plural	Neuter
este	estos	éste	éstos	esto
esta	estas	ésta	éstas	
ese	esos	ése	ésos	eso
esa	esas	ésa	ésas	
aquel	aquellos	aquél	aquéllos	aquello
aquella	aquellas	aquélla	aquéllas	

Chichén Itzá, ruinas de la antigua ciudad maya al norte de Yucatán. Al centro, la figura de Chac Mool, divinidad maya-tolteca de la lluvia.

The demonstratives are used to indicate distance in space or time.

este	*(this)*	close to the person that speaks
ese	*(that)*	close to the person spoken to
aquel	*(that over there)*	far from the speaker and listener

Aunque ha pasado mucho tiempo, no olvido **aquella** experiencia traumática.
Although a long time has elapsed, I can't forget that traumatic experience.
Siempre recordaré **estos** momentos felices que pasé contigo.
I will always remember these happy moments I spent with you.

1. *Demonstrative adjectives.* Demonstrative adjectives go in front of the noun and agree with it in gender and number. Note that demonstrative adjectives don't require an accent mark.

Aquí tienes **esta** carta. Léela y contéstala.
Here is this letter. Read it and answer it.

Déme **ese** informe que acaba de escribir.
Give me that report that you just wrote.

Siempre recuerdo **aquellos** días cuando no existían las computadoras.
I always remember those days when computers did not exist.

2. *Demonstrative pronouns.* Demonstrative pronouns are used instead of nouns and agree in gender and number with the nouns they replace. The demonstrative pronouns require an accent mark.

Escogí estos zapatos y **aquéllos**.	*I chose these shoes and those.*
¿Cuál cartera prefiere: **ésta** o **ésa**?	*Which handbag do you prefer, this one or that one?*
Aquélla sí fue una semana inolvidable.	*That really was an unforgettable week.*

a. The pronoun **éste (-os, -a, -as)** is used as the equivalent of the English expression *the latter.*

b. **Aquél, aquéllos, aquélla, aquéllas** are used as the equivalent of the English expression *the former.*

Rita es mayor que Anita; **ésta** tiene diez años y **aquélla** tiene quince. *Rita is older than Anita; the latter is ten years old and the former is fifteen.* (**Ésta** refers to Anita; **aquélla** refers to Rita.)

3. The neuter forms **esto, eso,** and **aquello** refer to an abstract idea, action, or thing. It is the equivalent of *this thing, that thing,* or *that thing far away.* The neuter forms do not have a written accent.

Ricardo, **esto** que escribiste está muy bien, puesto que aclaras que **aquello** que parecía humo era sólo niebla. Por **eso** la gente del pueblo estaba tan alarmada.
Ricardo, what you wrote is very good, because you clarify that that which looked like smoke was really fog. That is the reason the people in the village were so upset.

Ejercicios

I. Cambie las siguientes oraciones de acuerdo con las palabras indicadas entre paréntesis y haga los cambios necesarios.

MODELO: Esas ideas son absurdas. (conceptos)
Esos conceptos son absurdos.

1. En aquella época el viaje a la luna era sólo un sueño. (tiempo)
2. Ese hotel nos pareció horrible. (cuartos)
3. Esta primavera regresarán las golondrinas (*swallows*). (verano)
4. Aquella excursión no nos gustó. (asientos)
5. Esta persona no hace más que molestar. (chicos)

II. Complete las oraciones empleando los demostrativos adecuados.

1. _____ mercado que está aquí parece ser bastante bueno.
2. Nunca olvidaré _____ casa adonde íbamos de vacaciones.

3. _____ misma tarde iré a la agencia de pasajes.

4. ¿Qué es _____ que trae Ud. en la mano?

5. ¿Qué vestido prefiere: éste que acabo de enseñarle o _____ que está allá?

III. Complete las oraciones con el equivalente en español de las palabras que están en inglés. Use los demostrativos necesarios.

1. (*this/that*) ¿Qué mesa prefiere, señor, _____ que está aquí, o _____ más lejos?

2. (*these*) Mis hijos me regalaron _____ cerámicas.

3. (*those long-ago*) _____ días que pasé en Puerto Rico fueron maravillosos.

4. (*that*) Te digo que _____ es un misterio.

5. (*this*) Aquí tiene _____ informe para Ud.

6. (*those*) No veo bien qué hay detrás de _____ árboles que están allá lejos.

IV. El siguiente párrafo trata del mexicano José Vasconcelos. Subraye la forma correcta del pronombre o adjetivo demostrativo que está entre paréntesis.

José Vasconcelos, uno de los más distinguidos hombres de letras de México, fue ministro de educación en 1921. (Este, Éste) filósofo de vida contradictoria y apasionada nació en Oaxaca, pero se educó en la Ciudad de México. Participó activamente a favor de la Revolución. (Esto, Esta) le llevó al Ministerio de Educación. En (aquellos, aquéllos) años el porcentaje de analfabetos era sumamente alto. (Esto, Este) le impulsó a hacer muchas reformas en la enseñanza. (Esas, Ésas) reformas incluían la enseñanza tanto a niños así como a adultos en sitios rurales.

V. Composición dirigida (oral o escrita). Conteste las preguntas en forma original usando en la respuesta algún demostrativo.

MODELO: ¿Qué restaurante le gusta más?
Me gusta más aquél que está en la esquina porque preparan unos tamales muy sabrosos y el vino de la casa es estupendo.

1. ¿Qué son todos esos papeles?
2. ¿Quién es esa mujer tan extraña?
3. ¿Por qué dice que esto no le gusta?
4. ¿Cuál de estos dos vuelos nos recomienda?
5. ¿Qué asientos prefieren en el teatro: éstos o aquéllos?

D Adverbs

Adverbs modify a verb, an adjective, or another adverb and are invariable, that is, they do not change in form.

La ópera empezó **muy** tarde, pero disfrutamos **mucho**. La soprano cantó **bien** y todos los cantantes eran **bastante** buenos.
The opera started very late but we enjoyed it a lot. The soprano sang well and all the singers were quite good.

1. Adverbs express relations of place, time, way, manner, quantity, affirmation, or negation.

El pueblo quedaba **lejos de** la capital.   *The town was far from the capital.*
Terminaré **mañana** lo que empecé hoy.   *I will finish tomorrow what I began today.*
Acaba **mal** lo que empieza **mal**.   *What begins badly ends badly.*
El pobre hombre bebe **mucho** y come **poco**. *The poor man drinks a lot and eats little.*
Me siento **verdaderamente** feliz.   *I feel truly happy.*
Nunca olvidaré el favor que me   *I will never forget the favor you have*
    has hecho.   *done for me.*

2. Adverbs are formed by adding **-mente** to adjectives. If the adjective ends in **-o** the feminine form is used. (The ending **-mente** corresponds to the English ending *-ly*.)

feo	**feamente**	rico	**ricamente**
fácil	**fácilmente**	amable	**amablemente**

NOTE: If the adjective has a written accent, it remains in the adverbial form.

dificil   **difícilmente**

NOTE: If there are two or more adjectives, **-mente** is added only to the last adjective.

Él habla **clara** y **lentamente**.   *He speaks clearly and slowly.*

3. Note that **bueno (-a, -os, -as)** and **malo (-a, -os, -as)** are adjectives; **bien** and **mal** are adverbs, therefore, these don't change.

Gutiérrez y Almeida son **buenos** artistas; tocan **bien** el piano y la guitarra.
Gutiérrez and Almeida are good artists; they play the piano and the guitar well.
Pepito es un niño **malo**; se porta **mal** en la escuela.
Pepito is a bad boy; he behaves badly in school.

NOTE: **Más, menos, poco, mucho, mejor, peor, demasiado,** and **bastante** can be used as adjectives or adverbs.

La señora tiene **muchas** ganas de viajar.   *The lady really feels like traveling.*
                  (adjective)

Alberto está **mucho** mejor.   *Albert is much better. (adverb)*
Tenemos **demasiados** gastos.   *We have too many expenses. (adjective)*
Elena es **demasiado** orgullosa.   *Elena is too proud. (adverb)*

The word **mas** does not have a written accent when it is an adverbial conjunction. It is the equivalent of **pero**:

> No la vi **mas** le escribí. (No la vi pero le escribí.)
> *I didn't see her but I wrote to her.*

4. The adverb **aún**, in affirmative sentences, corresponds to the English *still*. In negative sentences it corresponds to *yet*.

> **Aún** están bailando.   *They are still dancing.*
> **Aún** no han llegado.   *They have not arrived yet.*

Aún más (menos) corresponds to the English *still (even) more* or *still (even) less*.

> Yo estudio mucho, pero tú estudias **aún más**.
> *I study a lot, but you study even more.*

NOTE: **Aún** (with a written accent) is the equivalent of **todavía**.

> **Aún (Todavía)** no ha llegado el avión.   *The plane has not arrived yet.*

Aun (without an accent mark) means **hasta** or **incluso** (*including*).

> **Aun** los tontos lo saben.   *Even the fools know it.*

Ejercicios

I. Complete las oraciones con la forma adecuada de la palabra entre paréntesis.

MODELO: (bastante) Practicamos **bastante** el español; tenemos **bastantes** amigos que hablan esa lengua.

1. (poco) Ella habla muy _____ ; tiene _____ amigos.

2. (mejor) Estos zapatos son _____ ; caminarás _____ con ellos.

3. (peor) Hoy hace _____ tiempo que ayer y anuncian _____ condiciones para mañana.

4. (demasiado) Ese niño tiene _____ cosas; los padres lo malcrían _____ .

II. Dé el adjetivo cuyo significado corresponde a los sustantivos. Después forme adverbios terminados en **-mente**.

	Sustantivo	Adjetivo	Adverbio
MODELO:	claridad	claro	claramente
1.	riqueza	_____	_____
2.	lealtad	_____	_____
3.	pereza	_____	_____
4.	alegría	_____	_____
5.	felicidad	_____	_____

III. Sustituya las frases subrayadas por un adverbio terminado en **-mente**.

> **MODELO:** El coro cantó los villancicos <u>con emoción</u>.
> **El coro cantó los villancicos emocionadamente.**

1. El cura de la iglesia habló <u>con humildad</u>.
2. La madre les habló <u>con amor</u>.
3. Nos recibieron en su casa <u>con alegría</u>.
4. Ella lo trató <u>con inteligencia</u>.
5. Nos despedimos de ellos <u>con tristeza</u>.

E Impersonal verbs

Impersonal verbs do not have a subject or a complement. They are used in the form corresponding to the third person singular (it) of all tenses.

1. In Spanish all verbs expressing atmospheric conditions are impersonal.

llover	*to rain*	**nevar**	*to snow*
lloviznar	*to drizzle*	**relampaguear**	*to lighten*
diluviar	*to pour, rain heavily*	**tronar**	*to thunder*
escampar	*to stop raining*	**amanecer**	*to dawn*
granizar	*to hail*	**anochecer**	*to grow dark at nightfall*

Anuncian que **lloverá** mañana.	*They are announcing that it will rain tomorrow.*
Nevó toda la noche.	*It snowed all night.*
Está **relampagueando** y tronando.	*It is lightning and thundering.*
Ha **lloviznado** todo el día.	*It has drizzled all day.*

NOTE: Observe that these verbs in English use the pronoun *it*, which is not required in Spanish. Spanish does not have an equivalent for the subject pronoun *(it)*.

> **Llueve mucho.**   *It rains a lot.*

2. The verbs **amanecer** and **anochecer** sometimes are used to express the idea of arrival at or being in a place at the beginning of the day or at nightfall.

> Salimos de Los Ángeles por la noche y **amanecimos** en La Habana.
> *We left Los Angeles at night and arrived in Havana at dawn.*

3. Other impersonal verbs are:

bastar	*to be enough*	**Basta** decir que es la persona más noble que existe.
		It's enough to say that he is the most noble person there is.
precisar	*to be necessary*	**Precisa** que salgamos temprano.
		It's important that we leave early.
importar	*to be important*	**Importa** que seas puntual.
		It's important (It matters) that you be punctual.
parecer	*to appear, seem*	**Parece** que el mundo está en crisis.
		It seems that the world is in a crisis.
convenir	*to be advisable*	**Conviene** estudiar español.
		It is advisable to study Spanish.

Ejercicios

I. Complete las respuestas usando el tiempo que sea necesario del verbo entre paréntesis.

1. ¿Cómo es el clima en el trópico?

   (llover) Es caliente y _____ mucho.

2. ¿Podremos ir a esquiar este fin de semana?

   (nevar) Creo que sí, porque es posible que _____ mucho.

3. ¿Te gusta el horario de verano?

   (anochecer) Sí, porque _____ tarde.

4. ¿Te levantas muy temprano?

   (amanecer) Generalmente cuando _____ ya yo me he desayunado.

5. Dicen que llovió mucho ayer en San Juan.

   (tronar / relampaguear) Sí, y también _____ y _____ mucho.

6. ¿A qué hora vamos a poner el despertador (*alarm clock*)?

   (precisar) A las cuatro y media. _____ que salgamos temprano.

7. ¿Por qué te disgustas tanto cuando lees el periódico por la mañana?

   (parecer) Porque _____ que no hay un solo lugar en el mundo sin problemas.

8. ¿Crees que debo de ir a ver al abogado?

   (convenir) Creo que sí. _____ hacerle algunas preguntas antes de firmar el contrato.

II. Composición dirigida (oral o escrita). Complete las oraciones en forma original usando un vocabulario relacionado con los fenómenos atmosféricos.

MODELO: Toda la noche…

Toda la noche estuvo lloviendo y es posible que haya una inundación.

1. El cielo está nublado…
2. El termómetro está bajando…
3. El viento…
4. En el momento de llegar a casa…
5. ¡Qué manera de…!
6. El pronóstico del tiempo para mañana…

F   Review of verbs that may be confusing

caber
(to fit)
Los juguetes no **caben** en esta caja tan pequeña.
The toys don't fit in this very small box.

quedar
(to fit)
Ese traje le **queda** muy bien a Margot.
This outfit fits Margot very well.

creer
(to believe)
Los niños **creen** en Santa Claus y en los Reyes Magos.
The children believe in Santa Claus and in the Three Wise Men.

criar
(to raise)
La madre **cría** a sus hijos con disciplina.
The mother raises her children with discipline.

crear
(to create)
El artista **crea** una obra de arte.
The artist creates a work of art.

dejar
(to leave behind)
Los señores **dejaron** las maletas sobre el mostrador.
The men left their suitcases on top of the counter.

salir
(to leave)
Los señores **salieron** sin sus maletas.
The men left without their suitcases.

darse cuenta de
(to realize)
Te das cuenta de lo lista que es Sofía?
Do you realize how smart Sofia is?

realizar
(to fulfill)
Ella **realizó** el sueño de su vida: llegar a ser ingeniera.
She realized (fulfilled) her life's dream: to become an engineer.

jugar)
(to play a game)
Ellos **juegan** bien al tenis.
They play tennis well.

tocar *(to play
an instrument)*
Alberto **toca** el violín y el clarinete.
Alberto plays the violin and the clarinet.

llevar
(to take)
Llevé a mi padre al médico.
I took my father to the doctor.

traer
(to bring)
Acabo de llegar del mercado y te **traje** las naranjas que querías.
I've just come back from the market and I brought you the oranges you wanted.

tomar
(to take)
Ellos **toman** el autobús que pasa por la esquina.
They take the bus that goes by the corner.

mirar
(to look at)
Lo **miraba** pero no lo veía.
She was looking at it but she didn't see it.

ver
(to see)
Miró a lo lejos y **vio** que se acercaban los enemigos.
He looked in the distance and saw that the enemy was approaching.

mover
(to move)
Moví todos los muebles de la sala para limpiar la alfombra.
I moved all the furniture in the living room in order to clean the carpet.

mudarse
(to move)
Nos mudamos a una casa nueva.
We moved to a new house.

parecer
(to seem)
¿Qué te **parece** este restaurante?
How does this restaurant seem to you? (What do you think of this restaurant?)

parecerse
(to look like)
Elisa **se parece** a su madre.
Elisa looks like her mother.

preguntar	Le **pregunté** al policía dónde estaba el correo.
(to ask)	*I asked the policeman where the post office was.*
pedir	Ella me **pidió** un favor.
(to ask for)	*She asked me for a favor.*

quedar	A María le **quedan** $20 para terminar el mes.
(to have left)	*Maria has $20 left until the end the month.*
(to be located)	Tijuana **queda** cerca de San Diego.
	Tijuana is (located) near San Diego.
quedarse	Vete tú que yo **me quedo** para esperar a los niños.
(to stay)	*You go and I'll stay to wait for the children.*
	Después de mirar muchos vestidos **me quedé** con el azul.
	After looking at a lot of dresses I kept the blue one.
quedar en	**Quedé** en encontrarme con mi amigo en el juego de pelota.
(to agree to)	*I agreed to meet my friend at the ball game.*

quitar	**Quitamos** las sillas que estaban en la terraza.
(to remove)	*We removed the chairs that were on the terrace.*
sacar	**Saqué** las llaves de la cartera y no sé dónde las puse.
(to take out)	*I took out the keys from my purse and I don't know where I put them.*

saber	Ella **sabe** mucho de astronomía.
(to know)	*She knows a lot about astronomy.*
conocer	No **conozco** la ciudad de Valparaíso.
(to know)	*I don't know (am not familiar with) the city of Valparaiso.*

salvar	Juan **salvó** al perro que se cayó en el río.
(to save)	*Juan saved the dog that fell into the river.*
ahorrar	Ellos **ahorran** dinero todos los meses.
(to save)	*They save money every month.*

Ejercicio

Escoja el verbo que sea correcto para completar el párrafo.

La familia que compró la casa al lado de la nuestra _____ (se movió / se mudó) ayer por la mañana. Por la tarde fui a saludarlos y les _____ (llevé / traje) una jarra (*pitcher*) con limonada fría, pues hacía mucho calor. La señora es joven y _____ (parece / se parece) muy simpática. Tiene dos niños, uno de nueve y otro de once años. Ella _____ (crea / cree) que las escuelas de esta área son mejores y por eso compraron la casa. Ella y su esposo quieren _____ (criar / crear) a sus hijos en un lugar lejos del centro de la ciudad. Ella no _____ (conocía / sabía) que yo era maestra de la escuela adonde irán sus hijos. Yo le dije que podría _____ (llevar / traer) a los niños de la escuela cuando ella no pudiera ir a buscarlos. Se puso muy contenta con mi ofrecimiento y _____ (se dio cuenta de / realizó) la buena suerte que tuvo al comprar la casa.

G Prefixes *des-*, *in-*, *re-*

1. The prefixes **des-** and **in-** are used to indicate the opposite meaning of the word.

acuerdo *(to agree)*	**desacuerdo**	comprensible *(comprehensible)*	**incomprensible**
hacer *(to do, make)*	**deshacer**	consciente *(conscious)*	**inconsciente**
heredar *(to inherit)*	**desheredar**	experto *(expert)*	**inexperto**
tejer *(to knit)*	**destejer**	satisfecho *(satisfy)*	**insatisfecho**
vestirse *(to get dressed)*	**desvestirse**	útil *(useful)*	**inútil**

A pesar del **desacuerdo** general del principio, los obreros llegaron a un acuerdo con el patrón.
In spite of the general disagreement at the beginning, the workers came to an agreement with the boss.
¡Qué hombre tan **inexperto**!   *What an inexperienced man!*

2. The prefix **re-** is used to emphasize or repeat the meaning of a word.

leer   **releer** *(to reread)* bonita   **rebonita** *(very pretty)*

hacer   **rehacer** *(to redo)*   tonta   **retonta** *(very foolish)*

Tuve que leer y **releer** las instrucciones varias veces para comprenderlas.
I had to read and reread the instructions several times in order to understand them.

Mural hecho en un edificio de San Francisco, California, por artistas méxicoamericanos.

Ejercicios

I. Dé el opuesto de las siguientes oraciones usando los prefijos **des-** e **in-**.

MODELO: El nuevo equipo resultó útil.
El nuevo equipo resultó inútil.

1. Raquel siempre habla en forma comprensible.
2. Tuvo una reacción consciente.
3. Acaban de alquilar el apartamento.
4. La vida es un continuo hacer.
5. Hay que vestirse rápidamente.

II. Transforme las frases según los modelos.

MODELOS: más que feo   **refeo**
volver a leer   **releer**

1. más que bueno
2. más que malo
3. más que linda
4. volver a hacer
5. volver a mirar

 # Composición

Antes de escribir, repase las siguientes reglas sobre las mayúsculas y la ortografía.

 ## A   Review of capitalization rules

Capital letters are used:

1. With all holidays and holy days

el Día de la Independencia   la Navidad
el Día de las Madres   la Semana Santa
el Día de la Amistad

2. With all abbreviations

Sr., Sra., Srta.   Dr., Dra.   Lic.   Uds.

3. After a colon when quoting an expression

Habló poco pero dijo mucho: "No dejes para mañana lo que puedas hacer hoy".
He spoke little, but said a lot: "Don't leave for tomorrow what you can do today."

B   Review of spelling rules: *ll, y, -ío, -illo, -illa*

1. Use **ll**:

   - In words ending in **-alla, -alle, -ello, -ella**:

     pantalla (*screen*), **calle, camello, paella**, except: **Pompeyo** (*Pompey*), **plebeyo** (*lower class*)

   - in the diminutive endings **-illa, -illo**:

     chiquilla, panecillo

   NOTE: Do not confuse the ending **-ía, -ío** with **-illa, -illo**. Use the dictionary if you are not sure.

mía (*mine*)	**milla** (*mile*)
comías (*you ate*)	**comillas** (*quotation marks*)
sombría (*gloomy*)	**sombrilla** (*beach umbrella*)

2. Use **y**:

   - In the preterite, imperfect subjunctive, and the present participle of verbs like **caer, creer, leer, oír**:

     cayó, creyera, leyendo, oyeron

   - In the present indicative and present subjunctive, the preterite, the imperfect subjunctive and the present participle of verbs, whose ending in the infinitive is **-uir**:

     atribuir   atribuyo   huir   huyó   contribuir   contribuyendo

   - The present subjunctive of **haber, ir**:

     haya, hayamos, vaya, vayan

   NOTE: The exercises corresponding to this section are included in the *Cuaderno de ejercicios*, Capítulo 6.

Ejercicio de composición (opcional)

Escriba una composición sobre el tema que se da a continuación. Use el esquema siguiente.

TEMA: El "graffiti" y los murales de una ciudad.

INTRODUCCIÓN: El "graffiti" ha sido usado como expresión de protesta y rebelión. Uso del "graffiti" por los movimientos políticos y los grupos de pandilleros (*gangs*) de una ciudad. Expresión de orgullo de una identidad cultural en los murales pintados en los muros y paredes de una ciudad.

DESARROLLO: Temas que aparecen en los "graffitis". Temas que predominan en los murales. ¿Existe sentido artístico en el "graffiti"? Diferencia entre los que pintan el "graffiti" y los que pintan los murales. Problemas que ocasiona el "graffiti" para las autoridades de una ciudad. Actitud del público con respecto al "graffiti" y con respecto a los murales. ¿Cómo son los murales que existen en su ciudad?

CONCLUSIÓN: Dé su apreciación personal del "graffiti" y de los murales. ¿Cree que se debe y se puede prohibir y controlar el "graffiti" en una ciudad? ¿Tiene algún comentario que hacer con respecto a estas dos manifestaciones de expresión pública?

Capítulo 7

Valle del río Aconcagua situado entre la Argentina y Chile con los majestuosos Andes al fondo.

LECTURAS

- Lectura 1: "Dos poetas chilenos: Mistral y Neruda"
- Lectura 2: "Yo no tengo soledad" de Gabriela Mistral
- Lectura 3: "Poema 20" de Pablo Neruda

GRAMÁTICA

- Subject pronouns
- Direct and indirect object pronouns
- Double object pronouns
- Reflexive pronouns
- Prepositional pronouns
- Expressions with **se**

COMPOSICIÓN

- Review of capitalization rules
- Review of spelling rules: **gue, gui, güe, güi**

189

Vocabulario

Antes de leer, repase el siguiente vocabulario que le ayudará a comprender la lectura.

Sustantivos

el **alma**   soul
el **campo**   field
la **carrera**   career
el **dolor**   pain, sorrow
el **extranjero**   abroad
la **fe**   faith
la **fuerza**   strength
el **inicio**   beginning

la **muerte**   death
la **naturaleza**   nature
la **noticia**   news
el **novio**   fiancé; boyfriend
el **poder**   force; power
el **puesto**   position; post, job
la **soledad**   solitude
el **título**   title

Verbos

cambiar   to change
crear   to create
combinar   to combine
convertir (ie) (i)   to convert
criar   to raise
dejar   to leave behind
esconder   to hide

entretenerse (g) (ie)   to amuse oneself
nacer (zc)   to be born
proporcionar   to provide; to supply
publicar   to publish
romper   to break
suicidarse   to commit suicide

Adjetivos

ambos   both
distinto   different

escondido   hidden
único   only

Adverbio

luego   later

Frases

llegar a + infinitivo   to come to…
cambiar de nombre   to change name

más tarde   later

Related words (Palabras relacionadas). The meaning of some words may be determined by thinking of related words familiar to you. Can you give in English the meaning of the underlined words derived from the words in parentheses?

1. (niño) … durante su <u>niñez</u> muy frecuentemente se entretenía conversando…
2. (nombrar) … combinó con éxito su mundo creativo con sus <u>nombramientos</u> diplomáticos…

3. (sentir) … Estos <u>sentimientos</u> de dolor… son evidentes en su obra.

4. (solo) … una profunda tristeza que se convirtió en gran <u>desolación</u>…

5. (triste) … Estas muertes llenaron el alma de Gabriela de una profunda <u>tristeza</u>…

NOTE: Some verbs change in meaning when they are used as reflexives.

cambiar	*to change*	cambiarse	*to change clothes*
convertir	*to convert; to change*	convertirse	*to become; to turn into*
entretener	*to entertain*	entretenerse	*to amuse oneself*

Be careful with these false cognates:

noticia	*news*	notar	*to notice*
éxito	*success*	salida	*exit*
extranjero	*abroad; foreigner*	extraño	*stranger*
único	*only* (la única obra)	único	*unique, original* (una obra única)

Lectura 1

Dos poetas chilenos: Mistral y Neruda

Gabriela Mistral y Pablo Neruda, dos grandes figuras de la poesía chilena, están unidos por más de una circunstancia común. Los dos nacieron en pueblos pequeños de Chile, ambos decidieron cambiar sus verdaderos nombres por otros y además recibieron el Premio Nobel de Literatura.

5   Lucila Godoy Alcayaga, quien más tarde cambió su verdadero nombre por el de Gabriela Mistral, nació en 1889 en un pequeño pueblo escondido en las montañas de los Andes, en el norte de Chile. Pasó los primeros años de su vida en perfecta comunión con la naturaleza, y durante su niñez muy frecuentemente se entretenía conversando con las

10 flores, los árboles y los pájaros.

    Gabriela Mistral comenzó a enseñar a la edad de quince años. El trabajo de maestra de pueblo pequeño fue el inicio de su carrera profesional de educadora y humanista. Más tarde, llegó a ocupar puestos importantes en el campo de la educación y en el servicio diplomático de

15 Chile en el extranjero.

    La vida de esta mujer estuvo siempre marcada por la tragedia. El primer y único novio de Gabriela Mistral se suicidó a los veintidós años y, luego, el sobrino que ella había criado y quería como a un hijo, se suicidó también. Estas muertes llenaron el alma de Gabriela de una profunda

Gabriela Mistral recibiendo el Premio Nobel de Literatura de manos del rey de Suecia en 1945.

Pablo Neruda, Premio Nobel de Literatura, 1971.

20   tristeza que se convirtió en gran desolación cuando recibió la noticia del suicidio, en el Brasil, de sus amigos más queridos e íntimos, Stefan Zweig* y su señora. Estos sentimientos de dolor, junto a una ternura maternal por los niños, y más tarde una fe vehemente en Dios, son evidentes en su obra poética.

25   En 1945 Gabriela Mistral recibió el Premio Nobel de Literatura. Su poesía refleja° su gran amor por todos los niños, un humanismo   *reflects* apasionado, un intenso poder emocional y gran fuerza lírica. En 1957 Gabriela Mistral murió en la ciudad de Nueva York.

Pablo Neruda, uno de los más altos valores° de la lírica hispana, nació   *worthy figures*
30   en Parral, Chile, en 1904. Su verdadero nombre era Neftalí Ricardo Reyes el cual cambió por el de Pablo Neruda al principio de su carrera poética. El paisaje chileno de montañas y desiertos ayudó a formar el alma del poeta y, siendo muy joven, se fue a vivir a la capital. A los veintitrés años, Neruda comenzó su carrera diplomática, la cual le proporcionó la
35   oportunidad de viajar por distintos países del Oriente, de Europa y de Latinoamérica.

De convicciones políticas marxistas, Neruda combinó con éxito su mundo creativo con sus nombramientos diplomáticos y actividades políticas, poniendo su gran talento poético, como miembro del Partido
40   Comunista, al servicio de una ideología totalitaria.

Neruda publicó sus dos primeros libros cuando tenía veinte años. La

*Stefan Zweig (1881–1942), escritor austriaco.

obra poética de Neruda se caracteriza por una evolución constante que
expresa las impresiones y cambios que tuvo en su vida. Sus primeros
poemas líricos y románticos se transforman más tarde en una creación
45   más espiritual, más introvertida y más enigmática. Rompió con las formas
tradicionales de la poesía y creó un mundo lleno de símbolos e imágenes
personales.

    Neruda recibió el Premio Nobel de Literatura en 1971. Al morir en
1973 en Chile, Neruda le dejó al mundo una extensa y magnífica obra
50   poética. Sus memorias fueron publicadas después de su muerte bajo el
título de *Confieso que he vivido*.

Complete las oraciones con la palabra que corresponde.

1. Ahora no puedo pasar por tu casa; pasaré a verte _____ .
2. Desde aquí no se puede ver el pueblo; está _____ detrás de la montaña.
3. En su juventud el escritor _____ _____ _____ ; no
   quiso usar su nombre verdadero.
4. _____ Gabriela Mistral y Pablo Neruda nacieron en Chile.
5. Gabriela Mistral salió de Chile y vivió varios años en _____ .
6. Gabriela Mistral _____ a su sobrino con mucha ternura.
7. Hace tiempo que el escritor trabaja allí porque tiene muy buen _____
   en el Ministerio de Educación.
8. Gabriela Mistral _____ jugando en el jardín.
9. El _____ del poeta se debió a la magnífica calidad de su talento poético.
10. Neruda pudo _____ su mundo creativo con su carrera diplomática.

Preguntas sobre la lectura

1. ¿Qué similaridades existen en la vida de Gabriela Mistral y Pablo Neruda?
2. ¿Qué sentimientos abundan en la poesía de Gabriela Mistral?
3. ¿Por qué se dice que la vida de Gabriela Mistral estuvo marcada por la tragedia?
4. ¿En qué aspectos de la vida piensan de manera diferente los dos poetas?
5. ¿Qué cambios se notan en la poesía de Neruda?
6. ¿Siguió Neruda las formas tradicionales de la poesía?

Temas de conversación

1. Si Ud. estuviera en el campo de la educación, ¿qué le interesaría más: estar en la
   administración o estar enseñando en contacto con los estudiantes? ¿Le gustaría ser
   decano, director de una escuela secundaria o consejero? ¿Ha tenido Ud. un
   consejero que le haya ayudado en su educación? ¿En qué sentido?
2. ¿Le gustaría a Ud. estar en el servicio diplomático de su país? Explique su respuesta.
3. Es importante proteger la naturaleza. ¿Cree Ud. que se están haciendo suficientes
   esfuerzos para no destruirla? ¿Comparte Ud. estas ideas?

ectura 2

"Yo no tengo soledad" de Gabriela Mistral

Es la noche desamparo°   *abandonment*
de las sierras hasta el mar.
Pero yo, la que te mece,°   *rocks*
¡yo no tengo soledad!°   *solitude*

5   Es el cielo desamparo
pues la luna cae al mar.
Pero yo la que te estrecha,°   *hugs*
¡yo no tengo soledad!

Es el mundo desamparo.
10   Toda carne triste va.
Pero yo, la que te oprime,°   *holds close to me*
¡yo no tengo soledad!

De *Ternura* (1924)

Preguntas sobre la lectura

1. En este poema la poeta termina las tres estrofas con las mismas palabras. ¿Qué efecto produce esto al leerlo?
2. La palabra "desamparo" se repite en el primer verso de cada estrofa. ¿Qué cosas no le ofrecen protección o consuelo (*consolation*) a la autora?
3. ¿Por qué dice la autora que no tiene soledad?
4. ¿Qué sentimiento principal predomina en este poema?

Uocabulario

Antes de leer, repase el siguiente vocabulario que le ayudara a comprender la lectura.

Sustantivos

el cielo sky; heaven	**el olvido** forgetfulness	**el rocío** dew
la estrella star	**el pasto** pasture	**el viento** wind

Verbos

acercar (qu) to bring or place near	**girar** to revolve
besar to kiss	**guardar** to keep
contentarse to be content	**tocar (qu)** to touch

Adjetivos

corto short	**estrellado** with stars	**largo** long

Lectura 3

"Poema 20" de Pablo Neruda

Puedo escribir los versos más tristes esta noche.

Escribir, por ejemplo, "La noche está estrellada,
y tiritan,° azules, los astros,° a lo lejos".   *twinkle / stars*

El viento de la noche gira en el cielo y canta.

5 Puedo escribir los versos más tristes esta noche.
Yo la quise, y a veces ella también me quiso.

En las noches como ésta la tuve entre mis brazos.
La besé tantas veces bajo el cielo infinito.

Ella me quiso, a veces yo también la quería.
10 ¡Cómo no haber amado sus grandes ojos fijos!

Puedo escribir los versos más tristes esta noche.
Pensar que no la tengo. Sentir que la he perdido.

Oír la noche inmensa, más inmensa sin ella.
Y el verso cae al alma como al pasto el rocío.

15 ¡Qué importa que mi amor no pudiera guardarla!
La noche está estrellada y ella no está conmigo.

Eso es todo. A lo lejos alguien canta. A lo lejos.
Mi alma no se contenta° en haberla perdido.   *is not happy*

Como para acercarla mi mirada la busca.
20 Mi corazón la busca, y ella no está conmigo.

La misma noche que hace blanquear° los mismos árboles.   *whiten*
Nosotros, los de entonces,° ya no somos los mismos.   *other times*

Ya no la quiero, es cierto, pero cuánto la quise.
Mi voz buscaba al viento para tocar su oído.°   *ear*

25 De otro. Será de otro. Como antes° de mis besos.   *As before*
Su voz, su cuerpo claro. Sus ojos infinitos.

Ya no la quiero, es cierto, pero tal vez la quiero.
Es tan corto el amor y tan largo el olvido.°   *forgetfulness*

Porque en noches como ésta la tuve entre mis brazos,
30 mi alma no se contenta con haberla perdido.

Aunque éste sea el último dolor que ella me causa,
y éstos sean los últimos versos que yo le escribo.

De *Veinte poemas de amor y una canción desesperada* (1924)

Preguntas sobre la lectura

1. ¿Cuál es la causa de la tristeza del poeta?
2. La naturaleza no ha cambiado, pero los amantes sí. ¿Qué cambios se han producido en ellos?
3. Mencione los dos versos en que se expresa más o menos lo siguiente: La noche le parece al poeta más enorme porque está sin la amada y el escribir poesía le hace bien a su alma.
4. ¿Cómo interpreta Ud. el verso: "Es tan corto el amor y tan largo el olvido"?
5. ¿Por qué cree Ud. que el poeta repite el primer verso varias veces?

Gramática

A Subject pronouns

PRONOUNS

Subject	Direct object	Indirect object	Reflexive	Prepositional pronouns
yo	me	me	me	mí
tú	te	te	te	ti
Ud.	lo, la	le (se)	se	Ud.
él	lo (le)*	le (se)	se	él
ella	la	le (se)	se	ella
nosotros/as	nos	nos	nos	nosotros/as
vosotros/as	os	os	os	vosotros/as
Uds.	los, las	les (se)	se	Uds.
ellos	los (les)*	les (se)	se	ellos
ellas	las	les (se)	se	ellas
ello (neuter)	lo (neuter)			ello (neuter)

*le, les, as direct objects, may be used instead of lo, los referring to *you* (m.) *him, them* (m.).

Yo visito a Juan.	Yo le visito.
I visit Juan.	*I visit him.*

1. Subject pronouns may be omitted when there is no ambiguity because the ending of the verb indicates person and number.

No **puedo** ir.	**Hablas** mucho.	**Salimos** tarde.
I can't go.	*You talk a lot.*	*We left late.*

2. Subject pronouns are used in the following cases:

   a. To emphasize the subject. In this case its use is only emphatic.

Yo se lo dije.	**Tú** estás loca.
I told it to him/her.	*You are crazy.*

Las impresionantes cataratas del Iguazú situadas entre la Argentina, el Brasil y el Paraguay.

b. With verb forms when there is ambiguity, to avoid confusion.

Yo
Ud.
Él   } iba a la plaza todas las mañanas.
Ella

(I, you, he, she) used to go to the square every morning.

c. When there are two verbs and two different subjects.

Ella va al centro, pero **yo** no voy.   *She goes downtown, but I don't go.*

3. The pronoun **usted** —**Ud.** or **Vd.**— is the formal way to address the person to whom we speak. It is derived from "Vuestra Merced," the form that was used in old times. In Spanish America, **Uds.** is used as the plural of **tú** and **Ud.**; in Spain, the form **vosotros (-as)** is used as the plural of **tú**.

4. The neuter pronoun **ello**, used as a subject, is used less frequently. It refers to an idea or situation that has been mentioned previously.

El gobierno quiere controlar   *The government wants to control*
    la inflación.   *inflation.*
Ello va a ser imposible.   *That's going to be impossible.*

NOTE: These days it is more common to use **esto** (*this*) or **eso** (*that*) instead of **ello**.

5. The English pronoun *it,* used as a subject, has no translation in Spanish.

    Llueve mucho.   *It rains a lot.*
    Es caro.   *It is expensive.*
    Es tarde.   *It is late.*
    Está sobre la mesa.   *It is on the table.*

6. In contrast to English, Spanish uses the subject pronouns **yo** and **tú** instead of the prepositional forms **mí** and **ti** after **excepto, según, incluso, como,** and **entre.**

    excepto él (ella, ellos, ellas)   *except him (her, them)*
    según él (ella, ellos, ellas)   *according to him (her, them)*
    incluso él (ella, ellos, ellas)   *including him (her, them)*
    como él (ella, ellos, ellas)   *like him (her, them)*
    entre tú y yo   *between you and me*

Ejercicios

I. Los pronombres sujeto se han omitido en estas oraciones porque el verbo indica el sujeto correspondiente. El usarlos sería redundante. Muestre su conocimiento y diga cuál es el sujeto que corresponde a cada verbo numerado.

José y Luis son muy divertidos y _____ bailan muy bien.

_____ quiero que _____ me des su número de teléfono

para que _____ podamos invitarlos a nuestra fiesta.

II. Traduzca las oraciones al español.

1. *It is easy.*
2. *It rained last night.*
3. *They all came, except him.*
4. *Felicia is not like her.*
5. *I invited all the students, including her.*
6. *According to them, the house is very big.*

B Direct and indirect object pronouns*

1. Pronouns

   a. A direct object pronoun refers to the direct object noun (person, place, or thing) previously mentioned. The direct object pronoun reflects the number and gender of the noun.

       Jorge mira el programa pero yo no **lo** miro.
       Jorge watches the program but I don't watch it.
       ¿Escribiste la carta? Sí, **la** escribí y **la** puse en el correo.
       Did you write the letter? Yes, I wrote it and I put it in the mail.
       ¿Llamaste a tu hermano? Sí, **lo** llamé por la mañana.
       Did you call your brother? Yes, I called him in the morning.
       ¿Quién tiene los pasajes? **Los** tengo yo.
       Who has the tickets? I have them.

---

*The definition of direct and indirect object appears in the Capítulo preliminar, page 18.

b. The English pronoun **it**, used as a direct object, is translated as **lo** or **la**.

¿Compró Pepe **un televisor** nuevo?	*Did Pepe buy a new television set?*
Sí, **lo** compró y **lo** tiene en su cuarto.	*Yes, he bought it and he has it in his room.*
¿Toca Elena **la guitarra**?	*Does Elena play the guitar?*
Sí, **la** toca, aunque no muy bien.	*Yes, she plays it, although not very well.*

As a prepositional pronoun, *it* is translated using the subject pronouns.

¿Salió el gato por **la ventana**?	*Did the cat go out through the window?*
Sí, salió por **ella**.	*Yes, he went out through it.*

c. Note that the direct and indirect object pronouns are identical, except in the third person singular and plural, where **le** and **les** are used as indirect object pronouns.

d. Note the meaning of the following sentences, which change according to the direct or indirect object pronoun.

(¿A Carmela?) **Le** pagué la renta.	*(Carmela?)I paid her the rent.*
	(I paid the rent for her.)
(¿La renta?) **La** pagúe ayer.	*(The rent?) I paid it yesterday.*

NOTE: Le refers to the indirect object (the person to or for whom I paid the rent); while in the example **la pagué ayer, la** is the direct object (the rent).

2. Position of direct and indirect object pronouns

a. Both direct and indirect object pronouns normally precede a conjugated verb.

Pepe **me** ve.	*Pepe sees me.*
Luis **me** escribió.	*Luis wrote to me.*
Los llamaré mañana.	*I'll call them tomorrow.*
Marta **les** ha regalado una bicicleta.	*Marta has given them a bicycle.*

b. Direct and indirect object pronouns follow and are attached to infinitives and present participles.

Para abrir**la** necesitamos la llave de esa gaveta.
In order to open it we need the key to that drawer.
Llamándo**lo**,* me di cuenta de que no estaba en casa.
By calling him, I realized he wasn't at home.

When the infinitive or present participle follows a conjugated verb there are two options: the object pronouns may either precede the conjugated verb or be attached to the infinitive or present participle.

Me quiere conquistar. Quiere conquistar**me**.	*He wants to win me over.*
Nos va a explicar. Va a explicar**nos**.	*He's going to explain to us.*
Lo está haciendo. Está haciéndo**lo**.	*She is doing it.*
Las desea escuchar. Desea escuchar**las**.	*She wants to listen to them.*

c. Object pronouns are attached to affirmative commands; they precede negative commands.

díga**me** *tell me*	no **me** diga *don't tell me*	ábran**las** *open them*	no **las** abran *don't open them*
haz**lo** *do it*	no **lo** hagas *don't do it*	dé**le** *give him*	no **le** dé *don't give him*

---

*Note that an accent mark is required when adding a pronoun to a present pariciple.

3. Redundant use of an indirect object pronoun and a prepositional phrase with **a** + a noun or pronoun

  a. A prepositional phrase is commonly used in combination with an indirect object.

Le escribo **a Ud.**	(Le → a Ud.)	*I write to you.*
Les doy los papeles **a Uds.**	(Les → a Uds.)	*I give the papers to you.*
Le enseño el mapa **a Ricardo**.	(Le → a Ricardo)	*I show the map to Ricardo.*
Les envío la carta **a Irene y a Rodolfo**.	(Les → a Irene y a Rodolfo)	*I send the letter to Irene and Rodolfo.*
Nos entregaron las llaves **a Enrique y a mí**.	(Nos → a Enrique y a mí)	*They gave the keys to Enrique and to me.*

  In the case of **le** and **les** the prepositional phrase may be used when there is ambiguity.

Le leo el cuento	⎰	**a Ud.** **a él.** **a ella.**	*I read the story*	⎰ to you. to him. to her.
Les muestro la casa	⎰	**a Uds.** **a ellos.** **a ellas.**	*I show the house*	⎰ to you. to them (m.). to them (f.).

  b. The explanatory prepositional phrase is rarely used with the direct object.

Lo admiro	⎰	(a Ud.). (a él).	*I admire*	⎰ you him.
Los vi	⎰	(a Uds.). (a ellos).	*I saw*	⎰ you. them.
La comprendo	⎰	(a Ud.) (a ella)	*I understand*	⎰ you. her.
Las esperé	⎰	(a Uds.) (a ellas)	*I waited for*	⎰ you. them (f).

  Sometimes the direct object precedes the verb and in this case the object pronoun is also used.

A Ofelia la conocí ayer.	(A Ofelia → la)	*I met Ofelia yesterday.*
El vestido lo lavé a mano.	(El vestido → lo)	*I washed the dress by hand.*
La paella la preparó mi padre.	(La paella → la)	*My father prepared the paella.*

Ejercicios

I. Ud. y su amigo van a ir al desfile. Conteste las preguntas que le hace su amigo usando un pronombre de complemento en la respuesta.

  MODELO: ¿Llevarás a tu familia al desfile?
  Sí, la llevaré. o No, no la llevaré.

  1. ¿Has visto alguna vez (*ever*) el Desfile de las Rosas de California?
  2. ¿Conoces la historia de este desfile anual?
  3. ¿Verán Uds. el desfile desde un balcón?

4. ¿Leíste en el periódico el orden del programa?

5. ¿Sacarás fotos de las carrozas (*floats*) llenas de flores?

6. ¿Tienes las entradas para el partido de fútbol después del desfile?

II. Ud. les va a comprar una computadora a sus hijos. Complete las frases, según el modelo, colocando los pronombres con los infinitivos y gerundios o participios presentes.

MODELO: ¿A quiénes les vas a comprar una computadora?

_____ una computadora a Rubén y a Carolina.

Voy a comprarles una computadora a Rubén y a Carolina.

1. ¿Quién les va a hacer una demostración?

El vendedor _____ una demostración a mis hijos.

2. ¿Cuándo la puede instalar el técnico?

El técnico _____ el próximo lunes.

3. ¿Le siguen interesando las ciencias a Rubén?

Sí, _____ las ciencias y también ahora las artes.

4. ¿Piensas usar tú también la computadora?

Sí, _____ para escribir mis cartas.

III. Ud. supervisa el trabajo de los camareros en un restaurante y contesta las preguntas que le hacen con un mandato.

MODELO: ¿Limpio las mesas?

Sí, límpielas.

1. ¿Doblo las servilletas?

2. ¿Traemos las copas de vino?

3. ¿Secamos los cuchillos?

4. ¿Pongo los platos en las mesas?

IV. Complete las oraciones con los pronombres de complemento indirecto que correspondan.

1. ¿Por qué Fernando no _____ dice la verdad a Luisa?

2. Él dice que yo comprendo sus problemas y por eso él _____ cuenta todo a mí.

3. Él _____ va a escribir a sus suegros (*in-laws*) y _____ pedirá ayuda a ellos.

4. Fernando _____ explicará sus planes a Luisa y a mí.

5. Ella dice que _____ dijo a ti mismo lo que ella quería hacer este verano.

V. Complete las oraciones con los pronombres de complemento indirecto que correspondan.

1. El agente _____ entregó los pasajes a los viajeros.

   _____ dio los horarios (*schedules*) de vuelo a mi marido y a mí.

2. El empleado de inmigración _____ ha devuelto el pasaporte a la Sra. Portera.

3. El guía _____ mostrará a los turistas todos los monumentos de la ciudad.

VI. Diálogo entre Elsa y su hermana. Complete las ideas con los pronombres de complemento que sean necesarios.

Hermana: ¿Qué sabes de Fefita?

Elsa: ¡Qué tonta soy! ¿No _____ dije que recibí una carta de ella que _____ escribió desde Barcelona?

Hermana: No _____ dijiste nada.

Elsa: _____ manda a ti un abrazo. _____ dice que España es un país muy interesante y que sus amigos españoles _____ han llevado a visitar muchos lugares hermosos. Pero _____ parece que ya tiene ganas de regresar. Dice que _____ extraña mucho a ti y a mí.

Hermana: El tiempo se va muy rápido. Ya pronto _____ tendremos aquí de vuelta.

Elsa: Eso es verdad. _____ voy a escribir mañana. ¿Quieres que _____ dé algún recado (*message*) tuyo?

Hermana: Sí, _____ dices que quiero que _____ traiga el plato de porcelana de Talavera que _____ pedí.

Elsa: ¿No _____ parece que es demasiado problema el traer una cosa tan frágil?

Hermana: Es verdad, pero ella _____ dijo que _____ traería cualquier cosa que yo _____ pidiera.

C Double object pronouns

1. When two object pronouns are used in the same sentence, the indirect precedes the direct. Remember that object pronouns precede a conjugated verb; they follow and are attached to infinitives, present participles and affirmative commands.

Pedro **me lo dice**.	*Pedro tells it to me.*
Voy a **preparártela**.	*I am going to prepare it for you.*
Ella **te la enseñará**.	*She will show it to you.*
Están **explicándonoslo**.	*They are explaining it to us.*
Ellos **nos los han dado**.	*They have given them to us.*
Muéstremelos.	*Show them to me.*

Note that an accent mark is required when adding pronouns to infinitives, present participles, and commands.

2. The pronoun **se** replaces **le, les** when used before **lo, la, los, las**.

Ernestina le escribe una carta a **su madre**.	*Ernestina writes a letter to her mother.*
Ernestina **le** escribe **una carta**.	*Ernestina writes her a letter.*
Ernestina **se la** escribe.	*Ernestina writes it to her.*
Les prestaré mi **libro** a Uds.	*I will lend you my book.*
Se lo prestaré a Uds.	*I will lend it to you.*
Ella **les** ha explicado **las lecciones**.	*She has explained the lessons to them.*
Ella **se las** ha explicado.	*She has explained them to them.*

3. The neuter pronoun **lo** refers to an idea or concept that has been previously expressed.

¿Crees que llueva mañana?	*Do you think it will rain tomorrow?*
—No, no **lo** creo.	*No, I don't think so.*
¿Está Ud. loco? —Seguramente **lo** estoy.	*Are you crazy? Surely I am.*
¿Son ellos uruguayos? —Sí, **lo** son.	*Are they Uruguayan? Yes, they are.*
¿Sabes que Julia se casó? —Sí, **lo** sé.	*Do you know that Julia got married? Yes, I know it.*

a. The construction of **lo** + a masculine singular adjective expresses the idea of "the thing or the part + adjective."

> **Lo extraño** es que el perro no ladró anoche.
> *The strange thing is that the dog did not bark last night.*
> **Lo bueno** es que no tenemos clase hoy.
> *The good thing is that we don't have class today.*

b. When used with adjectives (masculine or feminine, singular or plural) **lo** is the equivalent of the English *how*.

No puedes imaginarte **lo cansada** que estoy.	*You can't imagine how tired I am.*
Tengo que decirte **lo feliz** que está mi sobrina.	*I have to tell you how happy my niece is.*

Ejercicios

I. Conteste afirmativamente las preguntas, usando en las respuestas pronombres de complemento. Haga los cambios necesarios.

> **MODELO:** ¿Les explicaste la situación a los accionistas (*shareholders*)?
> **Sí, se la expliqué.**

1. ¿Le dejó ella el contrato al abogado?
2. ¿Me trajiste los papeles?
3. ¿Me puedes firmar estas cartas?
4. ¿Te dieron los certificados?
5. ¿Les vas a enviar el dinero a los accionistas?

II. Ud. tiene un amigo que es muy preguntón (*nosy*). Conteste sus preguntas usando en las respuestas la información que está entre paréntesis y los pronombres de complemento.

> **MODELO:** ¿A quién le pides ayuda cuando necesitas algo? (a mi padre)
> **Se la pido a mi padre.**

1. ¿A quiénes les prestas tus discos? (a mis amigos)
2. ¿A quiénes les dio sus libros el profesor? (a los estudiantes)
3. ¿A quién le regaló Roberto una enciclopedia? (a su sobrino)
4. ¿A quién le cuentas tus problemas? (a mi mejor amigo)
5. ¿A quién le envió tu hermano un telegrama? (al rector de la universidad)

III. Usando la información dada, escriba oraciones reemplazando los nombres subrayados por pronombres de complemento.

> **MODELO:** di / los libros / al profesor
> **Se los di.**

1. mi primo / escribió / una carta / al director
2. mandé / las flores / a la cantante
3. los turistas / visitaron / las ruinas mayas
4. escribí / a Matilde / la carta de recomendación
5. ¿pidieron / las llaves del carro / al abuelo?

IV. Conteste las preguntas traduciendo al español las frases que están en inglés. Después cambie esos mandatos al negativo.

> **MODELO:** ¿Los periódicos? (*Take them with you.*)
> **Lléveselos.**
> **No se los lleve.**

1. ¿La verdad? (*Tell it to me.*)
2. ¿Los exámenes? (*Give them to him.*)
3. ¿El paquete? (*Send it to Luisa.*)
4. ¿Las flores? (*Bring them to us.*)
5. ¿El café? (*Serve it to us.*)

V. Su compañero de clase le hace preguntas sobre el escritor Gabriel García Márquez. Conteste sus preguntas usando el pronombre neutro **lo** en la respuesta.

> **MODELO:** ¿Es bueno ese libro?
>
> **Sí, lo es.**

1. ¿Son interesantes las obras de García Márquez?
2. ¿Es colombiano?
3. ¿Estás de acuerdo con la crítica de sus obras?
4. ¿Están traducidas sus novelas al inglés?

VI. Traduzca al español las frases que están en inglés para contestar las preguntas. Use una construcción con el pronombre neutro **lo**.

1. ¿Qué dice Camila? (*How tired she is.*)
2. ¿Cómo es la novia de Andrés? (*You cannot imagine how pretty she is.*)
3. ¿Qué vas a hacer con tu carro? (*The best thing is to change it.*)
4. ¿Vamos en autobús? (*The bad thing is that it is always late.*)
5. ¿Qué dices? (*How difficult it is to learn a language.*)

VII. Complete las oraciones con un complemento directo. Construya después una oración usando un pronombre de complemento directo.

> **MODELO:** Yo hago...
>
> **Yo hago ejercicios. Los hago todos los días porque quiero tener buena figura.**

1. Visito a...
2. Compré...
3. Elena lleva…
4. Queremos ver…

VIII. ¿Qué hace Ud. normalmente en las circunstancias que se mencionan a continuación? En sus oraciones use pronombres de complemento directo o indirecto.

> **MODELO:** Es el cumpleaños de un amigo.
>
> **Yo le compro un regalo a mi amigo y se lo llevo.**

1. Su abuelo está en el hospital.
2. Su amigo necesita dinero.
3. Su hermana se gradúa.
4. Es el aniversario de bodas de sus padres.
5. Es el Día de las Madres.

IX. Ud. conversa con una amiga sobre su viaje a Puerto Rico. Complete el diálogo con los pronombres que correspondan.

Ud.: Mañana salgo para Puerto Rico para asistir a la conferencia de hispanistas.

Amiga: ¿Conoces la ciudad de San Juan?

Ud.: No _____ conozco. Por eso principalmente voy a la reunión.

Amiga: ¿ _____ avisaste a tu amiga Aida para que _____ espere en el aeropuerto?

Ud.: Sí, _____ llamé por teléfono y _____ dije la hora de mi llegada. Ella _____ va a hacer el favor de hacer la reservación del hotel. _____ va a hacer en un hotel antiguo que está en el Viejo San Juan.

D Reflexive pronouns

1. The reflexive pronouns **me, te, se, nos, se** are used with reflexive verbs, that is, when the receiver of the action is the same as the doer. As we shall see later, reflexive verbs may also be used to express a reciprocal relationship between two or more persons, and to assign a special meaning to a verb when used reflexively.

Alberto **se afeita, se baña** y **se desayuna** antes de ir al trabajo y siempre sale tarde.	*Alberto shaves, takes a bath, and eats breakfast before going to work and he always leaves late.*
Pablo y Virginia **se aman** con locura.	*Pablo and Virginia love each other madly.*
Ellos y yo no **nos hablamos**.	*They and I do not speak to one another.*

a. Many transitive verbs* can be used as reflexive verbs.

Lavo la ropa.	**Me lavo** la cara.
I wash the clothes.	*I wash my face.*
Elisa **peina** a la niña.	Elisa **se peina**.
Elisa combs the girl's hair.	*Elisa combs her hair.*
Ponemos el abrigo en el armario.	**Nos ponemos** el abrigo.
We put the coat in the armoire.	*We put on our coat.*
¿**Bañaste** al perro?	**Te bañaste** de prisa.
Did you give the dog a bath?	*You bathed in a hurry.*

b. Some verbs, due to their meaning, are used reflexively. In some cases they are followed by the prepositions **a, de,** or **en**.

arrepentirse (de)	*to repent, to regret*	**empeñarse (en)**	*to insist on*
asomarse (a)	*to look out of*	**enterarse (de)**	*to find out*
alegrarse (de)	*to rejoice*	**equivocarse**	*to make a mistake*
atreverse (a)	*to dare*	**portarse bien (mal)**	*to behave (misbehave)*
burlarse (de)	*to make fun of*	**resignarse**	*to resign oneself*
darse cuenta (de)	*to realize*	**suicidarse**	*to commit suicide*

*See Capítulo preliminar, page 17.

Me **resigno** a mi suerte.	*I resign myself to my luck.*
Ella **se dio cuenta de** su error.	*She realized her error.*
La niña **se ha empeñado** en que la llevemos a patinar.	*The girl has insisted that we take her skating.*
El pobre hombre **se suicidó** anoche.	*The poor man committed suicide last night.*
Me **arrepiento** de lo que dije.	*I regret what I said.*

2. Position of reflexive pronouns. Like direct and indirect object pronouns, reflexive pronouns precede a conjugated verb; they are attached to infinitives, present participles, and affirmative commands, but precede negative commands.

Nos sentamos a descansar.	*We sat down to rest.*
Esperan **despertarse** temprano.	*They hope to wake up early.*
Estaba **desayunándose** cuando la llamé.	*She was having breakfast when I called her.*
¡Cállense!	*Be quiet!*
No **se bañen** en el río porque es peligroso.	*Don't bathe in the river because it is dangerous.*

a. When there are two pronouns, the reflexive pronoun precedes the direct object pronoun.

Luisa **se lo** pone.	*Luisa puts it on.*
Me los probé.	*I tried them on.*
Nos los quitamos.	*We took them off.*

b. In the affirmative commands with **nosotros**, the final **-s** of the verb form is omitted when adding the reflexive pronoun **nos.** (The equivalent of this construction in English is *let's . . .*).*

Sentémonos. *(Let's sit down.)*	**No nos sentemos.** *(Let's not sit down.)*
Vistámonos. *(Let's get dressed.)*	**No nos vistamos.** *(Let's not get dressed.)*

NOTE: The command for **irse** is:

Vámonos. *(Let's go.)*   **No nos vayamos.** *(Let's not go.)*

c. In affirmative commands with **vosotros**, the final **-d** of the verb form is omitted when adding the reflexive pronoun **os.**

Lavad (vosotros) las ventanas *(Wash the windows.)*
No **lavéis** las ventanas. *(Don't wash the windows.)*
Lavaos. *(Wash yourselves.)*
No os lavéis. *(Don't wash yourselves.)*

3. Some verbs change meaning when used as reflexives.

abonar	*to fertilize; to pay*	**abonarse**	*to subscribe*
acordar	*to agree to*	**acordarse de**	*to remember*
acostar	*to put to bed*	**acostarse**	*to go to bed*
alegrar	*to cheer up*	**alegrarse de**	*to be glad; to rejoice*
casar	*to marry*	**casarse**	*to get married*
conducir	*to drive*	**conducirse**	*to behave*

---

*See the imperative, Capítulo 4, page 119.

despedir	to dismiss	despedirse	to say good-bye
ir	to go	irse	to go away, to leave
levantar	to lift	levantarse	to get up, to stand up
llamar	to call	llamarse	to be called
llevar	to carry; to take	llevarse	to take away
negar	to deny	negarse	to refuse
parecer	to seem; to look like	parecerse	to look alike
poner	to put	ponerse	to put on
probar	to taste; to try	probarse	to try on
quitar	to take away	quitarse	to take off
volver	to return	volverse	to turn around; to become

Él **parece** un payaso.	*He looks like a clown.*
Ella **se parece** a su madre.	*He looks like his mother.*
El ministro **casó** a los novios.	*The minister married the bride and groom.*
Ellos **se casarán** en la primavera.	*They will get married in spring.*
Llevo a los niños a la escuela.	*I take the children to school.*
El ladrón **se llevó** las joyas.	*The thief carried off the jewels.*

Ejercicios

I. Conteste las preguntas usando en las respuestas un verbo reflexivo y la información que está entre paréntesis.

> **MODELO:** ¿Qué hace Ud. cuando tiene frío? (un abrigo)
> **Me pongo un abrigo.**

1. ¿Qué hace Ud. cuando le duelen los pies? (los zapatos)
2. ¿Cuál es el nombre del mecánico? (Gilberto Rojas)
3. ¿Para qué va su hermano a la barbería? (el pelo)
4. ¿Qué hace Ud. cuando quiere ver si está bien peinado? (en el espejo) *(mirror)*
5. ¿Qué hace Ud. cuando tiene sueño? (en la cama)

II. Conteste las preguntas con respuestas originales usando los verbos reflexivos que están entre paréntesis.

> **MODELO:** ¿Qué le pasó al niño que está llorando? (cortarse)
> **Se cortó un dedo con el cuchillo.**

1. ¿Qué le pasó a Pedro en el examen? (equivocarse)
2. ¿Cómo la pasaron tus primos en la fiesta? (divertirse)
3. ¿Qué haces para no llegar tarde al trabajo? (levantarse)
4. ¿Qué le pasa a tu papá cuando tardas en llegar por la noche? (preocuparse)
5. ¿Por qué no te gusta que te visiten los niños de tu hermana? (portarse)
6. ¿Qué les pasa a tus abuelos cuando los visitas? (alegrarse)

III. Escoja el verbo correcto y complete las frases. Use el tiempo verbal que sea necesario.

1. (probar / probarse) Ayer en la tienda Elena _____ un traje que le quedaba muy bien.

2. (negar / negarse) Anoche en la cena Lupita _____ a comer el postre porque está a dieta.

3. (acostar / acostarse) Marta siempre _____ a los niños a las ocho, pero ella no _____ hasta las once.

4. (ir / irse) Yo _____ a la reunión la semana pasada, pero a las diez _____ porque estaba muy cansado.

5. (casar / casarse) Humberto _____ mañana por la tarde con la hija del alcalde.

6. (llevar / llevarse) Todos los días (yo) _____ a los niños a la escuela.

7. (quitar / quitarse) Cuando compré la casa _____ el papel de las paredes porque no me gustaba.

8. (despedir / despedirse) Cuando _____ de ellos estábamos todos muy tristes.

9. (acordar / acordarse) Estela nunca _____ donde deja las llaves.

10. (parecer / parecerse) Alicia _____ mucho a su madre.

IV. Cambie la construcción **ir a** + infinitivo a un mandato.

MODELO: Vamos a acostarnos temprano.
   Acostémonos temprano.

1. Vamos a sentarnos en el parque.
2. Vamos a ponernos el sombrero.
3. Vamos a vestirnos para salir en seguida.
4. Vamos a irnos con Maricusa.
5. Vamos a despedirnos de los amigos.
6. Vamos a levantarnos temprano.

V. Complete las oraciones con la traducción al español de los verbos entre paréntesis. Use la forma verbal que sea necesaria.

1. (*to dare*) Fernando no _____ a esquiar en esa montaña tan peligrosa.

2. (*to regret*) Mi compañero _____ del negocio que hizo.

3. (*to sit down*) Estábamos tan cansados que _____ un rato a descansar.

4. (*to have breakfast*) Ellos _____ todos los días a las siete.

5. (*to agree*) Llamé a Felipe y _____ con él encontrarnos en su oficina.

6. (*to realize*) Lo que ocurre es que muchas veces mi amigo no _____ de que ofende cuando dice ciertas cosas.

7. (*to find out*) Ayer (yo) _____ de esa noticia.

8. (*to insist on*) Cuando Fifina _____ en una cosa, no está contenta hasta que la obtiene.

 ## Prepositional pronouns

El reloj es para **mí**. — *The watch is for me.*
Tengo muchas esperanzas en **ti**. — *I have a lot of hope for you.*
Ignacio desea hablar con **ella**. — *Ignacio wishes to speak with her.*
Marcela está sentada detrás de **nosotros**. — *Marcela is seated behind us.*
Él se sacrificó por **Uds**. — *He sacrificed himself for you.*

NOTE: The pronoun **mí** (*me*), has a written accent to distinguish it from the adjective **mi** (*my*). **Ti** does not need a written accent because the corresponding adjective is **tu**.

Pronouns used after a preposition may refer to persons and things.

¿Te gusta el libro? Quédate con **él**. — *Do you like the book? You may keep it.*
Hablé con **él**. — *I spoke with him.*

NOTE: In contrast to English, the personal pronouns are used after **como, entre**, and **menos** and not the prepositional pronouns.

Entre tú y **yo** nunca hay problema. — *Between you and me there is never a problem.*

Todos bailaron **menos** yo. — *Everyone danced except me.*
Como él, quiero ser médico. — *Like him, I want to be a doctor.*

1. The preposition **con** followed by **mi** or **ti** becomes **conmigo, contigo**.

Él no quiere hablar **conmigo**. — *He doesn't want to talk with me.*
Saldré **contigo**. — *I will go out with you.*

2. The form **sí** when used after a preposition means **himself, herself, themselves**.

Él sólo vive para **sí**. — *He lives only for himself.*
Ellos quieren todo para **sí**. — *They want everything for themselves.*

NOTE: **con + sí** = consigo (*with him/her*)

Él siempre lleva el llavero **consigo**. — *He always takes the keychain with him.*

3. **Mismo (-a, -os, -as)** are often used after prepositional pronouns to mean *myself, yourself, himself, herself, themselves.*

> Yo trabajo para **mí mismo**.   *I work for myself.*
> Ella tiene mucha seguridad en **sí misma**.   *She has a lot of confidence in herself.*
> Ellos ahorran el dinero para **sí mismos**.   *They save the money for themselves.*

NOTE: Mismo (-a, -os, -as) are also used after the personal pronouns and after a noun.

> **Yo misma** escribí la carta.   *I myself wrote the letter.*
> **Pedro mismo** hizo el trabajo.   *Pedro did the work himself.*

Ejercicios

I. Traduzca al español los pronombres que están entre paréntesis para completar las oraciones.

   1. (*it*) El agua es necesaria para vivir. Sin _____ moriríamos.

   2. (*it*) Ese verano fue maravilloso, siempre me acordaré de _____ .

   3. (*us*) Llevaremos el perro a la playa con _____ .

   4. (*you*) Sra. Costa, estos lirios son para _____ .

   5. (*with me*) Juanita vino _____ .

   6. (*himself*) Pedro siempre habla de _____ .

   7. (*among themselves*) Ellos discutían _____ .

   8. (*with you*) (*tú*) No puedo salir esta noche _____ .

   9. (*you*) (*Uds.*) Me gustaría estar con _____ .

  10. (*herself*) Raquel siempre escoge lo mejor para _____ .

II. Complete las oraciones con el pronombre adecuado.

MODELO: El sofá está delante de la ventana.
El sofá está delante de _____ .
El sofá está delante de ella.

   1. La sala está sin cortinas.
La sala está sin _____ .

   2. La lámpara estaba sobre el piano.
La lámpara estaba sobre _____ .

   3. Este reloj es para Justina.
Este reloj es para _____ .

   4. El ladrón entró por la puerta.
El ladrón entró por _____ .

   5. Ellos irán con Enriqueta y conmigo.
Ellos irán con _____ y conmigo.

F Expressions with *se*

1. To express something that occurs involuntarily or unexpectedly, the following structure is used: **se** + indirect object pronoun + the verb in the third person singular or plural, which is dependent on the subject.

Singular	*Plural*
Se me quitó el dolor de cabeza.	**Se te ocurrieron** algunas ideas.
My headache is gone.	*Some ideas occurred to you.*
Se le cayó el florero.	**Se me perdieron** los anteojos.
She dropped the vase.	*I lost my eye glasses.*
Se nos descompuso el carro.	**Se le rompieron** las copas.
Our car broke down.	*Her wine glasss broke.*
Se les acabó la gasolina.	
They ran out of gasoline.	

2. The equivalent in Spanish of the impersonal subject in English of *one, they, people* is **se** + verb in the third person singular.

Se vive bien aquí.	*One lives well here.*
No **se debe** decir eso.	*One should not say that.*
¿Qué **se dice** del presidente?	*What do they say about the president?*

3. When the doer is not mentioned or implied, the preferred construction in Spanish is **se** + the verb in the third person singular or plural instead of the passive voice with **ser**.* Note that in such constructions the subject generally follows the verb.

Se habla portugués en el Brasil.	*Portuguese is spoken in Brazil.*
Se descubrió América en 1492.	*America was discovered in 1492.*
Se anunciaron los resultados del examen.	*The results of the exam were announced.*

Summary of the different uses of **se**. Se is used:

• Instead of **le** or **les** in front of **lo, la, los,** and **las**.

Se lo dije a Manolo.	*I told it to Manolo.*

• As a third person reflexive pronoun and also to express reciprocal actions.

Luis **se despertó** tarde.	*Luis woke up late.*
Ellos **se quieren** mucho.	*They love each other a lot.*

• In front of the indirect object pronoun to express an involuntary action.

Se me olvidó tu dirección.	*I forgot your address.*

• In impersonal constructions.

Se prohíbe fumar.	*Smoking is forbidden.*

---

*See Capítulo 10, the passive voice.

Ejercicios

I. Complete las oraciones con los pronombres necesarios para expresar una acción involuntaria o inesperada.

1. A mi esposo _____ _____ olvidó nuestro aniversario de bodas.
2. ¿(A ti) _____ _____ paró el reloj, Rosita?
3. Cuando yo lavaba las copas _____ _____ rompieron dos de ellas.
4. A nosotros _____ _____ descompuso el carro en la autopista.
5. Cuando los chicos jugaban con el perro éste _____ _____ escapó.
6. Pedro salió de prisa y _____ _____ olvidaron los anteojos.

II. Escriba las siguientes frases usando **se** para expresar acción involuntaria o accidental.

MODELO: Olvidaron el número de teléfono.
Se les olvidó el número de teléfono.

1. Rompieron los platos.
2. ¿Perdiste las llaves?
3. Quemé el asado.
4. Olvidamos el teléfono celular.

III. De acuerdo con los sujetos, escriba el verbo que está entre paréntesis en la forma correcta del pasado.

1. (olvidar) A ella se le _____ los regalos.
2. (parar) A nosotros se nos _____ el carro en la autopista.
3. (perder) ¿Se te _____ los anteojos?

IV. Conteste las preguntas usando en las respuestas las palabras entre paréntesis y haga una oración que contenga una construcción con **se** para expresar una acción involuntaria o accidental.

MODELO: ¿Qué les pasó a Uds. en la oficina? (dañar la computadora)
Se nos **dañó** la computadora.

1. ¿Dónde dejaste los mapas? (perder en la calle)
2. ¿Por qué no compraste el vino? (olvidar)
3. ¿Qué les pasó a los niños? (perder el perro)
4. ¿Por qué llegaron tarde Uds.? (parar el reloj)
5. ¿Qué le pasó al camarero (*waiter*)? (caer las cervezas)

V. Conteste las preguntas que le hace su compañero(a). Use en sus respuestas una construcción con **se**.

1. ¿Qué idioma hablan en la Argentina?
2. ¿A qué hora abren los mercados?
3. ¿Cómo se dice en español *smoking is not permitted*?
4. ¿A qué hora sirven la cena en tu casa?
5. ¿En qué países cree Ud. que la gente vive bien?

VI. Traduzca al español las siguientes oraciones usando una construcción con **se**.

1. *We ran out of bread.*
2. *Many complaints are received every day.*
3. *They forgot the address.*
4. *One eats well in this restaurant.*
5. *Fresh apples are sold here.*
6. *His watch stopped.*
7. *She dropped her glasses.*
8. *They say the president will speak tomorrow.*

Jugadores de fútbol en un partido en Punta Arenas, Chile.

VII. Composición dirigida (oral o escrita). Diga lo que piensa Ud. de las siguientes opiniones de la gente.

1. Se dice que para conseguir un buen empleo es necesario tener una educación universitaria.
2. Se cree que los estudiantes tienen una vida muy fácil.
3. Se piensa que las universidades tienen fondos (*funds*) especiales para ayudar a los estudiantes con el costo de la educación.
4. Se dice que muchos estudiantes han tomado drogas.
5. Se piensa que muchos estudiantes tienen grandes problemas en la universidad por falta de preparación y porque no saben estudiar.

Composición

Antes de escribir, repase las siguientes reglas de las mayúsculas y la ortografía.

A Review of capitalization rules

A capital letter is used:

1. When the definite article is part of the name of the city or country.

   El Salvador   La Habana   El Ferrol   La Coruña   La Paz

2. With acronyms that identify commercial, political, or other organizations.

   OTAN (*NATO*)   **ABC** (*American Broadcasting Co.*)   **OEA** (*OAS*)

B Review of spelling rules: *gue, gui, güe, güi*

1. The strong sound of **g** with the vowels **e, i** is spelled **gue, gui**. The **u** is not pronounced:

   guerra (*war*), **juguete, pague, guitarra, Guillermo, águila** (*eagle*)

2. The **u** with diaresis (two dots) is pronounced: **güe, güi**:

   vergüenza (*shame*), **bilingüe, lingüista, pingüino** (*penguin*)

NOTE: The exercises corresponding to this section are included in the *Cuaderno de ejercicios*, Capítulo 7.

Ejercicio de composición (opcional)

Haga una composición, oral o escrita, sobre el tema que se da a continuación. Use el esquema siguiente.

TEMA: La tecnología moderna en el mundo actual.

INTRODUCCIÓN: Efectos producidos por la tecnología moderna (computadoras, calculadoras, correo electrónico, etc.)
                     Importancia de la computadora en todos los aspectos de la vida.

DESARROLLO: Cambios experimentados en el mundo de los negocios (*business world*).
                     Nuevos medios para facilitar las comunicaciones.
                     Equipos y aparatos especiales en el campo de la medicina.
                     ¿Cree Ud. que la tecnología estimula y aumenta la creatividad y hace que el hombre viva más feliz?

CONCLUSIÓN: ¿Cómo cree Ud. que será el mundo dentro de cincuenta años?
                     Dé una evaluación personal de los aspectos positivos y negativos producidos por los adelantos (*advances*) tecnológicos.

Vista aérea de la ciudad de Buenos Aires, capital de la Argentina.

LECTURAS

- Lectura 1: "Argentina"
- Lectura 2: "Sala de espera" de Enrique Anderson Imbert

GRAMÁTICA

- Nouns
- Uses of the infinitive
- Adjectives
- Comparatives
- Superlatives

COMPOSICIÓN

- Review of capitalization rules
- Review of spelling rules: **b, v**

Uocabulario

Antes de leer, repase el siguiente vocabulario que le ayudará a comprender la lectura.

Sustantivos

el arco iris   rainbow
el bosque   the forest
la confitería   coffee shop; pastry shop
la cordillera   mountain range
la costura   sewing
el/la cuentista   storyteller; short-story writer
el ganado   cattle
el grano   grain
el gaucho   Arg. expert horseman
la hierba (yerba)   grass
la imprenta   printing
la llanura   flatland; plain
la nieve   snow

el orgullo   pride
la orilla   shore
el pastel   pastry, pie, cake
el pasto   pasture
el/la periodista   journalist
el rascacielos   skyscraper
el sabor   taste, flavor
el taller   shop; workshop
el terreno   land, piece or plot of land
la trucha   trout
la uva   grape
el vaquero   cowboy

Verbos

destacarse (qu)   to stand out
empapar   to soak
encabezar (c)   to be at the top of, at the head of
esquiar   to ski

habitar   to live on
justificar (qu)   to justify
pescar (qu)   to fish
sobrecoger (j)   to fill with awe

Adjetivos

sedoso   silky

impresionante   impressive

Frases

al alejarse de   upon leaving
al pie de   at the foot of

dejar atrás   to leave behind
lugar de temporada   resort

Related words (Palabras relacionadas). The meaning of some words may be determined by thinking of related words familiar to you. Can you give in English the meaning of the underlined words derived from the words in parentheses?

1. (cultivar) ... el clima es templado y el terreno fértil para el cultivo de granos...
2. (llover) ... en la Tierra del Fuego, donde las lluvias son abundantes.
3. (cubrir) ... las majestuosas montañas cubiertas de nieve...
4. (habitar) ... los muchos millones de habitantes que tiene este país...
5. (densidad) ... ocupa una parte de los Andes que es famosa por sus densos bosques...
6. (nieve) ... los picos nevados de los Andes...

Preliminary view of some expressions (Vista preliminar de algunas expresiones).

1. Note the use of the adjective in front of the noun to give more emphasis to the description:

> Sus **densos bosques** y las **majestuosas montañas**
> *Its dense forests and majestic mountains*
> Una **magnífica metrópoli** con **grandes edificios, numerosos rascacielos y espléndidas avenidas**
> *A magnificent metropolis with big buildings, numerous skyscrapers, and splendid avenues*
> Los **excelentes vinos**   *The excellent wines*

2. Note the use of **gran** and **grande** in the following examples. **Grande** becomes **gran** when it goes in front of a noun and it means *great*. The plural **grandes** can be used before or after the noun. Note the difference: **grandes edificios** (*great buildings*) (*big buildings*: emphasis on *big*) and **edificios grandes** (*big buildings*: without emphasis).

> Un clima subtropical en el norte, y frío y con **grandes** vientos…
> *A subtropical climate in the north, and cold with great winds . . .*
> **Gran** parte de los muchos millones de habitantes…
> *A great part of the many millions of inhabitants . . .*
> Una magnífica metrópoli con **grandes** edificios…
> *A magnificent metropolis with great buildings . . .*
> Domingo Faustino Sarmiento, el **gran** político, escritor y pedagogo…
> *Domingo Faustino Sarmiento, the great politician, writer, and educator . . .*

*L*ectura 1

Argentina

La Argentina es un país fascinante que se encuentra al sur del continente americano y se extiende hasta la Tierra del Fuego. Con la excepción del Brasil, es el país de mayor extensión de Hispanoamérica y tiene fronteras con Chile, Bolivia, el Paraguay, el Brasil y el Uruguay. Su gran extensión
5 hace que tenga un clima subtropical en el norte, y frío y con grandes vientos en la Patagonia y en la Tierra del Fuego, donde las lluvias son abundantes.

Las pampas son extensas llanuras cubiertas de hierba que ocupan más de la mitad del territorio central de la Argentina. Aquí, el clima es
10 templado y el terreno fértil para el cultivo de granos y la cría de ganado, debido al abundante pasto. La ganadería, que es la primera del mundo, así como la producción agrícola de esta región, contribuyen a que la Argentina tenga una economía basada en estas dos importantes riquezas de exportación. Gran parte de los muchos millones de habitantes que
15 tiene este país vive en esta región central.

Los Andes separan a la Argentina de Chile y presentan un espectáculo grandioso que sobrecoge cuando se contemplan al volar sobre ellos. Las ciudades que están al pie de la cordillera, como San Luis, Mendoza y San

Juan, gozan de un clima ideal. Aquí llueve poco, hace sol, la temperatura
es templada° y abundan los hermosos valles donde se cultivan las uvas   *temperate, mild*
que producen los excelentes vinos argentinos.

20   Posiblemente, la región más hermosa del continente americano es
Neuquén, que se encuentra en las riberas° del río Negro. Neuquén ocupa   *banks*
una parte de los Andes que es famosa por la hermosura de sus lagos, sus
densos bosques y las majestuosas montañas cubiertas de nieve.

Bariloche, famoso lugar de temporada situado a orillas del lago
25   Nahuel Huapi (en araucano quiere decir Isla del Tigre), es de una belleza
impresionante. Estando a unas dos horas de vuelo de la ciudad de
Buenos Aires, en el invierno está lleno de visitantes que van a esquiar. En
el verano, la pesca de la trucha y los deportes acuáticos atraen a miles de
turistas que vienen de todas las partes del mundo. En una península del
30   lago están los incomparables bosques de los arrayanes° que sirvieron de   *wax myrtles*
inspiración a Walt Disney para su película "Bambi". Estos maravillosos
árboles, con troncos° amarillo-ámbar y hojas verdes sedosas, sólo crecen   *trunks*
en esta región de la Argentina. El visitante, al alejarse de Bariloche, sale
con la nostalgia de dejar atrás los múltiples arco iris que diariamente

35 mueren en los picos nevados de los Andes, y con el sabor y el perfume
    de los conocidos chocolates que allí se elaboran.°   *are made*

    Buenos Aires, capital de la Argentina, es una magnífica metrópoli con
    grandes edificios, numerosos rascacielos y espléndidas avenidas. La
    Avenida de Mayo, que se extiende entre la Casa Rosada (Palacio
40 Presidencial) y el Congreso, es el centro administrativo e intelectual de la
    ciudad. En ella abundan los cafés y confiterías que son centros de
    reunión de políticos, periodistas, escritores y artistas. En la Avenida 9 de
    Julio está el Teatro Colón que desde 1908, año en que se construyó, ha
    sido centro importante de la vida musical de Buenos Aires. Este teatro
45 cuenta con una orquesta propia, una compañía de ópera permanente y
    otra de ballet, así como talleres de costura, carpintería e imprenta. El
    orgullo que sienten los porteños —nombre que se les da a los habitantes
    de Buenos Aires— está muy justificado, ya que poseen una capital
    hermosa con una rica tradición.

50 El pueblo argentino ha creado una rica cultura, tanto en el aspecto
    popular como en el culto. En el aspecto popular son famosos los bailes y
    la música, especialmente el tango, que se hizo famoso en Europa y los
    Estados Unidos durante la primera guerra mundial. En el campo de la
    música culta, la Argentina contaba en el siglo XX con compositores de
55 fama internacional, sobresaliendo entre ellos Alberto Ginastera
    (1916–1983).

    Son muchos los escritores argentinos que han enriquecido la
    literatura hispánica. En el siglo pasado, Jorge Luis Borges (1899–1986)
    encabezó la lista de su generación abriendo nuevos caminos para la
60 renovación literaria en Hispanoamérica. Muchos nombres más siguieron
    a Borges: poetas, novelistas y cuentistas de excelente calidad, como, por
    ejemplo, Julio Cortázar (1914–1984), que se destacó con sus cuentos y
    novelas fantásticos.

    La literatura gauchesca ocupa un lugar especial en el mundo de las
65 letras argentinas. El gaucho, el vaquero que habita las pampas, es la
    figura central de esta literatura. Domingo Faustino Sarmiento
    (1811–1888), el gran político, escritor, pedagogo y además Presidente
    de la República argentina, fue quien primero describió con gran
    claridad y fuerza al gaucho en su obra *Civilización y barbarie: Vida de*
70 *Juan Facundo Quiroga* (1845). Más tarde, José Hernández (1834–1886),
    empapado del espíritu gauchesco, escribe su conocido poema *Martín*
    Fierro donde deja hablar la voz auténtica del gaucho. Martín Fierro
    tiene un doble público: se dirige a los lectores cultos° y a los gauchos.   *well-read people*
    Ante los cultos, reclama° justicia para el gaucho. Ante los gauchos,   *claim*
75 procura° darles lecciones morales que mejoren su condición.   *tries*

    Como hemos visto, la Argentina es un país donde los colores de su
    geografía, historia y tradición han producido un arco iris de insuperable
    belleza, vastedad y alcance.°   *scope*

Llene los espacios en blanco con la palabra que sea correcta.

1. Los niños jugaban _____ del río.

2. Bariloche es _____ muy hermoso.

3. El pelo de la niña era muy finito y _____ ; daba gusto peinarla.

4. Entre los escritores de Hispanoamérica el que más _____ es Borges.

5. En Buenos Aires _____ están muy concurridos por los sabrosos pasteles que tienen.

6. El gaucho vive en la pampa y se le compara al _____ americano.

7. Me sorprendió el aguacero (*heavy rain*) en la calle y llegué _____ a mi casa.

8. En Buenos Aires, como en Nueva York, hay edificios altísimos. Se ve el perfil de la ciudad con todos los _____ .

Preguntas sobre la lectura

1. Explique por qué cree Ud. que gran parte de los habitantes de la Argentina viven en la región central.
2. ¿Cuáles son las dos exportaciones más importantes de la Argentina?
3. ¿Qué palabras usa el autor para describir la belleza de los Andes que separan a la Argentina de Chile?
4. ¿Qué se dice de la región al pie de la cordillera donde están las ciudades de San Luis, Mendoza y San Juan?
5. ¿Por qué cree el autor que la región de Neuquén es tan hermosa?
6. ¿Qué cosas menciona el autor sobre Bariloche que Ud. no sabía?
7. ¿Qué nombre se le da en la Argentina a la casa donde vive el Presidente de la República?
8. ¿Qué dice el autor del Teatro Colón?
9. ¿Qué nombre se les da a los habitantes de Buenos Aires?
10. ¿Qué frases usa el autor para expresar la importancia que tiene Jorge Luis Borges en la literatura hispanoamericana?
11. ¿Qué importancia tiene Domingo Faustino Sarmiento en la historia de la Argentina?
12. ¿Por qué dice el autor que el poema *Martín Fierro* tiene un doble público?

Temas de conversación

1. En la Argentina el "asado" (*beef grilled on an open fire*) es una de las comidas más populares y típicas. ¿Ha comido Ud. asado alguna vez? ¿Conoce Ud. algún restaurante que sirva comida argentina? Narre su experiencia si ha estado en un restaurante argentino.
2. Muchas personas no comen carne porque piensan que es cruel matar los animales. ¿Qué piensa Ud. de esta actitud? ¿Es Ud. vegetariano? ¿Tiene Ud. animales en su casa? ¿Cómo es su relación con ellos?
3. Las telenovelas argentinas son muy populares. ¿Puede mencionar alguna que Ud. haya visto? ¿Cree Ud. que hay algunas diferencias entre una telenovela mexicana y una argentina? Dé su opinión.

ocabulario

Antes de leer, repase el siguiente vocabulario que le ayudará a comprender la lectura.

Sustantivos
la aspiradora   vacuum cleaner
el andén   railway platform
el bostezo   yawn
el fantasma   ghost, phantom
la joya   jewel
la valija   suitcase

Verbos
asesinar   to murder
fingir (j)   to pretend
quedarse con   to keep
robar   to steal

Adjetivos
fastidiado   annoyed
mudo   mute; speechless

Adverbio
entonces   then

ℒectura 2

Enrique Anderson Imbert

Enrique Anderson Imbert (1910–2000) es un reconocido escritor argentino que tuvo una exitosa carrera de profesor, novelista, historiador y crítico literario, tanto en su tierra natal como en los Estados Unidos. El cuento "Sala de espera" forma parte de *El gato de Cheshire* (1965) y es representativo de los "microcuentos" de Anderson Imbert. En él el autor combina el mundo de la fantasía con el de la realidad.

Sala de espera°

waiting room

Costa y Wright roban una casa. Costa asesina a Wright y se queda con la valija llena de joyas y dinero. Va a la estación para escaparse en el primer tren. En la sala de espera, una señora se sienta a su izquierda y le da conversación. Fastidiado, Costa finge con un bostezo que tiene sueño y que
5 va a dormir, pero oye que la señora continúa conversando. Abre entonces los ojos y ve, sentado a la derecha, el fantasma de Wright. La señora atraviesa° a   *pierces*
Costa de lado a lado con la mirada, y charla con el fantasma, quien contesta con simpatía. Cuando llega el tren, Costa trata de levantarse, pero no puede. Está paralizado, mudo y observa atónito° cómo el fantasma toma   *astonished*
10 tranquilamente la valija y camina con la señora hacia el andén, ahora hablando y riéndose. Suben, y el tren parte. Costa los sigue con los ojos. Viene un hombre y comienza a limpiar la sala de espera, que ahora está completamente desierta. Pasa la aspiradora por el asiento donde está Costa, invisible.

Preguntas sobre la lectura

1. ¿Por qué mata Costa a Wright?
2. ¿Qué contiene la valija?
3. ¿Para qué va Costa a la estación?
4. ¿Quién es la otra persona que está en la sala de espera? ¿Quién cree Ud. que es esta persona?
5. Costa finge que tiene sueño. ¿Qué ve cuando abre los ojos? ¿Cómo interpreta Ud. la aparición del fantasma?
6. ¿Qué hacen la señora y el fantasma?
7. ¿Qué pasa cuando llega el tren?
8. ¿Por qué no sube Costa al tren?
9. ¿Qué hace el hombre que viene a la sala de espera?
10. ¿Cómo interpreta Ud. el final de este cuento?

Gramática

A Nouns

1. Gender of nouns

    a. Most masculine nouns end in **-o**; most feminine nouns end in **-a**.

el muchacho	la puerta
los escritorios	las chicas

    b. There are exceptions to this rule: there are masculine nouns that end in **-a** and feminine nouns that end in **-o**.

Masculine nouns ending in *-a*		Feminine nouns ending in *-o*
el clima	el drama	la mano
el problema	el telegrama	la soprano
el tema	el mapa	la foto (la fotografía)
el programa	el planeta	la moto (la motocicleta)
el sistema	el día	
el poema		

En **estos días** Luisa tiene **varios problemas**: perdió **los poemas** que
escribió, recibió **un telegrama** con malas noticias y le robaron **la moto**
que compró el mes pasado.
*These days Luisa has several problems: she lost the poems she wrote, she received
a telegram with bad news, and they stole the motorcycle she bought last month.*

c. Nouns ending in **-d**, **-umbre**, **-ción**, **-sión**, and **-ez** are generally feminine.

la lealtad (*loyalty*)	la nación	la honradez (*honesty*)
la juventud (*youth*)	la porción	la madurez (*maturity*)
la costumbre (*custom*)	la pasión	la sencillez (*simplicity*)
la muchedumbre (*crowd*)	la misión	la vejez (*old age*)

La muchedumbre llenaba la plaza. *The crowd filled the square.*
Las misiones de California fueron fundadas por franciscanos españoles.
The missions in California were founded by Spanish franciscans.

d. The letters of the alphabet are feminine.

la a   las efes

e. The names of oceans, rivers, and mountains are masculine.

el Pacífico	el Caribe
el Amazonas	el Nilo
el Aconcagua	el Popocatépetl

f. Nouns ending in **-e**, **-sis**, and **-l** can be masculine or feminine.

	Masculine		*Feminine*	
-e:	el parque	el chiste (*joke*)	la calle	la nube (*cloud*)
	el coche	el valle	la nave (*ship*)	la nieve
	el postre	el billete	la gente	la fuente (*fountain*)
	el viaje	el paisaje (*landscape*)	la noche	la torre (*tower*)
	el nombre	el baile	la suerte	la pirámide
	el cine	el tomate	la leche	la parte
-sis:	el análisis	el oasis	la crisis	la tesis
-l:	el árbol	el mantel	la piel	la postal
	el rosal	el tamal	la cárcel (*jail*)	la sal

El flamenco es **un baile** andaluz. *The flamenco is an Andalucian dance.*
La gente llenó el estadio. *The people filled the stadium.*
Beatriz terminó **la tesis** doctoral. *Beatriz finished the doctoral thesis.*
Metieron al ladrón en **la cárcel**. *They put the thief in jail.*

g. Nouns ending in **-ante**, **-ente**, and **-iente** referring to people or animals, change the **-e** to **-a** to form the feminine.

el comediante	la comedianta
el elefante	la elefanta
el asistente	la asistenta
el presidente ⟶	la presidenta
el confidente	la confidenta
el pariente	la parienta
el dependiente	la dependienta

Tengo **una asistenta** muy eficiente.
I have a very efficient assistant.
La Sra. Presidenta leyó el discurso de despedida
The (Madam) President read the farewell address.

h. The days of the week are masculine.

el lunes	los viernes

i. Most masculine nouns ending in **d, l, n, r, s**, and **z**, referring to people or animals, add an **-a** for the feminine form.

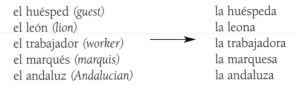

el huésped *(guest)*	la huéspeda
el león *(lion)*	la leona
el trabajador *(worker)* ⟶	la trabajadora
el marqués *(marquis)*	la marquesa
el andaluz *(Andalucian)*	la andaluza

j. There are nouns that use the same form for both masculine and feminine; the definite article distinguishes the gender.

el artista	la artista
el novelista	la novelista
el pianista	la pianista
el masajista	la masajista
el testigo	la testigo
el joven ⟶	la joven
el juez	la juez o la jueza
el astronauta	la astronauta
el mártir	la mártir
el cantante	la cantante
el atleta	la atleta
el compatriota	la compatriota

El flautista tocó acompañado de **una pianista** argentina.
The flutist played accompanied by an Argentine pianist.
Los atletas españoles ganaron varias medallas en las Olimpiadas.
The Spanish athletes won several medals in the Olympics.

k. There are nouns referring to people or animals, that have different words for each gender.

el actor (actor)	la actriz (actress)
el alcalde (mayor)	la alcaldesa
el caballero (gentleman)	la dama (lady)
el caballo (horse)	la yegua (mare)
el compadre	la comadre
el emperador (emperor)	la emperatriz (empress)
el gallo (rooster) ⟶	la gallina (chicken)
el héroe	la heroína
el marido, el esposo	la esposa
el padrastro	la madrastra
el padrino	la madrina
el príncipe	la princesa
el rey	la reina
el toro (bull)	la vaca (cow)
el varón, el macho (male)	la hembra (female)
el yerno (son-in-law)	la nuera (daughter-in-law)

Tanto **el actor** como **la actriz** me parecieron excelentes.
The actor as well as the actress seemed excellent to me.
Ramiro siempre monta (*rides*) **la yegua** blanca.
Ramiro always rides the white mare.

NOTE: The word **macho** applies mainly to animals; **varón** to male persons.

Mis tíos tienen dos **varones**.
My aunt and uncle have two boys. (sons)
Entre los animales, el **macho** generalmente es más agresivo.
Among animals, the male is generally more aggressive.

l. Some nouns may be either masculine or feminine, depending on their meaning.

el guía	guide	**el** frente	front
la guía	phone book	**la** frente	forehead
el policía	policeman	**el** Papa	Pope
la policía	police force	**la** papa	potato
el parte	communiqué; dispatch	**el** orden	order
la parte	part; portion	**la** orden	order; command
el capital	capital (money)	**el** modelo	example; pattern
la capital	capital (city)	**la** modelo	female model
el cura	priest		
la cura	cure; healing		

La policía de **la capital** se encargó de mantener **el orden**.
The police from the capital were in charge of maintaining order.
Le pedí la dirección a **un policía** de tráfico.
I asked a traffic policeman for the address.

2. Plural of nouns

   a. Nouns ending in an unstressed vowel or in **-é** (with a written accent) add **s** to form the plural.

cuadro	**cuadros**	almirante *(amiral)*	**almirantes**
sobrina	**sobrinas**	café	**cafés**

   b. Nouns ending in a consonant or in a stressed vowel, except **-é**, add **-es** to form the plural.

flor	**flores**	origen	**orígenes**
ley	**leyes**	danés *(Danish)*	**daneses**
reloj	**relojes**	rubí	**rubíes**
cárcel	**cárceles**	hindú	**hindúes**
carbón	**carbones**	ají	**ajíes**

   Exceptions:

mamá	**mamás**	menú	**menús**
papá	**papás**	esquí	**esquís**
sofá	**sofás**		

   NOTE: Words ending in a consonant with a written accent on the last syllable drop the accent mark in the plural form.

pasión	**pasiones**	inglés	**ingleses**
nación	**naciones**	alemán	**alemanes**

   NOTE: Words stressed on the next to the last syllable require a written accent on this same syllable in the plural form.

examen	**exámenes**	origen	**orígenes**

   c. Nouns ending in **-z** change **-z** to **-c** when adding **-es** to form the plural.

   luz **luces**   lápiz **lápices**   cruz **cruces**

   d. Nouns ending in an unstressed syllable ending in **-s** have the same form in the singular and plural.

el sacacorchos *(corkscrew)*	**los sacacorchos**
el salvavidas *(lifeguard)*	**los salvavidas**
el abrelatas *(can opener)*	**los abrelatas**
el tocadiscos *(record player)*	**los tocadiscos**
la crisis *(crisis)*	**las crisis**
la tesis *(thesis)*	**las tesis**
el viernes *(Friday)*	**los viernes**
el rompecabezas *(puzzle)*	**los rompecabezas**
el paraguas *(umbrella)*	**los paraguas**
el lavaplatos *(dishwasher)*	**los lavaplatos**

e. In Spanish, last names are not pluralized; first names, however, can be used in the plural.

> Anoche cenamos en casa de **los González.**
> *Last night we had supper at the Gonzalez' home.*
> Allí estaban **las Salcedo.** *The Salcedos were there.*
> Después llegaron los **dos Antonios** de la familia Pérez.
> *Afterwards the two Antonios of the Perez family arrived.*

f. Some words are only used in plural.

> las gafas *(sunglasses)*
> las vacaciones *(vacation)*
> los anteojos *(eyeglasses)*
> las cosquillas *(tickling)*

3. Diminutives

a. The most common diminutive suffixes are **-ito** and **-cito,** added to nouns and adjectives. In general, the ending **-cito** is used with nouns and adjectives ending in **e, n,** or **r.**

-cito		-ito
rincón **rinconcito**	amor **amorcito**	vaso **vasito**
lápiz **lapicito**	parque **parquecito**	papel **papelito**
suave **suavecito**	limón **limoncito**	silla **sillita**
madre **madrecita**	lugar **lugarcito**	árbol **arbolito**
corazón **corazoncito**	café **cafecito**	poco **poquito**
		muñeca **muñequita**
		lago **laguito**

NOTE: When a word ends in **-co** or **-go** the following spelling changes occur:

> -co → **-qui**   poco   **poquito**
> -go → **-gui**   amigo   **amiguito**

b. The endings **-illo, -ico,** and **-uelo** are also used to express the diminutive.

pájaro	**pajarillo**	pan	**panecillo**	mano	**manecita**
	pajarito		**panecito**		**manita**
flor	**florecilla**				
	florecita				
gato	**gatillo**	chico	**chiquillo**		
	gatito		**chiquito**		
	gatico		**chicuelo**		

NOTE: Some words, mainly those with one syllable, insert an **e** before the diminutive ending. Other words insert **ce** before the diminutive ending: **pie, piececito.**

Tres gauchos argentinos disfrutando de un día de fiesta y diversión.

c. In Spanish, the diminutive is used frequently not only to express smallness in size, but also to express affection. Sometimes, it is also used in a sarcastic or ironic way.

> El **abuelito** siempre llevaba a su **nietecito** a pasear.
> *The granddad would always take his little grandson for a ride.*
> El **gatico** estaba echado en un **rinconcito** del cuarto.
> *The kitten was lying in a small corner of the room.*

4. Augmentatives

a. The most common endings to form the augmentative are **-ote (-ota), -azo (-aza)**, and **-ón (-ona)**. Augmentatives are used to denote large size or scorn.

libro	**librote**	perro	**perrazo**
hombre	**hombrón**	mujer	**mujerona**
muchacho	**muchachón**		

Ejercicios

I. Escriba de nuevo los párrafos haciendo los cambios necesarios al cambiar los sustantivos subrayados del masculino al femenino.

MODELO: El <u>asistente</u> parecía cansado.
        La asistenta parecía cansada.

Tengo un <u>compatriota</u> que es un buen <u>masajista</u>. Cuando voy para que me dé masaje en la espalda le sirvo de <u>confidente</u> y conversa tanto que ya conozco su vida. Creo que es un <u>héroe</u> y un <u>mártir</u> por todo lo que pasó durante la revolución que hubo en su patria.

El <u>artista</u> de ópera que cantó anoche era el <u>yerno</u> del <u>director</u> de orquesta. Es un <u>cantante</u> magnífico y se viste que parece un <u>emperador</u>.

II. Usando los artículos definidos que sean necesarios, complete las siguientes ideas.

1. _____ problemas principales que existen en _____ sociedad son _____ hambre, _____ drogas y _____ gente sin trabajo.

2. _____ habitantes de _____ ciudad han perdido _____ fe y _____ esperanza de tener _____ alcalde que necesitan.

3. _____ cualidades que más aprecio son _____ honradez, _____ lealtad, _____ nobleza y _____ sencillez.

III. Usando los artículos indefinidos, complete la descripción de Carlos.

Carlos tiene _____ inteligencia clara y es _____ estudiante brillante. Es _____ amigo sincero y tiene _____ buen carácter. Además es _____ atleta dinámico.

Pero tiene _____ problema que no me gusta. Tiene _____ bigote muy grande y _____ nariz muy larga.

IV. Cambie las palabras al singular.

1. los abrelatas
2. las tesis
3. las cruces
4. los reyes
5. los claveles
6. los jóvenes
7. los ingleses
8. las naciones
9. las aguas
10. los exámenes

V. Escoja el artículo que sea correcto.

1. (un / una) El pájaro tiene _____ ala rota.

2. (el / la) El astronauta está en _____ nave espacial.

3. (el / la) Llegó _____ telegrama urgente para el director.

4. (el / la) Los alumnos discutieron _____ tema de las drogas.

5. (los / las) Se fueron muy rápido _____ días felices.

6. (un / una) Ella vive en _____ torre del Parque Central.

VI. Escriba los artículos —definidos o indefinidos— que correspondan, de acuerdo con el género de los sustantivos. Use las contracciones **al** o **del** donde sea necesario.

1. Cuando fuimos _____ Perú _____ guía que nos acompañó sabía mucho de _____ civilización de _____ incas. Tuvimos _____ suerte de estar con él cuando visitamos _____ ruinas de Machu Picchu. Además de ser _____ fuente (*source*) de información excelente, hablaba perfectamente _____ inglés.

2. _____ juez aplicó _____ ley correctamente cuando condenó _____ asesino que cometió _____ crimen de asaltar _____ banco y herir a _____ empleado que estaba en _____ mostrador (*counter*).

3. Son muchos _____ problemas que tienen que resolver _____ ciudades grandes. _____ sistema de educación y _____ programas de asistencia social necesitan cambios importantes.

4. _____ atleta alemán que tomó parte en _____ competencia de natación recibió _____ mención de honor que le dio _____ ciudad donde vive. Recibió las felicitaciones _____ público y hasta el Presidente de _____ nación le envió _____ telegrama.

5. _____ clima _____ estado de California es lo que atrae a _____ gente que vive en lugares fríos donde _____ nieve cubre todo durante _____ mayor parte _____ invierno.

VII. Escoja las palabras que más convengan para completar las oraciones.

1. (el guía / la guía) _____ que nos enseñó el Teatro Colón era muy simpático.

2. (el orden / la orden) El índice del libro sigue _____ de los temas.

3. (el cura / la cura) _____ del enfermo fue lenta.

4. (el capital / la capital) Rubén perdió todo _____ en malos negocios.

5. (el guía / la guía) No encuentro el número en _____ de teléfonos.

6. (el parte / la parte) Ellos comieron _____ que les correspondía.

7. (el frente / la frente) Me dieron un golpe en _____ del carro.

8. (el policía / la policía) _____ de toda la nación se movilizó en un día.

VIII. Usando el diminutivo de las palabras subrayadas, lea el siguiente párrafo para hacer la descripción del hijo de su amiga.

El bebé de mi amiga nació hace un mes y parece un muñeco. El pelo y los ojos son oscuros y tiene la cara como la de un ángel. Las manos y los pies son muy pequeños y suaves. La abuela está feliz con el nieto y lo va a ver todos los días.

Le llevé a mi amiga un traje azul y blanco para el niño y un cesto de flores que tenía unas rosas blancas combinadas con claveles rosados.

IX. Composición dirigida (oral o escrita). Complete las frases con ideas originales usando las palabras entre paréntesis.

MODELO: (paraguas) Anoche cuando salí…
   Anoche cuando salí llovía mucho y usé el paraguas para no mojarme.

1. (sacacorchos) Me regalaron una botella de vino…
2. (telegrama) Mi hermano envió…
3. (rascacielos) En la ciudad…
4. (restaurantito) Me han recomendado…
5. (salvavidas) En la playa…

B Uses of the infinitive

1. The infinitive can be used right after a conjugated verb or after a verb followed by a preposition. As a rule, the verb and the infinitive have the same subject. When there is a change of subject, a subordinate clause, with the verb in subjunctive, takes the place of the infinitive.

> **Prefieren salir** esta tarde. *They prefer to go out this afternoon.*
> **Prefieren que yo salga** esta tarde. *They prefer that I go out this afternoon.*
> **Han ido a ver** el juego de pelota. *They've gone to see the ball game.*
> **Me alegré de terminar** el trabajo. *I was happy to finish the work.*

2. In Spanish, the infinitive may be used as a noun, therefore, it can be used as the subject, predicate, or direct object in a sentence. It may or may not be accompanied by the masculine article **el**. English uses the **-ing** form instead of the infinitive.

> **(El) salir** de compras contigo   *Shopping with you is*
>   es un dolor de cabeza.   *a headache.*
>
> **Ver** es **creer**.   *Seeing is believing.*

3. In Spanish, the infinitive is always used after a preposition, and not the **-ing** form, which is used in English.

> Salieron **sin terminar** el trabajo.
> *They left without finishing the work.*

> La pluma es **para escribir**.
> *The pen is for writing.*

> **Antes de hablar**, piensa lo que vas a decir.
> *Think before talking.*

> **Después de conocer** la historia, comprendo los problemas del país.
> *After knowing the history, I understand the country's problems.*

4. **Al** + infinitive means **en el momento de** + infinitive. The English translation is *upon* + *present participle*.

> **Al salir**, perdí la bufanda.
> *Upon leaving, I lost the scarf.*
> (En el momento de salir, perdí la bufanda.)

> **Al oír** la explosión, llamé a la policía.
> *Upon hearing the explosion, I called the police.*

Ejercicios

I. Cambie las oraciones de dos sujetos a uno, usando el infinitivo.

MODELO: Desean que vayas a la reunión.
   Desean ir a la reunión.

1. Esperamos que vuelvan pronto.
2. ¿Quieres que prepare el postre?
3. Sintió que no fueras a la playa.
4. Lamentan que vendas la casa.

II. Complete los párrafos traduciendo al español las palabras que están en inglés.

_____ (*Upon seeing*) a Julita, Roberto se enamoró de ella. Fue un amor a primera vista. Roberto comprendió que Julita era la mujer de sus sueños _____ (*after talking*) con ella. Desde el momento en que la conoció Roberto no pudo vivir _____ (*without being*) a su lado.

_____ (*Living*) sin Julita era la muerte para Roberto, pero ella insistió en _____ (*waiting*) un poco de tiempo _____ (*before getting married*).

Decidí trabajar con el Cuerpo de Paz porque creo que hay que _____ (*educate*) y _____ (*help*) a la gente pobre que vive en el campo de Guatemala. _____ (*Knowing*) el idioma es importante y empecé a _____ (*study*) español para _____ (*to be able to talk*) con los habitantes del país. _____ (*Upon arrival*) voy a _____ (*rent*) una casa pequeña porque no me gusta _____ (*living*) en un hotel. Creo que el _____ (*working*) con el Cuerpo de Paz será una experiencia interesante que siempre recordaré.

III. Complete las oraciones en forma original usando infinitivos y las palabras necesarias para completar sus ideas.

> **MODELO:** Yo lo vi antes de…
> **Yo lo vi antes de salir de viaje.**

1. Ella los abrazó al…
2. Nos divertimos sin…
3. Insiste en…
4. Me alegro de…
5. El… es poder…

Glaciar en la Patagonia, Argentina.

C Adjectives

An adjective modifies a noun or a pronoun, qualifying (describing) or restricting (limiting) its meaning. Both descriptive and limiting adjectives agree in gender and number with the words they modify.

NOTE: When there are two nouns in a sentence, one masculine and the other feminine, the adjective that modifies them will be masculine.

> Miguel y Elisa son **argentinos**.

1. Limiting adjectives. Limiting adjectives restrict the meaning of a noun through different kinds of relationships which may be:

of place (demonstrative adjectives): **aquellas** guitarras *those guitars*
possessive (possessive adjectives): **nuestra** cultura *our culture*
indefinite (indefinite adjectives): **cualquier** cosa, **algún** amigo *any thing, some friend*
quantitative (adjetives of quantity): **poca** experiencia, **tres** pueblos *little experience, three towns*

   Limiting adjectives usually precede the noun.

2. Descriptive adjectives. Descriptive adjectives inform us about a particular quality or characteristic. As a rule, they follow the noun when we want to differentiate it from the rest of its class.

> hombre **inteligente** árboles **frutales** tierra **fértil**
> *intelligent man*   *fruit trees*   *fertile land*

NOTE: In Spanish a noun may not modify another noun. Spanish uses **de** + noun.

> el libro **de español** (*the Spanish book*)
> las clases **de verano** (*the summer classes*)

   Descriptive adjectives are sometimes placed before the noun to refer to an essential or inherent quality of the noun or to emphasize that quality.

La **blanca** nieve cubría todo el paisaje.
The white snow covered all the landscape.
Las **impresionantes** montañas se reflejan en el lago.
The impressive mountains are reflected on the lake.
La **inocente** niña temblaba de hambre y miedo.
The innocent child was trembling from hunger and fear.
La **hermosa** muchacha lloraba al alejarse de la **vieja** casa donde pasó su niñez.
The beautiful girl was crying upon leaving the old house where she spent her childhood.

3. Gender of adjectives

   a. Adjectives that end in **-o** change the **-o** to **-a** to form the feminine.

> un camino **estrecho** *a narrow road*   una calle **estrecha** *a narrow street*

   b. Adjectives ending in **-ón, -án, -or**, and adjectives of nationality that end in a consonant add **a** to form the feminine.

juguetón (*playful*)	**juguetona**	español (*Spanish*)	**española**
holgazán (*lazy*)	**holgazana**	alemán (*German*)	**alemana**
traidor (*traitorous*)	**traidora**	francés (*French*)	**francesa**
soñador (*dreaming*)	**soñadora**	andaluz (*Andalucian*)	**andaluza**

un joven **soñador**   *a dreaming young man/a young dreamer*
una joven **soñadora**   *a dreaming young woman/a young dreamer*
un pueblo **andaluz**   *an Andalucian town*
una casa **andaluza**   *an Andalucian house*

NOTE: The following adjectives ending in **-or** (all comparative) don't change and have only one form for both genders:

superior	**exterior**	**mayor**	**mejor**	**interior**
posterior	**menor**	**peor**	**inferior**	**ulterior**

un libro **inferior** *an inferior book*   una calidad **inferior** *an inferior quality*
el hijo **mayor** *the oldest son*   la hija **mayor** *the oldest daughter*

  c. The diminutives and augmentatives ending in **-ete** and **-ote** change the final **-e** to **-a** to form the feminine.

un niño **regordete** *a chubby little boy*   una niña **regordeta** *a chubby little girl*
un cuerpo **grandote** *a huge body*   una mano **grandota** *a huge hand*

  d. Adjectives ending **-a, -e, -l, -r, -s, -z,** have only one form for both genders.

un hombre **entusiasta**	*an enthusiastic man*	una sociedad **entusiasta**	*an enthusiastic society*
un día **triste**	*a sad day*	una noticia **triste**	*sad news*
un niño **débil**	*a weak child*	una salud **débil**	*weak health*
un actor **popular**	*a popular actor*	una actriz **popular**	*a popular actress*
un empleado **cortés**	*a courteous employee*	una empleada **cortés**	*a courteous employee*
un obrero **capaz**	*a capable worker*	una persona **capaz**	*a capable person*

4. Plural of adjectives

  a. Adjectives that end in a vowel add **-s**; adjectives that end in a consonant add **-es.**

unas ideas **interesantes** *some interesting ideas*   unos paisajes **tropicales** *some tropical landscapes*

NOTE: Words that end in a consonant with a written accent on the last syllable drop the accent mark when **-a** is added to form the feminine, and **-es** or **-as** to form the plural.

holgazán	**holgazana**	**holgazanes**	**holgazanas**
inglés	**inglesa**	**ingleses**	**inglesas**

  b. Adjectives that end in **-z** change **-z** to **-c** to form the plural.

un año **feliz** *a happy year*   unos días **felices** *some happy days*

5. Shortening of adjectives

  a. The adjectives **bueno, malo, primero, tercero, alguno,** and **ninguno** drop the final **-o** before a masuline singular noun.

un **buen** libro *a good book*   **primer** grado *first grade*
algún mercado *some market*   un **mal** negocio *bad business*
tercer cuaderno *third notebook*   **ningún** automóvil *no car*

  b. **Grande** becomes **gran** before a masculine or feminine noun.

un **gran** concierto *a great concert*   una **gran** fiesta *a great party*

c. **Santo** becomes **San** in front of masculine names.

San Juan   **San** Antonio   **San** José   **San** Cristóbal

NOTE: **Santo Tomás**, **Santo Toribio**, and **Santo Domingo** are exceptions.

d. **Ciento** becomes **cien** in front of a noun.

cien pesos   **cien** caballos

6. Some adjectives change meaning depending on whether they are placed before or after the noun.

un hombre **grande**	*a big man*
un **gran** hombre	*a great man*
un hombre **pobre**	*a poor man, without money*
un **pobre** hombre	*an unfortunate man*
un traje **nuevo**	*a brand new suit*
un **nuevo** traje	*a new (different) suit*
un libro **único**	*a unique book*
un **único** libro	*a single book*
el médico **mismo**	*the doctor himself*
el **mismo** médico	*the same doctor*
el vendedor **dichoso**	*the lucky salesman*
el **dichoso** vendedor	*the disagreeable (persistent) salesman*
la casa **antigua**	*the old, ancient house*
la **antigua** casa	*the former, previous house*

7. Adjectives derived from nouns. Some adjectives are derived from nouns and are therefore related in meaning to those nouns.

alegría *happiness*	**alegre** *happy*	humildad *humility*	**humilde** *humble*
amistad *friendship*	**amistoso** *friendly*	inteligencia *intelligence*	**inteligente** *intelligent*
amor *love*	**amoroso** *amorous*	lealtad *loyalty*	**leal** *loyal*
calor *heat*	**caluroso** *hot*	maravilla *marvel*	**maravilloso** *marvelous*
capacidad *capability*	**capaz** *capable*	montaña *mountain*	**montañoso** *mountainous*
debilidad *weakness*	**débil** *weak*	nobleza *nobility*	**noble** *noble*
delgadez *thinness*	**delgado** *thin*	palidez *paleness*	**pálido** *pale*
egoísmo *egotism*	**egoísta** *egotist*	pereza *lazyness*	**perezoso** *lazy*
envidia *envy*	**envidioso** *envious*	piedra *rock*	**pedregoso** *rocky*
estrechez *narrowness*	**estrecho** *narrow*	pobreza *poverty*	**pobre** *poor*
felicidad *happiness*	**feliz** *happy*	riqueza *wealth*	**rico** *wealthy*
fidelidad *fidelity*	**fiel** *faithful*	tierra *earth*	**terrestre** *earthly*
frialdad *coldness*	**frío** *cold*	tristeza *sadness*	**triste** *sad*
gordura *fatness*	**gordo** *fat*	vanidad *vanity*	**vanidoso** *vain*

Ejercicios

I. Coloque los adjetivos que están entre paréntesis delante o después de las palabras subrayadas.

MODELO: México se siente ligado a su <u>pasado</u>. (indígena)
México se siente ligado a su pasado indígena.

1. (primeros) (preazteca) (otras) Uno de los <u>pueblos</u> que llegó al valle de México fue el de los toltecas, <u>civilización</u> que influyó en las <u>culturas</u> que se desarrollaron en la región.
2. (maravillosas/toltecas) Teotihuacán es famoso por las <u>ruinas</u>.
3. (dos/impresionantes) Aquí se encuentran las <u>pirámides</u> que se conocen como la del Sol y la de la Luna.
4. (ceremonial) Teotihuacán, que quiere decir en náhuatl "Ciudad de los Dioses", fue el <u>centro</u> de una gran civilización.
5. (sagrado) (artístico) La serpiente era el <u>animal</u> que aparecía como <u>motivo</u> tallado en piedra.

II. Cambie las frases basándose en las palabras que están entre paréntesis.

MODELO: un alumno inteligente (decisión)
una decisión inteligente

1. un joven cortés (empleadas)
2. una película idiota (programa)
3. un deportista audaz (políticos)
4. un pintor irlandés (católicos)
5. la tercera puerta (piso)
6. algunos precios (producto)
7. aquella buena mujer (empleado)
8. otro perro juguetón (gata)
9. un cuadro gris (nubes)
10. un día inolvidable (noche)

III. Dé los adjetivos cuyos significados correspondan a los siguientes sustantivos. Después haga una oración con ellos.

MODELO: piedra
pedregoso
El camino era pedregoso y árido.

1. riqueza
2. vanidad
3. egoísmo
4. pereza
5. calor
6. frialdad
7. palidez
8. maravilla
9. envidia
10. estrechez

IV. Complete las oraciones con los equivalentes en español de las palabras en inglés.

1. (*a great woman*) Mi amiga es _____ .

2. (*a brand-new boat*) Horacio tiene _____ .

3. (*a big boy*) Juanito es _____ .

4. (*a unique book*) Éste es _____ por las ilustraciones que tiene.

5. (*The doctor himself*) _____ le puso la inyección.

6. (*The unfortunate man*) _____ perdió el trabajo.

V. Composición dirigida (oral o escrita). Complete las frases en forma original usando por lo menos tres adjetivos.

MODELO: El español es una lengua…
El español es una lengua musical, bella e interesante.

1. El año pasado pasé unas vacaciones…
2. El trabajo que tengo me parece…
3. Ricky Martin es un cantante…
4. Fui a ver una película…
5. El viaje que hice fue…

D Comparatives

Comparison can be made on three different levels to denote equality, superiority, or inferiority.

1. Equality

tan + adjective or adverb	
tanto (**-a, -os, -as**) + noun	como
tanto	

tan alta **como**	*as tall as*
tan tarde **como**	*as late as*
tanto dinero **como**	*as much money as*
tantas fichas **como**	*as many chips as*
tanto como	*as much as*

Las ruinas aztecas son **tan** interesantes **como** las ruinas incas.	*The Aztec ruins are as intresting as the Inca ruins.*
El avión llegó a Rosario **tan** tarde **como** el tren.	*The airplane arrived in Rosario as late as the train.*
Hoy hizo **tanto** calor **como** ayer.	*Today it was as hot as yesterday.*
Mi madre tiene **tanta** paciencia **como** mi padre.	*My mother has as much patience as my father.*
Había **tantos** turistas en el Museo de Bellas Artes **como** en la calle Florida.	*There were as many tourists at the Museum of Fine Arts as on Florida Street.*
Silvia tiene **tantas** amigas **como** Rosita.	*Silvia has as many friends as Rosita.*
Los viejos trabajan **tanto como** los jóvenes.	*The old ones work as much as the young ones.*
Ella habla **tanto como** su hermana.	*She talks as much as her sister.*

NOTE: In the two examples above, **tanto** is used as an adverb and doesn't change.*
Note the English equivalent of **tanto** and **tan** in the following sentences:

No debes beber **tanto**.	*You shouldn't drink so much.*
¡Esa casa tiene **tantos** defectos!	*That house has so many defects!*
¡Ella es **tan** bonita!	*She is so pretty!*

2. Superiority and inferiority

	Superiority			*Inferiority*	
más ⎰ adjective ⎱ adverb noun	**que**		**menos** ⎰ adjective ⎱ adverb noun	**que**

más viejo **que**	*older than*	**menos** orgulloso **que**	*less proud than*
más temprano **que**	*earlier than*	**menos** rápido **que**	*less fast than*
más camisas **que**	*more shirts than*	**menos** tiempo **que**	*less time than*

Los días del verano son **más** largos **que** los del invierno.
Summer days are longer than winter ones.
José camina **más** rápido **que** Antonio. *Jose walks faster than Antonio.*
El naranjo tiene **más** frutas **que** el limonero.
The orange tree has more fruit than the lemon tree.
Esta tela es **menos** suave **que** la otra. *This fabric is less soft than the other one.*
Lima tiene **menos** habitantes **que** Buenos Aires.
Lima has fewer inhabitants than Buenos Aires.
Un Ford pequeño consume **menos** gasolina **que** un Lincoln.
A small Ford takes less gasoline than a Lincoln.

NOTE: When an adjective is used in a comparison, it agrees with the first name or noun
mentioned. In case of adverbs, remember that adverbs are invariable.

Ernesto es tan **alto** como Susana. *Ernesto is as tall as Susana.*
La madre es más **orgullosa** que los hijos. *The mother is prouder than the children.*

a. The equivalent in English of **más que** and **menos que** is *more than* and *less than.*

Él trabaja **más que** tú. *He works more than you.*
Luisa estudia **menos que** sus compañeros. *Luisa studies less than her companions.*

b. With numbers, **más de** and **menos de** are used instead of *más que* and *menos que.*

Tengo **más de** veinte años. *I am more than twenty years old.*
Pagué por la casa **menos de** $50.000. *I paid less than $50,000 for the house.*

c. In negative sentences **más que** is used before a number, and is the equivalent of
the English *only.*

No tengo **más que** un buen amigo. *I have only one good friend.*
No compré **más que** dos vestidos. *I bought only two dresses.*

---

*See adverbs, pages 180 and 181.

d. When there are two clauses and the comparison in the second clause refers to a specific person or thing in the first clause, **de** + definite article + **que** is used.

Vendieron la casa en más dinero **del que** pagaron por ella.
They sold the house for more money than (the money) they paid for it.
Ella tiene menos amigos **de los que** tú crees. *She has less friends than (the friends) you think.*
Alfredo tiene más paciencia **de la que** parece. *Alfredo has more patience than it seems.*
Compré menos frutas **de las que** necesito. *I bought less fruit than (the fruit) I need.*

De lo que is used when the comparison refers to an adjective or an adverb or an idea (not to a specific person or thing) expressed in the first clause.

Vendieron la casa en más **de lo que** pagaron por ella.
They sold the house for more than (what) they paid for it.
El vestido cuesta menos **de lo que** yo creía. *The dress costs less than (what) I thought.*
El cuarto es más grande **de lo que** yo pensaba. *The room is bigger than (what) I thought.*

e. **Más** and **menos** can be modified by an adverb (**mucho, bastante, poco, algo, tanto**) to intensify or diminish the level of comparison.

Ella trabaja **mucho más** que yo. *She works much more than I.*
Elena habla **bastante menos** que su esposo. *Elena talks much less than her husband.*
Su casa es **algo más** moderna que la mía. *Her house is somewhat more modern than mine.*

3. Irregular comparatives

The following adjectives and adverbs have irregular forms to express the comparative. These comparatives agree only in number. **Mejor** and **peor** may be used as either **adjectives** or **adverbs**.*

bueno, bien	**mejor**	grande	**mayor**
malo, mal	**peor**	pequeño	**menor**

Los años que viví en Madrid fueron los **mejores** de mi vida.
The years I lived in Madrid were the best of my life.
Uds. nadan **mejor** que yo. *You swim better than I.*
Esta carretera está en **peores** condiciones que el año pasado.
This highway is in worse condition than last year.
Tu automóvil funciona **peor** que el mío. *Your automobile runs worse than mine.*

a. **Grande** and **pequeño**, when referring to size, use a regular comparison with **más** and **menos.**

La casa nueva es **más grande** que la que teníamos antes.
The new house is bigger than the one we had before.
La ventana de la sala es **más pequeña** que la del comedor.
The living room window is smaller than the one in the dining room.

b. When referring to age, **mayor** and **menor** are used to express **más viejo** and **más joven.**

Pedro es **mayor** que Enrique.	*Pedro is older than Enrique.*
Yo soy **menor** que mi hermano.	*I am younger than my brother.*
El senador es un señor ya **mayor.**	*The senator is a rather old man.*

*See adjectives, page 236.

c. **Más viejo** can be used for persons and things.

> Pedro es **más viejo** que Enrique. *Pedro is older than Enrique.*
> El edificio de la biblioteca es **más viejo** que el de ingeniería.
> *The library building is older than the engineering one.*

d. **Más joven** refers only to persons. **Más nuevo** is used when referring to things.

> Mi casa es **más nueva** que la suya. *My house is newer than his/hers/yours.*

Ejercicios

I. De acuerdo con la oración dada construya una oración comparativa que indique igualdad.

MODELO: Clemente y Nicolás son egoístas.
Clemente es tan egoísta como Nicolás.

1. Tu impresora (*printer*) y la mía son buenas.
2. Los cuentos de Borges y los de Cortázar son fascinantes.
3. Juan y Manuel están cansados.
4. Tus ojos y el cielo son azules.

II. De acuerdo con la oración dada construya una oración comparativa que indique superioridad y otra comparativa que indique inferioridad.

MODELO: Luisa y Ana son muy dinámicas.
Luisa es más dinámica que Ana.
Ana es menos dinámica que Luisa.

1. Mi padre y mi abuelo son ricos.
2. Pedro y Juan son vanidosos.
3. Mi tío y mi tía están bien.
4. Juan y Pedro llegaron tarde.

III. Ud. habla con un compañero de clase y éste presenta su punto de vista haciendo una comparación. Llene los espacios en blanco para conocer la opinión del compañero.

1. —Gloria Estefan es buena cantante.

   —Sí, pero Linda Ronstadt es _____ .

2. —El correo electrónico es rápido.

   —Claro que sí, pero algunos creen que el fax es _____ .

3. —Me gusta viajar en avión por muchas razones.

   —Yo prefiero el tren porque aunque es _____ rápido

   _____ el avión, es _____ cómodo.

IV. Complete las oraciones con los equivalentes en español de las palabras que están en inglés.

1. (*more than*) Ella tiene _____ dos hermanos.
2. (*so much*) El médico me dijo que no debo trabajar _____ .

3. (*so*) El estudiante es _____ bueno que se llevó el premio.

4. (*less than*) Ella gasta _____ su esposo.

5. (*older*) Ricardo es _____ que Rodolfo.

6. (*younger*) Mi madre es _____ que mi tío.

7. (*as much as*) Él quiere a su tía _____ a su madre.

8. (*only*) No tengo _____ 20 dólares en la billetera.

V. Complete las frases con los comparativos que sean correctos.

MODELO: Eva cocina muy bien, pero su madre cocina _____ .
Eva cocina muy bien, pero su madre cocina mejor.

1. El postre está malo, pero el vino está _____ .

2. El niño lee bien, pero su hermanito lee _____ .

3. Mi casa es grande, pero la de Antonio es _____ .

4. Ella tiene treinta años y yo tengo veinticuatro. Ella es _____ que yo.

5. Estos productos son malos, pero los otros son _____ .

VI. Composición dirigida (oral o escrita). Compare las siguientes cosas y personas. Haga por lo menos tres oraciones.

1. Un aeropuerto con una estación de trenes
2. Una ciudad grande con un pueblo pequeño
3. Una dictadura con una democracia
4. El verano con el otoño

E Superlatives

Ways to express a superlative idea:

el (la, los, las) { **más** + adjective
menos + adjective
irregular comparative

adjective
adverb } + **-ísimo** (-a, -os, -as)

1. By using the definite article

La hija menor es **la más linda de** la familia.
The youngest daughter is the prettiest in the family.
El fertilizante que compré es **el menos caro**.
The fertilizer that I bought is the least expensive.
Armando es **el peor** estudiante que conozco. *Armando is the worst student that I know.*
Éstas son las **mejores** piñas que encontré. *These are the best pineapples that I found.*

NOTE: In the first example the preposition **de** is used in Spanish to translate the English preposition *in*.

2. By adding the suffix **-ísimo (-a, -os, -as)** to the adjective or adverb when it ends in a consonant. Notice that when the adjective or adverb ends in a vowel, the vowel is dropped before adding the suffix. Observe the changes in the following words: **amable, fiel, fuerte.**

amable	**amabilísimo**
antiguo	**antiquísimo**
fácil	**facilísimo**
feliz	**felicísimo**
feo	**feísimo**
fiel	**fidelísimo**
fuerte	**fortísimo**
grande	**grandísimo**
inteligente	**inteligentísimo**
lejos	**lejísimos**
lindo	**lindísimo**
malo (mal)	**malísimo**
rico	**riquísimo**
sucio	**sucísimo**
tarde	**tardísimo**
viejo	**viejísimo**

Estamos **cansadísimas**. *We are extremely tired.*
Anoche nos divertimos **muchísimo**.
Last night we enjoyed ourselves very much.

Words ending in **-co, -go**, and **-z** have the following spelling changes.

c → **qu**	poco	**poquísimo**
g → **gu**	amargo	**amarguísimo**
z → **c**	feliz	**felicísimo**

NOTE: **Pésimo** is another superlative form of **malo**.

Pasé una noche **pésima**. El ruido de la calle no me dejó dormir.
I spent a terrible night. The street noise didn't let me sleep.

3. By placing certain adverbs (**muy, sumamente, extraordinariamente, extremadamente**) before the adjective or adverb.

Ella es **sumamente** inteligente.
She is extremely intelligent.

NOTE: In Spanish, the equivalent of *very much* is **muchísimo**. The equivalent of *very little* can be **poquísimo** or **muy poco**.

Ejercicios

I. Complete las oraciones con la palabra apropiada para expresar una idea comparativa o superlativa.

1. Carlos es tan capaz _____ su primo.
2. Esta novela tiene más _____ trescientas páginas.
3. Ella habla _____ bien como su padre.
4. Ese médico es menos respetado _____ la Dra. García.
5. Esa decisión es _____ mejor _____ todas las decisiones que has tomado.
6. No quiero para la cena _____ un plato de sopa.
7. Estos pueblos son _____ pueblos más antiguos _____ Guatemala.
8. El río Amazonas es más grande _____ el río Orinoco.
9. Ellos obtuvieron _____ beneficios como yo.
10. Éstas son _____ mejores toallas que encontré.

II. Sustituya las palabras subrayadas por un superlativo terminado en **-ísimo**.

MODELO: Es una casa muy antigua.
Es una casa antiquísima.

1. Vivimos <u>muy lejos</u>.
2. La Torre Latinoamericana, en la Ciudad de México, es <u>muy alta</u>.
3. Laura está <u>extremadamente flaca</u>.
4. Ellos se quieren <u>mucho</u>.
5. El café de Colombia es <u>muy bueno</u>.
6. La casa está <u>sumamente sucia</u>.

Composición

Antes de escribir, repase las siguientes reglas sobre las mayúsculas y la ortografía.

A Review of capitalization rules

A capital letter is not used:

1. With the days of the week, months, and seasons of the year
   lunes, mayo, la primavera

2. With adjectives of nationality:
   americano, salvadoreño, japonés

3. With names of languages:
   inglés, italiano, ruso

4. With adjectives referring to religion:
   católico, metodista, presbiteriano

5. With the names of academic courses when they don't refer to the discipline as such:
   La **Psicología** se considera importante para los educadores.
   Psychology is considered important for educators.
   Es necesario entender la **psciología** de los niños.
   It is necessary to understand the psychology of children.

B Review of spelling rules: *b, v*

1. Use **b**:
   - In the syllables **bur, bus,** and **b** followed by **l** or **r**:
     burla, buscar, hablar, brazo, libre
   - In the combinations **rab, rib, rob, rub**:
     rabia, arriba, robar except: **rival, Rivera**
   - In the prefixes **bi-, bis-, biz-**:
     bisnieto (biznieto), bilingüe
   - In the verbs ending in **-bir** and **-buir**:
     recibir, escribir, contribuir except: **servir, hervir** *(to boil)*, **vivir**
   - In the endings of the imperfect indicative:
     íbamos, trabajaba, estudiaban
   - After **m**:
     rumbo *(direction)*, **mambo, embajada** *(embassy)*
   - In the prefixes **abs-, sub-, biblio-, obs-**:
     abstinencia, submarino, bibliotecario *(librarian)*, **obstinación**
   - In the suffixes **-able, -ible**:
     comparable, discutible
   - In the endings **-bilidad, -bundo**:
     responsabilidad, moribundo except: **movilidad, civilidad**

2. Use **v**:

- After **b, d, n, le, di**:

  obvio, adverso, invierno, levantar, divino

- In the preterite of the indicative and the imperfect subjunctive of the verbs **tener, andar, estar**:

  tuvieron, anduvieron, estuve.

- In words beginning with **vice-, villa-**:

  viceversa, villanía, Villarreal except: **bíceps, billar** (*billiards*)

- In words beginning with **ave-, avi-, eva-, eve-, evi-, evo-**:

  avenida, avispa (*wasp*), evaporar, evento, evidente, evolucionar (*to evolve*)

- Words that begin with **sal-, sel-, sil-, sol-, ser-**:

  salvavidas, selva, Silva, solvente, servidumbre (*servants*)
  except: **silbar** (*to whistle*)

3. Words frequently confused:

tuvo *he/she/you had*	**tubo** *tube*	**bello** *beautiful*	**vello** *hair, fuzz*
botas *boots*	**votas** *you vote*	**barón** *baron*	**varón** *male*
haber *to be/to have*	**a ver** *let's see*		

NOTE: The exercises that correspond to this section are included in the *Cuaderno de ejercicios*, Capítulo 8.

Ejercicio de composición (opcional)

Escriba una composición sobre el tema que se da a continuación. Use el esquema siguiente.

TEMA: Un deporte para cada gusto.

INTRODUCCIÓN: A través de los siglos los deportes han sido importantes para las diferentes civilizaciones del mundo.
Interés que tienen los deportes.

DESARROLLO: El fútbol y el béisbol en los Estados Unidos. Equipos profesionales y equipos de aficionados.
Popularidad del baloncesto. Equipos de mujeres que compiten a nivel nacional en las competencias de baloncesto.
El golf y el tenis: equipos integrados por mujeres y hombres.
Los deportes de invierno: esquiar y patinar en el hielo.
La natación. El buceo submarino (*scuba diving*).
Los deportes más peligrosos y los más violentos.

CONCLUSIÓN: ¿Por qué cree Ud. que los deportes han sido siempre tan populares?
Evaluación personal del significado de los deportes.

Niños puertorriqueños en una clase de tercer grado en Brooklyn, Nueva York.

LECTURAS

- Lectura 1: "Inmigraciones hispanas en los Estados Unidos"
- Lectura 2: "Recuerdo intimo" de Lucha Corpi
- Lectura 3: "La mejor tinta" de Armando Valladares

GRAMÁTICA

- Prepositions
- Uses of **por** and **para**
- Uses of **pero** and **sino**
- Verbs that are used with the preposition **a** followed by an infinitive, and the ones that are used without it
- Verbs that are followed by prepositions

COMPOSICIÓN

- Review of accentuation
- Review of spelling rules: **r, rr**

Vocabulario

Antes de leer, repase el siguiente vocabulario que le ayudará a comprender la lectura.

Sustantivos

la banca   banking
la cifra   number
la ciudadanía   citizenship
la empresa   company
el ejército   armed services
la escasez   shortage
la fábrica   factory
el habitante   inhabitant
el negocio   business
el obrero   worker, laborer

la oferta   offer
la población   population
el puesto   position, job
el reconocimiento   recognition
el refugio   refuge
el suroeste   southwest
el trabajador   worker, laborer
la travesía   voyage
la vivencia   personal experience

Verbos

agrupar   to group, to assemble
aportar   to contribute
citar   to cite
establecer (zc)   to found
evolucionar   to evolve
expatriarse   to go into exile
fluir (y) (como huir)   to flow
fortalecer (zc)   to strengthen

hacerse   to become
mantener (como tener)   to maintain
narrar   to narrate
regresar   to go back (physically)
remontarse   to go back (to some date in the past)
surgir (j)   to appear
triunfar   to be successful, to triumph
valorar   to value

Adjetivos

agudo   keen, sharp
duro   hard

propio   one's own
trabajador   hardworking

Preposición

según   according to

Frases

debido a   due to
en busca de   looking for
en su época   in his/her/their time

segunda guerra mundial   World War II
sentido de humor   sense of humor

Related words (Palabras relacionadas). The meaning of some words may be determined by thinking of related words familiar to you. Can you give in English the meaning of the underlined words derived from the words in parentheses?

1. (fundar) … Cuando en 1607 se fundó Jamestown,…
2. (documento) … millones de indocumentados que viven en el país.

3. (agricultura) (brazo) … muchos de ellos trabajadores <u>agrícolas</u> o <u>braceros</u>.
4. (pintar) (vivir) … han tratado de expresar, a través de la <u>pintura</u>, su historia y sus <u>vivencias</u>.

Be careful with the following false cognates.

fábrica *factory*	tela *fabric*
actualmente *at present*	realmente *actually*
fundar *to found*	encontrar *to find*
calidad *quality*	cualidad *qualification*
época *time; epoch, era*	tiempo *time; duration of time; weather*
rato *short time*	vez *time (in a series)*

*L*ectura   1

Inmigraciones hispanas en los Estados Unidos

Históricamente, gran parte del territorio ocupado hoy por los Estados Unidos podría haber sido parte del mundo hispanoamericano. La presencia hispana en el suroeste de este país se remonta a la llegada de los españoles a América. Cuando en 1607 se fundó Jamestown, en Virginia,
5 el español Pedro Martínez de Avilés ya había fundado, en 1565, la ciudad de San Agustín en la Florida, y otros españoles habían navegado por el río Misisipí y explorado áreas de Tejas, Arizona, Nuevo México y California. En este último estado el fraile español Junípero Serra estableció las famosas misiones que, en su época, no sólo fueron centros religiosos, sino
10 también centros económicos y de educación. Como consecuencia de este pasado hispánico, en el suroeste de los Estados Unidos hay innumerables ciudades y pueblos, calles y avenidas con nombres españoles.

En el siglo XX ese pasado hispano se fortaleció, debido a las inmigraciones hispanas que actualmente representan un aspecto importante
15 de la vida y la cultura de los Estados Unidos. Según el último censo,° se   *census* calcula que la población hispana pasa de los veinte y dos millones, cifra que no incluye a los millones de indocumentados que viven en el país. Se calcula que para el año 2010 los hispanos serán la minoría más grande de los Estados Unidos. Las mayores inmigraciones que forman esta gran población
20 hispana han venido de México, Puerto Rico, Cuba y Centroamérica.

La principal inmigración, y la que más impacto ha tenido, es la mexicana, que representa un gran porcentaje de la población hispana, con grandes concentraciones en California, Arizona, Nuevo México y Chicago.

Durante la segunda guerra mundial, debido a la gran escasez de
25 trabajadores que había en los Estados Unidos, miles de mexicanos vinieron
en busca de trabajo. La vida de estos mexicanos, muchos de ellos
trabajadores agrícolas, era dura y se veían forzados° a ir de un lado para   *forced*
otro según las ofertas de trabajo. Aunque estos inmigrantes asimilaron una
nueva forma de existencia, no abandonaron sus tradiciones ni costumbres.
30 En el suroeste de los Estados Unidos la influencia de la cultura mexicana
es notable, ya que esta parte del país era territorio de México.
Lógicamente, la población de origen mexicano aportó varios elementos
culturales que han quedado incorporados a la vida norteamericana.
El chicano o mexicoamericano, como grupo, presenta gran variedad.
35 Se caracteriza por su bilingüismo y su biculturalismo. La cultura chicana
es el producto final de la vida y las experiencias del inmigrante mexicano
en los Estados Unidos. Los chicanos han producido una literatura propia
que evoluciona y crece constantemente y que, aunque muy variada, se
caracteriza por los elementos que definen la vida del chicano en conflicto
40 con la cultura norteamericana. Entre los muchos autores se deben citar a
Tomás Rivera, Rolando Hinojosa y Sandra Cisneros. Esta última escritora
ha iniciado su carrera literaria con dos novelas que han tenido mucho
éxito y resonancia. En ellas Sandra Cisneros narra las experiencias del
mexicoamericano en un estilo original, donde predomina su sentido de
45 humor poético. Asimismo, el arte muralista mexicano ha sido imitado en
muchas ciudades estadounidenses por artistas chicanos, los cuales han
tratado de expresar, a través de la pintura, su historia y sus vivencias.
Es importante mencionar que en la actualidad muchos chicanos
ocupan puestos en el gobierno, en las universidades y en las escuelas
50 desde donde defienden y luchan por su cultura. En el mundo de los
negocios y del comercio, son muchos los chicanos que han triunfado
estableciendo y desarrollando fábricas y empresas importantes.
Los puertorriqueños son el segundo grupo (en número y en
antigüedad) de inmigrantes hispanos que se encuentran por todo el país.
55 Puerto Rico pasó a ser parte de los Estados Unidos en 1898, y
actualmente es un Estado Libre Asociado.° Los habitantes de la isla tienen   *Commonwealth*
la ciudadanía norteamericana y sirven en el ejército de los Estados
Unidos, pero no votan en las elecciones presidenciales ni tienen
representantes en el Congreso. Después de la segunda guerra mundial, los
60 puertorriqueños, lo mismo que los mexicoamericanos, venían a los
Estados Unidos para buscar trabajo. Más de un 70% de los
puertorriqueños viven en Nueva York, donde forman un núcleo
sociocultural definido y vital. Muchos de ellos han asimilado la cultura
norteamericana y han tenido éxito, otros mantienen una dualidad°   *duality*
65 cultural y otros aun están agrupados solamente entre ellos mismos.
Últimamente la inmigración puertorriqueña ha disminuido, debido al
gran desarrollo económico de Puerto Rico, y algunos de los que vivían en
el clima frío de Nueva York han regresado a su hermosa isla tropical.

La influencia cubana es evidente en los comercios de la calle ocho en Miami, Florida.

70   En los últimos años han surgido escritores y poetas puertorriqueños
que, desde tierra° norteamericana, han creado una literatura genuina de   land
importancia. Entre ellos se pueden citar a Rosario Ferré y a Julia de
Burgos, poeta independiente, sincera y rebelde que vivió y murió en
Nueva York. En su poesía expresa la nostalgia de su tierra natal° y del   native country
75   campo de su isla del Caribe. Entre los compositores puertorriqueños de
música seria que enseñan en universidades de los Estados Unidos se
puede citar a Roberto Sierra, cuya música es cada vez más conocida.
A diferencia de los otros dos grupos anteriores, los cubanos empezaron
a venir a los Estados Unidos, buscando refugio político, a partir de 1959.
80   Al triunfar en esa fecha la revolución dirigida por Fidel Castro, miles de
profesionales, artistas, escritores, oficinistas, campesinos y obreros
tuvieron que expatriarse por no poder vivir bajo la dictadura comunista
existente en Cuba. Cuando en 1962 se suspendieron los vuelos

comerciales entre los Estados Unidos y Cuba, la salida de la isla se hizo
85 casi imposible y muchas familias completas escapaban en barcos
pequeños, muriendo muchos de ellos en la travesía. En 1965 el presidente
de los Estados Unidos, Lyndon Johnson, autorizó los "vuelos de la
libertad" y más de 300.000 cubanos llegaron, en corto tiempo, a las costas
de Miami. Actualmente los cubanos que residen en este país pasan del
90 millón.

Los cubanos se han incorporado a la vida estadounidense, ocupando
puestos importantes en las universidades y escuelas, en el comercio y en
la banca, y estableciendo negocios propios. Los comerciantes cubanos han
tenido un papel importante en el desarrollo de la economía de Miami,
95 centro bancario importante para las conexiones de negocios entre el
Caribe y la América del Sur. Se puede decir que la ciudad de Miami está
totalmente "cubanizada", ya que se ha convertido en una extensión de
Cuba en tierra norteamericana. A pesar de los cuarenta y tres años de
exilio, el cubano mantiene el uso del español en el hogar° y las   home
100 generaciones jóvenes son hoy día totalmente bilingües.

La producción literaria del exilio cubano es abundante y de gran
calidad. Novelistas, cuentistas y poetas, así como pintores, compositores
y escultores,° forman un núcleo creativo en el área de Nueva York y   sculptors
Miami. Entre los escritores que han alcanzado fama y reconocimiento
105 están Guillermo Cabrera Infante, que vive en Londres desde 1966, y que
recibió el valioso Premio Cervantes en 1997, y Reinaldo Arenas que dejó
una extensa lista de obras que han sido traducidas a muchos idiomas. La
autobiografía de éste último escritor, *Antes que anochezca* es un
estremecedor° testimonio personal y político que Arenas terminó de   shocking
110 escribir unos días antes de ponerle fin a su vida. Esta obra ha sido
llevada al cine y la película ha sido muy elogiada° por la crítica   praised
cinematográfica.

En la pintura varios pintores cubanos ocupan una posición sólida en
los círculos del mundo del arte, destacándose Cundo Bermúdez, cuyos
115 cuadros han alcanzado precios muy altos, y Ramón Alejandro, que al
igual que Bermúdez vive en Miami. En el campo de la música clásica
entre los compositores que han trascendido las fronteras de este país se
pueden citar a Julián Orbón, a Aurelio de la Vega y a Tania León.

En los años ochenta, grandes grupos de refugiados políticos de
120 Nicaragua llegaron a Miami, aumentando así el número de
hispanohablantes en esa ciudad. Más tarde, debido a la guerra civil en El
Salvador que duró hasta 1992, muchos salvadoreños vinieron a los
Estados Unidos y se establecieron en Miami, Nueva York y Los Ángeles,
que es donde reside el núcleo mayor de ellos.

125 Todas las inmigraciones mencionadas se han incorporado al fluir de la
vida norteamericana, dejando en ella las huellas de la cultura y las
tradiciones hispanas, produciendo un enriquecimiento en la forma de
vida, en las costumbres y hasta en la lengua.

Grupo folklórico colombiano durante la Celebración del Día Hispanoamericano en la ciudad de Nueva York.

Llene los espacios en blanco con la palabra que sea correcta.

1. En el siglo pasado un viaje a Europa demoraba varios días, _____ que no había aviones y el viaje se hacía en barco.

2. La presencia hispana en el suroeste de los Estados Unidos _____ a la llegada de los españoles a América.

3. Después de la segunda guerra mundial, en los Estados Unidos hacía falta gente para trabajar. Debido a esta _____ de trabajadores, vinieron muchos mexicanos a distintas partes del país.

4. Los puertorriqueños tienen que servir en el _____ norteamericano.

5. Muchos de los inmigrantes cubanos que venían en botes pequeños murieron en la _____.

6. En todo el suroeste de los Estados Unidos se ve la _____ dejada por la cultura mexicana.

7. Un fraile español _____ las misiones de California.

8. La inmigración grande de cubanos, a partir de 1959, _____ nuevas costumbres a la vida norteamericana.

9. El pasado hispano se ha _____ y se ha enriquecido con las inmigraciones de México, Puerto Rico y Cuba.

10. La literatura chicana tiene muchos escritores que han alcanzado _____ y fama.

11. Miami es un centro importante para las conexiones de _____ entre el Caribe y la América del Sur.

12. Debido al desarrollo económico de Puerto Rico, muchos puertorriqueños están _____ a la isla tropical.

Preguntas sobre la lectura

1. ¿Por qué dice el autor que parte de los Estados Unidos podría haber pertenecido al mundo hispanoamericano?

2. ¿Cuál de las tres inmigraciones hispanas que han venido a los Estados Unidos es la que más huellas ha dejado en la vida norteamericana? Mencione algunas de las influencias que se notan en la lengua, en las comidas, en la ropa, en el estilo de las casas.

3. Mencione las circunstancias que hicieron que miles de trabajadores mexicanos vinieran a los Estados Unidos.

4. ¿Qué narra la escritora chicana, Sandra Cisneros, en sus novelas?

5. En los últimos años, ¿en qué campos de la vida norteamericana se desenvuelve y triunfa el mexicoamericano?

6. Al ser Puerto Rico un Estado Libre Asociado, ¿qué ciudadanía tienen sus habitantes?

7. ¿Por qué ha disminuido en los últimos años la inmigración puertorriqueña que venía a Nueva York?

8. ¿Qué circunstancia produce la inmigración cubana a los Estados Unidos? Compare esta inmigración con las otras dos inmigraciones.

9. ¿Cómo interpreta Ud. el hecho de que muchas familias cubanas se decidieran a escapar, abandonando todas las pertenencias y posesiones, en lugar de quedarse en su patria? En iguales circunstancias, ¿haría Ud. lo mismo?

10. Si Ud. ha estado en Nueva York, entre los puertorriqueños, o en Miami, entre los cubanos, describa algunas de las costumbres de ambos grupos.

Temas de conversación

1. Se dice que este país es un mosaico de culturas. ¿Está de acuerdo con esta afirmación? Explique su respuesta. ¿Cuáles fueron las principales inmigraciones venidas de Europa en el siglo XIX? ¿En qué aspectos de la cultura popular norteamericana es evidente la influencia de los esclavos negros?

2. La inmigración ilegal de mexicanos y centroamericanos a los Estados Unidos es un problema muy discutido y existen muchas opiniones sobre ese tema. Algunas personas creen que es beneficiosa porque los inmigrantes ilegales hacen trabajos que nadie quiere hacer. Otros piensan que les quitan trabajos a los que ya viven aquí. ¿Cuál es su opinión?

3. ¿Viene Ud. de una familia de inmigrantes llegados recientemente a los Estados Unidos? Hable sobre las experiencias que han tenido en este país. ¿Qué diferencia cree Ud. que existe entre un turista y un inmigrante?

4. ¿Cree Ud. que la tecnología moderna ha creado o eliminado puestos de trabajo? Explique su respuesta. ¿Por qué cree Ud. que hay tanta inmigración del campo hacia las ciudades grandes? ¿Cree Ud. que el Gobierno Federal debe proporcionar (provide) trabajo a todos los que estén desempleados (unemployed)?

Vocabulario

Antes de leer, repase el siguiente vocabulario que le ayudará a comprender la lectura.

Sustantivos
el tejado   tile roof
la tina de baño   bathtub

Verbos
destrozar (c)   to destroy
meterse   to get inside

Adjetivo
infame   horrible

Frase
por si acaso   just in case

Lectura 2

Lucha Corpi

Lucha Corpi, escritora mexicoamericana, nació en Veracruz. Habiendo publicado varios libros, tanto en inglés como en español, esta escritora se destaca no sólo por su prosa, sino también por su poesía. "Recuerdo íntimo" narra en primera persona una anécdota del pasado en un tono melancólico y evocador.

Recuerdo íntimo

Para Arturo y Finnigan

No había llovido así
desde aquel día en que los perros
destrozaron los únicos zapatos que tenías
y mi bolsa estaba llena solamente
5   de papeles y palabras.

Llovía tanto aquella tarde
que Finnigan el gato, tú y yo,
a falta de arca,° decidimos meternos   *ark*
a la tina de baño, por si acaso....

10   Esta tarde llueve igual que entonces
pero mi razón se niega a reandar°   *to remember*
aquel infame invierno:
Sólo escucho la lluvia en el tejado,
el ronroneo° del gato en la tina de baño,   *purring*
15   veo la suave luz de tu sonrisa de dos años.

Es todo lo que necesito recordar.

Preguntas sobre la lectura

1. ¿Qué recuerdos le trae la lluvia a la poeta?
2. ¿A quién se dirige la poeta?
3. ¿Quién cree Ud. que es el tú de la segunda estrofa?
4. ¿A qué se refiere la poeta al mencionar, también en la segunda estrofa, la palabra "arca"?
5. ¿Cómo interpreta Ud. la expresión de "aquel infame invierno"?
6. ¿Qué cosas no quiere olvidar la poeta?

Vocabulario

Antes de leer, repase el siguiente vocabulario que le ayudará a comprender la lectura.

Sustantivos
la cárcel   jail
el castigo   punishment
la rebeldía   rebelliousness
la sonrisa   smile

Verbos
ahogar   to choke; to drown
hundir   to sink
quitar   to take away
sacar   to take out

Frases
ni así   not even then
mi propia sangre   my own blood

Lectura 3

Armando Valladares

Armando Valladares (1937–   ), poeta cubano, estuvo preso (*in prison*) veintidós años (1960–1982) por sus convicciones religiosas y políticas, contrarias a las ideas marxistas de la dictadura (*dictatorship*) de Fidel Castro en Cuba. Su poesía, parte de ella escrita en prisión y sacada (*taken out*) en secreto del país, se publicó en dos libros, *El corazón con que vivo* (1984) y *El alma de un poeta* (1988).

La mejor tinta

Me lo han quitado todo
las plumas
los lápices
la tinta
5 porque ellos no quieren
que yo escriba
y me han hundido
en esta celda de castigo
pero ni así ahogarán mi rebeldía.
10 Me lo han quitado todo
—bueno, casi todo—
porque me queda la sonrisa
el orgullo° de sentirme un hombre libre   *pride*
y en el alma un jardín
15 de eternas florecitas.
Me lo han quitado todo
las plumas
los lápices
pero me queda la tinta de la vida
20 —mi propia sangre—
y con ella escribo versos todavía.

Original escrito con mi sangre y una astillita de madera°   *wooden chip*
en abril de 1981 en las celdas de castigo de la cárcel° del   *jail*
Combinado del Este,° en La Habana.   *name of the prison*

De *El alma de un poeta* (1988)

Preguntas sobre la lectura

1. ¿En qué lugar estaba el poeta cuando escribió el poema?
2. ¿Por qué le han quitado todo?
3. ¿Qué cosas no le han podido quitar al poeta?
4. ¿Qué tinta usó para escribir los versos?
5. ¿Qué sentimiento cree Ud. que se expresa con mayor fuerza en este poema?

Ejercicio oral. Mire el dibujo por Armando Valladares en la página 260. Conteste las siguientes preguntas.

1. ¿Qué contraste ve Ud. entre los dos objetos del dibujo: la rosa y el alambre de púas (*barbed wire*)? ¿Qué cree Ud. que simbolizan?
2. ¿Qué sentimientos cree Ud. que se expresan en este dibujo?
3. ¿Cómo interpreta Ud. el dibujo?

Dibujo de Armando Valladares que aparece en el libro El alma de un poeta.

Gramática

A Prepositions

A preposition links or relates two elements of a sentence.

Árbol **sin** hojas…	*Tree without leaves…*
Salimos **para** la capital.	*We leave for the capital.*
Difícil **de** comprender…	*Difficult to understand…*

Besides single word prepositions, there are prepositional phrases that function like prepositions.

1. Prepositions.

a	de	hasta	sobre
ante	desde	para	tras
bajo	en	por	
con	entre	según	
contra	hacia	sin	

a. As in English, the use of the prepositions in Spanish is quite arbitrary. Some prepositions in Spanish can have different equivalents in English. For example:

a	*at, by, on, to*
de	*about, from, of, to*
en	*at, in, into, on*

Salí **a** las cuatro.	*I went out at four.*
Lavé la blusa **a** mano.	*I washed the blouse by hand.*
Llegó **a** tiempo.	*He arrived on time.*
Vamos **a** la playa.	*We go to the beach.*

b. Some verbs that in English are followed by a preposition, need only the verb in Spanish.

mirar	*to look at*	**buscar**	*to look for*
escuchar	*to listen to*	**pedir**	*to ask for*
esperar	*to wait for*		

Mientras **esperábamos** el autobús para ir al aeropuerto, Fernando pagó la cuenta del hotel, Susana **escuchó** las noticias y yo **miré** la televisión.
While we were waiting for the bus to go to the airport, Fernando paid the hotel bill, Susana listened to the news, and I watched television.

NOTE: The preposition **a** ("personal **a**") is used before a direct object referring to a person.

| Miro **a** los niños. | *I look at the children.* |
| Escuchamos **a** Plácido Domingo. | *We listen to Plácido Domingo.* |

2. General rules for the use of some prepositions. **A** is used:

a. With verbs that express movement or direction.

| Voy **al** banco. | *I go to the bank.* |
| Llegó **a** la casa. | *He (She) arrived home.* |

NOTE: Remember that **a + el = al** and **de + el = del**.

b. With direct and indirect objects.

| Visito **a** mis primos. | *I visit my cousins.* |
| Le doy las flores **a** Luisa. | *I give the flowers to Luisa.* |

c. To indicate the time of an event or an action.

| La cena es **a** las ocho. | *Dinner is at eight.* |

d. In idiomatic expressions to indicate how something is made.

| El mantel está hecho **a** mano. | *The tablecloth is made by hand.* |
| El suéter está tejido **a** máquina. | *The sweater is knitted by machine.* |

e. With the verb **estar** to indicate distance regarding another point of reference.

La capital **está a** 100 kilómetros de este pueblo.
The capital is (at) one hundred kilometers from this town.

f. In front of **quien** (the "personal **a**") to mean *whom* in English.

¿**A quién** invitaste?   *Whom did you invite?*

3. En is used:

a. To indicate position or place.

Estoy **en** la frontera del Canadá.   *I am at the Canadian border.*
Dejé los papeles **en** la oficina.   *I left the papers in the office.*

b. With some expressions using the words **momento, instante, tiempo,** or **época.**

Llegué al aeropuerto **en el instante** en que salían los pasajeros del avión.
I arrived at the airport at the moment the passengers were coming out of the plane.
En aquel tiempo vivíamos en Barcelona.
At that time we were living in Barcelona.
En esa época pocas mujeres usaban pantalones.
In those times few women wore pants.

c. To indicate means of transportation.

Viajaremos **en avión** hasta Guadalajara, pero después iremos **en tren** a la capital.
We will travel by plane to Guadalajara, but later we will go by train to the capital.
Ellos piensan ir **en barco** a Europa.
They plan to go to Europe by ship.
Los niños van a ir **en bicicleta** al parque, pero yo voy a ir **en coche.**
The children are going to go by bicycle to the park, but I'm going to go by car.

But we say:

Montamos **a caballo** en el campo.
We go horseback riding in the country.
Fuimos **a pie** hasta llegar a la catedral.
We went walking (We walked) until we got to the cathedral.

4. De is used:*

a. To indicate possession, origin, and material from which something is made.

La casa **de** Delia es hermosa.   *Delia's house is beautiful.*
Miguel Hidalgo era **de** Guanajuato.   *Miguel Hidalgo was from Guanajuato.*
Compré una cafetera **de** plata en Taxco.   *I bought a silver coffepot in Taxco.*

b. In front of ¿**quién?** to form an expression equivalent to the English *whose.*

¿**De quién** es esta computadora?   *Whose computer is this?*

c. In the following constructions that in English require the preposition *in:*

After a superlative:

Ella es la más bonita **de** la familia.   *She is the prettiest in the family.*

To indicate time of day:

Eran las ocho **de** la noche.   *It was eight o'clock in the evening.*

---

*See page 93, phrases with **estar** that use the preposition **de.** See page 274 in this Capítulo.

5. Other prepositions:

a. **Desde** is used to indicate beginning; **hasta** indicates end.

> Fuimos a pie **desde** mi casa **hasta** la escuela.
> *We went on foot (We walked) from my home to the school.*
> Estudia siempre **desde** las ocho **hasta** las once.
> *He (she) always studies from eight to eleven.*

De and **a** can substitute **desde** and **hasta**.

> Estudia siempre **de** las ocho **a** las once. *He (she) always studies from eight to eleven.*

b. **Según** means the same as **de acuerdo con**.

> Él actúa **según** las circunstancias. *He acts according to the circumstances.*

c. The equivalent of **tras** is **detrás de** or **después de**.

> Los automóviles salieron uno **tras** otro. *The cars left one after the other.*
> **Tras** la primavera, el verano. *After spring, comes summer.*

Tras also means the same as **además de**.

> El carro, **tras** ser (o **tras de** ser) económico, es muy cómodo.
> *The car, besides being economical, is very comfortable.*

6. Prepositional phrases. In general, these phrases have adverbial characteristics.*

antes de (*before*)	**detrás de** (*behind*)
acerca de (*about*)	**encima de** (*on top of*)
adentro de (*inside*)	**en contra de** (*against*)
alrededor de (*around*)	**en lugar de** (*instead of*)
a través de (*throughout*)	**en vez de** (*instead of*)
cerca de (*near*)	**frente a** (*in front of*)
después de (*after*)	**fuera de** (*outside of*)
delante de (*in front of*)	**junto a** (*next to*)

> Hay un parque **delante de** la iglesia. *There is a park in front of the church.*
> Los ciudadanos están **en contra de** esa ley. *The citizens are against that law.*
> Se me quedaron las llaves **encima de** la mesa. *I left the keys on top of the table.*
> El perro corrió **a través de** la calle. *The dog ran through the street.*

Ejercicios

I. Usando la preposición que corresponda, complete la narración que hace Jaime Blanco, donde habla de las vacaciones que piensa pasar en Puerto Rico.

Pienso pasar las vacaciones _____ Puerto Rico. Viajaré

_____ avión de Nueva York _____ San Juan, que está

_____ pocas horas de vuelo. Mis padres viven _____ el

Condado, frente _____ la playa. Mi amigo Ernesto vive

_____ otro lugar _____ la isla, en Ponce. Los dos haremos

---

*See Capítulo 10, Review of prepositional phrases.

varias excursiones _____ caballo y _____ pie. Si tengo

tiempo, me gustaría ir _____ barco _____ las Islas

Vírgenes. Allí se pueden comprar guayaberas bordadas (*embroidered*)

_____ mano más baratas que _____ los Estados Unidos.

Espero divertirme mucho estando _____ la familia y los amigos queridos.

II. Complete las oraciones con la preposición adecuada.

1. Ellas estuvieron _____ la playa desde julio _____ septiembre.

2. Le escribí una carta _____ lugar _____ llamarlo por teléfono.

3. ¿Dónde están los pañuelos? _____ el cajón.

4. Los pasajeros entraron al avión uno _____ otro.

5. Las plantas _____ jazmín están junto _____ la ventana.

6. ¿ _____ quién es el abrigo azul? Es de Isabel.

7. _____ mis predicciones astrológicas voy a casarme este año.

8. ¿Quién crees que es la muchacha más simpática _____ la clase?

9. Los niños montan _____ bicicleta todas las tardes.

10. Mi casa está _____ tres cuadras de la estación del metro.

III. Ud. se encuentra con su amigo Arturo en la calle. Complete el diálogo con la preposición que sea correcta.

Ud.: Te invito _____ tomar una cerveza. Estamos frente _____ café Versalles.

Arturo: ¡Qué buena idea! Salí _____ casa _____ las ocho _____ la mañana y no he bebido ni agua. Ya son las tres _____ la tarde.

Ud.: _____ mí me pasó lo mismo. Salí _____ casa muy temprano y no he almorzado.

Arturo: En vez _____ pedir una cerveza, ¿no crees que debemos ya almorzar? Yo tengo hambre. ¿Y tú?

Ud.: Yo también. Voy _____ pedir una tortilla _____ camarones (*shrimp*) y una sopa _____ verduras.

Arturo: Yo quiero una chuleta _____ cordero (*lamb chop*) y papas fritas.

Ud.: Y para completar el buen almuerzo, yo quiero una botella _____ vino tinto _____ lugar _____ la cerveza que íbamos a tomar.

IV. Traduzca al español las palabras que están en inglés y complete los párrafos.

El equipo _____ (*of*) mi escuela juega _____ (*against*) los

Leones el próximo sábado. _____ (*After*) la práctica de ayer nos

reunimos _____ (*with*) el entrenador (*coach*) y _____ (*we*

looked at) un video de fútbol muy interesante. Nuestro entrenador es

_____ (*from*) la Argentina y dicen que él es el mejor entrenador

_____ (*in*) la ciudad. _____ (*According to*) él, vamos a

ganar el campeonato (*championship*).

Por fin llegué _____ (*on*) tiempo _____ (*to the*)

aeropuerto. _____ (*Before*) salir tuve que hacer muchas cosas y creí que

iba a perder el avión. Llegué _____ (*at*) San Francisco _____

(*at*) las once _____ (*in*) la noche. _____ (*Instead of*) llamar

por teléfono a mi amiga Josefina, tomé un taxi que me llevó _____ (*to*)

su casa. _____ (*At*) el momento que me bajaba del taxi, mi amiga salió

a recibirme y pagué los veinte dólares que cobró el taxista.

B Uses of *por* and *para*

1. **Por** explains the motive or cause of an action. It is used in the following cases:

   a. To introduce the agent in the passive voice.

   > América fue descubierta **por** Colón. *America was discovered by Columbus.*
   > La novela *Cien años de soledad* fue escrita **por** el escritor colombiano
   > Gabriel García Márquez.
   > *The novel* One Hundred Years of Solitude *was written by the Colombian*
   > *writer Gabriel García Márquez.*

   b. To express duration of time.

   > Fui a Cuernavaca **por** tres semanas. *I went to Cuernavaca for three weeks.*
   > Todos los días nadamos **por** una hora. *Every day we swim for one hour.*

   c. With expressions that indicate time in general, or approximate moment.

   > Trabajo tanto **por** la mañana como **por** la tarde.
   > *I work as much in the morning as in the afternoon.*

   In time expressions when a definite time is expressed, **de** is used instead of **por**.

   > El poema de García Lorca, "Llanto por Ignacio Sánchez Mejías", comienza
   > así: "A las cinco **de** la tarde. Eran las cinco en punto **de** la tarde".
   > *García Lorca's poem "Llanto por Ignacio Sánchez Mejías", begins like this: "A*
   > *las cinco **de** la tarde. Eran las cinco en punto **de** la tarde".*

   d. To indicate reason or motive. It is equivalent to **a causa de**. It also indicates the
   person or thing for whom or in favor of whom something is done.

Hace el trabajo tan bien **por** la experiencia que tiene.
He does the work so well because of the experience he has.
Se cerró el aeropuerto **por** la niebla. *The airport was closed because of the fog.*
Fracasé en el examen **por** no estudiar. *I failed the exam because of not studying.*
Los soldados murieron **por** la patria. *The soldiers died for the homeland.*
Todo lo hice **por** ti. *I did everything for you.*

e. To indicate price or equivalent. It denotes exchange of one thing for another.

Pagó $200 **por** la cámara fotográfica. *He paid $200 for the camera.*
Cambié la camisa **por** un cinturón. *I exchanged the shirt for a belt.*
Compré tres piñas **por** un dólar. *I bought three pineapples for a dollar.*

f. As the equivalent of the English *per*.

El banco presta el dinero al siete **por** ciento.
The bank lends money at seven percent.
Ella distribuirá los juguetes a uno **por** niño.
She will distribute the toys at one per child.
Es peligroso manejar a ochenta millas **por** hora.
It is dangerous to drive at eighty miles per hour.

g. To indicate means or manner.

Te llamé **por** teléfono. *I called you by phone.*
¿Mandaste el paquete **por** avión? *Did you send the package by air mail?*
Se casaron **por** poder. *They were married by proxy.*

h. To indicate *through* or *throughout*.

El barco va a cruzar **por** el Canal de Panamá.
The ship is going to go through the Panama Canal.
Cuando empezó el fuego el humo salía **por** las ventanas.
When the fire started, the smoke was coming out through the windows.
Actualmente ellos están viajando **por** Tejas.
At present they are traveling through Texas.
La última vez que supe de Pepe andaba **por** la Florida.
The last time I had news from Pepe he was around Florida.
El ladrón entró **por** la ventana.
The burglar entered through the window.

i. To express the object of an action with verbs such as **ir, venir, mandar, enviar,**
and **preguntar.**

Ha ido a la escuela **por** los niños y dijo que vendría en seguida.
He has gone to school to pick up the children and said he would come immediately.
Envió **por** los libros que dejó olvidados.
He sent for the books he left behind.
En cuanto llegue preguntará **por** ti.
He will ask about you as soon as he arrives.

NOTE: The verb **preguntar** means *to ask a question.* **Preguntar por** means *to ask about
someone or something.*

¿Le **preguntaste** cuál era su dirección?	*Did you ask him what his address was?*
Ellos me **preguntaron por** ti.	*They asked me about you.*

j. To indicate a concept or opinion.

Pasa **por** rico.	*He is considered a rich man.*
Se le tiene **por** un gran hombre.	*He is considered a great man.*

k. To express preference for something or someone.

Voté **por** el candidato demócrata.	*I voted for the democratic candidate.*
El gobernador dijo que está **por** la pena de muerte.	*The governor said he is for the death penalty.*

l. For multiplication of numbers.

Tres **por** cuatro son doce.	*Three times four is twelve.*

m. **Estar por** + infinitive indicates disposition for an act or an action that has not occurred.

Estamos por tomar vacaciones, pero no sé cuando será.	*We are to take a vacation, but I don't know when it will be.*
Estuve por decirle que se callara la boca.	*I was going to tell him to shut up.*
El postre **está por** prepararse.	*The dessert is to be prepared.*

n. In phrases with adjectives or adverbs + **que**.

Por mucho que hables no me convencerás.
(Aunque hables mucho no me convencerás.)
No matter how much you talk, you will not convince me.
Por mucho que come no engorda.
No matter how much he eats, he does not get fat.

o. With exclamations and expressions.

por ahora	*for the time being*	por suerte	*luckily, fortunately*
por casualidad	*by chance*	por supuesto	*of course*
por cierto	*in fact*	por todas partes	*everywhere*
por consiguiente	*therefore; consequently*	por una vez	*once and for all*
por desgracia	*unfortunately*	por el estilo	*something like that*
¡Por Dios!	*For heaven's sake!*	¡Por lo que más quiera!	*For goodness sake!*
por ejemplo	*for example*		
por eso	*for that reason*	por lo general	*in general*
por favor	*please*	por lo menos	*at least*
por fin	*finally*	por lo pronto	*for the moment*
por otra parte	*on the other hand*	por lo tanto	*consequently*
por si acaso	*just in case*	por lo visto	*apparently*

2. Para expresses finality or the end of something. It is used in the following cases:

a. To indicate the end of a movement or direction.

Salgo **para** San Francisco.
I am leaving for San Francisco.
Nos mudamos **para** esta casa el año pasado.
We moved to this house last year.

b. To indicate purpose or finality of a thing or action.

La pluma es **para** escribir.	*The pen is for writing.*
El regalo es **para** ti.	*The gift is for you.*
Llamó **para** saber de nosotros.	*He called to know about us.*
Estudia **para** (ser) abogado.	*He studies to be a lawyer.*

c. To indicate time or specified date. (It is not used to indicate duration of time.)

Quiero el vestido **para** mañana.	*I want the dress for tomorrow.*
Terminará los estudios **para** el año que viene.	*He will finish his studies by next year.*

d. To express relation or comparison.

Para los hijos, los padres nunca tienen razón.
For the children, the parents are never right.
Para ser español, no es muy individualista.
For a Spaniard, he is not very individualistic.
Se ve muy joven **para** su edad.
She looks very young for her age.

NOTE: Note the difference:

Sabe mucho **para** su edad.	*He knows a lot for his age.*
Sabe mucho **por** su edad.	*He knows a lot because of his age.*

e. **Estar para** + infinitive indicates that an act or action is about to occur.

El tren **está para** salir.	*The train is about to leave.*
Ella **estaba para** llamar al médico.	*She was about to call the doctor.*

NOTE: Note the difference between **estar por** and **estar para**.

El tren **está por** salir.	(The train has everything ready to leave, but we don't know if it is going to leave immediately.)
El tren **está para** salir.	(The train is ready to leave. The train will leave soon.)

Ejercicios

I. Haga una nueva oración usando **por** o **para** según la sugerencia dada entre paréntesis.

MODELO: Viene corriendo. la playa (a través)
Viene corriendo por la playa.

1. No compré el vestido. no tener dinero (razón)
2. Fui al mercado. comprar frutas (finalidad)
3. Le avisamos. telegrama (medio)
4. Me dio las flores. el favor que le hice (a cambio)
5. Salió. Nueva York. Madrid (a través / destino)
6. Estudia. médico (finalidad)
7. Nadó. una hora (duración de tiempo)
8. Quiero el boleto. el día quince (plazo determinado)
9. Habla bien el español. ser ruso (comparación)
10. Dio el dinero. generosidad (motivo)

II. Complete los párrafos con **por** y **para**.

_____ ser tan joven, Inés es una muchacha muy cosmopolita y
sofisticada. Ayer salió _____ San Francisco _____ visitar
las galerías de arte y ponerse en contacto con los artistas de California. Estará en la
costa del oeste _____ tres semanas. Ella quiere adquirir algunas
pinturas _____ la galería que acaba de comprar en Nueva York. Espera
regresar _____ avión _____ estar _____ la
apertura (*opening*) de la galería. Ella piensa llevar con ella algunas obras de arte.
_____ muchas cosas que lleve no tendrá que pagar exceso de equipaje
_____ ser dueña (*owner*) de una galería de arte.

El huracán (*hurricane*) causó gran destrozo _____ todos los lugares
_____ donde pasó. _____ poder reconstruir todo el daño
causado será necesario esperar, _____ lo menos, un año. El gobierno y
las instituciones privadas están cooperando _____ proporcionar todo lo
necesario a las personas que han sufrido daños (*damage*) grandes. _____
el momento, la gente se ayuda mutuamente y lucha _____ normalizar
sus vidas. _____ mucho que uno trate de imaginarse lo que es un viento
que sopla (*blows*) a 160 millas _____ hora, no puede verdaderamente
comprenderlo hasta que no lo siente. Muchas donaciones han sido hechas
_____ personas e instituciones _____ enviar alimentos y
medicinas a las zonas afectadas _____ el huracán. Este gesto generoso
es apreciado _____ todos los que experimentaron el huracán.

III. Transforme las oraciones sustituyendo las palabras subrayadas por la preposición
por o **para**.

MODELO: Estamos <u>a punto de</u> servir la comida.
        Estamos para servir la comida.

1. Los aviones no salieron <u>a causa de</u> la niebla.
2. Todo lo que poseo será <u>destinado a</u> ti.
3. Nos quedamos en el desierto <u>durante</u> tres semanas.
4. El perro saltó <u>a través de</u> la ventana.
5. Estudio <u>con el fin de</u> aprender.
6. Me resfrié <u>a causa de</u> no llevar abrigo.
7. Te llamé <u>utilizando</u> el teléfono.
8. Voy a la panadería <u>en busca de</u> pan.
9. Voy a la peluquería <u>con el fin de</u> cortarme el pelo.
10. En cuanto me vio preguntó <u>acerca de</u> ti.
11. Se le tiene <u>en el concepto de</u> genio.
12. El chico está muy alto <u>considerando</u> su edad.

IV. Sustituya las palabras subrayadas por la preposición **por** o **para**.

A fin de evitar el tráfico grande de la ciudad, salimos a las cinco de la mañana <u>en dirección a</u> las montañas. Fuimos <u>a través de</u> la carretera nueva, que es más directa, <u>con el propósito de</u> llegar temprano. Pero al poco rato de salir de la ciudad, tuvimos que pararnos <u>durante</u> una hora <u>a causa de</u> un accidente grande que interrumpió el tráfico.

La Cruz Roja siempre está preparada <u>a fin de</u> ayudar cada vez que hay una catástrofe mundial. <u>A través de</u> muchos años esta institución ha socorrido (*helped*) a muchas naciones. <u>Debido a</u> su carácter humanitario el emblema de esta institución es símbolo de esperanza y amor.

V. Traduzca al español las frases que están en inglés y complete las oraciones usando **por** o **para**.

1. (*is about*) El ómnibus _____ salir.
2. (*because of*) _____ la lluvia no pudimos jugar al tenis.
3. (*for*) Las copias estarán listas _____ mañana.
4. (*for*) Mi padre fue al mercado _____ leche.
5. (*in order*) Quiero ir a México _____ estudiar español.
6. (*for*) _____ un atleta es muy importante el mantener una dieta balanceada.
7. (*to be*) Ella estudia _____ ingeniera.
8. (*per*) El carro iba a noventa millas _____ hora.
9. (*because*) El policía le puso una multa _____ ir tan rápido.
10. (*for*) Pienso votar _____ el candidato que haga menos promesas.
11. (*about*) Juan José está loco _____ ella.
12. (*through*) Debemos pasar primero _____ la aduana.
13. (*by*) Envié las cartas _____ correo aéreo.
14. (*about*) ¿Preguntó Elena _____ mí?
15. (*for*) El niño está muy alto _____ su edad.

VI. Entre las siguientes expresiones que llevan **por**, seleccione la que mejor corresponda a las frases en inglés.

por Dios	por suerte	por supuesto
por desgracia	por fin	por lo menos
por favor	por eso	

1. (*at least*) Pedro nunca saluda, pero hoy, _____, dijo: "buenos días".
2. (*Unfortunately*) ¿Vas al baile? _____ tengo que trabajar.
3. (*luckily*) Se me paró el carro en la autopista, pero _____ vino un policía a ayudarme.
4. (*for heaven's sake*) Niño, ¡_____!, no hagas tanto ruido.
5. (*finally*) Después de tomar varias clases, _____ aprendió a manejar.
6. (*Of course*) ¿Tienes que pagar los impuestos? _____.

7. (*Please*) _____, ¿me permite pasar?

8. (*That's why*) Después de la discusión, ella le dijo: "_____ no quiero salir contigo".

VII. Complete las oraciones usando **por** o **para** en lugar de la preposición inglesa *for*.

1. El pomo (*bottle*) de perfume es _____ Elisa.

2. No dijo la verdad _____ miedo al castigo.

3. No he visto a mis tíos _____ largo tiempo.

4. Tengo una cita con la dentista _____ el lunes.

5. Ese trabajo es muy importante _____ mí.

6. Ellos vivieron fuera de los Estados Unidos _____ tres años.

7. _____ un niño de dos años, habla muy claro.

8. No votaré _____ ese congresista.

C Uses of *pero* and *sino*

The equivalent of the conjunctions **pero** and **sino** is *but* in English.

1. **Pero** introduces a clarification of the first part of the sentence. It has the meaning of **sin embargo** (*nevertheless*).

> Le dijeron que no saliera, **pero** no hizo caso.
> *They told him not to go out, but he did not pay attention.*
> Le escribiré, **pero** estoy segura de que no contestará.
> *I will write him, but I am sure he will not answer.*

2. **Sino** is used when there is a negative statement followed by an opposite or contrary idea.

> **No** leí el libro, **sino** la crítica. *I did not read the book, but the critique (review).*
> **No** fui al cine, **sino** al teatro. *I did not go to the movies, but to the theater.*
> **No** quería comer, **sino** dormir. *He did not want to eat, but to sleep.*

3. **Sino que** is used when the opposite negative idea has a conjugated verb and a subject.

> No leí el libro, **sino que** leí la crítica.
> *I did not read the book, but I read the critique (review).*
> No le han regalado la enciclopedia, **sino que** la ha comprado.
> *They have not given him the encyclopedia, but he has bought it.*

Ejercicio

Combine los elementos dados y haga oraciones usando **pero**, **sino** o **sino que**.

MODELO: No es argentino / chileno.
  No es argentino sino chileno.

1. Salí tarde / pude hacer todo lo que quería.

2. Le escribí / no contestó.

3. No me llamó / vino a verme.
4. No ha comprado manzanas / naranjas.
5. No iba caminando / iba corriendo.
6. No necesita una chaqueta / un abrigo.
7. Quiero salir temprano / no sé si podré.
8. Su novia no es rubia / morena.
9. Le dije que cerrara la puerta / se le olvidó.
10. No quiero helado de fresas / de chocolate.

D Verbs that are used with the preposition *a* followed by an infinitive, and the ones that are used without it

1. Verb + **a** + infinitive. This construction is used with verbs that express movement, displacement, or beginning; with some reflexive verbs; and with other verbs outside these groups.

acertar a	*to manage to*	invitar a	*to invite to*
acostumbrarse a	*to get used to*	ir a	*to go to*
aprender a	*to learn to*	llegar a	*to get to (the extreme of)*
apresurarse a	*to hasten; to rush to*	negarse a	*to refuse*
asomarse a	*to lean out to*	obligar a	*to force to*
aspirar a	*to aspire to*	ofrecerse a	*to offer or volunteer to*
atreverse a	*to dare to*	oponerse a	*to oppose*
ayudar a	*to help to*	pararse a	*to stop to*
comenzar a	*to begin to*	ponerse a	*to begin to*
convidar a	*to invite to*	prepararse a	*to get ready to*
decidirse a	*to decide to*	principiar a	*to begin to*
dedicarse a	*to devote oneself to*	resignarse a	*to resign oneself to*
detenerse a	*to stop to*	salir a	*to go; to come out to*
dirigirse a	*to go to; to address, to speak to*	sentarse a	*to sit down to*
disponerse a	*to be about or ready to*	venir a	*to come to*
echar(se) a	*to begin to*	volver a	*to . . . again*
enseñar a	*to teach to*		

El cuento dice que el burro **aprendió a** tocar la flauta por casualidad, pero mi amigo, que es muy inteligente, nunca **llegó a** aprender a tocarla. Por eso **se dedicó a** ser pelotero.
The story says that the donkey learned to play the flute by chance, but my friend, who is very intelligent, never learned to play it. That is why he devoted himself to becoming a baseball player.

Hace un día tan bello que **convida a** pasear y **nos vamos a** ir a almorzar al lago.
It is such a beautiful day that it invites one to go out, and we are going to go to the lake for lunch.

El niño **se echó a** correr cuando sintió que **echaron a** andar el carrusel y en seguida **se dispuso a** montar el caballito negro que tanto le gusta.
The child began to run when he heard they started running the carousel and he immediately got ready to ride the little black horse he likes so much.

NOTE: There are other verbs that are never followed by an infinitive, but require the preposition **a** when followed by a noun.

asistir a   jugar a   oler a   parecerse a

Ayer **asistimos a** la apertura del curso.	*Yesterday we attended the opening of the classes.*
Ellos **juegan al** tenis en la cancha del club.	*They play tennis in the club's tennis court.*
La casa **huele a** jazmín.	*The house smells of jasmine.*
Beatriz **se parece a** su madre.	*Beatriz looks like her mother.*

2. Verb + infinitive. The following verbs do not require the **a** when they precede an infinitive.

aceptar	gustar	poder
aconsejar (*to advise*)	hacer	preferir
deber	intentar	prohibir (*to forbid*)
decidir	necesitar	prometer
dejar	odiar (*to hate*)	querer
desear	oír	rehusar (*to reject*)
detestar	olvidar	saber
elegir (*to choose*)	ordenar	soler (*to be accustomed to*)
esperar	pensar	ver
evitar (*to avoid*)	permitir	

Amelia **solía dar** largos paseos por el parque y, aunque prefería ir sola, le **gustaba encontrar** a alguien conocido con quien charlar.
Amelia used to take long walks in the park, and although she preferred to go alone, she liked to meet someone with whom to chat.

Ellos **saben hacer** el trabajo, pero **necesitan encontrar** a una persona que los dirija.
They know how to do the work, but they need to find a person to direct them.

¿**Quieres ir** al cine o **prefieres quedarte** en casa?
Do you want to go to the movies or do you prefer to stay home?

Ejercicio

Complete los párrafos con la preposición **a**, si es necesario.

Detesto _____ tener que tomar el examen de conducir. Aunque sé _____ conducir muy bien, voy _____ repasar el manual antes del examen escrito porque no quiero _____ fallar ninguna pregunta. La vez pasada, cuando renové la licencia de manejar, acerté _____ contestar todas las preguntas.

Vamos _____ celebrar el cumpleaños de Julieta y hemos decidido _____ tener una fiesta el sábado próximo. Pensamos _____ invitar a varios de sus amigos y Benito prometió _____ traer algunos de las grabaciones (*recordings*) de música bailable que tiene. Ojalá que puedan _____ venir todas las personas que

queremos _____ invitar. Todavía no sabemos qué vamos _____ servir de
comida. Yo prefiero _____ tener comida fría, pero mi hermana está dispuesta
_____ cocinar un buen arroz con pollo. Mi madre, por otro lado, aconseja
_____ servir sólo postre y café.

Desde muy pequeña mi prima ha querido _____ ser actriz. Siempre le gustaba
_____ tomar parte en las obras de teatro que presentaban en la escuela y en esas
representaciones demostró _____ tener talento teatral. Después de estudiar drama
en la universidad, ella espera _____ poder trabajar en alguna película y así aspirar
_____ ser conocida. Está dispuesta _____ hacer grandes sacrificios, y sé que
llegará _____ ser famosa algún día, porque tiene talento y una voluntad de hierro.

Verbs that are followed by prepositions

1. Verb + **de**.

acabar de	*to finish*	**enamorarse de**	*to fall in love with*
acabar de + inf.	*to have just . . .*	**encargarse de**	*to take charge of*
acordarse de	*to remember*	**enterarse de**	*to find out*
alegrarse de	*to be happy about*	**excusarse de**	*to decline; to excuse oneself*
arrepentirse de	*to repent*	**lamentarse de**	*to lament*
burlarse de	*to laugh at*	**olvidarse de**	*to forget*
cansarse de	*to get tired of*	**quejarse de**	*to complain about*
cesar de	*to stop; to cease*	**reírse de**	*to laugh at*
dejar de	*to stop; to cease*	**salir de**	*to get out of; to leave from*
depender de	*to depend on*	**terminar de**	*to finish*
despedirse de	*to say good-bye to*	**tratar de**	*to try to*

Nos alegramos de que ellos vengan a visitarnos.	*We are happy they come to visit us.*
En la escuela todos los compañeros **se burlaban de** Juan.	*At school all the classmates made fun of Juan.*
¿Cuándo **dejaste de** fumar?	*When did you stop smoking?*
Mario dijo que **se encargaría de** distribuir la mercancía.	*Mario said that he would take care of distributing the merchandise.*
¿Qué **piensas del** nuevo gobierno?	*What do you think about the new government?*

NOTE: The verb **acordarse de** is used to mean *to remember*. The equivalent of **recordar** is *to remember* and *to remind*.

Siempre **me acuerdo de** Uds.	*I always remember you.*
Siempre los **recuerdo**.	*I always remember them.*
Recuérdame que tengo que llevar esta carta al correo	*Remind me that I have to take this letter to the post office.*

NOTE: The meaning of the expression **acabar de** + inf. depends on the verb tense of **acabar**.

(present)	**Acabo de escribir** la carta. *I have just written the letter.*
(imperfect)	**Acababa de escribir** la carta. *I had just written the letter.*
(preterite)	**Acabé de escribir** la carta. *I finished writing the letter.*

2. Verb + **en**.

confiar en	to trust	**fijarse en**	to notice
consentir en	to consent; to agree to	**influir en**	to bear upon
consistir en	to consist of	**insistir en**	to insist on
convenir en	to agree to	**pensar en**	to think about
convertirse en	to turn into	**persistir en**	to persist in
creer en	to believe	**quedar en**	to agree
empeñarse en	to be bent on	**tardar en**	to delay in
entrar en	to enter		

Habíamos convenido en encontrarnos en el centro a las tres.
We had agreed to meet downtown at three.
¿**Cree** tu hijo **en** los Reyes Magos?
Does your son believe in the Three Wise Men?
Pienso mucho **en** mi hermano que vive en Costa Rica.
I think a lot about my brother who lives in Costa Rica.
Es extraño que Arturo **tarde** tanto **en** llegar. **Quedó en** venir tan pronto
como terminase en la oficina.
It is strange that Arturo takes so long in coming. He agreed to come as soon as he would finish in the office.

3. Verb + **con**.

acabar con	to put an end to	**dar con**	to find
amenazar con	to threaten with	**encontrarse**	to meet; to
casarse con	to get married to	**con**	come across
conformarse con	to be satisfied with	**enojarse con**	to get angry with
contar con	to count on	**quedarse con**	to keep
cumplir con	to fulfill one's	**soñar con**	to dream of
	obligations	**tropezar con**	to bump into

Al salir del cuarto **tropecé con** la mesa y se cayó el florero.
Coming out of the room I bumped into the table and the flower vase fell.
Él siempre **cuenta con** la ayuda de sus buenos amigos.
He always counts on the help of his good friends.
Maximiliano **se casó con** Carlota mucho antes de venir a México como
Emperador.
Maximiliano married Carlota long before coming to Mexico as Emperor.
Tanto caminó que al fin **dio con** la iglesia que estaba buscando.
He walked so much that he finally found the church he was looking for.
Mi hermano **se quedó con** los libros de papá.
My brother kept father's books.

Ejercicios

I. Complete las oraciones con la preposición adecuada.

Luis se enamoró _____ Conchita y se casó _____ ella despúes _____ dos años de relaciones (*courtship*). Los dos trataron _____ ajustarse a la nueva vida, pero pronto comenzaron _____ pelear y no tardaron _____ separarse. Al fin, convinieron _____ divorciarse y tropezaron _____ muchos inconvenientes. Los padres de Conchita se empeñaron _____ disuadirlos, pero ellos insistieron _____ terminar el matrimonio. Conchita se dispuso _____ trabajar y aprendió _____ ganarse la vida. Luis se volvió _____ casar al poco tiempo y se encargó _____ los negocios del nuevo suegro.

II. Decida si para llenar los espacios necesita **a, de, en** o **con**. Si no necesita ninguna preposición, use el símbolo Ø.

1. El profesor de filosofía enseña _____ pensar.
2. Lo han invitado _____ cenar.
3. Ya terminó _____ llover.
4. Prometo _____ escribirte todas las semanas.
5. Yo sueño _____ mi novia.
6. Pienso constantemente _____ mi madre.
7. Ella no sabe _____ coser.
8. Elisa se ha enamorado _____ Luis Guzmán.
9. Quedé _____ ir a buscarlo a las tres.
10. No me pidas _____ salir esta noche. Estoy muy cansada.
11. Cuando me casé _____ Alberto, él era muy delgado.
12. Ellos insistieron _____ salir muy temprano.
13. La esposa del hijo se encargó _____ los negocios de la familia.
14. Caminamos mucho, pero al fin dimos _____ la librería que buscábamos.
15. ¿Te fijaste _____ el vestido de Luisa? Era muy lindo.

III. Traduzca al español las frases que están en inglés y complete las oraciones.

1. María Luisa _____ (*dreams about*) su futura vida universitaria. Ella _____ (*tries to*) obtener una beca y _____ (*counts on*) la ayuda de sus profesores.
2. _____ (*We wanted to go*) al teatro para ver *La vida es sueño*, de Pedro Calderón de la Barca.* _____ (*I hurried up to*) comprar las entradas, pero no las pude encontrar porque el teatro entero estaba vendido. _____ (*I hope to*) tener mejor suerte la próxima vez.

_____
*Pedro Calderón de la Barca (1600–1681), famoso dramaturgo español.

3. _____ (*I could not*) obtener la visa porque _____

    (*I bumped into*) muchas dificultades para reunir todos los documentos necesarios.

4. ¿ _____ (*Did you notice*) lo atlética que es la novia de Ismael? Ella

    _____ (*looks like*) su madre que, aunque _____

    (*she has just*) cumplir cincuenta años, es todavía una campeona en gimnasia.

5. Eugenia _____ (*complains*) que sus hijos _____ (*don't*

    remember) sacar al perro por las noches y que ella tiene que hacerlo. Ella

    _____ (*hopes to*) resolver este problema y _____

    (*is going to*) mandar al perro a la estancia (*farm*) del abuelo.

IV. Decida qué preposición necesita, o si no necesita ninguna preposición, para llenar
los espacios.

Voy _____ ver al Sr. Gerardo Gómez porque necesito _____ hablar con él.

Él suele _____ estar siempre muy ocupado, pero convinimos _____

encontrarnos en su oficina a las diez de la mañana. No debo _____ tardar

_____ llegar porque él tiene una reunión muy importante esa misma mañana con

los directores de la compañía. Él aspira _____ ser vicepresidente y no dudo que,

con el tiempo, llegue _____ ocupar el puesto de presidente.

Agustín se ha enamorado _____ una muchacha que conoció en el trabajo. Él

quiere _____ llamarla por teléfono para invitarla _____ cenar, pero no sabe su

número. Llama a otra compañera de la oficina y comienzan _____ conversar y

_____ reírse. Tanto hablan que Agustín se olvida _____ pedir el número de la

muchacha a quien quería llamar. A esta conversación le siguen muchas más y, desde

luego, cenas y paseos juntos. ¿Cuál es el fin del cuento? Agustín se casa _____ la

muchacha del teléfono.

Composición

Antes de escribir, repase las siguientes reglas de acentuación y la ortografía.

A Review of accentuation

1. Some words require an accent mark in order to distinguish the meaning and the
   different grammatical use from other words that have the same pronunciation. (See
   pages 7–8.)

mi *my*	**mí** *me*	**el** *the*	**él** *he, him*	**te** *you, yourself*	**té** *tea*
si *if*	**sí** *yes*	**tu** *your*	**tú** *you*	**de** *of, from*	**dé** *give*

NOTE: In general, one-syllable words do not have a written accent when the meaning of the word is clear: **fui, fue, vi, vio, di, dio**

2. Interrogative and exclamatory words, whether direct or indirect, have a written accent:

¿**Cuánto** dinero pidieron? Dime **cuánto** les debo.
How much money did they ask for? Tell me how much I owe them.
¿**Quiénes** son aquellos señores? No sé **quiénes** son.
Who are those gentlemen? I don't know who they are.
¡**Cómo** llueve en estas partes! Dice que **cómo** llueve por aquí.
How it rains in these parts! He says how much it rains around here.

3. Words that end in **n** or **s** with an accent mark on the last syllable (agudas), drop the accent mark in the plural form.

corazón corazones	avión aviones	lección lecciones
autobús autobuses	jardín jardines	francés franceses

NOTE: The stress of a word should not change when pluralized. For this reason, an accent is needed when adding a syllable that did not exist in the singular form. There are a few cases, however, in which the stress and the accent mark change. Observe the following examples:

lápiz lápices	país países	examen exámenes
orden órdenes	carácter caracteres	régimen regímenes
espécimen especímenes		

B Review of spelling rules: *r, rr*

1. The multiple sound of **r** can be written **rr** or **r**. Write **rr** between vowels and in compound words:

perro, carro, irracional, grecorromano

2. Write **r**:

- after a consonant:

   Israel, subrayar, Enrique, alrededor

- at the beginning of words:

   Rosa, rojo, redondo, Rubén

3. The sound of single **r** is written **r** and corresponds to all orthographic **r**'s that are not at the beginning of a word nor preceded by **n, l,** or **s**:

coral, suspiro (*sigh*), **prieto** (*dark*), **sobre**

4. Note the difference in meaning:

caro (*expensive*)	**carro** (*car*)
coral (*coral*)	**corral** (*corral*)
para (*for*)	**parra** (*grape vine*)
cero (*zero*)	**cerro** (*mountain*)
foro (*forum*)	**forro** (*lining*)

NOTE: The exercises corresponding to this section are included in the *Cuaderno de ejercicios*, Capítulo 9.

Ejercicio de composición (opcional)

Escriba una composición sobre el tema que se da a continuación. Use el esquema siguiente.

TEMA: Los estereotipos. El "latino".

INTRODUCCIÓN: La fuerza que tienen los estereotipos en el público en general.
La imagen que tenemos del "latino".
Rasgos físicos y de carácter que le aplicamos.
El estereotipo del norteamericano, del italiano y del alemán.

DESARROLLO: Entre los "latinos" que Ud. ha conocido, ¿cuáles son las diferencias que ha notado?
Diferencia entre un argentino, que desciende de italianos y españoles, y un venezolano que desciende de indio y español. ¿Puede Ud. agruparlos bajo el estereotipo de "latino"?
Diferencias sutiles que existen.
Errores que cometemos.
Importancia que tiene el conocer bien la historia de los países que están al sur de los Estados Unidos.

CONCLUSIÓN: Dé su opinión personal con respecto al estereotipo que existe del "latino".
¿Cómo difiere el estereotipo de la realidad?
¿Contribuye el estereotipo del "latino" a comprenderlo mejor?

10 Capítulo

Vista de la Plaza de Armas en la ciudad de Lima, capital del Perú.

LECTURAS

- Lectura 1: "Países en la costa del Pacífico: Ecuador, Perú y Chile"
- Lectura 2: "El nacimiento de la col" de Rubén Darío

GRAMÁTICA

- Relatives
- Passive constructions
- Verbs that express the idea of change or *to become*

- Phrases that denote obligation
- Expressions with **hacer**. **Hace** + time + **que**
- Review of prepositional phrases
- Idiomatic expressions

COMPOSICIÓN

- Review of accentuation
- Review of spelling rules: differences between Spanish and English

Vocabulario

Antes de leer, repase el siguiente vocabulario que le ayudará a comprender la lectura.

Sustantivos

la bahía	bay	**la meseta**	plateau
el barco	ship	**la pesca**	fishing
la carretera	highway	**el propósito**	purpose
el imperio	empire	**la selva**	jungle
la espada	sword	**el tamaño**	size
el ferrocaril	railroad	**el trozo**	piece

Verbos

atravesar (ie)	to cross	**cesar**	to cease, to stop
bañar	to bathe	**cruzar (c)**	to cross
beneficiar	to benefit	**disfrutar**	to enjoy

Adjetivos

alegre	merry; happy	**imponente**	imposing
antiguo	ancient	**irlandés**	Irish
caluroso	warm; hot	**maravilloso**	marvelous
desértico	desert-like	**pintoresco**	picturesque
ecuatoriano	from Ecuador	**valioso**	valuable
estrecho	narrow	**vistoso**	attractive; showy

Frases

al igual	the same	**Escuela de Derecho**	law school
a raíz de	soon after	**junto a**	next to; near
de pie	standing	**junto con**	together with

Related words (Palabras relacionadas). The meaning of some words may be determined by thinking of related words familiar to you. Can you give in English the meaning of the underlined words derived from the words in parentheses?

1. (alto) ... situada a más de nueve mil pies de <u>altura</u>...

2. (calor) ... El clima de este país debe ser <u>caluroso</u>...

3. (gigante) ... aquí se encuentran <u>gigantescos</u> galápagos...

4. (tierra) ... toma su nombre del Ecuador <u>terrestre</u>...

5. (desierto) ... El norte de Chile es <u>desértico</u>...

Preliminary view of some expressions (Vista preliminar de algunas expresiones).

A passive construction may be expressed with the verb **ser** or **estar** + a past participle, and also with **se** + a verb in the third person singular or plural. Note the following examples:

… cuyas costas **están bañadas** …	… *whose coasts are washed* …
… razón por la que **han sido declaradas** …	… *reason for which they have been declared*
… la ciudad del Cuzco **ha sido llamada** …	…*the city of Cuzco has been called* …
… aquí **se encuentran** unas gigantescas estatuas …	…*here some gigantic statues are found* …
… **se celebra** anualmente el Festival de la Canción …	…*the Song Festival is celebrated annually* …

Reminder: In comparative superlative sentences **de** is used to translate *in*.

El lago Titicaca, el más alto **del** mundo …
Lake Titicaca, the highest in the world …

El paisaje chileno es uno de los más hermosos **del** continente …
The Chilean landscape is one of the most beautiful on the continent …

Lectura I

Países en la costa del Pacífico: Ecuador, Perú y Chile

El Ecuador, cuyas costas están bañadas por el océano Pacífico, toma su nombre del ecuador terrestre que lo atraviesa dividiendo su territorio en dos partes. El clima de este país debería ser caluroso, como lo es en otros lugares situados sobre el ecuador terrestre, pero debido a su altura° —lo *altitude*
5 atraviesa de norte a sur la cordillera° de los Andes— tiene un clima *mountain range* maravilloso, excepto en las costas donde es tropical y muy caliente.

Las principales ciudades ecuatorianas son Quito, la capital del país, situada a más de 9.000 pies de altura, Guayaquil, Cuenca, Riobamba y Ambato. La ciudad de Quito tiene su parte española con sus antiguas
10 construcciones, y la parte moderna con anchas calles y vistosos edificios.

Guayaquil, ciudad alegre con vida muy activa, es el puerto principal por donde pasan todos los productos de exportación, entre los que se encuentran frutas, plátanos, cacao y café. Riobamba, en la provincia del Chimborazo, es la ciudad ecuatoriana que tiene el paisaje andino más
15 pintoresco, ya que se puede ver el pico que da nombre a la provincia y que siempre está cubierto de nieve.

Las islas Galápagos pertenecen al Ecuador y aquí se encuentran gigantescos galápagos,° algunos de los cuales pesan más de 600 libras. *giant turtles* Estos animales que viven más de doscientos años, han sido motivo de
20 atracción para los que visitan las islas, razón por la que han sido declaradas como Parque Nacional.

Después de México, el Perú era la posesión más valiosa que tenía
España en el Nuevo Mundo. Lima, junto con la ciudad de México, eran
los dos centros culturales más importantes. Esta importancia colonial,
25 debido, tanto a la riqueza natural del país, como al substrato cultural
incaico, se mantuvo hasta el siglo XIX. Desde el siglo XX el Perú ha
estado luchando por establecer las reformas políticas, económicas y
sociales necesarias para el progreso económico, industrial y comercial
del país.
30   El Perú, lo mismo que el Ecuador, puede dividirse en tres regiones: la
costa, la sierra y la selva. La costa es una estrecha franja° de terreno entre   *strip*
el mar y los Andes que tiene todas las características de un desierto,
excepto por pequeños trozos de tierra cultivable. En lo que se llama la
sierra la altura oscila entre los 7.500 y 13.000 pies, y comprende la región
35 del sistema montañoso de los Andes que atraviesa el país. Aquí se
encuentran hermosos valles y áridas mesetas, y en una de éstas, en la
frontera con Bolivia, está el lago Titicaca, el más alto del mundo.
    La comunicación entre estas tres regiones es uno de los grandes
problemas del Perú, pues sus ferrocarriles y carreteras tienen que subir
40 altas montañas. El Ferrocarril Central, que es uno de los más altos del
mundo, va en ascensión desde Lima hasta el centro minero de La Oroya,

donde comienza a descender. La carretera que tiene que pasar por
innumerables puentes° y túneles, alcanza una altura de 16.000 pies. La   *bridges*
zona del río Amazonas, al otro lado de los Andes, es un mundo
45   completamente distinto. De un clima frío con picos° siempre cubiertos de   *peaks*
nieve se pasa a una selva con exuberante vegetación y ríos caudalosos.°   *abundant*

El Perú tiene ciudades de origen prehistórico y colonial. La ciudad del
Cuzco ha sido llamada la capital arqueológica de Sudamérica, debido a las
muchas ruinas prehispánicas que se encuentran en sus alrededores. Cuzco
50   fue por muchos años la capital del imperio incaico y se cree que Machu
Picchu, descubierto por el norteamericano Hiram Bingham en 1911, era la
ciudad sagrada de los incas.

Chile parece una espada estrecha y larga que se extiende al sur del Perú
entre los Andes y el Pacífico. El paisaje chileno, debido a su posición, es
55   uno de los más hermosos del continente. En los Andes hay imponentes
picos de gran elevación, como el Aconcagua que es el más alto del
continente americano con 23.000 pies de altura. El norte de Chile es
desértico y el desierto de Atacama es considerado el más seco del mundo
a pesar de tener un lago en el centro. En sus costas Chile tiene varios
60   archipiélagos e islas, entre las que se encuentran las Islas de Juan
Fernández, donde vivió Robinson Crusoe, el héroe de la novela de Daniel

Ruinas de Machu Picchu en el Perú.

Defoe, y la Isla de Pascua° que está a dos mil millas de la costa y presenta   *Easter Island*
una cultura de tipo polinesio.° En esta isla se encuentran unas gigantescas   *Polynesian*
estatuas llamadas "Moais", algunas con más de cinco metros de altura y
65   varias toneladas de peso.° Las figuras de estas estatuas están en varias   *weight*
posiciones, algunas de pie, otras en el suelo, rotas o semienterradas.°   *half buried*
Hasta ahora nadie sabe el origen y el propósito de estas figuras tan llenas
de misterio.

Las principales ciudades de Chile son: Santiago —la capital—
70   Valparaíso, Concepción y Valdivia, todas en la región central. La capital,
debido a la posición que tiene, es un lugar privilegiado. Está junto a la
cordillera° de los Andes y cerca del mar, lo que hace que sus habitantes   *mountain range*
puedan disfrutar de los deportes de esquí en las montañas y de las
hermosas playas. Santiago es una ciudad internacional con amplias
75   avenidas, magníficos edificios, elegantes barrios residenciales y bellos
parques. Valparaíso es el primer puerto de Chile y en su bahía hay
siempre barcos mercantes° de todo el mundo. En esta ciudad están la   *merchant ships*
Escuela de Derecho de la Universidad de Chile, la Universidad Católica y
la Escuela Naval, que es una de las más importantes de Hispanoamérica.
80   Muy cerca de Valparaíso está Viña del Mar, famosa por sus playas, clima
excelente, magnífica pesca y sus centros culturales y de diversión. Esta
ciudad está llena de elegantes y modernos edificios y hoteles, y es un
lugar ideal de atracción en el verano. En ella se celebra anualmente el
conocido Festival de la Canción.
85   Al igual que los otros países hispanoamericanos, Chile empezó su
lucha independentista en 1810. Bernardo O'Higgins —de madre chilena
y padre irlandés— luchó por la independencia de su patria y ayudado
por el general argentino José de San Martín que cruzó los Andes con su
ejército, O'Higgins vio su patria libre de la dominación española en 1817.
90   La tradición cultural chilena es extremadamente rica. Desde que Pedro
de Valdivia tomó posesión de la región en nombre del rey de España en
1540, Chile no ha cesado de contribuir al enriquecimiento de la cultura
hispánica.

Llene los espacios en blanco con la palabra correcta para completar la oración.

1. El panorama de los Andes es _____ por sus enormes picos cubiertos de
   nieve.
2. El padre de O'Higgins era de Irlanda; era _____.
3. Se dice que Chile parece una _____ porque es un país estrecho y largo.
4. La joven es abogada; estudió en la _____.
5. La ciudad de Santiago está _____ a los Andes.

6. Riobamba en el Ecuador es la ciudad que tiene el paisaje andino más

_____.

7. El lago Titicaca está en una _____ en la frontera con Bolivia.

8. El Cuzco fue por muchos años la capital del _____ incaico.

Preguntas sobre la lectura

1. ¿Qué explicación tiene el nombre que se le dio al Ecuador?
2. ¿Qué puede decir de las ciudades de Quito y Guayaquil?
3. ¿Por qué las islas Galápagos han sido declaradas Parque Nacional?
4. ¿Qué factores contribuyeron a la importancia colonial que tuvo el Perú hasta el siglo XIX?
5. ¿Qué contrastes presentan las distintas regiones del Perú?
6. ¿Por qué fue difícil establecer las vías de comunicación entre las diferentes regiones del Perú?
7. La ciudad del Cuzco en el Perú ha sido llamada la capital arqueológica de Sudamérica. Explique por qué.
8. ¿Qué comparación se hace al hablar del aspecto físico de Chile?
9. ¿Qué dice el autor de las islas que están en la costa de Chile?
10. ¿Qué atractivos ofrece la ciudad de Santiago en Chile?
11. ¿Qué cosas importantes hay en Valparaíso?
12. El autor dice que en el siglo XIX el general argentino José de San Martín cruzó los Andes con su ejército para ayudar a Bernardo O'Higgins a obtener la independencia de Chile. ¿Qué cree Ud. de esta hazaña (*heroic feat*)?

Temas de conversación

1. Si Ud. pudiera ir al Ecuador, ¿qué ciudades le interesaría visitar? ¿Por qué? En la lectura se mencionan varias ciudades. ¿Conoce Ud. alguna de ellas? Prepare un pequeño informe sobre Quito para compartir con la clase.
2. ¿Por qué cree Ud. que ciudades como Machu Picchu y Cuzco atraen a tantos visitantes? ¿Hay zonas en los Estados Unidos que atraen de la misma manera? Piense en algunos sitios del Sudoeste.
3. En la lectura se dice que "Santiago es una ciudad privilegiada". ¿Por qué? ¿Conoce Ud. una ciudad privilegiada como Santiago? Descríbala.
4. Los Andes, así como los Alpes en Suiza, han dado el nombre a un deporte: el alpinismo o el andinismo (*mountain climbing*). Puesto que es un deporte peligroso y exigente (*demanding*), ¿qué cree Ud. que motiva a los alpinistas? ¿Participa Ud. en algún deporte difícil?
5. Mucha gente va a las montañas porque quiere respirar aire puro y no contaminado como en la ciudad. ¿Qué hacen los movimientos ecológicos para proteger la naturaleza? ¿Cree Ud. que han tenido éxito?

Ciudad y puerto de Valparaíso, Chile.

Vocabulario

Antes de leer, repase el siguiente vocabulario que le ayudará a comprender la lectura.

Sustantivos

el alba dawn
la bellota acorn
la caricia caress
la col cabbage
la muchedumbre multitude

el nacimiento birth
la palidez paleness
el paraíso paradise
la utilidad usefulness

Verbo

tentar (ie) to tempt

Adjetivos

frondoso leafy
maligno evil

Lectura 2

Rubén Darío

Rubén Darío (1867–1916), uno de los grandes poetas del mundo hispano, nació en Nicaragua. Durante su adolescencia leyó e imitó a los poetas españoles y franceses, los cuales tuvieron gran influencia en su formación literaria. En su primera obra, *Azul* (1888), Rubén Darío mostró su gran sensibilidad y su originalidad en el verso. Fue el líder de la revolución artística que dio paso al Modernismo, movimiento que se caracterizó por las innovaciones métricas, la riqueza musical, el lenguaje preciosista y el mundo refinado y sensual que describía. El cuento "El nacimiento de la col" apareció en 1893 en el periódico argentino *La Tribuna*, y en él Darío nos transporta al paraíso terrenal en el quinto día de la creación del mundo.

El nacimiento de la col

En el paraíso terrenal,° en el día luminoso en que las flores fueron creadas, y antes de que Eva fuese tentada por la serpiente, el maligno espíritu se acercó a la más linda rosa nueva en el momento en que ella tendía,° a la caricia del celeste° sol, la roja virginidad de
5 sus labios.

    —Eres bella.
    —Lo soy —dijo la rosa.
    —Bella y feliz —prosiguió el diablo—. Tienes el color, la gracia y el aroma. Pero…
10   —¿Pero?…
    —No eres útil. ¿No miras esos altos árboles llenos de bellotas?
Ésos, a más de ser frondosos,° dan alimento a una muchedumbre de seres animados° que se detienen bajo sus ramas. Rosa, ser bella es poco…

15   La rosa entonces —tentada como después lo sería la mujer— deseó la utilidad, de tal modo° que hubo palidez en su púrpura.
Pasó el buen Dios después del alba siguiente.

    —Padre —dijo aquella princesa floral, temblando en su perfumada belleza—, ¿queréis hacerme útil?
20   —Sea, hija mía —contestó el Señor, sonriendo.
    Y entonces vio el mundo la primera col.

Garden of Eden

was offering / celestial

besides being leafy

living things

so much

Preguntas sobre la lectura

1. ¿Dónde y cuándo ocurrió este cuento?
2. ¿Quién se acercó a la más linda rosa nueva?
3. Según la narración, ¿qué tienen los árboles que no tiene la rosa?

4. ¿Con qué tentó el diablo a la rosa?
5. ¿Qué le pidió la rosa a Dios?
6. ¿Cómo complació (*pleased*) Dios a la rosa?

Gramática

A Relatives

que	lo que
quien (-es)	lo cual
el (los, la, las) que	cuyo (-os, -a, -as)
el (la) cual, los (las) cuales	

Relatives are used to connect clauses to the words they modify. The antecedent is the noun, pronoun, or concept to which the relative refers.

Hay pocos **hombres**   **que**   son héroes.   *There are few men*
    antecedent   *relative*   *who are heroes.*

Laura compró el **traje**   **que**   estaba en la tienda.   *Laura bought the dress*
    antecedent   *relative*   *that was in the store.*

1. **Que** is invariable and is the most commonly used relative when it immediately follows the antecedent. It can refer to persons, things, places, or concepts. It is the equivalent of the English *that, which, who*.

> Los niños **que** fueron a la excursión están emocionados.
> *The children that went to the excursion are thrilled.*
> Las personas **que** los acompañaron están contentas.
> *The persons that accompanied them are happy.*
> El árbol **que** plantamos el año pasado está lleno de fruta.
> *The tree that we planted last year is full of fruit.*
> La fruta **que** da es muy dulce.
> *The fruit (that) it produces is very sweet.*

NOTE: In conversational English, the relative *that* is often omitted. In Spanish **que** may not be omitted.

> Él es el profesor **que** tuve el año pasado. *He is the professor (that) I had last year.*

Que is used after the prepositions **a**, **con**, **de**, **en**, only when referring to things, not to people. The equivalent of **en que** is **donde**.

> La carta **a que** te refieres no la recibí, ni tampoco el informe **de que** me hablaste.
> *I didn't receive the letter you refer to, nor the information you told me about.*
> La compañía **en que** trabajo tiene muy buenos equipos, pero ayer se descompuso la computadora **con que** trabajo.
> *The company where I work has very good equipment, but yesterday the computer I work with broke down.*

2. **Quien (-es)** refers only to people and agrees in number with the antecedent. The equivalent in English is *who, whom, whomever*.

   a. **Quien (-es)** is used after prepositions.

   > La chica **a quien** conociste en mi casa es peruana y el muchacho **con quien** vino es un artista muy conocido. Ella es **de quien** te hablé hace tiempo y es la persona **para quien** se creó el puesto en el museo.
   > *The girl whom you met in my house is Peruvian and the boy with whom she came is a very well known artist. She is about whom I talked to you some time ago and is the person for whom they created the position in the museum.*

   NOTE: One may also say: La chica **que** conociste en mi casa es peruana. *The girl that you met in my house is Peruvian.* See letter **d**.

   b. **Quien (-es)** is used instead of **que** when it is the subject of an appositive clause separated by commas.

   > El director, **quien** acaba de llamar, vendrá esta tarde.
   > *The director, who has just called, will come this evening.*
   > Me quedaré en la oficina para escribirle a mis hijos, **quienes** están estudiando en San Diego.
   > *I will stay in the office in order to write to my children, who are studying in San Diego.*

   c. In some cases, **quien** includes the antecedent and is the equivalent to **la persona que**.

   > **Quien** habla mucho hace poco.
   > *He/She (The person) who talks a lot does little.*
   > **Quien** trajo el paquete se fue en seguida.
   > *Whoever (The person) who brought the package left immediately.*

   d. **Quien** is not used immediately after the antecedent. In this case **que** is used.

   > La persona **que** viste no era mi prima.
   > *The person (that) you saw was not my cousin.*
   > El hombre **que** tocó en la puerta vendía seguros.
   > *The man who knocked at the door was selling insurance.*

3. **El (los, la, las) que** or **el (la) cual, los (las) cuales** refer to people or things. They are more specific relatives than **quien** or **que**.

   a. **El que** or **el cual** are used when there are two possible antecedents to refer to the one that is farther away and to resolve the ambiguity.

   > El primo de María, **el que (el cual)** vive en Nuevo México, quiere venir a pasar las vacaciones con nosotros.
   > *María's cousin, the one that lives in New Mexico, wants to come to spend the holidays with us.*
   > Acabo de hablar con la mujer de Joaquín, **la que** quiere alquilar mi casa.
   > *I have just talked to Joaquin's wife, who wants to rent my house.*

   b. **El que** or **el cual** are used after prepositions (except after **a**, **con**, **de**, or **en**).

   > La razón por **la que (la cual)** dejé el trabajo es muy simple.
   > *The reason why I left the job is very simple.*

Vista de la Plaza de San Martín en la ciudad de Lima, Perú.

NOTE: In general, **que** is used to refer to things after **a**, **con**, **de**, or **en**. **El que** or **el cual** can also be used after prepositional phrases.

> La casa, delante de **la que (la cual)** dejé el carro, es de estilo californiano.
> *The house in front of which I left the car is Californian style.*

c. **El que**, **Los que** are sometimes used instead of **quien** as the equivalent of **la persona que**. **El cual** cannot be used in this case.

> **El que** estudia aprende. (**Quien** estudia aprende.)
> *The one who studies learns.*
> **Los que** hablan mucho saben poco. (**Quienes** hablan mucho saben poco.)
> *The ones who talk a lot know little.*
> Josefina fue **la que** llamó. (Josefina fue **quien** llamó.)
> *Josefina was the one who called.*

NOTE: **El que**, **Los que**, **La que**, **Las que** are also used as the equivalent of the English *the one that* or *the ones that*.

> Estos zapatos son muy cómodos. **Los que** compré ayer no lo son.
> *These shoes are very comfortable. The ones I bought yesterday are not.*
> La novela **que** estoy leyendo es romántica, pero **la que** leí antes es muy cómica.
> *The novel I'm reading is romantic, but the one I read before is very funny.*

4. The neuter relatives **lo que** and **lo cual** are used when referring to an idea, an action, or a deed previously mentioned.*

> Juan llegó tarde, **lo que (lo cual)** no le gustó a su mujer.
> *Juan came home late, which did not please his wife.*
> Salieron a tiempo, **lo que (lo cual)** me sorprendió.
> *They left on time, which surprised me.*

---

*See Comparatives, Capítulo 8, page 242.

NOTE: **Lo que** (and not **lo cual**) is used when referring to an abstract idea not mentioned previously. It is equivalent to **la cosa que**. The English equivalent is *what*.

> **Lo que** pasó anoche fue interesante, sin embargo ella no sabe **lo que** yo opino, pues no comprende **lo que** yo expliqué.
> *What happened last night was interesting, nevertheless, she doesn't know what opinion I have because she doesn't understand what I explained.*

Lo que can be used with the verb in the indicative if it refers to something specific, or with the verb in the subjunctive if it refers to something indefinite or undetermined.

> Di **lo que** tienes que decir.　　*Tell what you have to say.*
> Di **lo que** tengas que decir.　　*Tell whatever you may have to say.*

5. **Cuyo (-os, -a, -as)** is a relative adjective. It agrees in gender and number with the noun it modifies and is used to indicate possession. The antecedent can be a person or a thing. The English equivalent is *whose*.

> Pedro, **cuya** madre es brasileña, habla portugués muy bien.
> *Pedro, whose mother is Brazilian, speaks Portuguese very well.*
> Los pescadores, **cuyas** canoas están en la playa, trajeron muchas sardinas.
> *The fishermen, whose canoes are on the beach, brought many sardines.*
> Las montañas, **cuyos** picos están nevados, tienen más de diez mil pies de altura.
> *The mountains, where peaks are covered with snow, are more than ten thousand feet high.*

NOTA: The equivalent in Spanish of whose in interrogative sentences is **¿de quién (-es)?**

> **¿De quién** es este abrigo?　　*Whose coat is this?*

Ejercicios

I. Combine las oraciones usando el relativo **que** para contarnos lo que Ud. hizo anoche.

MODELO: Leo un libro. Es una biografía.
El libro que leo es una biografía.

1. Invité al cine a una muchacha. Es de Lima.
2. Vimos dos películas españolas. Son magníficas.
3. Después tomamos chocolate con churros. Estaban sabrosísimos.
4. Ella me regaló un libro. Tiene fotografías hermosas de Machu Picchu.

II. Combine las oraciones usando el relativo **que** o **quien**.

MODELOS: Ésta es la máquina de escribir. De ella te hablé anoche.
Ésta es la máquina de escribir de que te hablé anoche.
Tengo muchos amigos. Con ellos hablo todos los días.
Tengo muchos amigos con quienes hablo todos los días.

1. Aquí tengo el ordenador. Con él voy a preparar los informes.
2. Conseguí el disco compacto. En él está el programa que necesito.
3. Copié todos estos documentos. En ellos encontraré la información necesaria.
4. Ayer visité a mi compañera de clase. Con ella pienso escribir el bosquejo (*outline*).
5. Conocí a su profesor. Con él estudia filosofía.

III. Complete el párrafo llenando los espacios en blanco con **que, quien** o **quienes**.

Los carros _____ circulan por las calles de la ciudad producen gran parte de los contaminantes _____ respiramos. Por eso, el alcalde de la ciudad, _____ se preocupa mucho por todos los asuntos ambientales, quiere desarrollar buenos sistemas de transporte público y evitar el aumento de contaminación en el aire. Un periodista con _____ habló el alcalde mencionó el problema del poco espacio de estacionamiento para tantos carros en la ciudad. Para _____ trabajan en el centro un sistema de transporte eficiente será una gran cosa. Pero el periodista parece ser un poco pesimista y terminó diciendo: " _____ mucho promete cumple poco".

IV. Una amiga suya le habla de la hermana de Jorge. Complete las oraciones usando **el que, los que, la que** o **las que** para saber lo que cuentan de ella.

1. La hermana de Jorge, _____ trabaja en el banco, es muy simpática.
2. Ésa es la razón por _____ tiene tantos amigos.
3. Los edificios delante de _____ ella vive son de estilo colonial.
4. El baile para _____ ella compró el vestido largo será el sábado.
5. Ella cree que _____ trabajan mucho triunfan en la vida.

V. Traduzca las siguientes oraciones.

1. *What he wants is to live in Mexico. What he must do first is to study Spanish.*
2. *The one who sang last night was Shakira.*
3. *These are the new shoes. The ones I had were very old.*
4. *Whose house is this? It belongs to a family whose name I don't remember.*

VI. Escoja la respuesta correcta y complete las oraciones.

1. (los que, que, cual) ¿Trajiste los esquís _____ te pedí?
2. (El cual, Lo que, El que) _____ mucho habla, hace poco.
3. (quienes, a quienes, que) Ellos son los jóvenes _____ les dieron las becas.
4. (la cual, que, lo que) Ésta es la oficina para _____ trabaja Ernesto.
5. (El que, Lo que, Lo cual) _____ no me gusta es levantarme temprano.
6. (el que, lo que, lo cual) No sé de _____ están hablando.
7. (de quien, cuyo, cual) Ése es el profesor _____ nombre es Alfredo Matilla.
8. (quienes, los que, que) Los jugadores _____ llegaron anoche fueron al hotel Casa Grande.

9. (quien, que, el cual) El médico, _____ acaba de llamar, vendrá mañana a verte.

10. (que, la cual, lo que) Se aprobó la ley contra _____ voté en las elecciones.

VII. Complete las oraciones con la forma apropiada del relativo **cuyo**.

1. El parque, _____ flores nos encantan, está cerca de aquí.

2. Me gusta el edificio _____ balcones tienen rejas de hierro (*iron rails*) y macetas (*flowerpots*) con geranios.

3. Ése es el chico _____ abuelo tiene una plantación de café.

4. Visité los lagos _____ belleza es fabulosa.

5. El salto Ángel (*Angel Falls*), _____ altura es mucho mayor que la del Niágara, está en Venezuela.

VIII. Complete las oraciones con el relativo adecuado.

1. Alicia, _____ tiene un resfriado, no vino a clase.

2. La prima de Isidoro, _____ estudia química, es muy bonita.

3. La pluma con _____ escribo es de plata.

4. Los chicos _____ entrevistamos recibirán una beca.

5. Las clases empiezan el día dos, _____ no me gusta.

6. Los edificios cerca de _____ dejamos el carro son muy modernos.

7. _____ come mucho, engorda.

8. Los amigos para _____ doy la fiesta llegaron ayer de Quito.

9. La casa, _____ precio me conviene, ya se alquiló.

10. Todo _____ te digo es verdad.

IX. Ud. conversa con un amigo venezolano sobre la regulación que ayuda a descongestionar el tráfico en Caracas. Esta regulación ordena días de parada para los carros particulares. Complete el diálogo con los relativos necesarios.

UD.:   ¿Cómo se sabe cuáles son los carros _____ no salen los días de parada?

AMIGO: Muy fácil. Todas las personas _____ tienen carro saben el día _____ no pueden sacarlo a la calle por el número de la chapa (*license plate*).

UD.:   ¿Por el número de la chapa?

AMIGO: Sí. _____ tienen números pares (*even numbers*) salen un día y

al siguiente _____ tienen números impares.

UD.: ¡Qué buena idea!

AMIGO: Exactamente. Así todas las personas _____ trabajan hacen sus

planes para ir en el metro o en taxi cuando no pueden usar el carro.

UD.: ¿Y los taxis no tienen que parar un día también?

AMIGO: No, _____ es muy bueno, pues los taxis son muy baratos.

X. Complete las oraciones con el equivalente en español de las palabras en inglés. Use los relativos necesarios.

1. ¿ _____ (*Whom*) vas a invitar?
2. Teresa es _____ (*the one who*) más necesita el librero.
3. Ella no sabe _____ (*what*) quiere estudiar.
4. _____ (*The one who*) llamó anoche fue Isidoro.
5. El señor _____ (*with whom*) trabaja mi esposo es el presidente del senado.
6. Puedes ordenar _____ (*whatever*) quieras.
7. La población _____ (*through which*) pasamos es muy pintoresca.
8. Su padre, _____ (*who*) acaba de cumplir ochenta años, es un médico famoso.
9. El puente _____ (*that*) cruzamos lo construyeron los romanos.
10. Los industriales _____ (*who*) acaban de llegar son de El Salvador.
11. El escritor _____ (*whose*) novela te regalé vino a la universidad ayer.
12. _____ (*What*) quiere la gente es que no aumenten los impuestos.

XI. Composición dirigida (oral o escrita). Complete las oraciones con ideas originales usando el relativo entre paréntesis.

MODELO: (cuyo) Ese artista…

Ese artista, cuyo nombre no recuerdo, es el que hizo la película que vi hace unos días.

1. (quien) Nunca sabemos para…
2. (el que) El novio de Celia…
3. (que) El refrigerador…
4. (lo que) Para hablar español…
5. (en que) Quiero visitar el pueblo…

Vista de la ciudad de Quito, capital del Ecuador.

B Passive constructions

Active voice and passive voice are different ways of structuring a sentence to inform about the same event. Generally, in conversation we use the active voice for sentences such as the following:

> El pueblo **eligió** al gobernador.
> *The people elected the governor.*

In this sentence, whoever did the action of electing, the people, (el pueblo) is the subject; the person who received the action of being elected, the governor, is the direct object. Using the passive voice one can inform about the same event from a different point of view, giving a more prominent place to the one who receives the action (el gobernador) than the one who does it (el pueblo).

> El gobernador **fue elegido** por el pueblo.
> *The governor was elected by the people.*

1. The passive voice is expressed with the verb **ser** + a past participle that agrees in gender and number with the subject. In general, the preposition **por** precedes the agent, the person that executes the action.

> La novela **fue escrita por** Isabel Allende.
> *The novel was written by Isabel Allende.*
> Los productos **son distribuidos por** el agente.
> *The products are distributed by the agent.*

The passsive voice, **ser** + past participle is used less in Spanish than in English, especially in conversational Spanish.

a. Note the change from active voice to passive voice in the following sentences:

> El cineasta León Ichaso **dirigió** la película.
> *The film producer León Ichaso directed the film.*
> La película **fue dirigida por** el cineasta León Ichaso.
> *The film was directed by the film producer León Ichaso.*

The subject of the sentence in the active voice becomes the agent, and the direct object becomes the subject in the passive voice.

b. The passive voice **ser** + past participle always implies an action received by the subject. **Estar** + past participle describes a state or condition of the subject, as well as the result of an action.*

> Las puertas **fueron abiertas** a las ocho.
> *The doors were opened at eight.*
> Las puertas **estaban abiertas** a las ocho.
> *The doors were (already) open by eight.*

NOTE: Any tense can be used in the passive voice:

> La reunión **ha sido cancelada**. *The meeting has been cancelled.*

2. Another form of expressing the passive voice is with the word **se**. This construction is more common in conversational Spanish. **Se** + verb in third person singular or plural is equivalent to the passive voice with **ser** + past participle. The person or thing that does the action is not mentioned. In general the verb precedes the subject. In English this construction is expressed with *to be* + past participle.

> **Se publicará** la entrevista en todos los periódicos.
> (La entrevista será publicada en todos los periódicos.)
> *The interview will be published in all the newspapers.*
> **Se cerraron** las tiendas a las ocho.
> *The stores were closed at eight.*
> **Se ha decidido** aumentar el presupuesto para las escuelas.
> *It has been decided to increase the budget for the schools.*
> **Se dice** que las próximas Olimpiadas serán en Sudamérica.
> *It is said that the next Olympic Games will be in South America.*

---

*See Capítulo 3, pages 92-93, uses of **ser** and **estar**.

NOTA: Remember that in impersonal constructions **se** is used with the verb in the third person singular. The equivalent in English is *one, they, people* + the verb.

Se vive bien aquí.	*One lives well here.*
Se come tarde en España.	*They eat late in Spain.*
Se habla mucho.	*People talk a lot.*

3. Sometimes, in conversation, the verb in third person plural is used, having the implicit subject **las personas**. It is equivalent to the passive construction with **se**.

Producen café en Colombia. (Se produce café en Colombia.)	*They produce coffee in Colombia.* *Coffee is produced in Colombia.*
Dicen que subirán los precios. (Se dice que subirán los precios.)	*They say prices will increase.* *It is said that prices will increase.*
Le enviaron los pedidos la semana pasada. (Se le enviaron los pedidos la semana pasada.)	*They sent him the orders last week.* *The orders were sent to him last week.*
¿Servirán café en la reunión mañana? (¿Se servirá café en la reunión mañana?)	*Will they serve coffee at the meeting tomorrow?* *Will coffee be served at the meeting tomorrow?*

NOTA: The word **se** always precedes the pronouns used as direct and indirect objects.

Ejercicios

I. Complete las oraciones con la voz pasiva de los verbos entre paréntesis. Use el tiempo de verbo que sea necesario.

1. (escribir) La novela que me regalaste _____ _____ por el autor peruano Mario Vargas Llosa.

2. (elegir) En México, el presidente _____ _____ por un período de seis años.

3. (entrevistar) Los inmigrantes que llegan a la frontera _____ _____ por las autoridades.

4. (recoger) El mes pasado, un grupo de exiliados cubanos _____ _____ en alta mar por un guardacostas (*coast guard*) norteamericano.

5. (aprobar) ¿Crees que la nueva ley de inmigración _____ _____ por el Congreso el próximo año?

II. Su amigo le hace preguntas acerca de las noticias que Ud. escuchó en la radio. Conteste sus preguntas usando una construcción pasiva con **se**.

MODELOS: ¿Aumentarán el precio de la gasolina?
Sí, se aumentará el precio de la gasolina.

¿Han pedido que bajen los impuestos?
Sí, se ha pedido que bajen los impuestos.

1. ¿Anunciaron que regularán los precios para fin de año?
2. ¿Han importado más petróleo de México y Venezuela?
3. ¿Están construyendo una refinería cerca de la costa?
4. ¿Dicen que fabricarán más carros económicos?
5. ¿Esperan que pronto se normalice esta situación?

III. ¿Qué se hace cuando se quiere conseguir alguna información en la universidad? Transforme las frases usando una construcción con **se**, según el modelo.

MODELO: Ir a la oficina de la universidad
Se va a la oficina de la universidad.

1. Hablar con un consejero
2. Explicar la información que se desea
3. Escuchar las recomendaciones del consejero
4. Pedir los folletos (*brochures*) necesarios
5. Preguntar las posibilidades para obtener una beca

IV. Describa la condición o estado producido por las siguientes acciones.

MODELO: El río inundó el valle.
El valle está inundado.

1. La nieve cubrió todo.
2. La lluvia destruyó las cosechas (*crops*).
3. El tornado destrozó los edificios.
4. El viento rompió los cristales.

V. Complete las frases del siguiente minidiálogo con **ser** o **estar**, usando el tiempo de verbo que sea necesario.

1. —¿No ibas a ir hoy a la playa?

   —Sí, pensé ir, pero cambié de idea porque _____ muy nublado.

2. —¿Entonces piensas ir al lago?

   —Sí, iré al lago por el puente antiguo que ya _____ reparado y _____ abierto al tráfico.

3. —¿Fuiste ayer al juego de pelota?

   —Sí, pero llegué tarde porque el reloj _____ atrasado. Después lo vi en casa porque _____ transmitido por televisión.

VI. Complete las oraciones con la traducción al español de las frases que están en inglés. Use una construcción pasiva con **ser** para informar sobre una acción, o **estar +** participio pasado para describir un estado o condición.

1. (*has been translated*) La obra _____ a muchos idiomas.
2. (*were approved*) Las peticiones de los obreros _____ por los directores.

3. (*is made*) La blusa _____ a mano.

4. (*will be covered*) La ciudad _____ de nieve mañana.

5. (*Is dinner served?*) ¿_____?

6. (*were announced*) Los premios _____ al final del banquete.

7. (*is painted*) La casa _____ de verde y blanco.

8. (*is made*) El pastel _____ con mantequilla.

9. (*were founded*) Las misiones _____ por un fraile español.

10. (*are signed*) Muchas de las cartas recibidas _____ por los estudiantes.

VII. Complete las oraciones con la traducción al español de las frases que están en inglés. Use una construcción con **se**.

1. (*One eats*) _____ bien en este restaurante.

2. (*They say*) _____ que van a construir otra autopista.

3. (*were signed*) Los contratos _____ el mes pasado.

4. (*Were distributed*) _____ los juguetes entre los niños.

5. (*opens*) El banco _____ a las nueve.

6. (*It's believed*) _____ que la economía mejorará este año.

C Verbs that express the idea of change or *to become*

1. The verbs **ponerse**, **volverse**, **hacerse**, and **llegar a ser** + adjective or noun are used to express change in condition or state. They express the idea of *to become* in English.

   a. **Ponerse** expresses a physical or emotional change, usually of short duration.

   > Alina **se puso** roja cuando oyó el chiste. *Alina turned red when she heard the joke.*

   b. **Volverse** indicates a more radical change of longer duration.

   > Ella **se volvió** loca al sufrir tantos horrores durante la guerra.
   > *She went crazy due to so much suffering during the war.*

   c. **Hacerse** indicates change obtained through effort. **Llegar a ser** also expresses change obtained through effort and can be used instead of **hacerse**.

   > Después de tantos años de estudio, Pedro **se hizo** médico (**llegó a ser** médico).
   > *After so many years of studies, Pedro became a doctor.*

2. **Quedarse** generally indicates a change that occurs as a consequence of something that took place before. It expresses the state or resulting condition of the person.

   > Roberto **se quedó** muy débil después del accidente.
   > *Roberto remained very weak after the accident.*
   > Lucía **se quedó** sin poder hablar al oír la noticia.
   > *Lucia became speechless when she heard the news.*

3. There are verbs whose very meaning expresses the idea of change, *to become* or *to get*.
Many of these verbs are reflexive.

adelgazar	*to get thin*	**alegrarse**	*to be happy*
enloquecer	*to go crazy*	**cansarse**	*to get tired*
envejecer	*to get old*	**enfermarse**	*to get sick*
palidecer	*to become pale*	**enojarse**	*to get angry*
enrojecerse	*to blush*	**mejorarse**	*to get better*
acostumbrarse	*to get used to*	**aburrirse**	*to get bored*

Ella **ha adelgazado** más de veinte libras.
She has lost more than twenty pounds.
¡Cómo **ha envejecido** esa señora!
How old that lady has become!
Se enojó mucho cuando le dijiste que se callara.
She got very angry when you told her to shut up.

Ejercicios

I. Transforme las frases según los modelos.

MODELOS: Se pone viejo.
Envejece.
Se puso enfermo.
Se enfermó.

1. Se pone delgado.
2. Se pone pálido.
3. Se vuelve loca.
4. Se puso enojado.
5. Se puso mejor.
6. Se puso rojo.

II. Llene los espacios en blanco con la traducción adecuada de *to become*.

1. Antonio _____ triste cuando se despidió de su amigo.
2. Al fin, mi sobrina terminó los estudios y _____ abogada.
3. Después de tantos años de trabajar en sus negocios, Rafael _____ rico.
4. Mi padre _____ contento cuando supo que había ganado el campeonato.
5. Después de perder a los dos hijos, la madre se enfermó y _____ loca.
6. Cuando terminó el concierto, el público _____ loco aplaudiendo a la pianista.
7. Mi esposo _____ muy delgado después de la operación.

III. Ud. se encuentra con su amigo Rubén a quien no veía desde hace tiempo.
Complete el diálogo traduciendo al español las frases que están en inglés. Use verbos
que expresen idea de cambio.

UD.:   Hola, Rubén, ¡qué alegría verte! Hacía mucho tiempo que no te veía.

RUBÉN: Es que _____ (*I became sick*) a finales del verano y no he salido

mucho. Por suerte, _____ (*I have improved*) bastante.

UD.:   Noto que _____ (*you have gotten thin*) y te ves muy bien.

RUBÉN: He estado con una dieta muy estricta; he dejado de fumar y ahora sólo bebo

agua. Al principio creí que _____ (*I was going to go crazy*).

UD.:   Me lo imagino. Tú sin fumar, sin comer y sin beber…

RUBÉN: No te rías, pero creo que si sigo con este régimen _____

(*I'll get to be*) un santo.

D Expressions that denote obligation

1. **Haber de** + infinitive expresses a sense of obligation imposed on ourselves. The
    equivalent in English is *to be supposed to.*

    Has de levantarte temprano si quieres   *You are (supposed) to get up early*
    llegar a tiempo.   *if you want to be on time.*
    He de estudiar más el año que viene.   *I am (supposed) to study more next year.*

2. **Hay que** + infinitive expresses obligation imposed from outside to an indefinite
    subject. The equivalent in English is *it is necessary* or *one must.*

    Hay que comprar los boletos para   *It is necessary to buy the tickets for*
    la corrida de toros.   *the bullfight.*
    Hay que estar en el aeropuerto a las seis.   *One must be at the airport at six.*

3. **Tener que** + infinitive expresses a more determined sense of obligation, also
    imposed from outside. The equivalent in English is *to have to.*

    Tienes que pintar la casa.   *You have to paint the house.*
    Han tenido que cancelar el viaje.   *They have had to cancel the trip.*

Ejercicios

I. Complete el siguiente diálogo entre una madre y su hijo pequeño llenando los
espacios en blanco con la traducción al español de las frases que están en inglés.

NIÑO: ¿Puedo ir a jugar a la pelota?

MADRE: No, _____ (*you have to*) hacer la tarea.

NIÑO: Todos los días me dices lo mismo.

MADRE: Claro, y te lo seguiré diciendo. _____ (*One must*) estudiar

para tener éxito en la vida.

NIÑO: Pero si me dejas jugar a la pelota _____ (*I'm supposed to*)

llegar a ser un pelotero famoso.

II. Haga oraciones originales usando como principio las siguientes frases.

> **MODELO:** He de salir muy temprano...
>
> **He de salir muy temprano porque quiero llegar a la capital antes de que sea de noche.**

1. Hay que escoger bien a los amigos...
2. Tengo que buscar otro empleo...
3. Hemos de evitar que destruyan la naturaleza...

E Expressions with *hacer. Hace* + time + *que*

1. **Hace** + time + **que** + verb in present tense indicates the time passed since the beginning of an action that still continues in the present.

> **Hace dos meses que** ella **está** de vacaciones.
> (Ella todavía sigue de vacaciones.)
> *She has been on vacation for two months.*
> **Hace tres horas que estamos** aquí.
> *We have been here for three hours.*
> **Hace un año que estudio** español.
> *I have been studying Spanish for one year.*

NOTE: Observe the following construction: verb in present + **desde hace** + time.

> **¿Desde cuándo** viven Uds. en Nicaragua?
> *How long have you been living in Nicaragua?*
> Vivimos en Nicaragua **desde hace** tres meses.
> *We have been living in Nicaragua for three months.*

2. **Hace** + time + **que** + verb in the preterite tense indicates the time elapsed since an action was completed. The English equivalent is *ago*.

> **Hace un año que regresé** de España.
> (Ha pasado un año desde que regresé de España.)
> *I came back from Spain a year ago.*
> **Hace seis meses que dejé** el trabajo del banco.
> *I left the job at the bank six months ago.*

3. **Hacía** + time + **que** + verb in imperfect indicates the time passed of an action that started in the past and was still going on at a moment in the past.

> **Hacía un año que** ellos **estaban** en El Paso cuando compraron la casa.
> (Ellos llevaban un año en El Paso cuando compraron la casa.)
> *They had been in El Paso for one year when they bought the house.*
> ¿Cuánto tiempo **hacía que** ellos **se conocían**?
> *How long had they known each other?*

NOTE: The expression with **hacer** can go at the beginning or at the end of the sentence. If it goes at the end, the word **que** is not necessary.

Hace tres meses que vivimos en Nicaragua.	*We have been living in Nicaragua*
Vivimos en Nicaragua **hace tres meses**.	*for three months.*
Hace un año que me gradué.	*I graduated a year ago.*
Me gradué **hace un año**.	
Hacía una semana que ella estaba enferma.	*She had been sick for a week.*
Ella estaba enferma **hacía una semana**.	

4. The verb **hacer** can be used in the preterite or the future depending on the idea we want to communicate. Note the following examples:

Ayer **hizo** tres meses que llegué de Chile.
I arrived from Chile three months ago yesterday.
Mañana **hará** dos años que me casé.
Tomorrow it will be two years since I got married.

5. The impersonal form of the verb **hacer** is used to express atmospheric conditions.

	Hace buen tiempo.	*The weather is nice.*
	Hace mal tiempo.	*The weather is bad.*
	Hace calor.	*It is hot.*
¿Qué tiempo **hace**?	**Hace frío.**	*It is cold.*
How is the weather?	Hace fresco.	*It is cool.*
	Hace sol.	*It is sunny.*
	Hace viento.	*It is windy.*

6. Expressions with the verb **hacer**.

hacer alusión	*to allude*	Juan no **hizo alusión** a lo que le dije.
		Juan did not allude to what I said.
hacer caso	*to pay attention*	Manolito no **hace caso** cuando lo llamo a comer.
		Manolito doesn't pay attention when I call him to eat.
hacer cola	*to stand in line*	Tuvimos que **hacer cola** para entrar en el cine.
		We had to stand in line to go into the theater.
hacer daño	*to harm; to make sick*	A ella le **hizo daño** el pescado que comió anoche.
		The fish she ate last night made her sick.
hacer el papel	*to play the role*	Ese artista **hace** muy bien **el papel** de Romeo.
		That actor plays the role of Romeo very well.
hacer escala	*to stop over*	El avión **hizo escala** en Lima.
		The plane made a stopover in Lima.
hacer falta	*to be necessary*	**Hace falta** que tengamos paciencia.
		It is necessary that we be patient.
hacer un favor	*to do a favor*	**Hágame el favor** de cerrar la puerta.
		Please (do me the favor) close the door.
hacer frente	*to face*	Tuvimos que **hacerle frente** a la situación.
		We had to face the situation.
hacer gestos	*to gesture*	Maricusa **hace** muchos **gestos** al hablar.
		Maricusa gestures a lot when she speaks.

hacer la maleta	to pack	Ya **hice las maletas** para el viaje.
		I already packed for the trip.
hacer pedazos	to break; to tear to pieces	El gato **hizo pedazos** la almohada.
		The cat tore the pillow to pieces.
hacerse pedazos	to break into pieces	El plato **se hizo pedazos** al caerse.
		The plate broke into pieces when it fell.
hacer saber	to inform; to make known	Le **hice saber** a Pepe lo que yo pensaba.
		I let Pepe know what I thought.
hacer señas	to signal	El policía **hacía señas** para desviar el tráfico.
		The policeman signaled to detour the traffic.
hacer una pregunta	to ask a question	**Hacemos** muchas **preguntas** en la clase.
		We ask a lot of questions in class.
hacer una visita	to pay a visit	Tengo que **hacer una visita**.
		I have to pay a visit.
hacer un pedido	to place an order	Ya **hice el pedido** de los libros.
		I already placed the book order.
hacer un viaje	to take a trip	Pensamos **hacer un viaje** el próximo año.
		We plan to take a trip next year.
hacerse	to become	Pedro **se hizo** médico; yo **me hice** abogada.
		Pedro became a doctor; I became a lawyer.
hacerse daño	to hurt oneself	El chico **se hizo daño** al caerse.
		The boy hurt himself when he fell down.
hacerse el sordo	to play deaf	**Se hizo el sordo** y no contestó.
		He played deaf and didn't answer.
hacerse el tonto	to play dumb	**Se hizo el tonto** y no me pagó la cuenta.
		He played dumb and didn't pay me the bill.
hacerse pasar por	to pretend to be	**Se hacía pasar por** médico, pero no lo era.
		He pretended to be a doctor, but he wasn't.
hacerse tarde	to get late	**Se hizo tarde** y no llegamos a tiempo. Siempre **se hace tarde**.
		It got late and we didn't arrive on time. It always gets late.

Ejercicios

I. Llene los espacios en blanco con las palabras necesarias para contestar las preguntas en una oración completa.

MODELO: ¿Cuánto tiempo hace que estudias español?

_____ tres años _____.

Hace tres años que estudio español.

1. ¿Cuánto tiempo hace que él trabaja de enfermero?

_____ dos años _____.

2. ¿Cuándo estuviste en Bogotá?

_____ un año _____.

3. ¿Cuánto tiempo hacía que esperabas a la doctora?

_____ veinte minutos _____.

4. ¿Cuánto tiempo hace que dejaste de fumar?

_____ cinco meses _____.

5. ¿Desde cuándo estás a dieta?

_____ a dieta _____ tres semanas.

6. ¿Cuánto tiempo hacía que conocías a Pedro cuando te casaste con él?

_____ cinco años _____ cuando _____.

II. Escriba las preguntas para las siguientes respuestas.

MODELO: ¿ _____ ?   Hace tres años que fui a Chile.
¿Cuántos años hace que fue a Chile?

1. ¿ _____ ? Hace una semana que vi esa película.
2. ¿ _____ ? Hace dos años que tengo novio.
3. ¿ _____ ? Hacía una hora que te esperaba.
4. ¿ _____ ? Hacía un año que vivían en Lima cuando compraron la casa.
5. ¿ _____ ? Juego al tenis desde hace tres años.
6. ¿ _____ ? Hace más de dos meses que ellos no me visitan.

III. De acuerdo con el sentido de las oraciones, use **hace, hacía, hizo** o **hará** para completarlas.

1. ¿ _____ mucho tiempo que Ud. no compra billetes de lotería (*lottery tickets*)?

2. Hoy _____ un año que ella se graduó de la universidad.

3. ¿Cuánto tiempo _____ que Ud. no patinaba?

4. El verano pasado _____ dos años que me visitó mi amigo José.

5. La semana que viene _____ cinco años que nos casamos.

6. _____ mucho tiempo que no veía a mis primas.

IV. Traduzca al español las frases que están en inglés y complete las oraciones usando expresiones con el verbo **hacer**.

1. ¿ (*How is the weather*) _____ en Madrid en el invierno?

   (*It is very cold / It is very hot*) _____ en el invierno y

   _____ en el verano.

2. (*it was very windy*) La semana pasada _____ y se quebraron varias ramas (*branches*) del naranjo.

3. (*it is cool*) Me gusta la primavera porque _____.

4. (*it is sunny*) Prefiero ir a la playa cuando _____.

5. (*will play the role*) Rosita _____ de Blanca Nieves (*Snow White*) en la producción de la escuela.

6. (*stand in line*) Había tanta gente para el estreno de la película que tuvimos que _____ por una hora.

7. (*he plays deaf*) Cuando mi hermano no quiere contestar una pregunta _____.

8. (*stops*) El vuelo que voy a tomar _____ en las Bahamas.

9. (*he pretends to be*) Ese joven es un charlatán; _____ artista y no sabe ni dibujar.

10. (*broke to pieces*) Se me cayó el plato y _____.

G Review of prepositional phrases

PREPOSITIONAL PHRASES

Preposition				
a	a caballo	*on horseback*	a menudo	*often*
	a causa de	*due to*	a pesar de	*in spite of*
	a eso de	*at about* (time)	a pie	*on foot*
	a la (misma) vez	*at the same time*	a tiempo	*on time*
	a mano	*by hand*	a veces	*sometimes*
con	con respecto a	*regarding*	con tal (de) que	*provided*
de	de buena (mala) gana	*willingly (unwillingly)*	de pie	*standing*
			de repente	*suddenly*
	de esta manera	*this way*	de veras	*really*
	de modo que	*so*		
	de vez en cuando	*once in a while*		
en	en cuanto a	*in regard to*	en vez de	*instead*
	en seguida (enseguida)	*right away*		
para	¿para qué?	*what for?*	para siempre	*forever*
por	por eso	*that is why*	por otra parte	*on the other hand*
	por fin	*finally*		
	por lo general	*as a rule*	por poco	*almost*
	por lo menos	*at least*	por supuesto	*of course*

Ejercicio

Complete el párrafo con las frases preposicionales que están en inglés.

El Uruguay es un país que _____ (*as a rule*) ofrece seguridad y tiene

una política seria para desarrollar las inversiones extranjeras (*foreign investments*).

_____ (*This way*) atrae el capital que _____ (*of course*)

contribuye al crecimiento económico del país.

H Idiomatic expressions

además de	*besides*	estar de moda	*to be fashionable*
a escondidas	*secretly*	estar de paso	*to be passing by;*
a fin de cuentas	*all things*		*to be on the way*
	considered	hablar entre dientes	*to mumble*
a lo largo de	*along*	hacer caso de* (o a)	*to pay attention to*
a menos que	*unless*	llover a cántaros	*to rain cats and dogs*
a menudo	*often*	más vale	*it's better*
a pesar de	*in spite of*	ni siquiera	*not even*
a propósito	*by the way*	no faltaba más	*that's the last straw*
a veces	*sometimes*	no hay (o tiene)	*it's hopeless*
caer bien (mal)	*to like (dislike)*	remedio	
dar en el clavo	*to hit the nail*	pasarlo bien (mal)	*to have a good*
	on the head		*(bad) time*
de dientes afuera	*insincerely*	paso a paso	*step by step*
de vez en cuando	*once in a while*	poco a poco	*little by little*
día a día	*day by day*	por lo tanto	*therefore*
en cualquier caso	*in any case*	por poco	*almost*
en lugar de	*instead of*	ser plato de	*to play second fiddle*
en un abrir y	*in the blink*	segunda mesa	
cerrar de ojos	*of an eye*	sobre todo	*above all*
estar al tanto	*to be up-to-date*	tarde o temprano	*sooner or later*
estar a punto de	*to be about to*	tener buen diente	*to have a big appetite*
estar conforme	*to be in agreement*	tener en cuenta	*to take into account*
estar de luto	*to be in mourning*	tomarle el pelo	*to kid; to pull your*
			leg

Ejercicio

Complete el párrafo con la traducción al español de las frases que están en inglés.

Uruguay es la patria de Horacio Quiroga cuya vida _____ (*step by step*)

estuvo marcada por la tragedia. La selva, donde _____ (*often*) vivió,

dejó huellas profundas para siempre que _____ (*along*) su vida lo

atormentaron. El amor, la selva, el horror y la muerte son sus temas preferidos.

Escribió una colección de cuentos bajo el título de *Cuentos de amor, de locura y de*

muerte que _____ (*besides*) mantener al lector en suspenso, muestra una

gran imaginación.

Composición

Antes de escribir, repase las siguentes reglas de acentuación y la ortografía.

A   Review of accentuation

The accent mark is used:

1. With interrogative words.

   ¿quién?   ¿dónde?   ¿cuándo?

2. In adverbs derived from adjectives with a written accent.

   fácilmente   rápidamente

3. To distinguish the grammatical function of words.

   No se sabe **quién** es ella.
   Nobody knows who she is.
   Aquí está la persona de **quien** te hablé.
   Here is the person about whom I talked to you.
   Siempre me pregunta **cómo** me llamo.
   He always asks me what my name is.
   Ella es **como** su madre.
   She is like her mother.

B Review of spelling rules: differences between Spanish and English

As we have seen, a cognate is a word that has the same origin in English and in Spanish. Some times the spelling is identical, sometimes it is similar. Compare the following:

English		Spanish	
ph	photography	f	fotografía
ch	orchestra, technology	qu	orquesta, c tecnología
sc	school	esc	escuela
sp	spy	esp	espía
st	student	est	estudiante
mm	immigrant	nm	inmigrante
ss	professor	s	profesor
ff	difficult	f	difícil
ll	stellar	l	estelar
th	theme	t	tema

NOTE: The exercises that correspond to this section are included in the *Cuaderno de ejercicios*, Capítulo 10.

Ejercicio de composición (opcional)

Haga una composición, oral o escrita, sobre el tema que se da a continuación. Use el esquema siguiente.

TEMA: El mundo de la astrología.

INTRODUCCIÓN: La astrología se ocupa de predecir el porvenir (*future*). Muchas personas creen en la influencia que los astros (*stars*) tienen en su vida. Consultan con astrólogos y respetan su horóscopo.

DESARROLLO: Ud. en relación con su signo del zodíaco. ¿Lee Ud. la sección del horóscopo en el periódico y revistas? Relate alguna circunstancia de su vida en que ocurrió lo que predijo su horóscopo. ¿Cree Ud. que creer en la astrología es lo mismo que creer en el destino?

CONCLUSIÓN: ¿Qué aspectos positivos o negativos puede tener el creer que toda la vida de la gente está guiada por los astros?

Parte 2

Lectura

Octavio Paz

Octavio Paz, una de las figuras más destacadas° de la literatura hispanoamericana, nació en 1914 en la Ciudad de Mexico, y murió en esta misma ciudad en 1998. Allí hizo todos sus estudios, recibiendo el Doctorado en Leyes de la Universidad Nacional de México. En los círculos literarios de todo el mundo, Paz es respetado y admirado por sus ideas y por la gran destreza° literaria que se observa en sus obras.

Octavio Paz recibió el Premio Nobel de Literatura en 1990 y la Academia de Letras de Suecia,° al otorgarle el premio, citó "la integridad humanística de Paz y el ancho horizonte que exhibe su obra". Ya en 1981, Paz había recibido el importante Premio Cervantes.

Durante muchos años Octavio Paz estuvo en el servicio diplomático de su país. Fue Embajador de México en Suiza, Francia, el Japón y la India, y también formó parte de la delegación mexicana en las Naciones Unidas. Cuando en 1968 el gobierno mexicano hizo uso de una política represiva contra las demostraciones estudiantiles, Paz renunció° a su puesto° en el servicio diplomático. A partir de 1970, actuando como comentarista° político, Paz expresó su desaprobación° de la intervención soviética y cubana en Latinoamérica.

El amor, la soledad y la angustia son temas que abundan en la obra de Octavio Paz. A través de innumerables símbolos que usa Paz en sus obras, percibimos al ser humano preso° en su soledad. El gran

outstanding

mastery, skill

Sweden

resigned / position
commentator / disapproval

imprisoned

313

conocimiento que tiene de los problemas del hombre contemporáneo hace que su obra tenga un sentido de universalidad. Al mismo tiempo, nadie como Octavio Paz conoce la psicología del mexicano, tal y como lo demuestra en *El laberinto de la soledad: Vida y pensamiento de México* (1950).

Entre las muchas obras de Octavio Paz se deben mencionar además del citado *Laberinto*, *El arco y la lira* (1956), *Las peras del olmo°* (1957) y *Tiempo nublado* (1983). Junto a la producción ensayística de Paz está su valiosa obra poética. Es de gran importancia el libro *Libertad bajo palabra*, que contiene 207 poemas que fueron reunidos en 1958.

"El ramo azul" apareció en *Arenas movedizas*, que fue publicado en 1949. El suspenso en este cuento está muy bien logrado y el diálogo entre los dos personajes principales es muy efectivo para llegar a la conclusión final del cuento.

elm

VOCABULARIO ÚTIL I

Sustantivos

el **ala** (las **alas**)	parte del cuerpo de algunos animales que les sirve para volar	*wing*
la **blancura**	de color blanco	*whiteness*
la **estrella**	astro	*star*
la **hamaca**	objeto que se cuelga de los extremos y sirve para dormir o mecerse	*hammock*
la **jarra**	recipiente para agua	*jug, pitcher*
el **ladrillo**	material de barro que se usa para la construcción	*brick*
la **mariposa**	insecto de cuerpo pequeño con alas grandes de colores brillantes	*butterfly*
el **mesón**	posada, venta	*inn*
el **muro**	pared grande, tapia	*outside wall*
el **pliegue**	doblez	*fold, pleat*
el **sudor**	agua que sale por los poros	*sweat*
el **trapo**	pedazo de tela viejo	*rag*

Adjetivos

descalzo	sin zapatos	*barefoot*
empapado	mojado con mucha agua	*soaking wet*
entrecerrado	medio cerrado	*half-closed*
grisáceo	que predomina el color gris	*grayish*
minúsculo	muy pequeño	*minute, tiny*
ronco	que tiene voz gruesa y áspera	*hoarse*
tuerto	que ve con un solo ojo	*one-eyed*

Verbos

acercarse (qu)	aproximarse, ponerse cerca	*to get near, approach*
alzar (c)	levantar	*to raise, lift*
aspirar	atraer el aire a los pulmones	*to inhale*
atravesar (ie)	cruzar	*to cross*
calzarse (c)	ponerse los zapatos	*to put on shoes*
encender (ie)	prender la luz o un fuego	*to light*
frotar	restregar	*to rub*
humedecer (zc)	mojar para producir humedad	*to dampen*
parpadear	abrir y cerrar los ojos	*to blink*
pisar	poner el pie sobre alguna cosa	*to step on*
regar (ie)(gu)	irrigar, mojar el suelo	*to water, sprinkle*
regresar	volver	*to return*
saltar	brincar	*to jump, skip*
secarse (qu)	quitarse el agua o la humedad	*to dry up*
soplar	echar aire	*to blow*
vaciar	sacar el contenido	*to empty*

Expresiones

apretar el paso	caminar más rápido	*to walk faster*
a tientas	sin ver, a ciegas	*feeling one's way, blindly*
dar una vuelta	dar un paseo	*to take a walk*
de pronto	de repente, súbitamente	*suddenly*
detenerse en seco	pararse abruptamente	*to stop abruptly*

ESTUDIO PRELIMIMAR DE VOCABULARIO

A. Sinónimos ◈ Dé una palabra o expresión que quiera decir lo mismo.

1. volver   2. posada   3. pequeño   4. atravesar   5. descalzo

B. Antónimos ◈ Busque antónimos en la lista de vocabulario.

1. apagar   3. con zapatos   5. mojarse
2. caminar lentamente 4. medio abierto

C. Escoja la palabra que no pertenece al grupo.

1. pestaña	ojo	párpado	sudor
2. mariposa	capricho	alas	insecto
3. hamaca	cielo	estrella	luna
4. muro	ladrillo	pared	pliegue

El ramo azul

(I)

Desperté cubierto de sudor. Del piso de ladrillos rojos,
recién regado, subía un vapor caliente. Una mariposa
de alas grisáceas revoloteaba encandilada alrededor del
foco° amarillento. Salté de la hamaca y descalzo atravesé
el cuarto, cuidando no pisar algún alacrán salido de su
escondrijo° a tomar el fresco. Me acerqué al ventanillo y
aspiré el aire del campo. Se oía la respiración de la
noche, enorme, femenina. Regresé al centro de la
habitación, vacié el agua de la jarra en la palangana de
peltre° y humedecí la toalla. Me froté el torso y las
piernas con el trapo empapado, me sequé un poco y,
tras de cerciorarme° que ningún bicho° estaba escondido
entre los pliegues de mi ropa, me vestí y calcé. Bajé

revoloteaba...
*fluttered blindly
around the light*
alacrán... *scorpion out
of its hiding place*

palangana... *pewter
washbasin*

tras... *after making
sure / insect*

saltando la escalera pintada de verde. En la puerta del
15 mesón tropecé con el dueño, sujeto tuerto y reticente.
Sentado en una silla de tule,° fumaba con el ojo
entrecerrado. Con voz ronca me preguntó:

—¿Ónde va,° señor?

—A dar una vuelta. Hace mucho calor.

20 —Hum, todo está ya cerrado. Y no hay alumbrado°
aquí. Más le valiera° quedarse.

Alcé los hombros, musité° "ahora vuelvo" y me metí
en lo oscuro. Al principio no veía nada. Caminé a
tientas por la calle empedrada. Encendí un cigarrillo.
25 De pronto salió la luna de una nube negra, iluminando
un muro blanco, desmoronado a trechos.° Me detuve,
ciego ante tanta blancura. Sopló un poco de viento.
Respiré el aire de los tamarindos.° Vibraba la noche,
llena de hojas e insectos. Los grillos vivaqueaban° entre
30 las hierbas altas. Alcé la cara: arriba también habían
establecido campamento las estrellas. Pensé que el
universo era un vasto sistema de señales, una
conversación entre seres° inmensos. Mis actos, el
serrucho del grillo,° el parpadeo de la estrella, no eran
35 sino pausas y sílabas, frases dispersas de aquel diálogo.
¿Cuál sería esa palabra de la cual yo era una sílaba?
¿Quién dice esa palabra y a quién se la dice? Tiré el
cigarrillo sobre la banqueta.° Al caer, describió una
curva luminosa, arrojando breves chispas,° como un
40 cometa minúsculo.

Caminé largo rato despacio. Me sentía libre, seguro
entre los labios que en ese momento me pronunciaban
con tanta felicidad. La noche era un jardín de ojos. Al
cruzar una calle, sentí que alguien se desprendía° de
45 una puerta. Me volví, pero no acerté a distinguir nada.
Apreté el paso. Unos instantes después percibí el
apagado rumor de unos huaraches° sobre las piedras
calientes. No quise volverme,° aunque sentía que la
sombra se acercaba cada vez más. Intenté correr. No
50 pude. Me detuve en seco, bruscamente. Antes de que
pudiese defenderme, sentí la punta de un cuchillo en
mi espalda y una voz dulce:

—No se mueva, señor, o se lo entierro.°

*bulrush, a reed-like
    wetland plant*

¿Ónde va? ¿Adónde va?

light

más... *it would be better*

mumbled

desmoronado...
    crumbling here and there

árboles tropicales

Los grillos... *The crikets
    were camping*

beings

serrucho... *the sawing
    sound of the cricket*

(Mex.) sidewalk

sparks

se separaba, salía

tipo de zapato propio de
    México
turn around

o se... *or I'll bury it in you*

VOCABULARIO ÚTIL II

Sustantivos

el **cabello**	pelo	*hair*
el **capricho**	antojo, deseo vehemente	*whim, caprice*
el **fósforo**	cerillo o cerilla	*match*
la **llama**	fulgor que sale del fuego	*flame*
el **párpado**	piel que cubre el ojo	*eyelid*
la **pestaña**	pelo que está al borde del párpado	*eyelash*
el **ramito**	ramillete pequeño	*small bouquet*
el **resplandor**	brillo, reflejo	*glare*

Adjetivos

apenado	avergonzado	*embarrassed, sorry*
mañoso	habilidoso, astuto	*skillful, cunning*
remilgoso	exageradamente delicado y afectado	*finicky*

Verbos

alumbrar	poner luz, iluminar	*to provide light*
arrodillarse	ponerse de rodillas	*to kneel*
arrojar	tirar	*to throw*
engañar	decir mentiras	*to deceive*
entrecerrar (ie)	poner a medio cerrar	*to half-close*
permanecer (zc)	quedarse	*to remain*

Expresiones

a ver	vamos a ver	*let's see*
dar la vuelta	volverse, virarse	*to turn around*
de improviso	imprevistamente	*unexpectedly*
volver la cara	virar la cara	*to turn one's face*

(II)

Sin volver la cara, le pregunté:

55   —¿Qué quieres?

—Sus ojos, señor —contestó la voz suave, casi apenada.

—¿Mis ojos? ¿Para qué te servirán mis ojos? Mira, aquí tengo un poco de dinero. No es mucho, pero es

60   algo. Te daré todo lo que tengo, si me dejas. No vayas a matarme.

—No tenga miedo, señor. No lo mataré. Nada más° voy a sacarle los ojos.

Nada más *Solamente*

65   Volví a preguntar:

—Pero ¿para qué quieres mis ojos?

—Es un capricho de mi novia. Quiere un ramito de ojos azules. Y por aquí hay pocos que los tengan.

—Mis ojos no te sirven. No son azules, sino
70   amarillos.

—Ay, señor, no quiera engañarme. Bien sé que los tiene azules.

—No se le sacan a un cristiano los ojos así. Te daré otra cosa.

75   —No se haga el remilgoso°—me dijo con dureza—. Dé la vuelta.

Me volví. Era pequeño y frágil. El sombrero de palma le cubría medio rostro. Sostenía con el brazo derecho un machete de campo, que brillaba con la luz
80   de la luna.

—Alúmbrese la cara.

Encendí y me acerqué la llama al rostro. El resplandor me hizo entrecerrar los ojos. Él apartó mis párpados con mano firme. No podía ver bien. Se alzó°
85   sobre las puntas de los pies y me contempló intensamente. La llama me quemaba los dedos. La arrojé. Permaneció un instante silencioso.

—¿Ya te convenciste? No los tengo azules.

—Ah, qué mañoso° es usted —respondió—. A ver,
90   encienda otra vez.

Froté otro fósforo y lo acerqué a mis ojos. Tirándome de la manga,° me ordenó:

—Arrodíllese.

Me hinqué.° Con una mano me cogió por los
95   cabellos, echándome la cabeza hacia atrás. Se inclinó sobre mí, curioso y tenso, mientras el machete descendía lentamente hasta rozar° mis párpados. Cerré los ojos.

—Ábralos bien —ordenó.

100 Abrí los ojos. La llamita me quemaba las pestañas. Me soltó de improviso.

—Pues no son azules, señor. Dispense.°

Y desapareció. Me acodé° junto al muro, con la cabeza entre las manos. Luego me incorporé. A

No se... *Don't be so finicky*

Se alzó *Se levantó*

qué mañoso *how clever*

Tirándome... *Pulling my sleeve*

Me hinqué *I knelt down*

touch lightly

Excuse me.

Me acodé *I reclined*

105 tropezones,° cayendo y levantádome, corrí durante una   **A tropezones** *Stumbling*
hora por el pueblo desierto. Cuando llegué a la plaza, vi
al dueño del mesón, sentado aún frente a la puerta.
Entré sin decir palabra. Al día siguiente huí de aquel
pueblo.

COMPRENSIÓN DEL CUENTO

A. Preguntas ◆

1. ¿Ocurre este cuento en una ciudad grande o en un pueblo pequeño? ¿Cómo lo sabemos?
2. ¿Por qué salió el narrador del mesón?
3. ¿Qué le dice el dueño del mesón al narrador cuando ve que éste sale a dar una vuelta?
4. ¿Qué es lo que el narrador siente, oye y ve al salir en la oscuridad de la noche?
5. Al cruzar una calle, ¿qué ruido sintió el narrador?
6. ¿Qué quería el hombre que amenazaba al narrador con el cuchillo?
7. ¿Para qué quería el hombre los ojos del narrador?
8. ¿Qué circunstancia es la que hace que el hombre no le saque los ojos al narrador?

B. Repaso ◆ Explique la situación a que se refieren las siguientes oraciones que aparecen en el cuento.

1. Me froté el torso y las piernas con el trapo empapado.
2. Más le valiera quedarse.
3. Percibí el rumor de unos huaraches.
4. No se mueva, señor, o se lo entierro.
5. Mira, aquí tengo un poco de dinero.
6. Es un capricho de mi novia.
7. Ay, señor, no quiera engañarme.
8. A tropezones, cayendo y levantándome, corrí durante una hora.

C. Temas para presentación oral o escrita ◆

1. ¿Cómo crea el autor el aspecto de suspenso en este cuento?
2. ¿Cómo interpreta Ud. el capricho de la novia que quiere los ojos azules, especialmente cuando el hombre dice que "por aquí hay pocos que los tengan"?
3. Comente Ud. la manera en que se hablan los dos hombres: el narrador le habla de "tú" al hombre, y éste se dirige al narrador con "usted". ¿Qué nos dice esto de los dos hombres?

REPASO DE VOCABULARIO

A. Llene los espacios en blanco escogiendo las palabras que mejor completen el sentido del párrafo.

Al despertarse, el narrador estaba cubierto de _____1_____ y salió de la hamaca _____2_____ por temor a _____3_____ un alacrán. _____4_____ el cuerpo con una toalla mojada y salió del cuarto. El dueño del _____5_____ era tuerto y tenía la voz _____6_____. El narrador salió a dar una vuelta y caminó _____7_____ porque no había alumbrado en las calles. _____8_____ un cigarrillo y _____9_____ salió la luna. El hombre que se acercó al narrador quería sus ojos porque su novia tenía un _____10_____. Ella quería un _____11_____ de ojos azules. Al convencerse el hombre que los ojos del narrador no eran azules _____12_____ rápidamente.

1. *resplandor / sudor*
2. *saltando / secando*
3. *soplar / pisar*
4. *Se frotó / Se calzó*
5. *muro / mesón*
6. *ronca / grisácea*
7. *a tientas / a ver*
8. *Encendió / Parpadeó*
9. *de pronto / de rodillas*
10. *capricho / cabello*
11. *murito / ramito*
12. *engañó / desapareció*

B. Indique en el cuento las oraciones donde aparece la siguiente información.

1. Salió de un salto del lugar donde había dormido.
2. Las calles no tienen luz eléctrica.
3. Lo que piensa el narrador sobre el universo.
4. Lo que sintió el narrador al cruzar la calle.
5. El hombre le ordena al narrador que encienda un fósforo para verlo bien.

C. Complete las oraciones de acuerdo con las indicaciones en inglés que están a la derecha.

1. El narrador salió a _____ y caminó _____ por un rato.   *(take a walk)* *(feeling his way)*
2. Cuando sintió que alguien se acercaba _____, pero un hombre apareció _____ y lo amenazó con un cuchillo.   *(he walked faster)* *(unexpectedly)*
3. El hombre le ordenó al narrador que _____ y que _____ para verle los ojos.   *(turn around)* *(turn his face)*
4. _____ el hombre desapareció cuando vio que el narrador no tenía los ojos azules.   *(Suddenly)*

5. Al despertarse el narrador estaba _____ y   *(covered with sweat)*

   saltó de _____ .   *(the hammock)*

6. Como _____ caminó con mucho cuidado   *(he was barefoot)*

   por miedo a _____ un alacrán.   *(to step on)*

7. _____ por poco le quema _____   *(The flame) (the eyelashes)*

   y _____ .   *(the eyelids)*

8. El hombre le ordenó al narrador que _____ .   *(kneel down)*

9. Con la luz de _____ el hombre pudo ver   *(a match)*

   el color de los ojos del narrador.

10. La novia del hombre tenía _____ y quería un   *(a whim)*

    _____ de ojos azules.   *(small bouquet)*

REPASO DE GRAMÁTICA

Llene los blancos con la forma correcta de la palabra que aparece a la derecha.

Al _____1_____ vi que una mariposa volaba cerca del foco y que

_____2_____ a quemarse _____3_____ ala. Yo

_____4_____ lentamente a _____5_____ luz,

_____6_____ no pisar un insecto en el suelo. _____7_____

movimientos asustaron a la mariposa y se alejó volando

como _____8_____ cometa.

1. *despertarse*
2. *ir*
3. *uno*
4. *acercarse*
5. *el*
6. *cuidar*
7. *Mi*
8. *uno*

Jorge Luis Borges

Jorge Luis Borges nació en Buenos Aires en 1899 y murió en Ginebra, Suiza, en 1986.

Borges es uno de los escritores hispanos más notables del siglo XX y uno de los que más influyó en la renovación literaria de Hispanoamérica. Vivió siempre en un mundo intelectual rodeado de libros e ideas que contribuyeron a la profundidad° de sus conocimientos° y de su cultura.

Cuando tenía catorce años su familia se trasladó° a Europa donde él continuó sus estudios en Suiza, Inglaterra y España. Dominaba a la perfección el español, el inglés y el francés, además del alemán y el latín. Desde muy niño mostró gran inclinación a la lectura. Leía incansablemente obras de la literatura inglesa, francesa y española, así como de historia y de filosofía. Debido a una enfermedad congénita,° Borges empezó a perder la vista° siendo muy joven. Gracias a su increíble memoria y a los secretarios que siempre le leían, continuó su labor de escritor aunque quedó completamente ciego.°

Borges ocupó los puestos de profesor de literatura inglesa en la Universidad de Buenos Aires y de director de la Biblioteca Nacional de Argentina, además de ser presidente de la Academia Argentina de Letras. Durante su larga vida recibió numerosos premios y honores.

Los cuentos de Borges ocupan un lugar prominente en la literatura

depth

knowledge

moved

congenital

sight

blind

universal. En ellos Borges desplaza° los elementos tradicionales del   *displaces*
espacio, el tiempo y la identidad. Sus cuentos trascienden° el mundo   *trascend*
de la realidad para proyectarse en esferas metafísicas que van más allá
del tiempo y el espacio. Borges poseía una rica imaginación, una
fabulosa habilidad lingüística y una gran erudición.

Los temas que más aparecen en los cuentos de Borges son: el
infinito, el universo como laberinto,° la contradicción entre la   *labyrinth*
apariencia° y la realidad, y el tiempo en forma circular. Para él, el   *appearance*
universo es un laberinto caótico que sólo se puede ordenar a través
de la inteligencia.

Entre las muchas obras de Borges se pueden citar las siguientes:
Fervor de Buenos Aires (1923), *Inquisiciones* (1925), *Ficciones* (1944), *El
Aleph* (1949), *Otras inquisiciones* (1952), *Obra poética* (1969), *La cifra*
(1981) y *Nueve ensayos dantescos* (1982).

El cuento "Pedro Salvadores" pertenece a la colección *Elogio de la
sombra* (1969). La narración ocurre en la Argentina durante la
dictadura de Juan Manuel Ortiz de Rosas,* que terminó en 1852. En
esta historia Borges presenta una narración en forma objetiva sin
añadir° nada de comentario personal. Al hablar de este cuento,   *adding*
Borges señaló lo siguiente:° "el texto no es una invención mía, es un   *observed the following*
hecho histórico, que he tratado de imaginar con cierta precisión. Un
bisnieto° del protagonista me visitó en la Biblioteca Nacional".   *great-grandchild*

VOCABULARIO ÚTIL

Sustantivos

el **amante**	persona con quien se tienen relaciones de amor	*lover*
el **casco**	uña de la pata de los caballos	*hoof*
la **cera**	substancia con que está hecho el panal de las abejas	*wax*
el **ejército**	fuerzas militares de una nación	*army*
el **griterío**	confusión de gritos; algazara	*shouting, uproar*
la **hondura**	profundidad	*depth*
la **madriguera**	cueva o guarida donde habitan ciertos animales	*burrow, hole*
el **paso**	pisada	*step*
el **personaje**	persona que se representa en una obra literaria	*character (in a literary work)*
la **servidumbre**	los sirvientes o los criados	*servants, maids*
el **sótano**	parte subterránea de un edificio	*basement*
la **vajilla**	platos, fuentes, tazas que se usan para poner la mesa	*chinaware*
el **zaguán**	vestíbulo de una casa	*lobby, entrance hall of a house*

*Juan Manuel Ortiz de Rosas (1793–1877), general y político argentino que gobernó dictatorialmente desde 1829 hasta 1852. Su modo tiránico de gobernar fue severamente combatido por los unitarios, partido político al cual pertenecían los principales hombres de letras y patriotas argentinos.

Adjetivos

acosado	perseguido, atormentado	*harassed*
amenazado	intimidado	*threatened*
atroz	horrible, espantoso	*atrocious*
cobarde	que no tiene valor o coraje	*cowardly*
fofo	blando	*flabby*
incierto	no cierto, falso	*untrue, doubtful*

Verbos

alzar (c)	levantar	*to lift*
azotar	dar latigazos o golpes	*to whip, beat*
coser	unir con hilo y aguja	*to sew*
delatar	denunciar	*to denounce*
derribar	echar abajo	*to knock down*
encarcelar	poner en la cárcel	*to imprison, incarcerate*
huir (y)	escapar, fugarse	*to flee, run away*
ocultar	esconder	*to hide*
registrar	buscar o examinar con cuidado	*to search, inspect*

Expresiones

acaso	tal vez, quizá	*perhaps, maybe*
al cabo de	al final de	*at the end of*
ni siquiera	ni aun	*not even*
pasar de largo	seguir y no detenerse	*to go on without making a stop*
por más que (+ verbo)	por mucho que	*no matter how much (+ verb)*

ESTUDIO PRELIMINAR DE VOCABULARIO

A. Sinónimos ◆ Dé una palabra o expresión que quiera decir lo mismo.

1. levantar   2. tal vez   3. esconder   4. espantoso   5. escapar

B. Antónimos ◆ Busque antónimos en la lista de vocabulario.

1. valiente   2. construir   3. al principio   4. liberar   5. seguro

C. Escoja la palabra que no pertenece al grupo.

1. ejército	general	soldado	servidumbre
2. zaguán	vajilla	sótano	patio
3. amante	fofo	novio	enamorado
4. amenaza	golpe	casco	azote

Pedro Salvadores

A Juan Murchison

Quiero dejar escrito, acaso por primera vez, uno de los
hechos más raros y más tristes de nuestra historia.
Intervenir lo menos posible en su narración, prescindir
de° adiciones pintorescas y de conjeturas aventuradas   **prescindir...** *leaving out*
5 es, me parece, la mejor manera de hacerlo.
    Un hombre, una mujer y la vasta sombra de un
dictador son los tres personajes. El hombre se llamó
Pedro Salvadores; mi abuelo Acevedo lo vio, días o
semanas después de la batalla de Caseros. Pedro
10 Salvadores, tal vez, no difería del común de la gente,
pero su destino y los años lo hicieron único. Sería un
señor como tantos otros de su época. Poseería (nos cabe
suponer°) un establecimiento de campo y era unitario.°   **nos...** *we suppose / name*
El apellido de su mujer era Planes; los dos vivían en la   *of political party*
15 calle Suipacha, no lejos de la esquina del Temple. La
casa en que los hechos ocurrieron sería igual a la otras:
la puerta de calle, el zaguán, la puerta cancel,° las   **puerta...** *inner door*

habitaciones, la hondura de los patios. Una noche, hacia
1842, oyeron el creciente y sordo rumor de los cascos
20   de los caballos en la calle de tierra y los vivas y mueras°
de los jinetes.° La mazorca,° esta vez, no pasó de largo.
Al griterío sucedieron los repetidos golpes; mientras los
hombres derribaban la puerta, Salvadores pudo correr
la mesa del comedor, alzar la alfombra y ocultarse en el
25   sótano. La mujer puso la mesa en su lugar. La mazorca
irrumpió,° venían a llevárselo a Salvadores. La mujer
declaró que éste había huido a Montevideo. No le
creyeron; la azotaron, rompieron toda la vajilla celeste,°
registraron la casa, pero no se les ocurrió levantar la
30   alfombra. A la medianoche se fueron, no sin haber
jurado volver.°
Aquí principia verdaderamente la historia de Pedro
Salvadores. Vivió nueve años en el sótano. Por más que
nos digamos que los años están hechos de días y los
35   días de horas y que nueve años es un término
abstracto y una suma imposible, esa historia es atroz.
Sospecho que en la sombra que sus ojos aprendieron a
descifrar, no pensaba en nada, ni siquiera en su odio ni
en su peligro. Estaba ahí, en el sótano. Algunos ecos de
40   aquel mundo que le estaba vedado° le llegarían desde
arriba: los pasos habituales de su mujer, el golpe del
brocal y del balde,° la pesada lluvia en el patio. Cada
día, por lo demás, podía ser el último.
La mujer fue despidiendo° a la servidumbre,° que
45   era capaz de delatarlos. Dijo a todos los suyos que
Salvadores estaba en la Banda Oriental. Ganó el pan de
los dos cosiendo para el ejército. En el decurso° de los
años tuvo dos hijos; la familia la repudió,°
atribuyéndolos a un amante. Después de la caída del
50   tirano, le pedirían perdón de rodillas.
¿Qué fue, quién fue, Pedro Salvadores? ¿Lo
encarcelaron el terror, el amor, la invisible presencia de
Buenos Aires y, finalmente, la costumbre? Para que no
la dejara sola, su mujer le daría inciertas noticias de
55   conspiraciones y de victorias. Acaso era cobarde y la
mujer lealmente le ocultó que ella lo sabía. Lo imagino
en su sótano, tal vez sin un candil,° sin un libro. La

vivas... *shouts of "long live" and "down with"* / *horsemen* / *secret police*

irrumpió *burst in*

azul

no... *not without swearing*

prohibido

brocal... *the bucket on the stones of the well*

dismissing / *sirvientes*

decurso... *course of time*
repudiated

oil lamp

sombra lo hundiría en el sueño. Soñaría, al principio,
con la noche tremenda en que el acero buscaba la
60 garganta, con las calles abiertas, con la llanura. Al cabo
de los años no podría huir y soñaría con el sótano.
Sería, al principio, un acosado, un amenazado; después
no lo sabremos nunca, un animal tranquilo en su
madriguera o una suerte de oscura divinidad.

65   Todo esto hasta aquel día del verano de 1852 en que
Rosas huyó. Fue entonces cuando el hombre secreto
salió a la luz del día; mi abuelo habló con él. Fofo y
obeso, estaba del color de la cera y no hablaba en voz
alta. Nunca le devolvieron los campos que le habían
70 sido confiscados; creo que murió en la miseria.
    Como todas las cosas, el destino de Pedro
Salvadores nos parece un símbolo de algo que estamos
a punto de comprender.

COMPRENSIÓN DEL CUENTO

A. Preguntas ◆

1. ¿Es pura ficción el cuento de Pedro Salvadores? ¿Por qué?
2. ¿Por qué vino la mazorca a casa de Salvadores?
3. ¿Qué hizo Salvadores cuando sintió que estaban derribando la puerta?
4. ¿Cómo reaccionó la mazorca cuando la mujer declaró que su esposo se había huido a Montevideo?
5. ¿Dónde estaba realmente Salvadores?
6. ¿Cómo fue la vida de Salvadores durante nueve años?
7. ¿Y cómo fue la vida de la mujer durante ese tiempo?
8. ¿Por qué la repudió la familia?
9. ¿Qué fin tuvo la vida de Pedro Salvadores?
10. Según el narrador, ¿por qué nos parece Salvadores un símbolo?

B. Repaso ◆ Explique la situación a que se refieren las siguientes oraciones que aparecen en el cuento.

1. La mazorca esta vez no pasó de largo.
2. No le creyeron, la azotaron, rompieron toda la vajilla celeste.
3. Cada día, por lo demás, podía ser el último.
4. Ganó el pan de los dos cosiendo para el ejército.
5. Después le pedirían perdón de rodillas.
6. Fofo y obeso, estaba del color de la cera.

C. Comprensión de la lectura ◆ Escoja las explicaciones que sean correctas.

1. ¿Qué hizo la mujer de Pedro Salvadores?
   a. Se unió al partido de los unitarios.
   b. Demostró inteligencia y valor.
   c. Aceptó la ayuda de la familia.
   d. Se fue a vivir a Montevideo.
2. La mujer se quedó sola en la casa, sin los sirvientes, porque…
   a. éstos no querían trabajar para ella.
   b. éstos sabían que el esposo estaba escondido.
   c. ella temía que fueran a descubrir su secreto.
   d. ella se dio cuenta de que eran enemigos.
3. La mujer pudo mantenerse durante esos años porque…
   a. sabía coser.
   b. cocinaba para el ejército.
   c. tenía dinero guardado.
   d. pudo vender su vajilla.
4. ¿Cómo se sentía Salvadores al salir del sótano?
   a. Dispuesto a vengarse de sus enemigos.
   b. Decidido a irse de la Argentina.
   c. Dispuesto a trabajar y a ganar dinero.
   d. Destruido física y espiritualmente.
5. El autor nos dice que Pedro Salvadores…
   a. trató de escaparse de la madriguera.
   b. se quedó ciego de tanto leer.
   c. posiblemente se acostumbró a vivir en su escondite.
   d. acaso por primera vez, ayudó a su esposa a coser.

D. Temas para presentación oral o escrita ◆

1. ¿Qué habría hecho Ud. si hubiera estado nueve años encerrado en un sótano?
2. ¿Qué habría hecho Ud. si hubiera estado en el lugar de la esposa de Salvadores?
3. ¿Cree Ud. que Pedro Salvadores es símbolo del terror que produce una dictadura o símbolo del hombre cobarde que no se enfrenta a luchar por su libertad? Explique el por qué de su respuesta.
4. ¿Conoce Ud. casos semejantes al de Pedro Salvadores? Compártalos con la clase. Piense en el caso de Anne Frank.

REPASO DE VOCABULARIO

A. Llene los espacios en blanco escogiendo las palabras que mejor completen el sentido del párrafo.

El sordo rumor de los _____1_____ de los caballos
anunció la llegada de la policía que con gran _____2_____

1. *cascos / jinetes*
2. *griterío / ejército*

comenzó a _____3_____ la puerta. Salvadores se pudo

_____4_____ en el sótano y la mujer le dijo a la policía

que su esposo había _____5_____ y estaba en

Montevideo. Después la mujer, poco a poco, fue

_____6_____ a la _____7_____ para que no fueran a

descubrir que su esposo estaba en el _____8_____ . No es

posible saber si Salvadores era _____9_____ o si se

acostumbró a vivir como un animal en su _____10_____ .

Cuando cayó el dictador Rosas, Pedro Salvadores salió a la luz

del día y estaba _____11_____ y tenía el color de la

_____12_____ .

3. *alzar / derribar*

4. *registrar / ocultar*

5. *huido / delatado*

6. *encarcelando /*
   despidiendo

7. *servidumbre / vajilla*

8. *zaguán / sótano*

9. *incierto / cobarde*

10. *hondura / madriguera*

11. *delgado / obeso*

12. *llanura / cera*

B. Complete las oraciones de acuerdo con las indicaciones en inglés que están a la derecha.

1. La policía esta vez _____ y, después de
   _____ a la mujer, rompió toda la vajilla azul.

   (didn't go by without stopping)
   (beating)

2. _____ tratemos, no podremos comprender
   cómo Salvadores pudo vivir nueve años encerrado en el
   sótano.

   (No matter how much)

3. Posiblemente Salvadores no pensaba en nada,
   _____ en su odio ni en el peligro que corría.

   (not even)

4. Cuando Salvadores salió del sótano _____
   mucho tiempo estaba fofo y obeso.

   (at the end of)

5. Esta historia es tan _____ que parece
   _____ .

   (atrocious)
   (doubtful)

REPASO DE GRAMÁTICA

Repase el uso del condicional en el Capítulo 3. Note el uso frecuente del condicional para indicar probabilidad o conjetura en el cuento "Pedro Salvadores". Después, traduzca las siguientes oraciones usando el condicional.

1. *Salvadores <u>was probably</u> like other men of his time. He <u>supposedly owned</u> a home in the country. The house in which the events occurred <u>was probably</u> the same as the others.*

2. *<u>Could his wife have given</u> him uncertain news about conspiracies? <u>Could she have thought</u> he was a coward?*

3. *At the end of many years <u>he would not be able</u> to escape and <u>he would dream</u> about the basement. <u>He would be</u>, at first, a harassed man. <u>He would die</u> in misery.*

Guillermo Cabrera Infante

Guillermo Cabrera Infante nació en 1929 en la provincia de Oriente, Cuba. La obra de este novelista cubano está impregnada de un divertido sentido de humor y, al mismo tiempo, de una gran melancolía. Esta paradoja hace que Cabrera Infante ocupe un lugar especial entre los escritores hispanoamericanos de su generación.

Cabrera Infante comenzó a escribir en 1947, cuando abandonó los estudios de una soñada carrera médica, ganando varios premios con sus cuentos. Su interés en el cine lo llevó a escribir crítica cinematográfica y a fundar la Cinemateca° de Cuba, la cual presidió de 1951 a 1956. En 1959 Cabrera Infante fundó la revista literaria *Lunes de Revolución*, la cual dirigió hasta 1961 cuando ésta fue clausurada por el gobierno. En 1962 salió de Cuba con el cargo de Agregado Cultural en Bruselas, y su posición de disidente frente al gobierno de Fidel Castro hizo que se quedara en Europa. Vivió primero en Madrid, y más tarde se estableció en Londres, donde vive desde 1966.

°film library

Entre sus muchos libros se pueden citar *Así en la paz como en la guerra, Tres tristes tigres,* que obtuvo el premio Biblioteca Breve en 1964, *Mea Cuba,* publicado en 1992, y en 1995 apareció una colección de tres cuentos bajo el título *Delito por bailar el chachachá.* En 1997 Cabrera Infante recibió el prestigioso Premio Cervantes.

"Abril es el mes más cruel" forma perte de su colección de cuentos *Así en la paz como en la guerra.* En esta narración el escritor presenta un momento de la vida de una pareja enamorada. Según progresa el diálogo nos damos cuenta de que la esposa ha estado enferma y que detrás de la aparente normalidad de la vida de estas dos personas, algo inesperado va a ocurrir.

VOCABULARIO ÚTIL

Sustantivos

la **ampolla**	bolsita que se forma en la piel	*blister*
el **bostezo**	acto de bostezar	*yawn*
la **botica**	farmacia	*drugstore*
el **crepúsculo**	cuando termina la luz del día	*dusk, twilight*
el **delantal**	prenda de vestir que se usa para que no se manche la ropa	*apron*
el **dormilón**	persona a quien le gusta dormir	*sleepyhead*
el **encargado**	persona que tiene a su cargo algunas cosas o tareas	*caretaker*
la **espuma**	burbujas que se forman en un líquido	*foam*
el **hoyo**	cavidad en la tierra; hueco	*hole*
la **loza**	platos y tazas	*dishes*
la **manteca**	grasa que se usa para cocinar	*lard*
la **nuca**	parte posterior del cuello	*nape of neck*
las **olas**	ondas en la superficie de las aguas	*waves*
el **olor**	aroma, fragancia	*smell, odor*

Adjetivos

bobo	tonto	*dumb, silly*
despierto	lo opuesto de dormido	*awake*
grueso	voluminoso; opuesto de delgado o fino	*full, thick*
hirviente	que hierve; muy caliente	*boiling*
hondo	profundo	*deep, profound*
relajado	que no está tenso	*relaxed*

Verbos

aspirar	atraer el aire a los pulmones	*to inhale*
besar	tocar con los labios en señal de amor, amistad o reverencia	*to kiss*
bostezar (c)	abrir la boca en señal de sueño, aburrimiento o debilidad	*to yawm*
bromear	hacer bromas, chistes como diversión o burla	*to joke*
dormitar	estar medio dormido	*to doze*
entrecerrar (ie)	poner medio cerrado	*to half-close*
estirarse	extenderse, desperezarse	*to stretch out*
fregar (ie)(gu)	lavar para limpiar (la loza)	*to wash (dishes)*
molestarse	incomodarse, ofenderse	*to get annoyed*
quemarse	calentarse mucho la piel con el sol	*to get sunburned*
retratar	sacar fotografías de	*to photograph*
secar (qu)	sacar la humedad de un cuerpo o cosa	*to dry*

Expresiones

darse cuenta de	tener conocimiento de algo	*to realize*
dentro de una hora	en una hora	*in an hour*
de perfil	postura del cuerpo de lado	*in profile*
de veras	de verdad	*truly, really*
echó a andar	empezó a caminar	*started to walk*
luna de miel	los primeros días que siguen al matrimonio	*honeymoon*
puesta de sol	momento en que el sol desaparece en el horizonte	*sunset*

ESTUDIO PRELIMINAR DE VOCABULARIO

A. Sinónimos ◆ Dé una palabra o expresión que quiera decir lo mismo.

1. onda   2. profundo   3. incomodarse   4. grasa   5. extenderse

B. Antónimos ◆ Busque antónimos en la lista de vocabulario.

1. dormido   2. delgado   3. frío   4. inteligente   5. tenso

C. Escoja la palabra que no pertenece al grupo.

1. nuca   cabeza   crepúsculo   cuello
2. relajar   dormitar   bostezar   fregar
3. espuma   delantal   agua   ola
4. despierto caliente   quemado   hirviente

Abril es el mes más cruel

No supo si lo despertó la claridad que entraba por la
ventana o el calor, o ambas cosas. O todavía el ruido
que hacía ella en la cocina preparando el desayuno. La
oyó freír huevos primero y luego le llegó el olor de la
5   manteca hirviente. Se estiró en la cama y sintió la tibieza
de las sábanas escurrirse° bajo su cuerpo y un amable   *to slide*
dolor le corrió de la espalda a la nuca. En ese momento
ella entró en el cuarto y le chocó° verla con el delantal   **le chocó** *it shocked him*
por encima de los shorts.° La lámpara que estaba en la   (anglicismo) *shorts*
10   mesita de noche ya no estaba allí y puso los platos y las
tazas en ella. Entonces advirtió que estaba despierto.

—¿Qué dice el dormilón? —preguntó ella,
bromeando.

En un bostezo él dijo: Buenos días.

15   —¿Cómo te sientes?

Iba a decir muy bien, luego pensó que no era exactamente muy bien y reconsideró y dijo:

—Admirablemente.

No mentía. Nunca se había sentido mejor. Pero se
20   dio cuenta que las palabras siempre traicionan.°   *betray*

—¡Vaya!° —dijo ella.   *Well! Indeed!*

Desayunaron. Cuando ella terminó de fregar la loza, vino al cuarto y le propuso que se fueran a bañar.

—Hace un día precioso —dijo.

25   —Lo he visto por la ventana —dijo él.

—¿Visto?

—Bueno, sentido. Oído.

Se levantó y se lavó y se puso su trusa.° Encima se   *bathing suit*
echó la bata de felpa° y salieron para la playa.   **bata de felpa** *plush*
                                                      bathrobe
30   —Espera —dijo él a medio camino—. Me olvidé de la llave.

Ella sacó del bolsillo la llave y se la mostró. Él sonrió.

—¿Nunca se te olvida nada?

—Sí —dijo ella y lo besó en la boca—. Hoy se me
35   había olvidado besarte. Es decir, despierto.

Sintió el aire del mar en las piernas y en la cara y aspiró hondo.

—Esto es vida —dijo.

Ella se había quitado las sandalias y enterraba° los   *buried*
40   dedos en la arena al caminar. Lo miró y sonrió.

—¿Tu crees? —dijo.

—¿Tú no crees? —preguntó él a su vez.

—Oh, sí. Sin duda. Nunca me he sentido mejor.

—Ni yo. Nunca en la vida —dijo él.

45 Se bañaron. Ella nadaba muy bien, con unas brazadas° largas de profesional. Al rato él regresó a la playa y se tumbó° en la arena. Sintió que el sol secaba el agua y los cristales de sal se clavaban en los poros° y pudo precisar dónde se estaba quemando más, dónde

50 se formaría una ampolla. Le gustaba quemarse al sol. Estarse quieto, pegar la cara a la arena y sentir el aire que formaba y destruía las nimias dunas° y le metía los finos granitos en la nariz, en los ojos, en la boca, en los oídos. Parecía un remoto desierto, inmenso y

55 misterioso y hostil. Dormitó.

Cuando despertó, ella se peinaba a su lado.

—¿Volvemos? —preguntó.

—Cuando quieras.

Ella preparó el almuerzo y comieron sin hablar. Se

60 había quemado, leve, en un brazo y él caminó hacia la botica que estaba a tres cuadras y trajo picrato.° Ahora estaban en el portal y hasta ellos llegó el fresco y a veces rudo aire del mar que se levanta por la tarde en abril.

La miró. Vio sus tobillos delicados y bien dibujados,°

65 sus rodillas tersas y sus muslos torneados sin violencia.° Estaba tirada° en la silla de extensión,° relajada, y en sus labios, gruesos, había una tentativa de sonrisa.

—¿Cómo te sientes? —le preguntó.

Ella abrió los ojos y los entrecerró ante la claridad.

70 Sus pestañas eran largas y curvas.

—Muy bien. ¿Y tú?

—Muy bien también. Pero dime… ¿ya se ha ido todo?°

—Sí —dijo ella.

75 Y… ¿no hay molestia?°

—En absoluto. Te juro que nunca me he sentido mejor.

—Me alegro.

—¿Por qué?

80 —Porque me fastidiaría° sentirme tan bien y que tú no te sintieras bien.

—Pero me siento bien.

---

strokes

se tumbó *lay down*

se clavaban… *got into his pores*

nimias dunas *small dunes*

ointment for sunburn

well shaped

muslos… *well proportioned /* **silla**… *deck chair* / **tirada** *stretched out /*

ya se… *are you feeling better?*

discomfort

me… *it would annoy me*

—Me alegro.

—De veras. Créeme, por favor.

85 —Te creo.

Se quedaron en silencio y luego ella habló:

—¿Damos un paseo por el acantilado?° ¿Quieres?   *rocky path*

—Cómo no. ¿Cuándo?

—Cuando tú digas.

90 —No, di tú.

—Bueno, dentro de una hora.

En una hora habían llegado a los farallones° y ella le   *cliffs*
preguntó, mirando a la playa, hacia el dibujo de
espuma de las olas, hasta las cabañas:

95 —¿Qué altura crees tú que habrá de aquí a abajo?

—Unos cincuenta metros. Tal vez setenta y cinco.

—¿Cien no?

—No creo.

Ella se sentó en una roca, de perfil al mar con
100 sus piernas recortadas° contra el azul del mar y del   *outlined*
cielo.

—¿Ya tú me retrataste así? —preguntó ella.

—Sí.

—Prométeme que no retratarás a otra mujer así.

105 Él se molestó.

—¡Las cosas que se te ocurren! Estamos en luna de
miel, ¿no? Cómo voy a pensar yo en otra mujer ahora.

—No digo ahora. Más tarde. Cuando te hayas
cansado de mí, cuando nos hayamos divorciado.

110 Él la levantó y la besó en los labios, con fuerza.

—Eres boba.

Ella se abrazó a su pecho.

—¿No nos divorciaremos nunca?

—Nunca.

115 —¿Me querrás siempre?

—Siempre.

Se besaron. Casi en seguida oyeron que alguien
llamaba.

—Es a ti.

120 —No sé quién pueda ser.

Vieron venir a un viejo por detrás de las cañas del
espartillo.°   **cañas**… *stalks of sparto grass*

—Ah. Es el encargado.

125   Los saludó.

—¿Ustedes se van mañana?

—Sí, por la mañana temprano.

—Bueno, entonces quiero que me liquide° ahora.   **me liquide** *pay me,*
¿Puede ser?   *settle your account*

130   Él la miró a ella.

—Ve tú con él. Yo quiero quedarme aquí otro rato
más.

—¿Por qué no vienes tú también?

—No —dijo ella—. Quiero ver la puesta de sol.

135   —No quiero interrumpir. Pero es que quiero ver si
voy a casa de mi hija a ver el programa de boseo* en la
televisión. Uste* sabe, ella vive en la carretera.

—Ve con él —dijo ella.

—Está bien —dijo él y echó a andar detrás del viejo.

140   —¿Tú sabes dónde está el dinero?

—Sí —respondió él, volviéndose.°   *turning his head*

—Ven a buscarme luego, ¿quieres?

—Está bien. Pero en cuanto oscurezca bajamos.
Recuerda.

145   —Está bien —dijo—. Dame un beso antes de irte.
Lo hizo. Ella lo besó fuerte, con dolor.

Él la sintió tensa, afilada por dentro.° Antes de   **afilada...** *edgy inside*
perderse tras la marea del espartillo° la saludó con la   **marea...** *waving*
mano. En el aire le llegó su voz que decía te quiero.   *sparto grass*

150   O tal vez preguntaba ¿me quieres?

Estuvo mirando el sol cómo bajaba. Era un
círculo lleno de fuego al que el horizonte convertía
en tres cuartos de círculo, en medio círculo, en
nada, aunque quedara un borboteo° rojo por donde   *gush*

155   desapareció.

Luego el cielo se fue haciendo violeta, morado, y el
negro de la noche comenzó a borrar los restos del
crepúsculo.

—¿Habrá luna esta noche? —se preguntó en alta

160   voz ella.

Miró abajo y vio un hoyo negro y luego más abajo la

---

*El autor, al imitar la forma de hablar del encargado, escribe boseo y Usté en lugar de boxeo y Usted.

costra° de la espuma blanca, visible todavía. Se movió   *crust*
en su asiento y dejó los pies hacia afuera, colgando en el
165   vacío. Luego afincó° las manos en la roca y suspendió el   *took hold*
cuerpo, y sin el menor ruido se dejó caer al pozo°   *hole*
negro y profundo que era la playa exactamente ochenta
y dos metros más abajo.

COMPRENSIÓN DEL CUENTO

A. Preguntas ◆

1. Describa las acciones de los dos protagonistas al empezar el cuento.
2. ¿Qué hace la pareja después del desayuno?
3. ¿Qué pregunta es la que se repite entre ellos dos con gran insistencia?
4. ¿Qué quiere el viejo encargado cuando viene a llamarlos?
5. ¿Qué significado tiene la pregunta que hace la esposa en relación con la altura del acantilado?
6. ¿Por qué cree Ud. que la esposa se quedó en el acantilado y no fue con el esposo para pagarle al encargado?
7. ¿Qué desenlace trágico tiene el cuento?
8. ¿Cómo se imagina Ud. que es la esposa? ¿Qué adjetivos usaría para describirla?
9. ¿Cree Ud. que el esposo sospechaba lo que iba a hacer su esposa? Explique su respuesta.
10. ¿Qué función importante tiene el encargado en este cuento?

B. Repaso ◆ Explique la situación a que se refieren las siguientes oraciones que aparecen en este cuento.

1. Cómo voy yo a pensar en otra mujer ahora.
2. Unos cincuenta metros. Tal vez setenta y cinco.
3. Muy bien también. Pero dime… ¿ya se ha ido todo?
4. Ve tú con él. Yo quiero quedarme aquí otro rato más.
5. ¿Habrá luna esta noche?

C. Temas para presentación oral o escrita ◆

1. Dé su interpretación del significado del título. ¿Por qué es cruel el mes de abril?
2. Escriba otro final para este cuento basándose en el hecho de que el esposo no se va con el encargado.
3. Analice la comunicación y la relación que hay entre la esposa y el esposo.
4. Analice los hechos que ocurren el día de la tragedia y lo que el lector descubre al final.

REPASO DE VOCABULARIO

A. Llene los espacios en blanco escogiendo las palabras que mejor completen el sentido de las oraciones.

1. Al despertarse le llegó el _____1_____ de lo que la esposa estaba _____2_____ . Cuando ella entró en el cuarto, a él le chocó verla con el _____3_____ por encima de los shorts.

   1. *olor / bostezo*
   2. *cocinando / retratando*
   3. *crepúsculo / delantal*

2. Después de desayunar decidieron ir a _____4_____ un rato y él se puso la _____5_____ .

   4. *dormitar / nadar*
   5. *trusa / loza*

3. El esposo se _____6_____ por la esposa y cuando ella se _____7_____ un poco en el sol, él temía que se le hicieran _____8_____ y fue a la botica para comprarle una pomada (*ointment*).

   6. *estiraba / preocupaba*
   7. *quemó / secó*
   8. *olas / ampollas*

4. El esposo retrató a la esposa _____9_____ y ella le pidió que nunca más le sacara fotografías a otra mujer en ese lugar. Él se _____10_____ con esa petición de su esposa, especialmente estando cómo estaba, en _____11_____ .

   9. *de perfil / de veras*
   10. *molestó / movió*
   11. *luna de miel / puesta de sol*

B. Indique en el cuento las oraciones donde aparece lo siguiente.

1. El esposo se preparó para ir a bañarse en el mar.
2. La esposa es una nadadora excelente.
3. Deseo que me pague lo que me debe.
4. Cuando ella lo besó fuertemente, él notó que ella estaba por dentro muy angustiada.
5. La descripción del atardecer.

C. Complete las oraciones de acuerdo con las indicaciones en inglés que están a la derecha.

1. Cuando le llegó el _____ de los huevos que la esposa estaba friendo, él _____ en la cama y comprendió que estaba _____ .

   (*smell*)
   (*stretched out*)
   (*awake*)

2. Al decir que se sentía admirablemente bien, _____ que las palabras engañan.

   (*he realized*)

3. Cuando ella terminó de _____ se fueron a la playa.

   (*wash the dishes*)

4. Después de nadar, él se tiró en la arena y _____ un rato.

   (*dozed*)

5. Ella _____ un poco y él temía que se le hicieran   *(got burned)*

   _____ . Por eso, fue a _____ para   *(blisters)(the drugstore)*

   comprarle una medicina.

6. Cuando ella estaba en la silla de extensión él notó una

   ligera sonrisa en los labios _____ de la esposa.   *(full)*

7. _____ cuando ella le dijo que le prometiera que   *(He got annoyed)*

   no retrataría a otra mujer en ese lugar.

8. "¿_____ esta noche?", —se preguntó ella en voz alta.   *(I wonder if there will be a moon)*

REPASO DE GRAMÁTICA

¿Pretérito o imperfecto? Escoja la forma correcta del verbo.

No supo si lo (despertó / despertaba) la claridad que (entró / entraba) por la ventana o el calor, o ambas cosas. O todavía el ruido que (hizo / hacía) ella en la cocina preparando el desayuno. La oyó freír huevos primero y luego le (llegó / llegaba) el olor de la manteca hirviente. (Se estiró / Se estiraba) en la cama y (sintió / sentía) la tibieza de las sábanas escurrirse bajo su cuerpo y un amable dolor le (corrió / corría) de la espalda a la nuca. En ese momento ella (entró / entraba) en el cuarto y le chocó verla con el delantal por encima de los shorts. La lámpara que (estuvo / estaba) en la mesita de noche ya no estaba allí y (puso / ponía) los platos y las tazas en ella. Entonces advirtió que (estuvo / estaba) despierto.

Ana María Matute

Ana María Matute nació en Barcelona, España, en 1926. Es una de las mejores escritoras de su generación y, posiblemente, una de las más fecundas por sus numerosas novelas y colecciones de cuentos.

Esta novelista contemporánea, de delicada sensibilidad, dedica preferente atención a los niños, presentando en sus obras la psicología infantil con ternura° maternal y profundo conocimiento de la misma.   *tenderness*

En sus cuentos, Ana María Matute vuelca° todas las impresiones de   *pours*
su niñez,° enriquecidas° por los cuentos que oyó a los campesinos,° a   *childhood | enriched | farmers | shepherds*
los pastores,° a su madre y a su abuela, así como un sentimiento de
rebeldía contra los valores de la vida española de su tiempo.

Los personajes en las obras de Matute se encuentran aislados° de   *isolated*
la sociedad en que viven y están rodeados de un sentimiento de
desolación y tragedia. La escritora logra° una presentación realista y   *obtains*
sombría° de la vida de esos personajes que no pueden escapar de su   *somber*
propio destino. El tema de la soledad del individuo aparece
frecuentemente en la obra de Matute.

La prosa de Ana María Matute es sencilla, cargada° de lirismo   *loaded*
poético, y sus descripciones de la naturaleza son ricas en imágenes
visuales.

Son muchas las novelas de Ana María Matute. Entre éstas hay tres
que han recibido premios importantes: *Pequeño teatro* (1954), Premio
Planeta, *Hijos muertos* (1958), Premio Nacional de Literatura, y *Primera
memoria* (1959), Premio Nadal. En el cuento se pueden citar las

siguientes colecciones: *Historias de la Artámila* (1961) y *Algunos muchachos* (1968).

"El árbol de oro" es uno de los cuentos más populares de *Historias de la Artámila*. En él, Matute combina lo real con el mundo de lo sobrenatural° y nos presenta la perspectiva realista del narrador junto al mundo imaginativo y poético del chico Ivo, quien nos dice que ve un árbol de oro a través de la rendija de la pared.

supernatural

La Artámila es el nombre que Ana María Matute usa para ese país imaginario que, en la realidad, viene a estar situado en el nordeste de España.

VOCABULARIO ÚTIL

Sustantivos

la **aldea**	pueblo pequeño	*small village*
la **bombilla** ⎫ el **bombillo** ⎭	globo de cristal que contiene los filamentos eléctricos para dar luz	*light bulb*
la **cadena**	conjunto de eslabones trabados	*chain*
la **cal**	óxido de calcio	*lime*
el **charco**	depósito de agua en el suelo	*puddle*
el **don**	gracia o habilidad natural	*natural ability*
el **juanete**	hueso del dedo del pie cuando es muy abultado	*bunion*
la **mosca**	insecto	*fly*
la **rama**	parte que sale del tronco del árbol	*branch*
el **recreo**	tiempo de recreación (en la escuela)	*recess, recreation time at school*
la **red**	objeto de hilo o soga que sirve para pescar o cazar	*net*
la **rendija**	abertura pequeña	*small crack*
el **sosiego**	tranquilidad, quietud, paz	*tranquility, calmness*
la **torre**	parte más alta de un edificio	*tower*
la **vuelta**	regreso, retorno	*return*
la **zozobra**	angustia, preocupación, inquietud	*uneasiness, anxiety, worry*

Adjetivos

aplicado	estudioso	*studious*
áspero	que no tiene suavidad	*rough*
bizco	que mira torcido	*cross-eyed*
codiciado	deseado	*desirable, coveted*
embustero	mentiroso	*deceitful*
gracioso	que tiene gracia, que es divertido	*funny, amusing, witty*
grasiento	lleno de grasa, mugriento	*greasy, grubby, grimy*
grueso	gordo, de mucho espesor	*fat, thick*
enrevesado	torcido, enredado	*nonsensical, complex, intricate*

pedregoso	lleno de piedras	*stony*
pegajoso	que se pega con facilidad	*sticky*
sosegado	calmado, tranquilo	*calm, quiet, peaceful*

Verbos

agacharse	doblarse o inclinarse	*to squat, bend down*
alargar (gu)	hacer una cosa más larga	*to lengthen, extend*
arrastrar	llevar a una persona o cosa por el suelo tirando de ella	*to drag, pull, haul*
asentir (ie)(i)	consentir, admitir como cierto	*to assent, agree*
asistir	hacer acto de presencia	*to attend*
avergonzarse (c)	sentir vergüenza	*to feel ashamed*
ceder	dar, dar preferencia a otra persona o cosa	*to yield, give in*
cegar (gu)	que no deja ni puede ver	*to blind*
codiciar	desear lo que otro tiene	*to covet, desire*
confiar	tener confianza	*to entrust*
disfrutar	gozar	*to enjoy*
enderezar (c)	poner derecho	*to straighten*
estafar	apoderarse del bien ajeno por medio de engaño	*to swindle*
guardar	conservar, retener para sí	*to keep, put away*
relampaguear	producir un resplandor fuerte de luz	*to lighten, flash*
resplandecer	brillar, despedir rayos de luz	*to shine*
retrasar	demorar	*to delay, retard*
tender (ie)	extender	*to extend*
vaciar	sacar el contenido de un lugar	*to empty*

Expresiones

andar bien (mal)	ir o estar todo bien (mal)	*to go well, run well*
dar con	tropezar con	*to come upon, come across*
dejarse (+ infinitivo)	permitir	*to let oneself be* (+ *past participle*)
de malos modos	de mala gana, sin deseos	*unwillingly*
de tal forma	de una manera especial	*in such a way*
hacer caso	obedecer, prestar atención	*to pay attention*
volverse de (+ sustantivo)	cambiarse	*to become, turn into*

ESTUDIO PRELIMINAR DE VOCABULARIO

A. Sinónimos ◆ Dé una palabra o expresión que quiera decir lo mismo.

1. gozar   2. brillar   3. gordo   4. tropezar   5. prestar atención

B. Antónimos ◆ Busque antónimos en la lista de vocabulario.

1. agitación   2. llenar   3. sincero   4. sencillo   5. suave

C. Escoja la palabra que no pertenece al grupo.

1. mentir   asistir   codiciar   estafar
2. charco   lluvia   cadena   tormenta
3. enderezar   enrevesar   alargar   asentir
4. aplicado   estudioso   trabajador   pegajoso

 El árbol de oro

Asistí durante un otoño a la escuela de la señorita
Leocadia, en la aldea, porque mi salud no andaba bíen
y el abuelo retrasó mi vuelta a la ciudad. Como era el

tiempo frío y estaban los suelos embarrados° y no se
veía rastro° de muchachos, me aburría dentro de la
casa, y pedí al abuelo asistir a la escuela. El abuelo
consintió y acudí a aquella casita alargada° y blanca de
cal, con el tejado pajizo° y requemado° por el sol y las
nieves, a las afueras del pueblo.

    La señorita Leocadia era alta y gruesa, tenía el carácter
más bien° áspero y grandes juanetes en los pies, que la
obligaban a andar como quien arrastra cadenas. Las
clases en la escuela, con la lluvia rebotando° en el
tejado y en los cristales, con las moscas pegajosas de la
tormenta y persiguiéndose alrededor de la bombilla,
tenían su atractivo. Recuerdo especialmente a un
muchacho de unos diez años, hijo de un aparcero° muy
pobre, llamado Ivo. Era un muchacho delgado, de ojos
azules, que bizqueaba° ligeramente al hablar. Todos los
muchachos y muchachas de la escuela admiraban y
envidiaban un poco a Ivo, por el don que poseía de
atraer la atención sobre sí en todo momento. No es que
fuera ni inteligente ni gracioso, y sin embargo, había
algo en él, en su voz quizás, en las cosas que contaba
que conseguía cautivar a quien le escuchase. También la
señorita Leocadia se dejaba prender de aquella red de
plata que Ivo tendía a cuantos° atendían sus
enrevesadas conversaciones, y —yo creo que muchas
veces contra su voluntad— la señorita Leocadia le
confiaba a Ivo tareas deseadas por todos, o distinciones
que merecían alumnos más estudiosos y aplicados.

    Quizá lo que más se envidiaba de Ivo era la posesión
de la codiciada llave de la torrecita. Esta era, en efecto,
una pequeña torre situada en un ángulo de la escuela,
en cuyo interior se guardaban los libros de lectura. Allí
entraba Ivo a buscarlos, y, allí volvía a dejarlos, al
terminar la clase. La señorita Leocadia se lo
encomendó a él, nadie sabía en realidad por qué.

    Ivo estaba muy orgulloso de esta distinción, y por
nada del mundo la hubiera cedido. Un día, Mateo
Heredia, el más aplicado y estudioso de la escuela,
pidió encargarse de la tarea —a todos nos fascinaba el
misterioso interior de la torrecita, donde no entramos
nunca—, y la señorita Leocadia pareció acceder. Pero

muddy

trace, sign

larga (long)

tejado... *straw-colored roof / muy quemado*

más... *rather*

bouncing

sharecropper

looked cross-eyed

a cuantos *a todos los que*

45 Ivo se levantó, y acercándose a la maestra empezó a
hablarle en su voz baja, bizqueando los ojos y
moviendo mucho las manos, como tenía por
costumbre. La maestra dudó un poco, y al fin dijo:

—Quede todo como estaba.° Que siga encargándose

50 Ivo de la torrecita.

A la salida de la escuela le pregunté:

—¡Qué le has dicho a la maestra?

Ivo me miró de través° y vi relampaguear sus ojos
azules.

55 —Le hablé del árbol de oro.

Sentí una gran curiosidad,

—¿Qué árbol?

Hacía frío y el camino estaba húmedo, con grandes
charcos que brillaban al sol pálido de la tarde. Ivo

60 empezó a chapotear° en ellos, sonriendo con misterio.

—Si no se lo cuentas a nadie...

—Te lo juro,° que a nadie se lo diré.

Entonces Ivo me explicó:

—Veo un árbol de oro. Un árbol completamente de

65 oro: ramas, tronco, hojas... ¿sabes? Las hojas no se caen
nunca. En verano, en invierno, siempre. Resplandece
mucho, tanto, que tengo que cerrar los ojos para que
no me duelan.

—¡Qué embustero eres! —dije, aunque con algo de

70 zozobra. Ivo me miró con desprecio.

—No te lo creas —contestó—. Me es completamente
igual que te lo creas o no... ¡Nadie entrará nunca en la
torrecita, y a nadie dejaré ver mi árbol de oro! ¡Es mío!
La señorita Leocadia lo sabe, y no se atreve a darle la

75 llave a Mateo Heredia, ni a nadie... ¡Mientras yo viva,
nadie podrá entrar allí y ver mi árbol!

Lo dijo de tal forma que no pude evitar preguntarle:

—¿Y cómo lo ves...?

—Ah, no es fácil —dijo, con aire misterioso—.

80 Cualquiera no podría verlo. Yo sé la rendija exacta.

—¿Rendija...?

—Sí, una rendija de la pared. Una que hay corriendo
el cajón° de la derecha: me agacho y me paso horas y
horas... ¡Cómo brilla el árbol! ¡Cómo brilla! Fíjate°

85 si algún pájaro se le pone encima° también se vuelve de

Quede... Que todo
continúe lo mismo

de... *sideways*

to splash

Te... *I swear to you*

caja grande

Imagine

on top

oro. Eso me digo yo: si me subiera a una rama, me
volvería acaso° de oro también?

tal vez

No supe qué decirle; pero, desde aquel momento,
mi deseo de ver el árbol creció de tal forma que me

90   desasosegaba.° Todos los días, al acabar la clase de
lectura, Ivo se acercaba al cajón° de la maestra, sacaba
la llave y se dirigía a la torrecita. Cuando volvía, le
preguntaba:

—¿Lo has visto?

95   —Sí —me contestaba. Y, a veces, explicaba alguna
novedad.

—Le han salido unas flores raras. Mira: así de
grandes, como mi mano lo menos,° y con los pétalos
alargados. Me parece que esa flor es parecida al arzadú.°

100   —¡La flor del frío! —decía yo, con asombro—. ¡Pero
el arzadú es encarnado!°

—Muy bien —asentía él, con gesto de paciencia—.
Pero en mi árbol es oro puro.

—Además, el arzadú crece al borde de los caminos...

105   y no es un árbol.

No se podía discutir con él. Siempre tenía razón, o
por los menos lo parecía.

Ocurrió entonces algo que secretamente yo deseaba;
me avergonzaba sentirlo, pero así era: Ivo enfermó, y la

110   señorita Leocadia encargó a otro la llave de la torrecita.
Primeramente, la disfrutó Mateo Heredia. Yo espié su
regreso, el primer día, y le dije:

—¿Has visto un árbol de oro?

—¿Qué andas graznando?° —me contestó de malos

115   modos, porque no era simpático, y menos conmigo.
Quise dárselo a entender,° pero no me hizo caso. Unos
días después, me dijo:

—Si me das algo a cambio, te dejo un ratito° la llave
y vas durante el recreo. Nadie te verá...

120   Vacié mi hucha,° y, por fin, conseguí la codiciada
llave. Mis manos temblaban de emoción cuando entré
en el cuartito de la torre. Allí estaba el cajón. Lo aparté
y vi brillar la rendija en la oscuridad. Me agaché y
miré.

125   Cuando la luz dejó de cegarme, mi ojo derecho sólo
descubrió una cosa: la seca tierra de la llanura

me... it made me restless / drawer

como... at least the size of my hand / una planta de flor que crece en el noreste de España / rojo

¿Qué... What are you chattering about?

dárselo... make him understand

a little while

piggy bank

alargándose hacia el cielo. Nada más. Lo mismo que se veía desde las ventanas altas. La tierra desnuda y yerma,° y nada más que la tierra. Tuve una gran

130 decepción y la seguridad de que me habían estafado.

barren

Olvidé la llave y el árbol de oro. Antes de que llegaran las nieves regresé a la ciudad.

Dos veranos más tarde volví a las montañas. Un día, pasando por el cementerio —era ya tarde y se anunciaba

135 la noche en el cielo: el sol, como una bola roja, caía a lo lejos, hacia la carrera terrible y sosegada de la llanura—, ví algo extraño. De la tierra grasienta y pedregosa, entre las cruces caídas, nacía un árbol grande y hermoso, con las hojas anchas de oro

140 encendido° y brillante todo él, cegador. Algo me vino a la memoria, como un sueño, y pensé: "Es un árbol de oro". Busqué al pie del árbol, y no tardé en dar con una crucecilla de hierro negro, mohosa° por la lluvia. Mientras la enderezaba, leí: IVO MÁRQUEZ, DE DIEZ

145 AÑOS DE EDAD.

full of light

rusty

Y no daba tristeza alguna, sino, tal vez, una extraña y muy grande alegría.

COMPRENSIÓN DEL CUENTO

A. Preguntas ◆

1. ¿Dónde quedaba la escuela a la que asistió la narradora?
2. ¿Por qué quería la narradora asistir a la escuela?
3. ¿Cómo era la maestra? Descríbala.
4. ¿Cómo era Ivo? Descríbalo.
5. ¿Por qué le tenían envidia los niños a Ivo?
6. ¿Qué había en la pequeña torre?
7. ¿Tenía conocimiento la maestra del secreto de Ivo del árbol de oro? ¿Cómo lo sabemos?
8. ¿Cómo describe Ivo su visión del árbol de oro?
9. Cuando Ivo se enfermó, ¿a quién le dio la llave la maestra para ir a la torrecita?
10. ¿Qué le dio la narradora a Mateo Heredia para que éste le diera la llave por un ratito para subir a la torre?
11. ¿Qué vio la narradora desde la rendija de la torre?
12. En este cuento Ana María Matute usa varios diminutivos (casita, torrecita, ratito, cuartito, crucecilla). ¿Qué efecto obtiene la narradora al usar los diminutivos?

B. Repaso ◆ Explique la situación a que se refieren las siguientes frases que aparecen en el cuento.

1. El abuelo consintió y acudí a aquella casita alargada y blanca.
2. La obligaban a andar como quien arrastra cadenas.
3. También la señorita Leocadia se dejaba prender de aquella red de plata que Ivo tendía.
4. Ivo estaba muy orgulloso de esta distinción.
5. Vacié mi hucha y por fin conseguí la codiciada llave.
6. Busqué al pie del árbol y no tardé en dar con una crucecilla de hierro negro.

C. Comprensión de la lectura ◆ Escoja las explicaciones que sean correctas.

1. La narradora dice que todos los muchachos admiraban a Ivo porque...
   a. tenía un don especial que llamaba la atención de los demás.
   b. era extremadamente inteligente y era el más aplicado de la clase.
   c. era muy gracioso y divertido.
   d. tenía unos ojos muy lindos y siempre miraba de frente.
2. ¿Cómo describe la narradora su experiencia en la escuela de la señorita Leocadia?
   a. Con gran melancolía y frustración.
   b. Con burla hacia los sueños infantiles.
   c. Con gran delicadeza y conocimiento del mundo infantil.
   d. Con admiración hacia el sistema de escuelas de su país.
3. ¿Qué se dice del árbol de oro que veía Ivo desde la torrecita?
   a. Que aparecía por la mañana y desaparecía por la noche.
   b. Que representaba para Ivo la realidad de su imaginación.
   c. Que existía para todos los que subían a la torre.
   d. Que servía de símbolo de la vida triste de Ivo.
4. La última línea del cuento "Y no daba tristeza alguna, sino, tal vez, una extraña y muy grande alegría", sugiere que...
   a. la narradora se alegra de la muerte de Ivo.
   b. el cementerio está bien ciudado.
   c. la narradora comprueba que Ivo era un embustero.
   d. la ilusión y la fantasía de Ivo seguirán siempre existiendo para otras personas.
5. ¿Cuál es el tema de este cuento?
   a. El materialismo de algunos niños en la escuela.
   b. La fantasía y las ilusiones frente a la realidad.
   c. El atractivo de la escuela de la aldea.
   d. La envidia entre los estudiantes de la clase.

D. Temas para presentación oral o escrita ◆

1. ¿Cómo explica Ud. la visión del árbol que veía Ivo?
2. ¿Tuvo Ud. alguna experiencia similar a la de Ivo? Hable sobre ella.
3. ¿Cree Ud. que si la señorita Leocadia contara el cuento produciría el mismo efecto?
4. Describa al maestro o maestra de su niñez que le haya hecho la mayor impresión.

REPASO DE VOCABULARIO

A. Llene los espacios en blanco escogiendo las palabras que mejor completen el sentido del párrafo.

La narradora asistió a la escuela de la _____1_____ durante el otoño porque no estaba bien de salud y el abuelo _____2_____ su _____3_____ a la ciudad.

El carácter de la señorita Leocadia era _____4_____ ; ella tenía grandes _____5_____ en los pies. Ivo era un muchacho que _____6_____ un poco al hablar. Los compañeros de la escuela admiraban en él el _____7_____ que tenía de atraer la atención de todos, cautivando a cuantos atendían sus _____8_____ conversaciones.

En la torrecita se _____9_____ los libros de lectura y todos los días Ivo era el encargado de buscarlos. Le contó a la narradora la visión que él veía, al _____10_____ a través de una _____11_____ que había en la pared de la torrecita. Ella pensó que Ivo era _____12_____ y no creyó lo que él decía. Cuando Ivo se enfermó, Mateo Heredia fue el encargado de la _____13_____ de la torrecita y la narradora le dio dinero para que la dejara ir, durante el _____14_____ , a visitar la misteriosa torrecita. Su desilusión fue grande cuando descubrió sólo la tierra de la llanura y no la visión del árbol de oro que Ivo _____15_____ . Cuando la narradora volvió a la aldea, al cabo de dos años, al pasar por el cementerio vio algo extraño que salía de la tierra grasienta y _____16_____ : un árbol de oro había nacido, y al pie de éste estaba una crucecilla con el nombre de Ivo Márquez.

1. *cadena / aldea*
2. *retrasó / confió*
3. *recreo / regreso*
4. *áspero / aplicado*
5. *juanetes / zozobra*
6. *codiciaba / bizqueaba*
7. *don / charco*
8. *embusteras / enrevesadas*
9. *estafaban / guardaban*
10. *avergonzarse / agacharse*
11. *rendija / rama*
12. *gracioso / embustero*
13. *cal / llave*
14. *recreo / charco*
15. *disfrutaba / enderezaba*
16. *pedregosa / codiciosa*

B. Indique en el cuento las oraciones donde aparece la siguiente información.

1. El motivo por el cual la narradora asistió a la escuela de la aldea.
2. Cualidad que tenía Ivo que hacía que lo admiraran los compañeros de la escuela.
3. Lo que hacía Ivo en la escuela que producía mucha envidia.
4. La descripción que hace Ivo de la visión que ve desde la torrecita.
5. Lo que ve la narradora cuando sube a la torrecita.
6. La experiencia extraña que tuvo la narradora cuando, dos años más tarde, pasó por el cementerio.

C. Repase las expresiones en la lista de vocabulario y después complete las oraciones de acuerdo con las indicaciones en inglés que están a la derecha.

1. La salud de la narradora _____ .   *(was not going well)*

2. Ivo decía que si un pájaro se subía al árbol que él veía desde
   la torrecita _____ .   *(it would turn into gold)*

3. El deseo que la narradora tenía de ver el árbol creció
   _____ que sólo pensaba en eso.   *(in such a way)*

4. Mateo Heredia _____ a lo que ella quiso decirle.   *(did not pay attention)*

5. La narradora no tardó en _____ una crucecilla   *(come upon)*
   que tenía el nombre de Ivo.

REPASO DE GRAMÁTICA

Diminutivos ◆ Repase la lección sobre los diminutivos en el Capítulo 8. Después escriba los diminutivos de las siguientes palabras y use cada una en una oración original.

1. torre _____
2. maestra _____
3. pies _____
4. rama _____
5. escuela _____
6. mosca _____
7. cajón _____
8. llave _____
9. flor _____
10. árbol _____

María Manuela Dolón

María Manuela Dolón, nacida y residente de Ceuta, es una escritora española cuyos cuentos han sido publicados en diversas revistas, como "Silueta", "La Estafeta Literaria", "Blanco y Negro", "Tribuna Médica" y "Lecturas", y también en periódicos, entre ellos, "Diario de León", "Diario Regional de Valladolid" y "Arriba". Dolón, que comenzó a escribir desde muy niña, se mantiene siempre muy productiva. Ha ganado gran número de premios en diversos concursos de cuentos y también recibió una Mención Honorífica del Círculo de Escritores y Poetas Iberoamericanos de Nueva York. En el año 2000, la Ciudad de Ceuta le concedió el Premio de las Artes y de la Cultura de Literatura y en el 2001, la Casa de Ceuta en Barcelona le otorgó el Premio de Narrativa en el Concurso anual con motivo de la Feria del Libro. Entre sus libros, se deben citar *Las raíces y otros relatos* y en 1999, *27 Historias* que es una recopilación de sus cuentos premiados.

VOCABULARIO ÚTIL

Sustantivos

el **barco**	embarcación, buque	*ship*
el **bulto**	volúmen, cosa que no se distingue bien	*form, bundle*
la **cantina**	lugar donde se vende bebida y comida	*bar, tavern*

la **carretera**	camino empedrado o asfaltado	*highway*
el **cenicero**	recipiente para poner la ceniza	*ashtray*
la **cita**	hora y lugar en que acuerdan encontrarse dos personas	*date, appointment*
la **flojedad**	pereza; debilidad	*laziness*
la **gabardina**	abrigo para la lluvia	*raincoat*
la **inquietud**	intranquilidad	*restlessness*
el **mostrador**	mesa grande en las tiendas	*counter*
la **niebla**	neblina, bruma	*fog*
la **pena**	sentimiento de dolor, tristeza	*sorrow*
el **pesar**	tristeza; disgusto	*sorrow*
la **pitada**	sonido de un pito	*toot, whistle*
el **rincón**	sitio apartado	*corner*
el **rostro**	cara	*face*
la **rueda**	objeto circular que gira y facilita el movimiento de un vehículo	*wheel*
el **sorbo**	líquido que se bebe de una vez	*sip*
el **tabernero**	el que trabaja en un bar	*bartender*
la **velocidad**	celeridad en un movimiento uniforme	*speed*
el **volante**	rueda de dirección en un vehículo	*steering wheel*

Adjetivos

alborozado	contento, regocijado	*overjoyed*
apurado	con prisa, apresurado	*hurriedly*
anhelante	con ansia, con deseos fuertes	*yearning, gasping*
dispuesto	preparado para algo	*ready*
espeso	denso, no transparente	*thick*
horrendo	horrible	*horrible, horrendous*
lejano	que está lejos	*distant, remote*
lúcido	de inteligencia clara	*lucid*
lúgubre	oscuro	*gloomy*
malhumorado	de mal humor	*ill-humored*
sobresaltado	asustado	*shocked, startled*
resuelto	decidido	*decided, resolved*
vacío	que no contiene nada	*empty*

Adverbios

| **acaso** | quizá, tal vez | *maybe, perhaps* |
| **precipitadamente** | rápidamente | *hastily* |

Verbos

abrochar	cerrar o unir con broches	*to fasten*
advertir (ie) (i)	notar; avisar	*to notice; warn*
aminorar	disminuir	*to diminish*
aplastar	aplanar, comprimir una cosa	*to crush*
apretar (ie)	estrechar; oprimir	*to tighten; to press*
colgar (ue)	suspender una cosa de otra	*to hang up*

demorar	retrasar, retardar	*to delay*
despachar	atender a los clientes	*to serve customers*
disimular	pretender que no se ve o se siente	*to conceal, hide*
fugarse	escaparse	*to flee, run away*
inquirir (ie)	preguntar, investigar	*to inquire*
huir (y)	escapar corriendo	*to run away*
latir	dar latidos	*to beat*
lograr	obtener, conseguir	*to attain, achieve*
morder (ue)	cortar con los dientes	*to bite*
obligar	imponer una obligación	*to force, obligate*
retroceder	volver atrás	*to move back*
retumbar	resonar	*to resound*
soborear	percibir con gusto el sabor de algo	*to savor*
tambalearse	moverse sin equilibrio	*to stagger*
temblar (ie)	moverse con movimiento frecuente	*to tremble*

Expresiones

al día siguiente	el próximo día	*next day*
a lo lejos	en la distancia	*far away*
de golpe	todo de una vez	*all at once*
de repente	de pronto, sin preparación	*suddenly*
dentro de diez minutos	en diez minutos	*in ten minutes*
hablar entre dientes	murmurar	*to mutter*
llevar a cabo	realizar, hacer	*to carry out*
rumbo a	en la dirección de	*in the direction of*

ESTUDIO PRELIMINAR DE VOCABULARIO

A. Sinónimos ◆ Dé una palabra o expresión que quiera decir lo mismo.

1. cara   2. quizá   3. asustado   4. contento   5. intranquilidad

B. Antónimos ◆ Busque antónimos en la lista de vocabulario.

1. lleno   2. claro, brillante   3. lentamente   4. tranquilo

C. Escoja la palabra que no pertenece al grupo.

1. cenicero	cigarillos	fumar	niebla
2. fugarse	barco	pitada	polvera
3. velocidad	carretera	acelerador	rincón
4. cantina	retumbar	tabernero	bebidas
5. morder	saborear	sorbo	disimular

Noche de fuga

—Al teléfono, señor Maurí.

Jorge Maurí se levantó, aplastó su cigarrillo contra el cenicero y lentamente se dirigió al teléfono.

—¿Qué hay? —preguntó.

5 —Soy yo, Jorge —se oyó una voz de mujer al otro lado del hilo°—. Todo me ha salido perfectamente. Estoy fuera de casa. En una cantina que hay en la carretera, ¿sabes cuál es?

—Sí, sí, ya sé —respondió él.

10 —¿Te espero entonces aquí mismo, Jorge? —inquirió la mujer. Jorge Maurí consultó su reloj.

—Sí, espérame ahí. Dentro de diez minutos estaré por ti.

La mujer también debió mirar su reloj porque le 15 advirtió en tono preocupado:

—Ya ha dado la primera pitada del barco, Jorge. Así es que tenemos el tiempo justo.

—Sí, ya lo sé. Te digo que dentro de diez minutos estoy ahí —volvió a repetir impacientándose.°

20 Colgó. Abrió su pitillera° y sacó un cigarrillo. Al encenderlo notó que la mano le temblaba un poco. ¡Pardiez!° —se dijo malhumorado. No sabía él que el

telephone line

becoming impatient

cigarette case

For God's sake!

hecho de huir con una mujer le fuera a poner tan
nervioso. Dio unas cuantas chupadas° al cigarro y   *puffs*

25   despacio, tratando de disimular el nerviosismo que
experimentaba, se fue acercando a la mesa de sus amigos.

—Chicos, os voy a tener que dejar —dijo queriendo
parecer natural y empezando a recoger ya su gabardina.

—¿Qué te vas? —le interrogó uno de los amigos,

30   mirándole sorprendido.

—¡Tú estás loco! Tú te tienes que quedar otra ronda.°   *round of drinks*

—Imposible. Tengo muchísima prisa.

—¡Ni prisa ni nada! —exclamó otro, cogiéndole la
gabardina y escondiéndosela.°   *hiding it from him*

35   Otro le sentaba a la fuerza° mientras le decía: **a la...** *against his will*

—Tú te quedas a beber otra copa. ¡Pues estaría
bueno...!

—¿Pero es que queréis que pierda la cita que tengo?
—se defendía él, aunque débilmente.

40   —¿Cita con una mujer? —le preguntó uno de ellos.
¡Estupendo! —gritó alborozado. Eso es lo bueno,
hacerlas esperar. Eso, además, hará la aventura
muchísimo más interesante —agregó riéndose
estrepitosamente.°   *boisterously*

45   Jorge Maurí volvió a mirar su reloj.

—No, no puedo, de verdad, quedarme —aseguró
apurado.

—Tú te quedas. Al menos hasta que te tomes otra
copa.

50   Y le obligaron a beber. Él se resistió al principio.
Sabía que no debía beber. Que debía conservar la
cabeza lúcida y serena. Pero por otra parte sabía
también que le vendría bien beber. Sentía una lasitud,°   *lassitude, weariness*
una flojedad —que le impedía moverse y reaccionar.

55   Era como si en el fondo, inconscientemente, tratara de
demorar lo más posible lo que iba a hacer. Como un
extraño temor a llevarlo a cabo, a llegar hasta el final. Y
eso sólo se quitaba bebiendo. Y bebió hasta que la
sirena de un barco le hizo incorporarse sobresaltado,

60   como si despertara de pronto de un sueño.

Cuando salió de allí tenía los ojos turbios y se
tambaleaba ligeramente sobre sus pies. Pero se metió
precipitadamente en su coche y cogiendo el volante

con una especie de furia, enfiló° la negra carretera a la   *followed*
65 máxima velocidad.

La muchacha salió de la cabina telefónica y pasó la
vista con inquietud alrededor suyo. No, no había nadie
conocido. Las gentes de su mundo no frecuentaban
estos lugares. En aquel momento se hallaba la cantina
70 casi vacía. Unos marineros en una mesa y dos hombres
más bebiendo en el mostrador. Iban mal trajeados° y   **mal**... *badly dressed*
parecían obreros.° Respiró. Y mirando su reloj, fue a   *laborers*
sentarse en un rincón, dispuesta a esperar los diez
minutos que él le dijera. Pidió un café, que bebió
75 lentamente, a pequeños sorbos, saboreándolo aunque
no estaba nada bueno. Después sacó una polvera° de   *compact*
su bolso y se retocó° el rostro, que lo tenía muy pálido.   *touched up*
Se pintó los labios...

Hasta ahora —pensó— todo le había salido bien.
80 Había logrado escapar de casa sin que nadie la viera,
sin que nadie la oyera. Al día siguiente sería el
escándalo. Al día siguiente toda la ciudad hablaría de
ella. Ella, una muchacha tan seria, tan formal, tan
decente, fugarse con el gamberro° y millonario Jorge   *libertine*
85 Maurí... Pero mañana, cuando todos se enteraran, ella
estaría ya lejos, en alta mar, con Jorge, rumbo a países
desconocidos, hacia un mundo nuevo y extraño que
nunca había imaginado.

Sonrió a su pesar.° ¡Menudo campanazo!° Bueno ¿y   **a su**... *in spite of herself* /
90 qué? Ella quería a Jorge, y Jorge no podía o no quería   **¡Menudo**... *What a scandal!*
casarse de momento con ella. Tenían, pues, que huir a
otros sitios donde la gente no se asustara de aquel
amor. Lo único que le dolía era dejar a sus padres. Le
apenaba enormemente el disgusto que les iba a dar.
95 Pero era necesario. No podía evitarlo sin perder a
Jorge. Y Jorge para ella significaba todo en su vida. Le
amaba de tal manera, estaba tan firme y resuelta a
seguirle aunque fuera al fin del mundo, que lo haría
aunque supiera fijamente que después le aguardarían
100 las penas más terribles, la muerte más horrenda. Con
él a su lado no le asustaba nada. Nada ya le podría
hacer retroceder.

De pronto oyó la segunda pitada del barco y
bruscamente se puso en pie. Habían pasado ya los diez

105 minutos que él le dijo. "¿Le habrá ocurrido algo? —
pensó alarmada—. ¡Es tan loco conduciendo...! ¿O..."
no se atrevió a concluir su pensamiento. No, no podía
ser que él se hubiera arrepentido.

Pagó su café y salió. El hombre que despachaba tras
110 el mostrador la vió salir, moviendo la cabeza en señal de
admiración. Afuera hacía frío y había niebla. Se abrochó
la mujer el abrigo, subiéndose el cuello hasta arriba,
mientras empezaba a andar por la solitaria carretera en
la dirección que él tenía que venir. No se veía nada. Ni
115 una luz siquiera en la oscuridad total que la rodeaba.
Advirtió de pronto que las piernas le temblaban. Y no
sabía si era de frío, del miedo a que le hubiera ocurrido
algo o se hubiera arrepentido. O acaso, tal vez, temor
ante el paso que iba a dar. No, no lo sabía. Sólo sabía
120 que por primera vez en la aventura estaba nerviosa.

Siguió andando mucho rato. Hasta que le pareció
distinguir a lo lejos, entre la niebla, como una luz que
se acercaba. Y respiró tranquilizada. ¡Sería él sin duda!
Y esperó ansiosa, con el corazón latiéndole anhelante.
125 Pero tan oscura la noche, tan espesa la niebla y cegada
además por los faros del coche que raudamente° se iba   *swiftly*
acercando, no podía precisar ella si se trataba de él. No
obstante, empezó a agitar un brazo a la vez que se
acercaba hacia el centro de la carretera, mientras una
130 sonrisa de felicidad flotaba en sus labios.

Y fue entonces cuando lúgubre, lejana, como
envuelta en bruma, se oyó la tercera pitada del barco.

Jorge Maurí no dejaba de apretar el acelerador. Cada
momento miraba el reloj, mordiéndose los labios
135 nerviosamente. Era espantoso lo rápido que corría el
reloj y lo despacio que debía de ir su coche. Le parecía
que no avanzaba nada o que aquella carretera era
siempre igual, interminable, como si no tuviera fin. Y
con furia, frenéticamente, apretaba más el acelerador.
140 De repente le pareció ver como un bulto en medio
de la carretera. "¡Pues solamente faltaba eso —exclamó
contrariado°—, que algo se interponga en mi camino!"   *annoyed*

Pero Jorge Maurí no aminoró la marcha. No podía,
en realidad, aminorarla aunque hubiera querido. Y
145 siguió conduciendo sin variar la velocidad, derecho
hacia aquello que parecía moverse en medio del

camino. En aquel momento sonó la sirena de un barco, pero Jorge Maurí no la oyó. Lo que oyó fue un grito terrible que retumbó en la noche, a la vez que sentía cómo las ruedas de su coche pasaban sobre algo. Todo fue rápido y al mismo tiempo. "¡Maldito sea!°" exclamó él entre dientes, pero sin detenerse en su loca carrera, sin mirar hacia atrás.

¡Maldito... *Damn it!*

Sólo se detuvo al llegar a la cantina. Allí se bajó apresuradamente y entró en el local mirando con ansiedad a todos lados. Al no verla en seguida pensó: "¿Será posible que se haya vuelto atrás y me dé chasco°...?"

me dé... *letting me down*

No obstante aún se acercó al mostrador con alguna esperanza.

—Oiga —le dijo al tabernero—, ¿no ha estado aquí una señorita que ha utilizado el teléfono hace un rato?

—Sí —contestó el hombre—. Aquí ha estado una señorita pero se ha marchado ya. Hacia ese lado ha ido —añadió, señalando por donde él había venido.

—¿Por ese lado? —murmuró Jorge Maurí pensativamente.

Y luego, de golpe° abriendo los ojos horrorizado, volvió a repetir:

de golpe *suddenly*

—Pero... ¿por ese lado dice usted?

COMPRENSIÓN DEL CUENTO

A. Preguntas ◆

1. ¿Dónde estaba la muchacha cuando llamó por teléfono a Jorge Maurí?
2. ¿Qué planeaban hacer ella y Jorge?
3. ¿Qué pensaba la muchacha acerca de la reacción que su fuga con Jorge iba a causar en su ciudad?
4. ¿Qué le apenaba enormemente a ella?
5. ¿Cómo se encontraba Jorge al salir de la taberna?
6. ¿Qué hizo la muchacha al salir de la cantina?
7. ¿Cómo era la noche?
8. ¿Cómo conducía Jorge el coche?
9. ¿Qué hizo Jorge cuando le pareció ver un bulto en la carretera?
10. ¿Qué le preguntó Jorge al tabernero?
11. ¿Qué supo Jorge al hablar con el tabernero?

B. Repaso ◆ Explique la situación a que se refieren las siguientes oraciones.

1. Estoy fuera de casa en una cantina que hay en la carretera.
2. Tú te quedas a beber otra copa.
3. Cuando salió de allí tenía los ojos turbios.
4. Al día siguiente sería el escándalo.
5. De repente le pareció ver como un bulto en la carretera.

C. Temas para presentación oral o escrita ◆

1. ¿Cómo prepara la autora al lector para la sorpresa al final del cuento? ¿Se imaginaba Ud. ese final?
2. Si Ud. hubiera escrito el cuento, ¿qué otro final le hubiera dado?
3. ¿Qué opina Ud. de la relación que existe entre los dos jóvenes?
4. ¿Con cuál de los dos jóvenes simpatiza Ud. más?

REPASO DE VOCABULARIO

Llene los espacios en blanco con la traducción al español de las palabras que están en inglés.

1. Jorge trató de _____ (*conceal*) el nerviosismo que sentía.
2. La muchacha se sentó en un _____ (*corner*) de la cantina.
3. Cuando Jorge salió de la taberna se metió en el carro _____ (*hastily*).
4. Hacía frío y la muchacha se _____ (*fastened*) el abrigo.
5. Ella no podía ver bien el camino porque había mucha _____ (*fog*).
6. El pensar que Jorge no viniera a reunirse con ella le causaba gran _____ (*restlessness*).
7. Ella tenía el _____ (*face*) pálido y por primera vez estaba nerviosa.
8. Jorge no aminoró la _____ (*speed*) cuando le pareció ver un bulto en la carretera.

REPASO DE GRAMÁTICA

Llene los espacios en blanco con el presente de indicativo de los verbos que están entre paréntesis.

1. (*huir*) Los jóvenes _____ de la ciudad donde viven.
2. (*tambalearse*) Jorge _____ al salir de la taberna.
3. (*advertir / temblar*) La muchacha _____ que le _____ las piernas.
4. (*disimular*) Jorge _____ el nerviosismo que siente.
5. (*colgar*) Ella _____ el teléfono cuando termina de hablar.
6. (*morder*) Ella se _____ los labios porque está disgustada.

Vocabulario

Note that the words beginning with **ch** or **ll** are listed under **c** or **l**.

~ A ~

abalanzarse *refl*   to rush to
abandonar   to abandon; to leave
abatimiento   depression
abeja   bee
ablandar   to soften
abogado   lawyer
abombado   sticking out; puffed out
abonar   to credit, pay; to fertilize, *refl* to subscribe; to buy a season ticket
abrazar   to embrace
abrelatas *m*   can opener
aburrir   to bore; *refl* to be bored
acabar   to finish, end
acabar con   to put an end to
acalambrado   having a cramp
acampanado   bell-shaped
acantilado   cliff
acariciar   to caress
acaso   maybe, perhaps
acceder   to accede, agree; to give in
acciones *f*   shares of stock
accionista *mf*   shareholder, stockholder
acechar   to spy on
aceite *m*   oil
acercar   to bring or place near or nearer; *refl* to approach, to draw near
acero   steel
acertar   to guess right
aclamar   to acclaim
acodarse   to lean on one's elbows
acoger   to welcome, to receive
aconsejar   to advise, to counsel

acordar   to agree
acordarse de   to remember
acosado   harassed
acosar   to harass; to pursue relentlessly
acostar   to put to bed; *refl* to go to bed, to lie down
acostumbrar   to accustom; *refl* to become accustomed to
actuar   to act, to perform
acudir   to go, attend; to resort
adelgazar   to get thin; to taper off
además   besides, moreover, in addition
adorno   ornament, adornment
aduana   customs; customhouse
advertir   to warn, to advise; to observe, to notice
afeitar   to shave; *refl* to shave oneself
afición *f*   liking, fondness
afincarse   to lean on, to get hold of
afligir   to afflict; to grieve
agacharse   to bend down; to crouch, to squat
agarrar   to grab, to grasp, to take hold of
agitar   to agitate, to shake
aglomerar   to cluster; to heap upon
agotar   to exhaust, to wear out; to use up, to consume completely
agradar   to please, to be pleasing
agronomía   agronomy
aguacate *m*   avocado
aguacero   rain, shower, downpour
aguantar   to tolerate, to put up with; to hold back; *refl* to endure, to suffer
aguardar   to wait for, to await
aguarse   to get watery

361

agudo   sharp

águila   eagle

agujero   hole

ahogarse   to drown; to choke

ahondar   to go deep into

ahorcar   to hang (as in an execution)

ahorrar   to save; to spare

aislado   isolated

ajeno   belonging to another; foreign, strange

ají *m*   bell or chili pepper

ala   wing

alabanza   praise

alacrán *m*   scorpion

alambrado   wire fence, wiring

alargar   to lengthen, to stretch; to prolong

alarido   howl, scream, cry, shout

alazán   sorrel-colored

alborotado   excited; noisy

alcalde *m*   mayor

alcanzar   to reach, to reach up

aldea   small village

alegar   to affirm, to allege

alegrar   to make glad; to brighten

alegrarse de   to be glad

alejarse   to move away, to go far away

alentar   to encourage

alero   eave of a roof

alfiler *m*   pin

alfombra   rug, carpet

algodón *m*   cotton

alhaja   jewel

alianza   alliance, league

alimentar   to feed, to nourish; to sustain

alimento   food, nutriment

aliviar   to alleviate, to ease; *refl* to be relieved; to get better

allanar   to level, to flatten

alma   soul

almendra   almond

almidonado   starched

almohada   pillow, cushion

alpaca   alpaca (South American animal)

alquilar   to rent

alrededor   around, about; *pl* surroundings

altivo   haughty, proud

alumbrado   street lights

alumno   student

alzar   to raise, to lift; *refl* to rise (in revolt)

amable   kind, courteous, amiable, friendly

amanecer   to dawn; to awaken in; *nm* dawn, daybreak

amante *mf*   lover; loving, fond

amargo   bitter

amarrar   to tie

ambiente *m*   environment

ambos   both

ambulante   traveling, moving; **vendedor ambulante** *m*   peddler

amenaza   threat, menace

amenazar   to threaten

amo   master (of the house); owner

amontonamiento   hoard, pile

amontonar   to pile up

amparar   to protect, to help, to shelter; *refl* to seek protection, to shelter

ampolla   blister

añadir   to add

anarquista *mf*   anarchist

anclar   to anchor

andaluz   Andalusian

andén *m*   train platform

angosto   narrow

ángulo   angle

angustia   anguish

angustioso   distressed; distressing

anhelar   to long for, to desire anxiously

anillo   ring

animar   to cheer up; *refl* to be encouraged

ánimo   mood; encouragement **estado de ánimo**   frame of mind

anochecer   to become dark; *nm* twilight, nightfall

ansiar   to crave

ansiedad *f*   anxiety

ansioso   eager

anticuado   old-fashioned

apacible   placid

apagado   soft; weak; dull; dim; extinguished

apagar   to put out, to extinguish; to turn off

apartarse   to go away, to withdraw; to leave

apego   fondness, affection, attachment

apenado   sorry, sad; embarrassed

apenar   to cause grief, embarrassment

apenas   hardly, scarcely; with difficulty

aperitivo   appetizer, cocktail

apertura   opening, beginning; commencement

aplastar   to crush, to flatten

aplaudir   to applaud

aplazar   to postpone

aplicado   studious

aportar   to contribute, to bring one's share; to provide support, help, backing

apresurarse a   to hurry up

apretar   to tighten; to press; to squeeze

   apretar el paso   to walk faster

apretón *m*   grip, squeeze;

   apretón de manos   handshake

aprisionar   to imprison; to capture

aprobar   to approve

apuntar   to take note

araña   spider

arbusto   shrub, bush

archivar   to file

arena   sand

argumento   plot, theme, subject; argument, reasoning

armadura   armor

arqueólogo   archaeologist

arquitectura   architecture

arraigar   to root, to establish firmly

arrastrar   to haul, to pull, to drag; *refl* to crawl; to drag oneself

arreglar   to arrange

arrepentirse   to repent, to regret

arrimarse   to take shelter; to come close to

arrodillarse   to kneel

arrojar   to throw

arroyo   brook, stream

arruinar   to ruin, to destroy

arrullar   to cuddle; to bill and coo to; to lull or sing to sleep

asado   roast

asalto   assault, attack

asar   to roast; *refl* to roast, to feel very hot

ascenso   promotion

ascético   ascetic

asco   disgust; nausea;   **dar asco**   to disgust

asegurar   to assure; to insure, to guarantee

asentir   to assent, to agree

asesinar   to murder

asiento   seat

asimilar   to assimilate

asimismo   likewise

asistir   to attend

asolear   to dry in the sun

asomar   to peep into; to show; to stick out; *refl* to appear at; to look out of (a door, window, etc.)

asombro   amazement

asombroso   astonishing, amazing

áspero   rough

aspiradora   vacuum cleaner

aspirar   to inhale, to breathe in; to aspire

astilla   splinter, chip

asunto   topic, subject; matter

atavío   dress, adornment; *pl* finery

atender   to pay attention, to take care of

aterrizaje *m*   landing

   pista de aterrizaje   landing strip

aterrizar   to land

aterrorizar   to terrify

atónito   astonished

atravesar   to cross, to go through

atrever   to dare

atreverse a   to venture to

atribuir   to attribute; to confer, to grant

atrio   atrium

atroz   atrocious, brutal, savage

audacia   audacity

audaz   audacious, daring, bold

aumentar   to augment, to increase

aun   even, yet

aún   yet, still

aureola   halo; aureole

autopista   freeway, turnpike

avanzar   to advance

avergonzado   ashamed, embarrassed

avergonzar   to shame, to embarrass; *refl* to be ashamed, to feel embarrassed

averiguar   to find out, to inquire into

avisar   to warn; to inform; to advise

ayuda   help

ayuntamiento   city hall

azafata   stewardess
azahar *m*   orange or lemon blossom
azotar   to flog, to beat, to whip

~ B ~

bailarín *m*   dancer
bajar   to go or come down; to bring or take down; to dismount
balcón *m*   balcony
balneario   bathing or beach resort
banqueta   *Mex* sidewalk
bañadera   bathtub
barba   beard
barca   boat
barco   boat, ship
barranca   ravine
barrer   to sweep
barroco   baroque
basura   garbage, trash
batalla   battle
batería   battery
   batería descargada   dead battery
bautizar   to baptize, to christen, to name
beca   scholarship
becerro   calf
beldad *f*   beauty
belleza   beauty
bendecir   to bless
bendición *f*   blessing
beneficio   benefit; profit
besar   to kiss
bicho   bug, insect
bigote *m*   mustache
billete *m*   bill
   billete de lotería   lottery ticket
billetera   wallet
bizco   cross-eyed
blancura   whiteness
boda   wedding
bodega   warehouse, storm room; wine cellar
bofetada   slap in the face
boina   beret
bombero   fireman
bombillo(a)   light bulb

bono   voucher, bond
borboteo   gushing, bubbling
bordar   to embroider
borde *m*   edge, side, fringe
borrachera   drunkenness
borrar   to erase; to fade away
borrasca   storm, tempest
bosque *m*   woods, forest
bostezar   to yawn
brazada   stroke (in swimming and rowing)
brillar   to gleam, to shine
brinco   jump, leap
bromear   to joke
brotar   to sprout, to bud; to break out, to appear; to spring (water)
brusco   rough
buey *m*   ox
bufanda   scarf
bufete *m*   lawyer's office
búho   owl
bulla   noise, uproar
bulto   bundle
burlarse de   to make fun of, to mock, to ridicule
buscar   to look for, to search for
búsqueda   search
buzón *m*   mailbox

~ C ~

caballería   chivalry
   novela de caballería   book of chivalry
caballero   gentleman; nobleman; knight
caballo   horse
cabaña   cabin
cabello   hair
caber   to fit
cabra   goat
cadena   chain
   cadena perpetua   life sentence, life imprisonment
cajero   cashier, teller
cajón *m*   big box or case; drawer
cal *f*   lime
calar   to pierce, to perforate; to soak, to drench

calentar to heat, to heat up

calificación mark, grade (on an examination)

callejón *m* alley

calzar to put on or wear shoes

camarero waiter

cambiar to change; to exchange; *refl* to change one's clothes

campamento camp

campeón *m* champion

campesino farmer, peasant

camposanto cemetery

canción *f* song

candela fire; light

candelero candlestick

candil *m* oil lamp

cansado tired

cansarse to get tired

cantante *mf* singer

cantina bar, tavern, canteen

canturrear or **canturriar** to hum, to sing in a low voice

caoba mahogany

caótico chaotic

capaz capable, competent

capitalino from the capital

capricho whim, caprice

captar to earn, to win (confidence, trust); to capture; to attract (attention)

carbón *m* coal, charcoal

carcajada outburst of laughter

cárcel *f* prison, jail

carecer to lack

carga load, burden; cargo

cargado loaded

cargar to charge (an electric battery); to load

caricia caress

cariño love, affection

carrera career; race, run

carretera highway

carroza hearse; float

casado married

casar to marry; *refl* to get married

casco hoof; helmet

castigar to punish

casulla chasuble (priest's vestment)

catarro cold, flu

catedral *f* cathedral

catedrático university professor

caudillo leader, chief

cautivar to captivate, to charm

cavar to dig; to dig up

cebada barley

ceder to cede, to yield; to transfer; to relinquish, to abandon, to give up

cegar to blind

ceguera blindness

celda cell (in a convent or prison)

celeste sky blue; celestial, heavenly

celo zeal; *pl* jealousy

celoso jealous

cenicero ashtray

ceniza ashes

cepillar to brush

cera wax

cerca fence; *adv* near

cercano nearby

cerciorarse to assure; to find out

cerrar to close

cerro hill

certero accurate, certain

certeza certainty

cerveza beer

cesar to stop, to cease

césped *m* lawn

cesto basket

chantaje *m* blackmail

chapalear to splash, to splatter

chapaleo splashing, gurgling

chaparro short

chapopote *m* tar; *Mex* chapapote

chapotear to splash

charco puddle

charol *m* patent leather

chaval *m* lad, youngster

chiflado *coll* crazy, mad, nuts

chiflido whistle

chispa spark

chiste *m* joke

chocar to collide, to crash

chorrete *m*   little stream

chorro   spurt, big stream

  avión a chorro   jet plane

chotear   to make fun of, to mock

churro   fritter

cicatrizar   to form a scar; to heal

ciclista *mf*   bicycle rider

ciclón *m*   storm

ciego   blind man; *adj* blind

cielo   heaven; sky

cinturón *m*   belt

cirugía   surgery

cirujano   surgeon

citar   to make an appointment with; to quote, to cite

ciudadanía   citizenship

claridad *f*   clarity, clearness

clavar   to nail

clavel *m*   carnation

clemencia   clemency, mercy

cobarde *mf*   coward

cobija   blanket, cover

cobrar   to collect; to charge; to cash (a check)

cocer; cocinar   to cook

cocinero   cook

codiciar   to covet, to desire

codicioso   greedy

coger   to pick; to seize; to grasp; to take

cojín *m*   cushion, pillow

cojo   lame

col *f*   cabbage

colar   to strain, to filter

colcha   blanket

colega *mf*   colleague

collar *m*   necklace

colmena   beehive

colocar   to place, to put (in place); to place or settle (a person in a job)

colorado   red

comadre *f*   name by which the mother of a child and the child's godmother call each other

comerciante *mf*   merchant, trader, dealer, businessman

compadecer   to feel sorry for, to pity, to sympathize with

compañero   companion

comparecer   to appear in court

compatriota *mf*   fellow countryman

competencia *f*   competition

complacer   to please

comprobar   to verify; to check; to prove

comunión *f*   communion

concurrencia   crowd; gathering; attendance

concurrido   with lots of people

concurrir   to attend; to gather

condenar   to condemn; to sentence

conejo   rabbit

conferir   to award, to grant

confianza   confidence, trust; self-confidence, assurance

confiar   to confide; to trust; to entrust

confiscar   to confiscate

conformarse   to be satisfied with

conjetura   conjecture, supposition

conocimiento   knowledge

conseguir   to get, to obtain

consentir   to consent, to agree to

consiguiente   resulting; consequent

  por consiguiente   consequently

consuelo   consolation, comfort

consultar   to consult

consultorio   doctor's office (or clinic)

contador *m*   accountant

contagiar   to infect with, to transmit

contar   to tell; to count

contemporizar   to temporize

contentarse   to be content or pleased

contestador automático *m*   answering machine

convenir   to be convenient; to suit; to agree

convidar   to invite

convivir   to live with, to live together

conyugal   conjugal

coraje *m*   anger; courage

corazón *m*   heart

cordillera   mountain range

coro   choir

correa   belt

corredizo   running, moving

correr   to run

corrido   *Mex* folk ballad
cortar   to cut, to cut into; to interrupt
cosecha   crop, harvest
coser   to sew
costilla   rib
costra   crust, scale, scab (of a wound)
costumbre *f*   custom; practice, habit
cotorra   parrot
crear   to create
crecer   to grow; to increase; to rise (as a river)
creciente *f*   flood; *adj* growing, crescent
crecimiento   growth
creer   to believe
crepúsculo   twilight, dusk
criar   to bring up, to raise
cristiano   Christian
cruz *f*   cross
cruzar   to cross
cuadra   block
cuadrarse   to stand at attention
cualquier   any
cuenta   bill, check; account
cuerda   cord, string
cuerdo   sane
cuerno   horn (of animals)
cuero   rawhide, leather
cuerpo   body
culebra   snake
culpa   blame, guilt
culpable   guilty
cumbre *f*   summit, crest, top
cumplir   to fulfill
   cumplir siete años   to reach the age of seven
cura *m*   priest; *f* cure

~ D ~

dado   die; *pl* dice
danés   Danish
daño   damage; harm
   hacerse daño   to hurt oneself
dar a luz   to give birth
dar con   to find, to meet

darse cuenta   to realize
dátil *m*   date (fruit)
dato   piece of information; fact; datum
deber   to owe; *m* duty
   deber de   ought to, must
decano   dean
décima   *Cuba* country ballad
declarar   to declare; to make known
   declararse   to propose, express one's love
dejar   to leave (something or someone behind one)
   dejar de   to stop or cease
delantal *m*   apron
delatar   to denounce
delgadez *f*   slenderness, thinness
demandar   to demand; to file suit against
demorar   to delay, to retard
denegar   to deny, to refuse
denotar   to denote
dependiente *m*   clerk
deplorar   to deplore, to lament, to regret
deporte *m*   sport
derecho   right, law; *adj* right; straight; upright
   derechos humanos   human rights
   no hay derecho   it's not fair, it's not right
derretir   to melt
derribar   to knock down
derrotar   to defeat
derrumbar   to collapse; to sink down; *refl* to collapse, cave in
desafiante   defiant
desamparar   to abandon
desarrollar   to develop, to promote; *refl* to develop oneself
desasosegado   restless
descalzo   barefoot
descartar   to discard
descifrar   to decipher
descomponer   to break down (a machine)
descompuesto   out of order; rude, impolite
descubierto   uncovered; discovered
descuidar   to neglect, overlook
desdén *m*   contempt, scorn, disdain
desdeñoso   disdainful, contemptuous

desfile *m*   parade

desgañitarse   to scream or yell at the top of one's voice

desgraciado   unfortunate, unlucky

desgreñado   disheveled, with unruly hair

deshacer   to undo

  deshacerse de   to get rid of

desheredar   to disinherit

designio   purpose, plan, intention

deslizar   to slide

deslumbrante   brilliant, dazzling, glaring; overwhelming, bewildering

deslumbrar   to dazzle, to blind; to baffle

desmayarse   to faint

desmerecer   to be inferior (to); to compare unfavorably; to be unworthy of

desmoronar   to crumble

desnudar   to undress; to strip

desnudo   naked, nude

despachar   to dispatch, send off

despacioso   slow, sluggish

despedida   farewell

despedir   to fire, to dismiss; *refl* to take leave, to say good-bye

despegar   to unglue; to separate; to detach; to take off (an airplane)

desperdiciar   to waste

despertar   to awaken, to wake up; to arouse, to stir up

desplazar   to displace; to move, to shift

despreciar   to despise, to disdain

desprecio   contempt, disdain, disregard

desprenderse   to detach, to become separated

destacar   to emphasize, to point out; to underline; *refl* to be distinguished, be outstanding or prominent

destino   destiny, fate

desventaja   disadvantage

desviar   to detour, to divert

detalle *m*   detail

detener   to stop, to detain; to arrest

deteriorado   damaged, worn out

deuda   debt

devolver   to return something

dibujar   to draw, to sketch, to outline

dictadura   dictatorship

diferir   to defer; to differ, to be different

dignidad *f*   dignity

diluviar   to pour rain

Dios   God

  por Dios   for heaven's sake

dirigir   to direct; to conduct; *refl* to go to, to address; to speak to

disco   disk; record

discusión *f*   discussion, argument

discutir   to argue; to discuss

diseñar   to design; to sketch

disfrutar   to enjoy

disimulado   dissembling, sly

disimular   to pretend; to cover up, to conceal; to overlook

disminuir   to diminish, to reduce

dispar   different, unequal, unmatched

disparar   to shoot, to fire; to throw, to hurl

disponer de   to dispose of

  disponerse a   to get ready to

distinto   different

disuadir   to discourage

diversión *f*   entertainment, amusement

divertir   to entertain; *refl* to have a good time

doblar   to turn

dolor *m*   pain, ache; grief

don *m*   natural ability

dondequiera   wherever, anywhere

dorado   golden, gilded

dormilón *m*   sleepyhead

dormitar   to doze

dudar   to doubt

dueño   owner

dulcero   candy vendor

dulzura   sweetness; gentleness, tenderness

duna   dune

durar   to last

～ E ～

echar   to throw; to throw out; to expel

  echarse a perder   to be ruined; to turn bad

eco   echo

ecuestre   equestrian

edad *f*   age

edificio   building
egoísta   selfish
ejemplar   exemplary
ejercer   to exercise; to exert; to practice a profession
ejército   army
elegir   to choose
elogiar   to praise
embarque *m*   shipment
embarrar   to smear, to splash with mud
embobado   stupefied, fascinated
emborracharse   to get drunk
embrollo   confusion, mess
embuste *m*   lie
embustero   liar
emigrar   to emigrate
empapado   soaking wet
empedrado   paved with cobblestones
empellón *m*   push, shove
empeñar   to pawn; *refl* to insist, to persist; to go into debt
  empeñarse en   to insist; to persist
emperador *m*   emperor
empleo   job, work
emplumado   feathered
empujar   to push
empujón *m*   push, shove
enamorado   in love
enamorar   to enamor; to woo, to court; *refl* to fall in love
encandilar   to blind; to dazzle
encantado   delighted, enchanted
encarcelar   to imprison, to incarcerate
encargarse   to be in charge of; to undertake
encender   to light
encerar   to wax
encerrar   to shut in, to lock up; to enclose, to contain, to include; *refl* to shut oneself up
encima   on top
encoger   to shrink
  encogerse de hombros   to shrug one's shoulders
encomendar   to entrust, to commend
encontrar   to find, to come across; to meet, to encounter
encuerarse   to strip, to undress

enderezar   to straighten; to put or stand up straight
endurecer   to harden, to make hard; to become hard or cruel
enfermarse   to become sick
enfermero   nurse
enfrentarse   to face, to confront; to come face to face
enfriar   to cool, to chill
engañar   to deceive
engordar   to fatten; to get fat
engrasar   to oil, to lubricate
enlagunado   covered with water
enlazar   to join, to link; to tie with cords or ribbons
enloquecer   to go mad
enmudecer   to become silent
enojarse   to get angry
enrevesado   nonsensical; complex, intricate
enriquecer   to enrich
enriquecimiento   enrichment
enrojecer   to blush, to turn red
enroscado   twisted
ensanchar   to widen; to enlarge, to extend
ensayar   to test, to try; to rehearse
ensayo   essay; rehearsal
enseñanza   teaching
enseñar   to teach; to show
ensombrecer   to darken; to dim
entender   to understand
entendimiento   understanding, comprehension
enterarse   to find out; to come to know
entero   entire, whole, complete
enterrar   to bury; to stick into
entierro   burial; funeral
entrada   entrance; entry; admission ticket
entrecerrado   half-closed
entregar   to hand over, to give; to deliver
entrenador *m*   coach, trainer
entretanto   meanwhile, in the meantime
entretener   to entertain, to amuse; *refl* to amuse onself; to be delayed
entrevista   interview
entullido   numb
envejecer   to get old, to age

envenenar   to poison
envidia   envy
envidiable   enviable
envidiar   to envy
envolver   to wrap
época   epoch, era
equipaje *m*   luggage
equipo   equipment, team
erigir   to build; to establish
erizado   bristly; spiky
erudición *f*   erudition, scholarship
esbelta   svelte, graceful, slender
escala   port of call; stopping point
  hacer escala   to stop over
escalón *m*   step of a stair
escampar   to stop raining
escarbar   to dig up
escenario   setting, background; stage, scenery
escoger   to choose, to select, to pick
escollo   reef
esconder   to hide, to conceal
escondrijo   hiding place
escritor *m*   writer
escudero   squire; shield bearer
escurrirse   to slide
esfera   sphere
esforzarse   to strive, to make an effort
espalda   back (of the body)
espectáculo   spectacle; sight; show, performance
esperanza   hope
espeso   thick
espiar   to spy
espuela   spur
espuma   foam, lather
esquiar   to ski
esquina   corner
establecer   to establish
estacionamiento   parking
estacionar   to park (a car)
estafador *m*   swindler, crook
estafar   to swindle; (legal) to defraud
estirar   to stretch
estrellado   with stars

estrenar   to present for the first time; *refl* to use for the first time
estropear   to spoil, to ruin; to mistreat
estruendo   noise, clamor
evitar   to avoid, to evade
evolucionar   to evolve, to develop
excusar   to excuse; *refl* to apologize; to excuse oneself
expatriarse   to go into exile
expectativa   expectation, hope
extranjero   foreigner, alien; *adj* foreign
extrañar   to miss; to wonder, to find strange
extrañeza   strangeness, oddness
extraño   strange, odd
extraviarse   to go astray; to get lost
extravío   losing one's way; going astray

～ F ～

fábrica   factory
factura   invoice
facultad *f*   faculty; school (of a university); faculty, authority
  facultades mentales   mental faculties
falda   foothill; skirt
falla   fault, defect, imperfection
faltar   to be missing; to be lacking
fantasma *m*   ghost
farmacéutico   pharmacist; *adj* pharmaceutical
fastidiar   to annoy, to bother
felicitar   to congratulate
fertilizante *m*   fertilizer
fidelidad *f*   faithfulness, fidelity; accuracy, precision
fiel   faithful
fijar   to fix; to set; *refl* to notice
fijo   fixed
fingir   to pretend
fiordo   fjord
firmamento   firmament, sky
firma   signature; business firm
firmar   to sign
flaco   thin, skinny
flamante   brand-new; bright, brilliant

flamboyán *m* royal poinciana (a tropical tree)

flan *m* baked custard

fleco fringe

florecer to flower, to blossom, to bloom

flotar to float

fluir to flow

foco light bulb

fofo spongy, soft

fondo bottom; back, rear

fortalecer to fortify, to strengthen

fortaleza fortress, stronghold; fortitude, strength

forzar to force

fósforo match

fracasar to fail

fraile *m* friar, monk

franco frank

fraternal brotherly

fregar to wash (dishes)

freír to fry

frenesí *m* frenzy; delirious excitement, rapture

frenético frantic

freno brake (of a car, etc.)

frialdad *f* coldness

frondoso leafy, luxuriant

frontera frontier, border

frotar to rub

fuego fire

fundador *m* founder

fundar to found

fuente *f* source

fusilar to execute by shooting (firing squad), to shoot

fusión *f* fusion; merging, union

~ G ~

gallina hen, chicken

gallinero chicken coop

gallo cock, rooster

gana desire

ganado cattle

ganador *m* winner

ganancia profit, gain

ganar to earn; to win

garganta throat

gastar to spend; to wear out

gaucho gaucho, cowboy

genial genial; brilliant, inspired

genio genius; temper; temperament, disposition

gente *f* people

geranio geranium

gerente *mf* manager

gesto gesture

gigante *m* giant; *adj* gigantic, huge

gigantesco gigantic, huge

gimnasia gymnastics

giro postal money order

gitano gypsy

gobernante *mf* ruler; *adj* governing, ruling

golondrina swallow

goloso sweet-toothed

golpe blow; knock

golpear to beat, to strike, to knock, to tap; *refl* to hurt oneself

gordura fatness

gota drop

gozar to enjoy

grabar to engrave; to record (music); to cut a record; *refl* to become engraved in the memory

gracioso funny, amusing; graceful

grado grade

graduarse to graduate

granizar to hail

granizo hail

grano grain; pimple

grasiento greasy, grubby, grimy

gravedad *f* gravity, seriousness

griego Greek

grillo cricket

grisáceo grayish

gritar to shout, to cry, to scream; to call out; to cry out

grito shout, cry, scream; outcry

grosería vulgarity, coarseness

grueso fat; thick

guagua   *Cuba & Puerto Rico* bus
guapo   handsome
guardar   to keep; to preserve; to put away; to guard
guerra   war
guiar   to guide

~ H ~

habitante *mf*   inhabitant
hacha   ax
hada   fairy
hallar   to find
hamaca   hammock
hecho   deed, fact
helado   ice cream
hembra   female
heredar   to inherit
heredero   heir
herencia   inheritance
herir   to wound
herradura   horseshoe
herramienta   tool
herrumbre *f*   rust
hiedra or **yedra**   ivy
hiel *f*   bitterness, gall
hielo   ice
hiena   hyena
hierro   iron
hincarse   to kneel, to kneel down
hincharse   to swell; to swell up, to fill up
hipódromo   racetrack
hipoteca   mortgage
hirviente   boiling
hoja   leaf
holgazán   lazy, indolent
hombro   shoulder
hondo   deep, profound
hondura   depth, profundity
honradez *f*   honesty, integrity
horario   timetable
hormiga   ant
horno   oven
hoyo   hole
huaraches *m pl*   *Mex* type of sandals
hueco   hole

huelga   strike
huella   trace, mark, footprint
huerta   orchard
hueso   bone
huésped *mf*   guest
huevo   egg
huir   to flee, to escape
humanista *mf*   humanist
humedecer   to dampen
humildad *f*   humility
humilde   humble
humo   smoke
hundimiento   sinking
hundir   to sink
húngaro   Hungarian; *fig* gypsy
huracán *m*   hurricane
hurtar   to steal; to eat away

~ I ~

iglesia   church
igualdad *f*   equality; uniformity
impasible   impassive, unfeeling
implacable   inexorable, relentless
imponer   to impose; to command, to order
impresionante   impressive
impuesto   tax
incapaz   incapable, unable, incompetent
incendiar   to set on fire
incienso   incense
inconmovible   firm, unyielding
incontenible   uncontainable; irrepressible
incredulidad *f*   incredulity, disbelief
increíble   incredible
indeleble   indelible
índice *m*   index; indication, sign; index finger
índole *f*   nature, character
indolente   lazy
indumentaria   clothing
ineludible   unavoidable
inequívoco   unmistakable, certain
inexorable   inexorable, unyielding, relentless
infalible   infallible
infarto   heart attack
influir   to influence
informática *f*   computer science

ingresar to enter, to become a member (of)
　ingresar en la universidad to enter the university (as a student)
ininteligible uninteligible
injusticia injustice, unfairness
inmovilizar to immobilize
inolvidable unforgettable
inquietud *f* uneasiness, restlessness
insistir en to insist on
insoportable insufferable, unbearable
insuperable insurmountable, unbeatable
intercambiable interchangeable
interrogar to question
intervenir to take part in, to participate; to intervene, to intercede
intimidar to threaten, to frighten; to intimidate
inundarse to become flooded
invadir to invade
irrumpir to burst in

jabón *m* soap
jaqueca headache, migraine
jarra pitcher
jazmín *m* jasmine
jesuita *m* Jesuit
jinete *m* horseman
joya jewel
juanete *m* bunion
jubilarse to retire (from work)
juez *m* judge
juguete *m* toy
juguetón playful
junto together, connected
　junto a next to
jurado jury
jurar to swear, to declare upon oath
justicia justice
juventud *f* youth

laberinto labyrinth
labor *f* labor, work

lacio limp, lifeless, flaccid, languid; straight (hair)
ladrar to bark
ladrillo brick
ladrón *m* thief
lágrima tear
laguna lagoon
lámpara lamp
lana wool
lanzar to throw
largarse to go away
lástima pity, compassion
lastimarse to hurt oneself; to get hurt
lavaplatos *m* dishwasher
lealtad *f* loyalty
lecho bed
lechón *m* young pig
lectura reading
lejano far away
lengua tongue, language
lento slow
leña firewood
letras *f pl* literature; liberal arts
　campo de las letras field of literature
letrero sign, poster
levantamiento uprising
levantar to raise, to pick up, to lift; *refl* to get up
leve light; trivial, unimportant
ley *f* law
librar to free; to save, to spare
ligado tied, bound, linked
llaga ulcer, sore
llama flame; llama (South American ruminant)
llano flatland; plain; level, flat, even
llanta tire
llanto weeping, crying
llanura plain, prairie
llave *f* key
llegar to arrive
llevar to take; to carry, to transport; to wear, to have on (clothes); *refl* to take away; to take with one
　llevar a cabo to carry out
llorar to cry

llover   to rain
lloviznar   to drizzle
loco   crazy
locutor *m*   radio announcer; commentator
lodo   mud
lograr   to achieve; to attain, to obtain
loza   dishes (dinnerware)
luchar   to fight; to struggle
lucir   to show, to display; to look
luminoso   bright
luna   moon
luto   mourning
luz *f*   light

~ M ~

maceta   flowerpot
madrastra   stepmother
madriguera   burrow, hole (of a rabbit, etc.)
madrina   godmother
madrugada   dawn, daybreak
  de madrugada   early, at daybreak
madurez *f*   maturity
majestuoso   majestic
maldecir   to curse, to damn
manantial *m*   spring of water; source
mancha   stain, spot (of oil, dirt, etc.)
manchar   to mar; to stain; to patch in a
  different color
mandado   errand
manejar   to drive
manejo   handling
manera   way, manner
manía   habit, whim, fad
manicomio   insane asylum
maniobra   maneuver, move
manojo   handful, bunch
manteca   lard
mañoso   cunning, tricky
maquillarse   to put on makeup
marfil *m*   ivory
mariposa   butterfly
marisco   seafood
Marte   Mars
masajista *mf*   masseur, masseuse

mata   bush, shrub, plant
matadero   slaughterhouse
mate *m*   South American herb, tea-like
  infusion
mayoría   majority
mecanógrafo   typist
mecer   to rock, to swing; to move to and fro
medir   to measure
mejorarse   to get better
melena   long, loose hair
mellizo   twin
mensaje *m* message
mentado   aforementioned
mentir   to lie
mentira   lie
merecer   to deserve
mesón *m*   inn
meter   to put in, to insert; *refl* to meddle; to
  get into; to enter
mezclar   to mix
mezquita   mosque
miedo   fear
miel *f*   honey
mimar   to pamper, to spoil; to pet, to fondle
mirada   look, glance
misa   Mass
mohín *m*   gesture, face
mohoso   rusty
mojar   to wet, to soak, to moisten; *refl* to get
  wet, soaked, moistened
molestar   to bother, to annoy
molino   mill
  molino de viento   windmill
monaguillo   altar boy
monedero   change purse
monja   nun
mono   monkey; *adj* cute
montar   to ride (a horse, bicycle, etc.)
montón *m*   heap, pile
morder   to bite
moribundo   dying
morir   to die
mortificar   to annoy, to bother
mosca   fly
mostrador *m*   counter

mostrar to show
motín *m* mutiny
mover to move
movilizar to mobilize
muchedumbre *f* crowd
mudarse to move; to change (clothes)
mudo dumb, mute
muerte *f* death
  pena de muerte death sentence
muestra sample, specimen; proof; demonstration
mujer *f* wife; woman
multitud *f* crowd, multitude
muñeca wrist; doll
muro wall; fence
musgo moss
muslo thigh

~ N ~

nadar to swim
natación *f* swimming
navaja switchblade; razor blade
nave *f* ship
  nave espacial spaceship
navegante *mf* navigator, sailor
navegar to sail, to navigate
neblina fog
necio foolish, stupid
negar to deny; to refuse; *refl* to decline to do
negocio business
nicaragüense from Nicaragua, Nicaraguan
niebla fog, mist, haze
nieve *f* snow
niñez *f* childhood
nobleza nobleness, nobility
nombramiento appointment
nombrar to appoint, to elect, to name
nopal *m* prickly pear
nota note; grade (in exam)
nublado cloudy
nublarse to become overcast or cloudy
nublazón *f* covered with clouds
nuca nape of the neck
nuera daughter-in-law

~ O ~

obedecer to obey
obispo bishop
obligatorio mandatory, compulsory
obra work; work (book, painting, etc.)
obrero worker, laborer
ocote torchwood (tropical American tree)
oculista *mf* eye doctor
ocultar to hide, to conceal
odiar to hate
odio hate
ojo eye
ola wave
oler to smell
olla pot
olor *m* smell
olvidar to forget
ómnibus *m* bus
oponer to oppose
oponerse a to be opposed to
oprimir to oppress
orar to pray
oreja outer ear
orgullo pride
orgulloso proud
orilla bank, border, edge; shoulder of a road
ortografía spelling
oscurecer to become dark
ovacionar to give an ovation to, to applaud, to acclaim
oveja sheep

~ P ~

pabellón *m* pavilion, canopy
pacifista *mf* pacifist
padecer to suffer; to endure
padrastro stepfather
padrino godfather
paella Spanish rice dish with seafood and chicken
paisaje *m* landscape
paisano fellow countryman

pájaro   bird
pala   shovel
palangana   washbasin
palidecer   to turn pale, to grow pale
palidez *f*   paleness, pallor
pampa   extensive grassy plain
pantalla   screen
pañuelo   handkerchief
papel *m*   role, part; paper
paquete *m*   package
paraguas *m*   umbrella
parar   to stop; *refl* to stand up
parecer   to look like, to seem; *refl* to look
   alike, to resemble one another
pareja   pair, couple
parpadeo   blinking
párpado   eyelid
partidario   supporter, follower
pasaje *m*   fare (price charged to transport a
   person)
pasajero   passenger, traveler; *adj* passing,
   transient
pasearse   to stroll, to walk; to take a ride; to
   go for a ride
paseo   walk, stroll; ride
paso   step
   abrirse paso   to get through
   apretar el paso   to hasten one's step
pastel *m*   pie, cake, pastry
pastor *m*   shepherd
pata   leg of an animal
paterno   paternal; from the male line
patinar   to skate
patria   native land; country
patrimonio   patrimony; heritage
payaso   clown
peatón *m*   pedestrian
pecado   sin
pecador *m*   sinner
pecho   breast; chest
pedalear   to pedal
pedido   order, purchase
pedir   to ask for; to order something
pedrada   blow with a stone
pedregoso   stony

pegajoso   sticky
pegar   to hit, to beat; to stick, to paste, to
   glue; to move or push close together; to pass
   on (a disease, bad habit, an opinion, etc.);
   to fire (a shot)
peinado   hairdo
peinar   to comb; *refl* to comb one's hair
pelar   to peel; *refl* to get a haircut
pelear   to fight, to struggle; to contend, to
   quarrel; *refl* to have a disagreement
peligro   danger
peligroso   dangerous
pelota   ball
peltre *m*   pewter
pena   embarrassment, shyness; sorrow; pain
   es una pena   it is a pity
   valer la pena   to be worthwhile
pensamiento   thought; idea
percatarse   to realize, to become aware
percibir   to perceive, to sense; to collect, to
   receive
perdición *f*   ruin, perdition
perdonar   to forgive
perezoso   lazy
perfil *m*   profile
periódico   newspaper
perjuicio   damage, injury
permanecer   to remain
perseguir   to persecute; to pursue, to chase
persignarse   to make the sign of the cross
personaje *m*   character (in literature, theater)
persuasivo   persuasive
pesado   heavy
pesadumbre *f*   grief, pain, sorrow
pesar   to weigh; *nm* sorrow, grief
pescado   fish
pescador *m*   fisherman
pescar   to fish; to catch
pésimo   very bad, terrible
pestaña   eyelash
petróleo   oil
picante   spicy
picar   to puncture, to pierce; to sting, to bite
   (insect, snake); to chop; to itch; to decay (a
   tooth)

picaresco picaresque; mischievous
pico peak, summit; beak (of bird)
pie *m* caption (under a photo or an illustration); foot
piel *f* skin
píldora pill
pináculo pinnacle, top
pincel *m* artist's paint brush
pintura paint; painting
piña pineapple
pisar to step on
piso floor
planta plant
plantar to set (foot) on; to plant
platino platinum
plato dish, plate
pleito fight
pleuresía pleurisy
pliegue *m* fold, pleat
plomo lead
pluma feather; pen
pobreza poverty
poco small amount;
  por poco almost, nearly
podar to prune
poderoso powerful
podrido rotten
pomo bottle
ponerse to put on
portar to carry, to bear; *refl* to behave
pos; en pos de after; in pursuit of
postal *f* postcard
postre *m* dessert
pozo pit, well, hole
prado meadow, field
precavido cautious, careful
preceder to precede, to go before
precisar to need
precolombino pre-Columbian
precoz precocious, advanced
predominar to predominate, to prevail
preguntón *m* nosey, (one) always asking questions
premiar to reward; to award a prize to
premio prize

prenda garment; jewel
prender to catch; to pin up; to seize; to turn on; to start (a motor)
preocuparse to worry
preparativos *pl* preparations
preponderancia preponderance, superiority
prescindir to do without
presentir to have a presentiment of something
préstamo loan
prestar to lend, to loan
presupuesto estimate, budget
prevalecer to prevail
prever to foresee
principio beginning
prisa haste, hurry
proceder to proceed, to go on; *m* conduct, behavior
proclama proclamation, announcement
profesar to profess; to practice
progenie *f* progency; descent
prohibir to forbid
prójimo fellow man; neighbor
prontitud *f* promptness
proporcionar to provide, to supply
proyectarse to project, to stick out
prueba trial, test; proof, evidence; sample, piece to be tested; ordeal
pudor *m* modesty, chastity
puente *m* bridge
puesta (de sol) sunset
puesto job, position
pulcro neat, tidy
pulir to polish
pulla caustic or cutting remark
pulmón *m* lung
pulque *m Mex* a drink (the fermented juice of the maguey plant)
pululante abundant, teaming
puntiagudo sharp-pointed
puntualizar to report or describe in detail
puño fist; handful; cuff (of a sleeve); handle (of an umbrella, cane, etc.)
pupila pupil of the eye
púrpura purple

～ Q ～

quebrar to break; *refl* to break

quechua *m* South American Indian; language of the Quechua Indians

quedar to be located

quedar en to agree; *refl* to remain, to stay, to be left behind

quehacer *m* chore, work, task

quejarse to complain; to groan, to moan

quemar to burn

quemazón *f* burning, fire

quiebra bankruptcy

quitar to take off, to remove

～ R ～

rabia anger, rage; rabies

radical *f* (grammar) stem

radiografía X-ray

ráfaga gust of wind

raíz *f* root; (grammar) stem

rama branch

ramillete *m* bouquet, cluster

ramo bouquet

ranchería settlement; camp

raro rare; odd, strange

rara vez seldom

rascacielos *m* skyscraper

rasgo characteristic

rastro vestige, trace, sign; track; store or market of secondhand goods; slaughterhouse

rato while, short time

a cada rato every now and then

a ratos at times

largo rato a long while

rayo ray

razón *f* reason

realizar to accomplish, to fulfill; to carry out

reanudar to resume

rebatir to refute, to rebut

rebelarse to revolt, to rebel

rebosar to overflow with; to abound

rebotar to bounce

recado message

recargar to overload; to charge extra; to recharge

receta recipe

rechazar to reject, to repudiate

recién recently

recinto space, area

reclamar to claim; to demand

recobrar to recover, to recuperate; to regain

recodo bend

recoger to pick up; to collect, to gather

recompensa reward

reconocer to recognize; to admit, to acknowledge

reconocimiento recognition

recordar to remember; to remind

recorrer to run through; to look over; to cross

recostarse to lean, to recline; to lie down (for a short while)

recrearse to amuse oneself

recreo recreation time at school

rector *m* president (of a university)

recuerdo memory, recollection, remembrance; *pl* regards, greetings

red *f* net; netting

reemplazar to replace

reflejar to reflect; to show; *refl* to be reflected

reflejo glare, reflection

refugiarse to take refuge

regalar to give, to treat

regalía bonus, gratuity

regañar to scold

regar to water

regazo lap

regio royal, regal

registrar to examine, to inspect, to search; to record

regresar to come back

rehusar to refuse, to turn down

reírse to laugh

reja railing, iron grillwork

relajado relaxed

relampaguear to lighten

relegar to put aside, to forget

reluciente shining
relucir to shine, to glitter; to excel
remilgoso finicky
remordimiento remorse
renacer to be reborn
rendija small crack
rendir to render; *refl* to surrender
renunciar to resign; to give up; to renounce
reñir to fight
reo *mf* criminal, offender, accused, defendant
reparo objection
repartir to distribute; to deliver
repasar to review, to go over
repente; de repente suddenly
repiquetear to ring gaily, to toll
repleto full
repudiar to repudiate
requemar to burn; to overcook, to roast too much
requisito requirement
res *f* beef
resbalar to slip
resbaloso slippery
reseco very dry
resfriado; resfrío head cold
resfriarse to catch a cold
resignarse to resign oneself
resollar to breathe noisily
respirar to breathe
resplandecer to shine, to glitter
resplandor *m* glare
responso response (prayer)
respuesta answer
restricción *f* restriction; restraint; limitation
retar to challenge, to dare
reticente deceptive, misleading; noncommital
retraído withdrawn, kept aloof from
retrasarse to delay; to be late; to be behind time
retratar to photograph
retrato portrait; portrait painting or photograph; image, exact likeness
retumbar to resound, to boom
reunirse to get together

revelar to reveal; to develop (a photograph)
revisar to revise, to check
revolcarse to roll on the ground
revolotear to flutter
rey *m* king
  Reyes Magos Three Wise Men
rezar to pray
rezo prayer
rezongón grumbling
rico rich
rincón *m* (inside) corner; remote place
risa laugh
robar to steal
rocío dew
rodar to roll
rodear to surround
rodilla knee
rogar to beg, to implore; to pray
rompecabezas *m* jigsaw puzzle
romper to break
ronco hoarse
rostro face
rozar to rub
ruego request, petition, plea
ruido noise
rumbo (a) en route to, on the way to

~ S ~

sábana bed sheet
sabor *m* taste, flavor
sabroso delicious, tasty
sacacorchos *m* corkscrew
sacar to take out
  sacarse la lotería to win the lottery
sacerdote *m* priest
sacudir to shake, to jolt
salpicar to splash
saltar to jump, to leap
salud *f* health
saludable healthy
saludar to greet, to salute
salvavidas *m* lifesaver; *mf* lifeguard
sandía watermelon
sangría wine and fruit drink

sarape *m* Mexican shawl or blanket
sastre *m* tailor
sauce *m* willow tree
secar to dry; to dry up
seco dry; dried up
sed *f* thirst
seguir to go on, to continue; to follow; to pursue
seguridad *f* assurance
seguro insurance
selva jungle; forest, woods
semblante *m* face; look, appearance
sembrar to plant; to seed; to sow
semilla seed
sencillez *f* simplicity, naturalness
seno bosom, heart; refuge
sentido sense; meaning; judgment
   los cinco sentidos the five senses
   perder el sentido to lose conciousness
   sin sentido meaningless
sentimiento feeling, sentiment
sentir to feel
señal *f* signal, sign
señalar to point out; to point at; to put a mark or sign on
sepultar to bury
serrucho handsaw
servible usable
servidumbre *f* servants, domestic help
siervo slave;
   siervo de Dios servant of God
siesta afternoon nap
siglo century
siguiente following, next
similitud *f* similarity
sindicato labor union
sinvergüenza *mf* scoundrel, rascal
sitio place
sobrar to have extra
sobrenatural supernatural
sobresalir to stand out
sobresaltado frightened
sobrevenir to happen, to take place
sobrevivir to survive
socio partner, member

socorrer to help, to aid
solar *m* lot, yard
soler to be accustomed to, to be used to
soldado soldier
soledad *f* solitude, loneliness
solicitud *f* application; request, petition
soltar to untie, to loosen; to let go, to free
soltero single, unmarried
solterón *m* old bachelor
solterona old maid
soltura ease, confidence, assurance
solucionar to solve, to resolve
sombra shade, shadow, darkness
sombrilla umbrella
sombrío somber, gloomy
sonar to strike (the hour); to sound
sondear to explore; to sound out
sonreír to smile
sonrisa smile
soñar to dream
soplar to blow; to blow away
soplido puff; blast of air
sordo deaf; muffled, dull
sorprender to surprise
sosegado calm, quiet, peaceful
sosiego calm, tranquility, quiet
sospecha suspicion
sotana cassock
sótano basement, cellar
suave soft
sublevarse to revolt
subrayar to underline; to emphasize
suceder to happen; to occur; to follow
sucursal *f* branch office
sudor *m* sweat
sueldo salary
suelo floor
suelto loose, free; at large
suerte *f* luck
suicidarse to commit suicide
sujeto fellow, individual; person; (grammar) subject
sumiso submissive, obedient
superar to overcome
suplente *mf* substitute, deputy, replacement

suplicar   to beg, to implore

surgir   to spring up, to arise; to present itself, to appear

suroeste *m*   southwest

suspender   to interrupt, to stop temporarily; to suspend, to hang up

suspirar   to sigh; to long for

sustantivo   (grammar) noun

sutil   subtle

~ T ~

tacaño   stingy

tallar   to carve

tamaño   size

tamarindo   tamarind; tamarind tree

tamboril *m*   small drum

tamborileo   the sound of a drum

taquilla   box office

tardar   to be long; to be late; to take a long time

tarea   task, homework

techo   roof, ceiling

tejado   roof; tile roof

tejer   to weave, to knit, to spin

telaraña   cobweb

telón *m*   drop curtain in the theater

temblar   to tremble, to shake

temer   to be afraid

temor *m*   fear

templado   lukewarm; temperate

tender   to extend; *refl* to stretch out; to hang (clothes) up or out to dry

tentar   to tempt

teñir   to dye

terceto   tercet; trio

ternura   tenderness

terremoto   earthquake

terso   smooth, glossy

tesoro   treasure

testigo   witness

tibieza   warmth

tibio   lukewarm, tepid

tientas; a tientas   gropingly

tierno   tender; soft; delicate

tinta   ink

tipejo   (*derog*) ridiculous little fellow

tirar   to throw

   tirar de   to pull

tiro   shot, shooting

títere *m*   puppet, marionette

toalla   towel

tobillo   ankle

tocadiscos *m*   record player

tocar   to touch; to play (musical instrument); to ring, to toll (bell); to be one's turn

tontería   foolishness, silliness

tonto   silly, foolish, stupid

torneado   shapely

torno   potter's wheel

   en torno a   about, in connection with

torre *f*   tower

torrencial   torrential

tortilla   omelette; *Mex* thin cornmeal pancake

toser   to cough

traer   to bring; to carry

traficante *mf*   trader, dealer

tragar   to swallow

traicionar   to betray

traidor *m*   traitor

traje *m*   dress, suit, gown; costume

   traje a la medida   made-to-order suit or dress

trampolín *m*   diving board; springboard

transcurrir   to go by, to pass, to elapse

transparencia   transparency

trapo   cloth, rag

tras   after; behind

trasladar   to transfer, to move; *refl* to move, to change residence

trasplantar   to transplant

trayectoria   path

trecho   stretch (of space or time)

trepar   to climb

trigo   wheat

trinar   to trill, to warble

trinchera   trench

triunfo   triumph

tronar   to thunder

tronco   trunk

tropezar   to stumble; to run into; to encounter

tropezar con   to bump into

tropezón *m*   stumbling

trusa   *Cuba* bathing suit

tuerto   one-eyed man

tule *m*   bulrush (a reedlike plant)

tumbarse   to lie down

tupido   dense, thick

turbar   to disturb, to upset; to confuse; to embarrass

~ U ~

ubicar   to locate, to situate; *refl* to be located

ultrajar   to offend, to affront, to insult

utilidad *f*   usefulness; profit, earnings

~ V ~

vaciar   to empty

vacío   emptiness; empty space; *adj* empty

vajilla   table setting, set of dishes

valer   to be worth

valija   suitcase; mailbag

vanidad *f*   vanity

vaquero   cowboy

varón *m*   male

vasco   Basque

vecindad *f*   neighborhood

vecindario   neighborhood

vecino   neighbor; *adj* neighboring, nearby

vedar   to prohibit, to forbid

vejez *f*   old age

velar   to watch; to watch over

velocidad *f*   speed

vengar   to avenge; *refl* to take revenge

ventaja   advantage

ventanilla   window (in airplane, railway coach, car, bank counter, etc.); ticket window (of box office, ticket office)

verduras *pl*   vegetables, greens

vergüenza   shame, bashfulness

vestuario   wardrobe, clothes

vez *f*   time

alguna que otra vez   occasionally, once in a while

de una vez   once and for all

de vez en cuando   from time to time

en vez de   instead of

rara vez   seldom

una y otra vez   again and again

vicuña   vicuna (South American ruminant)

videocasetera *f*   VCR

vidrio   glass

vigoroso   vigorous, strong

villancico   Christmas carol

virreinal   viceregal

virreinato   viceroyalty

vista   view

viudo   widower

vivaquear   to bivouac, to camp

vivencia   personal experience

volante *m*   steering wheel

volcar   to turn over, to overturn

voltereta   tumble, somersault

volverse   to become

vuelta   turn; return

a la vuelta   on returning; around the corner

dar una vuelta   to take a walk, stroll

darse vuelta   to turn around

~ Y ~

yedra; hiedra   ivy

yegua   mare

yermo   barren

yerno   son-in-law

~ Z ~

zafar   to rip; to loosen; to untie

zafarrancho   rumpus, quarrel

zaguán *m*   vestibule

zorro   fox

zozobra   uneasiness, anxiety, worry

Apéndice

▲ Verbs with spelling changes

▲ Irregular verbs

▲ List of irregular verbs

▲ Synopsis of a verb conjugation

▲ Practical vocabulary — false cognates

Verbs with spelling changes

Infinitive	Preterite	Present subjunctive	Imperative
1. Verbs ending in -car. Change **c** to **qu** before **e.**			
sacar	saqué	saque saques	saque saquemos saquen
buscar, tocar, colocar, dedicar, evocar, acercarse, chocar			
2. Verbs ending in -gar. Change **g** to **gu** before **e.**			
llegar	llegué	llegue llegues	llegue lleguemos lleguen
pagar, jugar, obligar, negar, regar, plegar, rogar			
3. Verbs ending in -zar. Change **z** to **c** before **e.**			
cruzar	crucé	cruce cruces	cruce crucemos crucen
empezar, gozar, alcanzar, avanzar, cazar, forzar, rezar			

	Present Indicative	Present subjunctive	Imperative
1. Verbs that end in -cer or -cir preceded by a consonant . Change **c** to **z** before **a, o.**			
vencer	venzo	venza venzas	venza venzamos venzan
convencer, ejercer, torcer, esparcir			

	Present Indicative	Present subjunctive	Imperative
2. Verbs that end in **-cer** preceded by a vowel add a **z** in the first person singular of the present indicative and present subjunctive.			
conocer	conozco	conozca	conozca
establecer, parecer, ofrecer, agradecer			
3. Verbs ending in **-ger** or **-gir**. Change **g** to **j** before **a, o**.			
escoger	escojo	escoja	escoja
		escojas	escojamos
			escojan
coger, recoger, proteger, regir, dirigir, elegir, corregir, fingir			
4. Verbs ending in **-guir**. Change **gu** to **g** before **a, o**.			
seguir	sigo	siga	siga
		sigas	sigamos
			sigan
conseguir, distinguir, perseguir			

	Preterite	Imperfect subjunctive	Present participle
1. Some verbs change the unstressed **i** to **y** when it goes between vowels.			
leer	leyó	leyera	leyendo
	leyeron	leyeras	
caer, creer, proveer			
2. Verbs with the stem ending in **ll** or **ñ** drop the **i** of some endings.			
bullir (*to boil*)	bulló	bullera	bullendo
	bulleron	bulleras	
reñir	riñó	riñera	riñendo
	riñeron	riñeras	
teñir, bruñir, ceñir, gruñir			

Irregular verbs

Infinitive *Present* *participle* *Past participle*	*Present*	*Preterite*	INDICATIVE *Imperfect*	*Future*	*Conditional*
1. andar andando andado	ando andas anda andamos andáis andan	anduve anduviste anduvo anduvimos anduvisteis anduvieron	andaba andabas andaba andábamos andabais andaban	andaré andarás andará andaremos andaréis andarán	andaría andarías andaría andaríamos andaríais andarían
2. caber cabiendo cabido	quepo cabes cabe cabemos cabéis caben	cupe cupiste cupo cupimos cupisteis cupieron	cabía cabías cabía cabíamos cabíais cabían	cabré cabrás cabrá cabremos cabréis cabrán	cabría cabrías cabría cabríamos cabríais cabrían
3. caer cayendo caído	caigo caes cae caemos caéis caen	caí caíste cayó caímos caísteis cayeron	caía caías caía caíamos caíais caían	caeré caerás caerá caeremos caeréis caerán	caería caerías caería caeríamos caeríais caerían
4. conducir conduciendo conducido	conduzco conduces conduce conducimos conducís conducen	conduje condujiste condujo condujimos condujisteis condujeron	conducía conducías conducía conducíamos conducíais conducían	conduciré conducirás conducirá conduciremos conduciréis conducirán	conduciría conducirías conduciría conduciríamos conduciríais conducirían
5. conocer conociendo conocido	conozco conoces conoce conocemos conocéis conocen	conocí conociste conoció conocimos conocisteis conocieron	conocía conocías conocía conocíamos conocíais conocían	conoceré conocerás conocerá conoceremos conoceréis conocerán	conocería conocerías conocería conoceríamos conoceríais conocerían

SUBJUNCTIVE		IMPERATIVE	
Present	*Imperfect*	*Affirmative*	*Negative*
ande	anduviera (anduviese)		
andes	anduvieras (-ses)	anda	no andes
ande	anduviera (-se)	ande	no ande
andemos	anduviéramos (-semos)	andemos	no andemos
andéis	anduvierais (-seis)	andad	no andéis
anden	anduvieran (-sen)	anden	no anden
quepa	cupiera (cupiese)		
quepas	cupieras (-ses)	cabe	no quepas
quepa	cupiera (-se)	quepa	no quepa
quepamos	cupiéramos (-semos)	quepamos	no quepamos
quepáis	cupierais (-seis)	cabed	no quepáis
quepan	cupieran (-sen)	quepan	no quepan
caiga	cayera (cayese)		
caigas	cayeras (-ses)	cae	no caigas
caiga	cayera (-se)	caiga	no caiga
caigamos	cayéramos (-semos)	caigamos	no caigamos
caigáis	cayerais (-seis)	caed	no caigáis
caigan	cayeran (-sen)	caigan	no caigan
conduzca	condujera (condujese)		
conduzcas	condujeras (-ses)	conduce	no conduzcas
conduzca	condujera (-se)	conduzca	no conduzca
conduzcamos	condujéramos (-semos)	conduzcamos	no conduzcamos
conduzcáis	condujerais (-seis)	conducid	no conduzcáis
conduzcan	condujeran (-sen)	conduzcan	no conduzcan
conozca	conociera (conociese)		
conozcas	conocieras (-ses)	conoce	no conozcas
conozca	conociera (-se)	conozca	no conozca
conozcamos	conociéramos (-semos)	conozcamos	no conozcamos
conozcáis	conocierais (-seis)	conoced	no conozcáis
conozcan	conocieran (-sen)	conozcan	no conozcan

Infinitive Present participle Past participle	INDICATIVE				
	Present	*Preterite*	*Imperfect*	*Future*	*Conditional*
6. contar contando contado	cuento cuentas cuenta contamos contáis cuentan	conté contaste contó contamos contasteis contaron	contaba contabas contaba contábamos contabais contaban	contaré contarás contará contaremos contaréis contarán	contaría contarías contaría contaríamos contaríais contarían
7. dar dando dado	doy das da damos dais dan	di diste dio dimos disteis dieron	daba dabas daba dábamos dabais daban	daré darás dará daremos daréis darán	daría darías daría daríamos daríais darían
8. decir diciendo dicho	digo dices dice decimos decís dicen	dije dijiste dijo dijimos dijisteis dijeron	decía decías decía decíamos decíais decían	diré dirás dirá diremos diréis dirán	diría dirías diría diríamos diríais dirían
9. dormir durmiendo dormido	duermo duermes duerme dormimos dormís duermen	dormí dormiste durmió dormimos dormisteis durmieron	dormía dormías dormía dormíamos dormíais dormían	dormiré dormirás dormirá dormiremos dormiréis dormirán	dormiría dormirías dormiría dormiríamos dormiríais dormirían
10. entender entendiendo entendido	entiendo entiendes entiende entendemos entendéis entienden	entendí entendiste entendió entendimos entendisteis entendieron	entendía entendías entendía entendíamos entendíais entendían	entenderé entenderás entenderá entenderemos entenderéis entenderán	entendería entenderías entendería entenderíamos entenderíais entenderían
11. estar estando estado	estoy estás está estamos estáis están	estuve estuviste estuvo estuvimos estuvisteis estuvieron	estaba estabas estaba estábamos estabais estaban	estaré estarás estará estaremos estaréis estarán	estaría estarías estaría estaríamos estaríais estarían

SUBJUNCTIVE		IMPERATIVE	
Present	*Imperfect*	*Affirmative*	*Negative*
cuente	contara (contase)		
cuentes	contaras (-ses)	cuenta	no cuentes
cuente	contara (-se)	cuente	no cuente
contemos	contáramos (-semos)	contemos	no contemos
contéis	contarais (-seis)	contad	no contéis
cuenten	contaran (-sen)	cuenten	no cuenten
dé	diera (diese)		
des	dieras (-ses)	da	no des
dé	diera (-se)	dé	no dé
demos	diéramos (-semos)	demos	no demos
deis	dierais (-seis)	dad	no deis
den	dieran (-sen)	den	no den
diga	dijera (dijese)		
digas	dijeras (-ses)	di	no digas
diga	dijera (-se)	diga	no diga
digamos	dijéramos (-semos)	digamos	no digamos
digáis	dijerais (-seis)	decid	no digáis
digan	dijeran (-sen)	digan	no digan
duerma	durmiera (durmiese)		
duermas	durmieras (-ses)	duerme	no duermas
duerma	durmiera (-se)	duerma	no duerma
durmamos	durmiéramos (-semos)	durmamos	no durmamos
durmáis	durmierais (-seis)	dormid	no durmáis
duerman	durmieran (-sen)	duerman	no duerman
entienda	entendiera (entendiese)		
entiendas	entendieras (-ses)	entiende	no entiendas
entienda	entendiera (-se)	entienda	no entienda
entendamos	entendiéramos (-semos)	entendamos	no entendamos
entendáis	entendierais (-seis)	entended	no entendáis
entiendan	entendieran (-sen)	entiendan	no entiendan
esté	estuviera (estuviese)		
estés	estuvieras (-ses)	está	no estés
esté	estuviera (-se)	esté	no esté
estemos	estuviéramos (-semos)	estemos	no estemos
estéis	estuvierais (-seis)	estad	no estéis
estén	estuvieran (-sen)	estén	no estén

Infinitive *Present* *participle* *Past participle*			**INDICATIVE**		
	Present	*Preterite*	*Imperfect*	*Future*	*Conditional*
12. haber habiendo habido	he has ha hemos habéis han	hube hubiste hubo hubimos hubisteis hubieron	había habías había habíamos habíais habían	habré habrás habrá habremos habréis habrán	habría habrías habría habríamos habríais habrían
13. hacer haciendo hecho	hago haces hace hacemos hacéis hacen	hice hiciste hizo hicimos hicisteis hicieron	hacía hacías hacía hacíamos hacíais hacían	haré harás hará haremos haréis harán	haría harías haría haríamos haríais harían
14. huir huyendo huido	huyo huyes huye huimos huís huyen	huí huiste huyó huimos huisteis huyeron	huía huías huía huíamos huíais huían	huiré huirás huirá huiremos huiréis huirán	huiría huirías huiría huiríamos huiríais huirían
15. ir yendo ido	voy vas va vamos vais van	fui fuiste fue fuimos fuisteis fueron	iba ibas iba íbamos ibais iban	iré irás irá iremos iréis irán	iría irías iría iríamos iríais irían
16. lucir luciendo lucido	luzco luces luce lucimos lucís lucen	lucí luciste lució lucimos lucisteis lucieron	lucía lucías lucía lucíamos lucíais lucían	luciré lucirás lucirá luciremos luciréis lucirán	luciría lucirías luciría luciríamos luciríais lucirían
17. mentir mintiendo mentido	miento mientes miente mentimos mentís mienten	mentí mentiste mintió mentimos mentisteis mintieron	mentía mentías mentía mentíamos mentíais mentían	mentiré mentirás mentirá mentiremos mentiréis mentirán	mentiría mentirías mentiría mentiríamos mentiríais mentirían

| SUBJUNCTIVE | | IMPERATIVE | |
Present	Imperfect	Affirmative	Negative
haya	hubiera (hubiese)		
hayas	hubieras (-ses)		
haya	hubiera (-se)		
hayamos	hubiéramos (-semos)		
hayáis	hubierais (-seis)		
hayan	hubieran (-sen)		
haga	hiciera (hiciese)		
hagas	hicieras (-ses)	haz	no hagas
haga	hiciera (-se)	haga	no haga
hagamos	hiciéramos (-semos)	hagamos	no hagamos
hagáis	hicierais (-seis)	haced	no hagáis
hagan	hicieran (-sen)	hagan	no hagan
huya	huyera (huyese)		
huyas	huyeras (-ses)	huye	no huyas
huya	huyera (-se)	huya	no huya
huyamos	huyéramos (-semos)	huyamos	no huyamos
huyáis	huyerais (-seis)	huid	no huyáis
huyan	huyeran (-sen)	huyan	no huyan
vaya	fuera (fuese)		
vayas	fueras (-ses)	ve	no vayas
vaya	fuera (-se)	vaya	no vaya
vayamos	fuéramos (-semos)	vayamos	no vayamos
vayáis	fuerais (-seis)	id	no vayáis
vayan	fueran (-sen)	vayan	no vayan
luzca	luciera (luciese)		
luzcas	lucieras (-ses)	luce	no luzcas
luzca	luciera (-se)	luzca	no luzca
luzcamos	luciéramos (-semos)	luzcamos	no luzcamos
luzcáis	lucierais (-seis)	lucid	no luzcáis
luzcan	lucieran (-sen)	luzcan	no luzcan
mienta	mintiera (mintiese)		
mientas	mintieras (-ses)	miente	no mientas
mienta	mintiera (-se)	mienta	no mienta
mintamos	mintiéramos (-semos)	mintamos	no mintamos
mintáis	mintierais (-seis)	mentid	no mintáis
mientan	mintieran (-sen)	mientan	no mientan

Infinitive Present participle Past participle	INDICATIVE				
	Present	Preterite	Imperfect	Future	Conditional
18. oír oyendo oído	oigo oyes oye oímos oís oyen	oí oíste oyó oímos oísteis oyeron	oía oías oía oíamos oíais oían	oiré oirás oirá oiremos oiréis oirán	oiría oirías oiría oiríamos oirías oirían
19. pedir pidiendo pedido	pido pides pide pedimos pedís piden	pedí pediste pidió pedimos pedisteis pidieron	pedía pedías pedía pedíamos pedíais pedían	pediré pedirás pedirá pediremos pediréis pedirán	pediría pedirías pediría pediríamos pediríais pedirían
20. pensar pensando pensado	pienso piensas piensa pensamos pensáis piensan	pensé pensaste pensó pensamos pensasteis pensaron	pensaba pensabas pensaba pensábamos pensabais pensaban	pensaré pensarás pensará pensaremos pensaréis pensarán	pensaría pensarías pensaría pensaríamos pensaríais pensarían
21. poder pudiendo podido	puedo puedes puede podemos podéis pueden	pude pudiste pudo pudimos pudisteis pudieron	podía podías podía podíamos podíais podían	podré podrás podrá podremos podréis podrán	podría podrías podría podríamos podríais podrían
22. poner poniendo puesto	pongo pones pone ponemos ponéis ponen	puse pusiste puso pusimos pusisteis pusieron	ponía ponías ponía poníamos poníais ponían	pondré pondrás pondrá pondremos pondréis pondrán	pondría pondrías pondría pondríamos pondríais pondrían
23. querer queriendo querido	quiero quieres quiere queremos queréis quieren	quise quisiste quiso quisimos quisisteis quisieron	quería querías quería queríamos queríais querían	querré querrás querrá querremos querréis querrán	querría querrías querría querríamos querríais querrían

SUBJUNCTIVE		IMPERATIVE	
Present	*Imperfect*	*Affirmative*	*Negative*
oiga	oyera (oyese)		
oigas	oyeras (-ses)	oye	no oigas
oiga	oyera (-se)	oiga	no oiga
oigamos	oyéramos (-semos)	oigamos	no oigamos
oigáis	oyerais (-seis)	oíd	no oigáis
oigan	oyeran (-sen)	oigan	no oigan
pida	pidiera (pidiese)		
pidas	pidieras (-ses)	pide	no pidas
pida	pidiera (-se)	pida	no pida
pidamos	pidiéramos (-semos)	pidamos	no pidamos
pidáis	pidierais (-seis)	pedid	no pidáis
pidan	pidieran (-sen)	pidan	no pidan
piense	pensara (pensase)		
pienses	pensaras (-ses)	piensa	no pienses
piense	pensara (-se)	piense	no piense
pensemos	pensáramos (-semos)	pensemos	no pensemos
penséis	pensarais (-seis)	pensad	no penséis
piensen	pensaran (-sen)	piensen	no piensen
pueda	pudiera (pudiese)		
puedas	pudieras (-ses)	puede	no puedas
pueda	pudiera (-se)	pueda	no pueda
podamos	pudiéramos (-semos)	podamos	no podamos
podáis	pudierais (-seis)	poded	no podáis
puedan	pudieran (-sen)	puedan	no puedan
ponga	pusiera (pusiese)		
pongas	pusieras (-ses)	pon	no pongas
ponga	pusiera (-se)	ponga	no ponga
pongamos	pusiéramos (-semos)	pongamos	no pongamos
pongáis	pusierais (-seis)	poned	no pongáis
pongan	pusieran (-sen)	pongan	no pongan
quiera	quisiera (quisiese)		
quieras	quisieras (-ses)	quiere	no quieras
quiera	quisiera (-se)	quiera	no quiera
queramos	quisiéramos (-semos)	queramos	no queramos
queráis	quisierais (-seis)	quered	no queráis
quieran	quisieran (-sen)	quieran	no quieran

INDICATIVE

	Present	Preterite	Imperfect	Future	Conditional
24. reír riendo reído	río ríes ríe reímos reís ríen	reí reíste rió reímos reísteis rieron	reía reías reía reíamos reíais reían	reiré reirás reirá reiremos reiréis reirán	reiría reirías reiría reiríamos reiríais reirían
25. saber sabiendo sabido	sé sabes sabe sabemos sabéis saben	supe supiste supo supimos supisteis supieron	sabía sabías sabía sabíamos sabíais sabían	sabré sabrás sabrá sabremos. sabréis sabrán	sabría sabrías sabría sabríamos sabríais sabrían
26. salir saliendo salido	salgo sales sale salimos salís salen	salí saliste salió salimos salisteis salieron	salía salías salía salíamos salíais salían	saldré saldrás saldrá saldremos saldréis saldrán	saldría saldrías saldría saldríamos saldríais saldrían
27. ser siendo sido	soy eres es somos sois son	fui fuiste fue fuimos fuisteis fueron	era eras era éramos erais eran	seré serás será seremos seréis serán	sería serías sería seríamos seríais serían
28. tener teniendo tenido	tengo tienes tiene tenemos tenéis tienen	tuve tuviste tuvo tuvimos tuvisteis tuvieron	tenía tenías tenía teníamos teníais tenían	tendré tendrás tendrá tendremos tendréis tendrán	tendría tendrías tendría tendríamos tendríais tendrían

	SUBJUNCTIVE	IMPERATIVE	
Present	*Imperfect*	*Affirmative*	*Negative*
ría	riera		
rías	rieras	ríe	no rías
ría	riera	ría	no ría
riamos	riéramos	riamos	no riamos
riáis	rierais	reíd	no riáis
rían	rieran	rían	no rían
sepa	supiera (supiese)		
sepas	supieras (-ses)	sabe	no sepas
sepa	supiera (-se)	sepa	no sepa
sepamos	supiéramos (-semos)	sepamos	no sepamos
sepáis	supierais (-seis)	sabed	no sepáis
sepan	supieran (-sen)	sepan	no sepan
salga	saliera (saliese)		
salgas	salieras (-ses)	sal	no salgas
salga	saliera (-se)	salga	no salga
salgamos	saliéramos (-semos)	salgamos	no salgamos
salgáis	salierais (-seis)	salid	no salgáis
salgan	salieran (-sen)	salgan	no salgan
sea	fuera (fuese)		
seas	fueras (-ses)	sé	no seas
sea	fuera (-se)	sea	no sea
seamos	fuéramos (-semos)	seamos	no seamos
seáis	fuerais (-seis)	sed	no seáis
sean	fueran (-sen)	sean	no sean
tenga	tuviera (tuviese)		
tengas	tuvieras (-ses)	ten	no tengas
tenga	tuviera (-se)	tenga	no tenga
tengamos	tuviéramos (-semos)	tengamos	no tengamos
tengáis	tuvierais (seis)	tened	no tengáis
tengan	tuvieran (-sen)	tengan	no tengan

	INDICATIVE				
participle *Past participle*	*Present*	*Preterite*	*Imperfect*	*Future*	*Conditional*
29. traer trayendo traído	traigo traes trae traemos traéis traen	traje trajiste trajo trajimos trajisteis trajeron	traía traías traía traíamos traíais traían	traeré traerás traerá traeremos traeréis traerán	traería traerías traería traeríamos traeríais traerían
30. valer valiendo valido	valgo vales vale valemos valéis valen	valí valiste valió valimos valisteis valieron	valía valías valía valíamos valíais valían	valdré valdrás valdrá valdremos valdréis valdrán	valdría valdrías valdría valdríamos valdríais valdrían
31. venir viniendo venido	vengo vienes viene venimos venís vienen	vine viniste vino vinimos vinsteis vinieron	venía venías venía veníamos veníais venían	vendré vendrás vendrá vendremos vendréis vendrán	vendría vendrías vendría vendríamos vendríais vendrían
32. ver viendo visto	veo ves ve vemos veis ven	vi viste vio vimos visteis vieron	veía veías veía veíamos veíais veían	veré verás verá veremos veréis verán	vería verías vería veríamos veríais verían
33. volver volviendo vuelto	vuelvo vuelves vuelve volvemos volvéis vuelven	volví volviste volvió volvimos volvisteis volvieron	volvía volvías volvía volvíamos volvíais volvían	volveré volverás volverá volveremos volveréis volverán	volvería volverías volvería volveríamos volveríais volverían

SUBJUNCTIVE		IMPERATIVE	
Present	*Imperfect*	*Affirmative*	*Negative*
traiga	trajera (trajese)		
traigas	trajeras (-ses)	trae	no traigas
traiga	trajera (-se)	traiga	no traiga
traigamos	trajéramos (-semos)	traigamos	no traigamos
traigáis	trajerais (-seis)	traed	no traigáis
traigan	trajeran (-sen)	traigan	no traigan
valga	valiera (valiese)		
valgas	valieras (-ses)	val	no valgas
valga	valiera (-se)	valga	no valga
valgamos	valiéramos (-semos)	valgamos	no valgamos
valgáis	valierais (-seis)	valed	no valgáis
valgan	valieran (-sen)	valgan	no valgan
venga	viniera (viniese)		
vengas	vinieras (-ses)	ven	no vengas
venga	viniera (-se)	venga	no venga
vengamos	viniéramos (-semos)	vengamos	no vengamos
vengáis	vinierais (-seis)	venid	no vengáis
vengan	vinieran (-sen)	vengan	no vengan
vea	viera (viese)		
veas	vieras (-ses)	ve	no veas
vea	viera (-se)	vea	no vea
veamos	viéramos (-semos)	veamos	no veamos
veáis	vierais (-seis)	ved	no veáis
vean	vieran (-sen)	vean	no vean
vuelva	volviera (volviese)		
vuelvas	volvieras (-ses)	vuelve	no vuelvas
vuelva	volviera (-se)	vuelva	no vuelva
volvamos	volviéramos (-semos)	volvamos	no volvamos
volváis	volvierais (-seis)	volved	no volváis
vuelvan	volvieran (-sen)	vuelvan	no vuelvan

List of irregular verbs

Each verb is followed by the model verb with which it is associated:

acertar (ie) (pensar)
acordarse (ue) (contar)
acostarse (ue) (contar)
adquirir (ie) (i) (mentir)
advertir (ie) (i) (mentir)
agradecer (z) (conocer)
almorzar (ue) (c) (contar)
aparecer (z) (conocer)
apostar (ue) (contar)
aprobar (ue) (contar)
atraer (g) (traer)
atravesar (ie) (pensar)
atribuir (y) (huir)
calentar (ie) (pensar)
cerrar (ie) (pensar)
colgar (ue) (contar)
comenzar (ie) (c) (pensar)
complacer (z) (conocer)
componer (g) (poner)
concluir (y) (huir)
confesar (ie) (pensar)
conseguir (i) (i) (pedir)
consentir (ie) (i) (mentir)
construir (y) (huir)
contener (ie) (tener)
convenir (ie) (venir)
convertir (ie) (i) (mentir)
costar (ue) (contar)
defender (ie) (entender)
demostrar (ue) (contar)
desaparecer (z) (conocer)
descender (ie) (entender)
deshacer (g) (hacer)
despedir (i) (i) (pedir)
despertar (ie) (pensar)
destruir (y) (huir)
detener (ie) (tener)
devolver (ue) (volver)
disolver (ue) (volver)

distraer (g) (traer)
distribuir (y) (huir)
divertir (ie) (i) (mentir)
doler (ue) (volver)
elegir (i) (i) (pedir)
empezar (ie) (c) (pensar)
encender (ie) (pensar)
encerrar (ie) (pensar)
encontrar (ue) (contar)
envolver (ue) (volver)
excluir (y) (huir)
extender (ie) (pensar)
favorecer (z) (conocer)
fluir (y) (huir)
forzar (ue) (c) (contar)
herir (ie) (i) (mentir)
hervir (ie) (i) (mentir)
impedir (i) (i) (pedir)
imponer (g) (poner)
incluir (y) (huir)
influir (y) (huir)
intervenir (ie) (i) (venir)
introducir (z) (conocer)
invertir (ie) (i) (mentir)
jugar (ue) (contar)
llover (ue) (volver)
manifestar (ie) (pensar)
mantener (ie) (tener)
merecer (z) (conocer)
morder (ue) (volver)
morir (ue) (u) (dormir)
mostrar (ue) (contar)
mover (ue) (volver)
nacer (z) (conocer)
negar (ie) (pensar)
nevar (ie) (pensar)
obtener (g) (ie) (tener)
ofrecer (z) (conocer)
oponer (g) (poner)

parecer (z) (conocer)
perder (ie) (entender)
permanecer (z) (conocer)
perseguir (i) (i) (pedir)
plegar (ie) (pensar)
preferir (ie) (i) (mentir)
probar (ue) (contar)
producir (z) (conducir)
proponer (g) (poner)
quebrar (ie) (pensar)
recomendar (ie) (pensar)
reconocer (z) (conocer)
recordar (ue) (contar)
reducir (z) (conducir)
referir (ie) (i) (mentir)
regar (ie) (pensar)
regir (i) (i) (pedir)
reír (i) (i) (pedir)
repetir (i) (i) (pedir)
reproducir (z) (conducir)
requerir (ie) (i) (mentir)
resolver (ue) (volver)
rogar (ue) (contar)
seguir (i) (i) (pedir)
sentir (ie) (i) (mentir)
servir (i) (i) (pedir)
soler (ue) (volver)
soltar (ue) (contar)
sonar (ue) (contar)
sonreír (i) (i) (pedir)
soñar (ue) (contar)
sugerir (ie) (i) (mentir)
temblar (ie) (pensar)
tender (ie) (entender)
tronar (ue) (contar)
tropezar (ie) (pensar)
volcar (ue) (contar)

Synopsis of a verb conjugation

Infinitive - **trabajar**
Present participle - **trabajando**
Past participle - **trabajado**

Indicative mood

Present	Cristina **trabaja** en una oficina de exportación.
Preterite	Anoche Rafael **trabajó** hasta muy tarde.
Imperfect	Cuando yo **trabajaba** en el centro siempre **llegaba** tarde a la oficina.
Future	El próximo verano ellos **trabajarán** en un campamento para niños.
Conditional	Yo no **trabajaría** en esa compañía que está tan desorganizada.
Present perfect	Pepe **ha trabajado** mucho este año.
Pluperfect	Yo ya **había trabajado** en ese banco dos años cuando me aumentaron el salario.
Future perfect	Juan **habrá trabajado** tanto este año como el pasado.
Conditional perfect	¿**Habrías trabajado** tú en esa oficina?

Subjunctive mood

Present	Esperamos que **trabajes** aquí con nosotros.
Imperfect	Federico dudaba que Maricusa **trabajara** para el Senador Valenzuela.
Present perfect	Es posible que Juana **haya trabajado** todos estos años en Santa Fe.
Pluperfect	¡Ojalá que ella **hubiera trabajado** conmigo!

Practical vocabulary—false cognates

The following list includes "false cognates"—words that are often confused because of their similarity in English and Spanish. Notice the difference in meaning.

actual = *present, current*
actual = **verdadero, real**

anticipar = *to act beforehand*
to anticipate = **esperar**

apreciar = *to esteem, to evaluate (a book, novel, a person)*
appreciate = **agradecer**

argumento = *plot summary of a story or novel*
argument = **disputa**

asistir = *to attend*
to assist, to wait on = **ayudar, atender**

asumir = *to adopt, to take on, to accept*
to assume, suppose = **suponer**

casualidad = *chance, opportunity, unforseen event*
casualty = **víctima; desgracia personal**

competencia = *competition, contest*
competence = **eficacia**

compromiso = *engagement, appointment*
compromise = **arreglo, convenio**

cualidad = *quality (of character)*
quality (of merchandise) = **calidad**

cuestión = *problem, issue*
question = **pregunta**

decepción = *disappointment*
deception = **engaño**

desgracia = *misfortune*
disgrace = **vergüenza**

educado = *well-mannered*
educated, schooled = **instruido**

emoción = *excitement*
emotion = **pasión, sentimiento**

entretener = *to amuse*
to entertain = **dar una fiesta**

éxito = *success*
exit = **salida**

facultad = *college or school in a university*
faculty = **profesorado**

fastidioso = *annoying, bothersome*
fastidious = **esmerado, exigente**

gracioso = *witty, funny*
gracious = **generoso, gentil**

honesto = *honorable, chaste*
honest = **honrado**

ignorar = *to be unaware of, be ignorant of*
to ignore = **no hacer caso de**

largo = *long*
large = **grande**

lectura = *reading*
lecture = **conferencia**

librería = *bookstore*
library = **biblioteca**

particular = *private*
particular = **exigente**

posición = *position, location*
position = **punto de vista; puesto, empleo**

pretender = *to seek, to claim*
to pretend = **fingir**

quitar = *to remove, to take away*
to quit = **dejar, abandonar**

realización = *achievement*
realization = **comprensión**

respecto = *referring to*
respect = **respeto**

restar = *to subtract*
to rest = **descansar**

reducir = *to reduce, to diminish*
to reduce (lose weight) = **adelgazar, bajar de peso**

remover = *to mix, to stir*
to remove = **quitar**

sensible = *sensitive*
sensible = **sensato, razonable**

sensitivo = *pertaining to the senses*
sensitive = **sensible**

simple = *simple (not multiple), single; stupid (simpleton)*
simple (not complicated) = **sencillo**

soportar = *to tolerate*
to support (a family) = **mantener, sostener**

suceso = *event, happening*
success = **éxito**

sugestión = *power of suggestion*
suggestion = **sugerencia, recomendación**

urgir = *to be urgent*
to urge = **persuadir**

Índice

~ A ~

a (in idiomatic expressions), 308
a (personal), 18, 261
a (preposition), 260-262, 271-273
a + noun or pronoun, 200
a verb + a + infinitive, 272
a + **alguien, nadie, alguno, ninguno**, 110
al + infinitive, 22, 234
"Abril es el mes más cruel"
  (Guillermo Cabrera Infante),
  333-338
Acabar de, 274
Accentuation
  rules, 6-9, 121-122, 277-278,
    309
  stressed syllables, **agudas,
    llanas, esdrújulas**, 6-7
  verbs ending in -**mente**, 180
Adjectives
  agreement, shortened forms,
    219, 236-238
  change of meaning, 238
  comparisons of equality, 240
  comparisons of inequality, 241
  demonstrative, 176-177, 237
  derived from nouns, 238
  descriptive, 236
  diminutives and augmentatives,
    237
  gender, 236-237
  irregular comparatives, 242
  limiting, 236

lo + possessive adjective, 175
  plural forms, 237
  possessives, 17, 174
  position, 219, 236, 238
  shortened forms, 237, 238
  superlative, 244, 245
  with **ser** and **estar**, 91-93
Adverbs
  accentuation of adverbs ending
    in -**mente**, 180
  comparisons of equality, 240
  comparisons of inequality,
    241-242
  forms and uses, 180-181
  of time, place, manner,
    quantity, affirmation or
    negation, 180
  present participle used as an
    adverb, 172
  superlative, 244-245
Affirmatives and negatives, 110-112
Alguna vez, 111
Algún, ningún, 110-111
América Central, 136-138
Anderson Imbert, Enrique, 223
"Apocalipsis" (Marco Denevi), 55
Argentina, 219-221
Art, muralist, 166-169
Articles
  agreement, 39, 42-43
  contractions **al** and **del**, 39
  definite, 39-40
  el + infinitive, 233
  el with feminine nouns, 39

  indefinite, 42-43
  neuter article **lo**, 41
  omission of definite article,
    40-41
  omission of indefinite article, 43
  un with feminine nouns, 43
  uses of definite article, 39-40
  uses of indefinite article, 43
Asturias, Miguel Ángel, 138
Augmentatives, 237
Averiguar, 58

~ B ~

Bien, mal, 180, 242
Borges, Jorge Luis, 323-324
Bueno, malo, 180, 237

~ C ~

Cabrera Infante, Guillermo, 331-332
Capitalization
  rules, 11
  review, 132, 162, 187, 215,
    246
Castellanos, Rosario, 109
Cervantes, Miguel de, 24, 36
Chile, 284-285
Chungara, Domitila Barrios de, 76
Cognates, 21, 49, 165
Cognates (false), 105, 136, 191,
  251, 400-401
Commands
  accentuation (with pronouns),
    121
  familiar, 120-121

forms, affirmative and negative,
    119-121
formal, 119
irregular verbs, 120-121
let's, 121
with pronouns, 121
with reflexives, 122
Como si, 155
Comparisons
    of equality, 240
    of inequality, 241
    irregular, 242
    superlative, 244
Con
    verb + **con**, 275
Conditional tense
    forms, 80-81
    irregular verbs, 81
    polite expressions, 82
    probability (conjecture), 82
    regular verbs, 80
    uses, 82
    with **si**, 82, 158
Conditional perfect tense
    forms, 88
    uses, 88
Conmigo, contigo, consigo, 210
Conocer, 63
    preterite and imperfect, 63
    vs. **saber**, 63
Contractions
    al, 22, 234, 261
    del, 39, 261
Corpi, Lucha, 257
Cortázar, Julio, 221
Cruz, Sor Juana Inés de la, 105-107
¿Cuál(es)?
    vs. **¿qué?**, 68-69

~ D ~

Darío, Rubén, 288
Darse cuenta de, 184
De
    de + infinitive, 234
    de + personal pronoun, 174
    uses of the preposition, 262
    verb + **de**, 274
Definite articles (See articles)
Demonstratives

adjectives, 176-177
neuter forms (**esto, eso,
    aquello**), 178
pronouns, 178
Denevi, Marco, 53
Desde/Hasta, 262-263
Díaz, Porfirio, 166
Diminutives, 229
Direct object pronouns,
    defined, 18
    with commands, 199
    with indirect object pronouns,
        198-199
    with present progressive, 171,
        199
Diphthongs, triphthongs, 4
Division of syllables, 4-5
Dolón, María Manuela, 352
Double object pronouns, 203, 207

~ E ~

Ecuador, 282
"El árbol de oro" (Ana María
    Matute), 344-348
"El eclipse" (Augusto Monterroso),
    142
"El nacimiento de la col" (Rubén
    Darío), 288
"El ramo azul" (Octavio Paz),
    316-320
Ello, 28, 197
En,
    verb + **en**, 275
    uses of the preposition, 262
España, 22-25
Estar
    + adjetive, 93
    + present participle, 93, 171
    + past participles, 93, 282, 297
    in expressions of time, 92
    in idiomatic expressions, 93
    uses, 92-93
    vs. **ser**, 93
Exclamations, 69, 155

~ F ~

Future tense
    forms, 80-81
    ir a + infinitive, 81

irregular verbs, 81
probability (conjecture), 81
regular verbs, 80
uses, 81-82
Future perfect tense
    forms, 88
    uses, 88

~ G ~

Gaucho
    Literatura gauchesca, 221
    Martín Fierro, 221
    Civilización y barbarie, 221
Gerund (See present participle)
Gustar, 97-98
    verbs similar to **gustar**, 98-99

~ H ~

Haber
    to express existence (**hay**, etc.),
        96-97
    to denote obligation, 302
    with the past participle
        (compound tenses), 86, 87-
        88, 147-148, 149
Haber de + infinitive, 302
Hacer
    expressions with **hacer**, 303-305
    hace + time, 303
    hacía + time, 303-304
    hace for weather expressions,
        304
Hay que + infinitive, 302
Hispanoamérica, 50-52
"Hombre pequeñito" (Alfonsina
    Storni), 79

~ I ~

Idiomatic expressions, 308
Imperative mood (See commands)
Imperfect tense
    indicative: forms, 61
    indicative: uses, 62
    indicative: irregular verbs (**ser,
        ir, ver**), 61
    subjuntive: forms, 124-125
    subjuntive: uses, 125
    vs. preterite, 55, 62-64
Impersonal expressions

subjunctive and indicative
  with, 144-145
Indefinite articles (See articles)
Indicative mood
  defined, 29, 114
  in adjective clauses, 154
  in adverbial clauses, 154
  vs. subjunctive, 114, 115, 145
Indirect object pronouns
  defined, 18, 199, 200
  with commands, 199
  with infinitives, 199
  with present progressive, 199
Infinitive
  al + infinitive, 22, 234
  el + infinitive, 233
  haber de + infinitive, 302
  hay que + infinitive, 302
  preposition + infinitive, 234
  tener que + infinitive, 302
  verb + **a** + infinitive, 272
Inmigraciones hispanas, 251-254
Interrogatives, 68-69
Ir + present participle, 171
-ísimo (superlative), 245

~ L ~

"La mejor tinta" (Armando
  Valladares), 259
"Lección sobre ruedas" (Domitila
  Barrios de Chungara), 76-77
Lo (neuter article), 41
Lo (direct object), 198-200
Lo + adjective or adverb, 41, 203
Lo + possessive, 175
Lo que, lo cual, 292

~ M ~

Más de, menos de, 241
Matute, Ana María, 341-342
mayas, 140
Mayor, menor, 237, 242
-mente, 180
Menchú, Rigoberta, 138
México, 166
Mistral, Gabriela, 191-192, 194
Monterroso, Augusto, 142
Mural art, 166-169

~ N ~

Negation, 110-111
Neruda, Pablo, 191-193
"Noche de fuga" (María Manuela
  Dolón), 355-359
Nouns,
  defined, 16
  gender, number, 224-228
  diminutives and augmentatives,
    229-230

~ O ~

Ojalá (que), 144-145
Orozco, José Clemente, 168-169

~ P ~

Para, uses, 267-268
  vs. **por**, 265-268
Past participle
  forms, 85
  uses, 86, 87-88
  with **estar**, 93, 297
  with **ser**, 92, 296-297
Paz, Octavio, 313-314
"Pedro Salvadores" (Jorge Luis
  Borges), 326-328
Pero and **sino**, 271
Perú, 283
Picasso, 37
Pluperfect
  indicative: forms, 87
  indicative: uses, 87
  subjunctive: forms, 149
  subjunctive: uses, 149
"Poema 20" (Pablo Neruda), 195
Poesía
  verso, estrofa, rima, 78
Ponerse, 300
Por, uses, 265-267
  vs. **para**, 267-268
¿Por qué?, 8
Porque, 8
Possessives
  adjectives, 174-175
  lo + possessive adjective, 175
  pronouns, 174-175
Premio Nobel
  Asturias, Miguel Ángel, 138

Menchú, Rigoberta, 138
Mistral, Gabriela, 192
Neruda, Pablo, 192
Prefixes **-des, -in, -re**, 186
Prepositions, 260-263
  prepositional phrases, 263, 307
  prepositional pronouns, 210-211
Present
  accentuation of verbs ending in
    -iar and **-uar**, 34
  indicative: forms, 30-34
  indicative: uses, 30
  indicative: irregular verbs, 31,
    32-34
  indicative: regular verbs, 30
  indicative: stem-changing
    verbs, 31
  indicative: spell-changing
    verbs, 31
  subjunctive, 114-117
Present Participle, 170-171
Present perfect
  indicative: forms, 87
  indicative: uses, 87
  subjuntive: forms, 147-148
  subjuntive: uses, 147-148
Preterite
  forms, 56-58
  irregular verbs, 56-57
  regular verbs, 56
  stem-changing verbs, 57-58
  spell-changing verbs: **-car, -gar,
    -zar**, 58
  uses, 55, 62
  vs. imperfect, 55, 62-64
Progressive tenses, 171-172
Pronouns
  demonstrative, 176, 178
  direct object (see Direct object
    pronouns),
  indirect (see Indirect object
    pronouns),
  prepositional (see Prepositional
    pronouns)
  possessive, 174-175
  reflexive, 38, 196, 206-207
  relative, 289-292
  subject, 196-198
  uses of **se**, 203

Punctuation 12-13
review of punctuation rules,
45, 71-72, 100-101

~ Q ~

¿Qué?
vs. ¿Cuál(es)?, 68-69

~ R ~

"Recuerdo íntimo" (Lucha Corpi),
257
Reflexives
pronouns, 38, 191
verbs, 38, 191, 370-371
se for impersonal expressions,
22, 212
se for involuntary actions, 212
se in passive voice, 212, 297-298
Relatives
antecedent, 289
cuyo, 292
el que, el cual, 290
lo que, lo cual, 292
que, 289
quien(es), 290
Revolución Mexicana de 1910,
166
Rivera, Diego, 167-168
Rosas, Juventino, 166

~ S ~

Saber
in preterite and imperfect, 63
vs. conocer, 63
"Sala de espera" (Enrique
Anderson Imbert), 223
Sarmiento, Domingo Faustino, 221
Se
impersonal, 22, 212
for involuntary actions, 212
in passive voice, 212, 297-298
Ser
+ adjetive, 91
as tener lugar, 92
in expressions of time, 92
in impersonal expressions, 92
with the past participle (passive
voice), 92, 282, 296-297

+ prepositions de and para, 91
+ noun or pronoun, 92
vs. estar, 93
Sequence of tenses, 150-151
Si clauses, 158
Sí (pronoun), 210
sí mismo, 211
Sino and pero, 271
Siqueiros, David Alfaro, 168
Sor Juana Inés de la Cruz, 105-107
Spelling rules
b, v, c, s, y, j, r, rr, h, 14-15
Differences between English
and Spanish, 310
Review of b, v, 247-248
Review of c, s, z, 46-47
Review of gue, gui, güe, güi,
215
Review of g, j, 162-163
Review of h, 132-133
Review of ll, y, ío, illo, 187
Review of que, qui, cue, cui,
101
Review of r, rr, 278
Review of sc, 72
Storni, Alfonsina, 79
Subjunctive
imperfect, 124,125
in adjective clauses, 154-155
in adverbial clauses, 153-154
in noun clauses, 128-129,
144-145
pluperfect, 149
present, 114-117
present perfect, 147-148
vs. indicative, 114, 115
Superlative, 244-245, 282

~ T ~

Tamayo, Rufino, 169
Tener
expressions with, 160
Tener que + infinitive, 302

~ U ~

"Una palmera" (Rosario
Castellanos), 109

~ V ~

Valladares, Armando, 258
Vasconcelos, José, 166
Verbs
conjugation, 27
impersonal, 182
irregular, 28, 32-34, 56-57, 61,
115, 386-398
mood, defined, 29-30
person, 27
reflexive, 38, 206-208
regular, 27
stem, 27-28, 31-32
spelling-changes, 31, 58,
384-385
stem-changing, 28, 31, 57-58
+ a, 272-273
+ de, 274-275
+ en, 272
+ con, 275
1st, 2nd, 3rd conjugation,
27-28
transitive/intransitive, 17

~ Y ~

"Yo no tengo soledad" (Gabriela
Mistral), 194

PHOTO CREDITS

Capítulo Preliminar   Page 3: Bettmann/Corbis Images.   **Capítulo 1**   Page 21: ©PhotoEdit. Page 24: Mark Antman/The Image Works. Page 25: Bettmann/Corbis Images. Page 36: ©Peter Menzel/Stock, Boston. Page 37: ©2002 Estate of Pablo Picasso/Artists Rights Society. Museo del Prado, Madrid, Spain/Giraudon/Art Resource.   **Capítulo 2**   Page 48: Stuart Cohen/The Image Works. Page 51: David Hiser/Stone. Page 55: Robert Frerck/Stone. Page 65: ©Stuart Cohen/The Image Works.   **Capítulo 3**   Page 74: Stuart Cohen/The Image Works. Page 76: Jay Silverman Productions/The Image Bank. Page 80: Yann Arthus-Bertrand/Corbis Images. Page 89: Bob Mahoney/The Image Works.   **Capítulo 4**   Page 103: Ulrike Welsch/Photo Researchers. Page 106: Laurie Platt Winfrey, Inc. Page 113: ©Peter Menzel/Stock, Boston. Page 117: Owen Franken/Stock, Boston. Page 127: Stuart Cohen/The Image Works.   **Capítulo 5**   Page 134: Carl Frank/Photo Researchers. Page 139: Jim Harrison/Stock, Boston. Page 141: Salvador Dali, *The Discovery of America by Christopher Columbus*, 1958-1959. Oil on canvas (161 1/2 x122 1/8 inches). Collection of The Salvador Dali Museum, St. Petersburg, Florida. Copyright 2001 Salvador Dali Museum, Inc. Page 152: Will & Deni McIntyre/Photo Researchers.   **Capítulo 6**   Page 164: Diego Rivera, *Sugar Cane,* 1931/Philadelphia Museum of Art: Gift of Mr. and Mrs. Herbert Cameron Morris. Page 168: Jose Clemente Orozco, *Zapatistas,* 1931. Oil on canvas (114.3 x 139.7cm). Given anonymously. Photograph 1997 The Museum of Modern Art, New York. Page 172: Macduff Everton/The Image Works. Page 177: Courtesy Mexican Government Tourist Office. Page 186: Peter Menzel/Stock, Boston.   **Capítulo 7**   Page 189: Carl Frank/Photo Researchers. Page 192 (left): Bettmann/Corbis Images. Page 192 (right): Henri Cartier-Bresson/Magnum Photos, Inc. Page 197: Peter Menzel/Stock, Boston. Page 214: Michael Dwyer/Stock, Boston.   **Capítulo 8**   Page 217: Georg Gerster/Photo Researchers. Page 230: Alicia Sanguinetti/Monkmeyer Press Photo.   **Capítulo 9**   Page 235: Michael Dwyer/Stock, Boston.   **Capítulo 8**   Page 249: Hazel Hankin.   **Capítulo 9**   Page 253: Ulrike Welsch. Page 255: Robert Brenner/PhotoEdit. Page 259: Courtesy Armando Valladares.   **Capítulo 10**   Page 280: Wesley Bocxe/The Image Works. Page 284: Andrew Rakoczy/Monkmeyer Press Photo. Page 287: Peter Menzel/Stock, Boston. Page 291: Rhoda Sidney/The Image Works. Page 296: Marcel and Eva Malherbe/The Image Works.   **Lecturas**   Page 313: Nola Tully/Corbis Sygma. Page 316: Ulrike Welsch/Photo Researchers. Page 323: Sophie Bassouls/Corbis Sygma. Page 326: Culver Pictures, Inc. Page 331: Courtesy Agencia Literaria Carmen Balcells, S.A. Page 334: Peter Menzel/Stock, Boston. Page 335: VCG /FPG International. Page 341: Courtesy Editorial Planeta, S.A., Barcelona. Page 345: Kees Van Den Berg/Photo Researchers.

TEXT CREDITS

Capítulo 2   Page 53: Marco Denevi, "Apocalipsis" from Salón de lectura, 1974. By permission of Librería Huemul, Buenos Aires.   **Capítulo 3**   Page 76: Domitila Barrios de Chungara, "Lección sobre ruedas," from *¡Aquí también, Domitila!,* 1985. By permission of Editores Siglo XXI, S.A. de C. V. Page 79: Alfonsina Storni, "Hombre pequeñito," from *Irremediablemente,* 1919. By permission of Editorial Losada, S.A., Buenos Aires.   **Capítulo 4**   Page 109. Rosario Castellanos, "Una palmera,"from *Meditación en el umbral: Antología poética, Primera edición.* ©1985, Fondo de Cultura Económica, México.
By permission of Fondo de Cultura Económica.   **Capítulo 5**   Page 142. Augusto Monterroso, "El eclipse," from *Obras completas y otros cuentos.* ©Augusto Monterroso, 1981. By permission of International Editors, Barcelona.
Capítulo 7   Page 194: Gabriela Mistral, "Yo no tengo soledad," from *Ternura.* ©Provincia Franciscana de la Santísima Trinidad, Santiago de Chile. ©Espasa-Calpe, S.A., Madrid. By permission of Espasa-Calpe, S.A. Page 195: Pablo Neruda, "Poema 20," from *20 poemas de amor y una canción desesperada.* ©Pablo Neruda, 1924, and Fundación Pablo Neruda. By permission of Agencia Literaria Carmen Balcells.   **Capítulo 8**   Page 223. Enrique Anderson Imbert, "Sala de espera," from *El gato de Cheshire,* 1965. By permission of Anabel Anderson Imbert.   **Capítulo 9**   Page 257: Lucha Corpi, "Recuerdo íntimo," from *Variaciones sobre una tempestad,* Third Woman Press, Berkeley, 1990. By permission of the author. Page 258: Armando Valladares, "La mejor tinta," from *El alma de un poeta,* ©1988. By permission of the author.   **Capítulo 10**   Page 288. Rubén Darío, "El nacimiento de la col," in "La Tribuna," 1893.   **Lectura 1.**   Page 316. Octavio Paz, "El ramo azul," from *Libertad bajo palabra,* 1960. Fondo de Cultura Económica, México.   **Lectura 2.**   Page 326. Jorge Luis Borges, "Pedro Salvadores," from *Elogio de la sombra,* ©Emecé Editores, S.A., Buenos Aires, 1967. By permission of Emecé Editores. **Lectura 3.**   Page 333. Guillermo Cabrera Infante, "Abril es el mes más cruel," from *Así en la paz como en la guerra,* 1971. By permission of the author.   **Lectura 4.**   Page 345. Ana María Matute, "El árbol de oro," from *Historias de la Artámila,* ©Ana María Matute, Barcelona, 1961. By permission of Agencia Literaria Carmen Balcells.   **Lectura 5.**   Page 355. María Manuela Dolón, "Noche de fuga." By permission of the author.